Jamal Mian

The Life of Maulana
Jamaluddin Abdul
Wahab of Farangi
Mahall, 1919–2012

Jamal Mian

The Life of Maulana
Jamaluddin Abdul
Wahab of Farangi
Mahall, 1919–2012

Francis Robinson

OXFORD
UNIVERSITY PRESS

OXFORD
UNIVERSITY PRESS

Oxford University Press is a department of the University of Oxford.
It furthers the University's objective of excellence in research, scholarship,
and education by publishing worldwide. Oxford is a registered trade mark of
Oxford University Press in the UK and in certain other countries

Published in Pakistan by
Ameena Saiyid, Oxford University Press
No.38, Sector 15, Korangi Industrial Area,
PO Box 8214, Karachi-74900, Pakistan

ISBN 978-0-19-940568-8

Printed on 80gsm Local Offset Paper

Printed by The Times Press Pvt. Ltd., Karachi

Dedication

For Patricia

Contents

viii CONTENTS

12. Politics, business, international engagements, and the   277
    break-up of Pakistan, 1958–71
13. Life in Karachi, 1971–2012   307
14. The nature of the man and the meaning of his life   335

Appendix 1. Maulana Ruhullah's Milad   367
Appendix 2. Jamal Mian's two Khutbas given on the Maidan   383
              in Calcutta, Eid October 1943

Glossary   399
Note on Sources   405
Bibliography   409
Index   415

Acknowledgements

RESEARCH OVER FIFTY YEARS HAS CONTRIBUTED TO THIS volume and many debts have been incurred. For help in research done in Lucknow at various times between 1968 and 1980 I thank Matin Mian, Raza Mian (Mufti Raza Ansari), and Abdul Rahman Sahib of Farangi Mahall alongside Mushir Mian Razzaqi and Asif Qidwai, all of whom were most generous with their time. Dr Iqbal Husain of Aligarh University made available to me his work on Farangi Mahall documents and early Farangi Mahalli newspapers. In 1968, Gail Minault was a kind and enabling host in Lucknow. Farid Faridi, Dr Faridi's son, was always a genial presence. Nabboo Mian, the Maharajkumar of Mahmudabad, was a wonderful host both in Lucknow and in Mahmudabad. But the key figure for me, as for so many who pursued research in Lucknow over that period, was the late Ram Advani, the great bookseller of Hazratganj who made it really pleasant for one to be in Lucknow day by day.

In Karachi in the 1970s I acknowledge the assistance of Kamal Habib and Aqil us-Zafar Khan alongside the general support of Hakim Said. This said, Jamal Mian himself gave me a great deal of his time as I worked on the family papers.

In Karachi from 2012 Bari Mian arranged for me to stay in the Sindh Club. Papers from the Jamal Mian Archive were brought to me there, and Mahmood would join me. It was a most pleasant arrangement. At times Farida, Amina, Humaira and Alauddin would appear to encourage the work forward. Some written contributions by members of the family have been of particular value, for instance, Matin Mian's essay on the Farangi Mahall Devotional Year, and Farida Jamal's two essays, one devoted to her grandmother and the second to her mother. This said, Bari Mian's oral contributions were of the first importance; he had lived closest to his father and was the best-placed to give weight and meaning to evidence. In Karachi I would also like to acknowledge the assistance of Raees Mian Ajmeri who (1) converted the minuscule shikast of Hasrat's diary into readable nastaliq, and (2) worked with Mahmood and Farida Jamal in producing the catalogue of Jamal Mian's library, without which much of chapter fourteen would not have been possible. Thanks are also due to the most helpful staff of the Sindh Archives, in particular Mr Advani. I also thank my very old friend, Masuma Hasan, who, like the Farangi Mahallis claims descent from Abu Ayub Ansari through Abdullah Ansari of Herat.

In the UK I am grateful for the assistance of the staff of the Royal Holloway, University of London Library, the Bodleian Library, Oxford, and the former British Library newspaper section at Colindale. For the first half of 2016 I was a visiting professor at the University of Chicago, where I enjoyed the welcoming environment of SALC in Foster Hall under the leadership of Ulrike Stark. Three graduate students were particularly supportive: Thomas Newbold, Aamer Bashir, and Daniel Morgan. The latter worked as my research assistant throughout my stay, amongst other things producing a version of Jamal Mian's library catalogue transliterated according to the *Encyclopaedia of Islam* (third edition).

The odd chapter of this biography has informed seminar presentations: at the Oxford Centre for Islamic Studies, at Emory University, and at the festschrift conference for Gail Minault at the University of Texas at Austin. I am grateful for the comments I was given, as I am for those of Joya Chatterji who read a chapter. Joya also made available to me copies of the fortnightly reports in the 1950s of the Indian High Commission in Karachi to the Foreign Ministry in Delhi.

Four people have read the complete text. One was the Chicago Urdu scholar, C. M. Naim, who must know the world of Farangi Mahall and Bara Banki that I have tried to evoke as well as anyone alive today. His comments have saved me from error and I am grateful. The other readers were Bari Mian, Mahmood, and Farida. Where possible I have tried to accommodate their concerns. For what remains, I am wholly responsible. I thank Farieha Shah and Sunehra Mehmood for their patient editing and Ameena Saiyid, Managing Director of OUP Pakistan for her longstanding interest in this book. Mahmood Jamal, who has travelled the journey of his father's life with me, has been a delightful companion. Finally I thank my wife, Patricia, for her forebearance; she has been beside me during my engagement of nearly fifty years with Farangi Mahall.

Francis Robinson
May 2017

Preface

MY RELATIONSHIP WITH THE FARANGI MAHALL FAMILY began, though initially at a distance, in 1967 when I was a PhD student in Cambridge, working on the Muslim politics of northern India in the late nineteenth and early twentieth centuries. I noticed that in the early twentieth century the ulama of Farangi Mahall (Lucknow) played a prominent political role, foremost among them Maulana Abdul Bari. This meant that when I went to India in December 1967, I was determined to meet members of the family and to see if they had any records they would permit me to consult. Through the kind offices of Professor Mohibbul Hasan, the head of the Department of History at Delhi's Jamia Millia Islamia, I and the US scholar, Gail Minault, were introduced to Farangi Mahall. There we were welcomed by Maulana Jalaluddin Abdul Matin and Mufti Raza Ansari and permitted to consult those Abdul Bari papers they had with them. The outcomes found their way into Gail Minault's book on the Khilafat movement (1919–24), which was published in 1982, and into my book on the emergence of separatist politics among the United Provinces' Muslims, which was published in 1974. During this encounter which took place in May 1968, Matin Mian and Raza Mian may have told me of the existence of Abdul Bari's son, Jamal Mian, who then lived in Dacca, but I had no recollection of it.

I was therefore a little surprised when, in May 1976, Jamal
Mian asked me to come and see him in London. First, he
wanted to tell me how pleased he was that a scholar had set
out the contributions of his family in general and his father
in particular to politics in the 1910s and 1920s. Then, there
were errors and misapprehensions in my book that he wished
to correct. After we had completed this business, conducted
with the personal and intellectual generosity which was typical
of Jamal Mian, we continued to talk for hours. He concluded
our meeting by saying that he had all of his father's papers in
Karachi and I was welcome to come and see them whenever
I wanted.

As any hungry young historian might do, I went to see
Jamal Mian's archive in Karachi as quickly as I could.
There, I found an extraordinary family archive. It began
with Mughal documents supporting the family in Awadh
in the sixteenth and seventeenth centuries and continued
to documents surrounding the killing of Mulla Qutbuddin
Sehalvi and the establishment of the family in Lucknow's
Farangi Mahall in the 1690s, and then followed through a
growing document trail in the eighteenth and nineteenth
centuries down to Abdul Bari's carefully-kept letter books
in the twentieth. I decided straightaway that my next project
would be on Farangi Mahall. I spent the next few years
tracking down materials in Lucknow, Aligarh, Hyderabad,
and Madras. Jamal Mian kindly enabled me to microfilm
substantial parts of his archive in Karachi. The research that
I did has influenced everything I have written up to this point.
Indeed, I developed a specific understanding that the central
spine of Islamic history was the transmission of the central
messages of Islam—the Quran and the Hadith—by ulama and
Sufis. Much of the substance of that Islamic history lay in the

interactions of these transmitters with, on the one hand, the
wielders of political power and, on the other, society at large.
This approach was most clearly expressed in the text of my
book, *Atlas of the Islamic World since 1500* (Oxford: Phaidon,
1982). I had always planned to write a monograph on Farangi
Mahall but, when in 2000 I seriously came to consider this,
I realized that I had already said much of what I wanted to
say in articles published over the previous twenty years. So
my research on Farangi Mahall was published as collected
essays, *The `Ulama of Farangi Mahall and Islamic Culture in
South Asia* (Delhi: Permanent Black, 2001/Lahore: Ferozesons
(Pvt) Ltd., 2002).

As I worked on Farangi Mahall I came to know Jamal Mian
quite well. I also came to know other members of his family,
in particular his eldest sons, Bari Mian, and Mahmood Jamal
who lived in London at that time. But it was Jamal Mian who
I came to see regularly—whether it was in Karachi, where he
made time for me on a daily basis, or in London, where we
would meet on his annual visits to the city. One particular
incident my wife likes to recall was when Jamal Mian came
to our home while she was wallpapering a room. I asked
her if she could make us some tea. Jamal Mian immediately
intervened saying: 'No, she is busy; you will go and make the
tea', making a point of his understanding of good manners.
Such incidents apart, we talked about everything under the
sun, including his family, his views on India and Pakistan,
and particular episodes in his life. At this stage I was tempted
to suggest that I write his biography. However, influenced
perhaps by the absorption of oral techniques in his upbringing,
the arc of his narrative, as he recounted an episode from his
life, took so long to reach a conclusion that I was discouraged
from taking on his biography in his lifetime.

After Jamal Mian died in 2012, it emerged in discussions between Bari Mian, Mahmood Jamal, and myself that they would be happy for me to write their father's life. Mahmood Jamal was in charge of his father's papers and it quickly became clear that they would be a rich source. There were diaries and notebooks covering almost every year from c. 1940 to the 1990s. There were letters, speeches, and unpublished writings, files on particular issues, tapes of recollections, his personal library with annotations of books, some excellent photographs, and Hasrat Mohani's diary which was a remarkable source depicting the atmosphere of the late 1940s. All these could be supplemented by newspapers for the more public aspects of Jamal Mian's life. Mahmood Jamal kindly agreed to help with the research. I went to Karachi to work with him whenever my teaching commitments permitted. On occasion, he came to London to work with me. Consequently, all translations from Urdu are his. This goes for excerpts from his father's and Hasrat's diaries, his father's poetry, his father's sister's poetry, his father's taped recollections and speeches, and letters from the Raja of Mahmudabad and Muhammad Shoaib. Farida Jamal translated the annotations to his books. Throughout this process, which has been very much a two-way process between Mahmood Jamal and myself, I have benefited from his glosses on the events described and on the weight which should be given to the meaning of particular words. This said, I take full responsibility for all final interpretations.

My aim in this book is to give a sense of what it was to be Maulana Jamal Mian. I have been concerned to assess the significance of his Farangi Mahall upbringing. I have explored what he thought he was doing as he worked for the Muslim League between 1937 and 1949. I have wished to show how a man who was determined to remain Indian came to work in Dacca from 1950 and how his constant movement across the Indo-Pakistan border seems to have helped create the conditions in which he had to take Pakistani citizenship. I have also been concerned to show how, against his better judgement, he became caught up in the politics of Pakistan and benefited from its economic patronage system so that, having lost almost everything in Dacca in the emergence of Bangladesh, he was able to bounce back in Karachi. I have also been concerned to show how, over the period from the 1950s to the 1980s, his spiritual focus shifted from the shrines of South Asia to the Hejaz, and to Medina in particular. Throughout this eventful life, I hope the reader will see how this warm and humane man was sustained by his faith, strong friendships, his family, and the cultural capital he gained from his Farangi Mahall background. Wherever possible, I enable him to speak in his own words.

Note on Transliteration

ONE OF THE PROBLEMS OF IMPOSING ONE SYSTEM OF transliteration on a text about a society which had English as one of its languages and in which individuals have often adopted distinctive forms for their names is that it will make some names that are familiar look odd. Of course, they will sound right, but they will still look odd. I have, therefore, adopted a practice designed to reduce the visual oddities but in doing so I have not avoided oddities altogether. All names in roman in the text are spelled as the individuals concerned spelled them. Where transliteration is required from Urdu, I have followed the Hunterian system adopted by the British Indian government and followed by subsequent governments. Words in italics in the text have been transliterated according to the *Encyclopaedia of Islam* 3rd ed., macrons, underdots, and Hamza being omitted. In the footnotes, the titles of books in Urdu and their author's names have been rendered after a similar fashion. Some oddities still exist, for instance, Qidwai spelled with both a 'Qaf' and a 'Kaf', and Altafur Rahman and Altaf al-Rahman in adjacent footnotes. I have taken the view that this may be less troubling than imposing a single system. In Appendices 1 and 2 Mahmood Jamal has used his own phonetic system for quotations in Arabic, Persian, and Urdu. Nothing is perfect.

Abbreviations

ABP   Abdul Bari Papers held by the Farangi Mahall family in Karachi and London

IDBP   Industrial Development Bank of Pakistan

JMP   Jamal Mian Papers held by the Farangi Mahall family in Karachi and London

NAI   National Archives of India

UNO   United Nations Organization

PICIC   Pakistan Industrial Credit & Development Organization

List of Illustrations and Map

Map

1

Jamal Mian announces himself

IN OCTOBER 1937, THE TWENTY-FIFTH SESSION OF THE ALL-
India Muslim League took place in Lucknow. After
the League session of 1916, this was the second of the
two momentous League sessions held in Lucknow; in
comparison, those of 1913 and 1923 were of minor
importance. The momentous meeting of December 1916
saw a pact made between the League and the Congress
to work together in pressing for the further devolution of
power which was expected after World War One. On this
occasion, the mood was very different. No longer did it
seem possible to work with the Congress against British rule.
Indeed, now the concern was to defend the League and its
supporters against Congress domination. In the elections
earlier in the year, under the 1935 Government of India
Act, the Congress had won majorities in seven out of eleven
provinces. One of those majorities, somewhat unexpectedly,
had been achieved in the UP. Congress leaders had then
made it clear first, that only one rather than two of their
members could enter G. B. Pant's cabinet, and second, that
they could only join the new government by renouncing
their allegiance to the League. 'The Muslim League group
in the United Provinces legislature,' Congress President
Azad told Choudhry Khaliquzzaman, 'shall cease to function

as a separate group.' The Congress had power now and was
going to exercise it.[1]

Given this background, the Congress could have construed
the very act of holding the League's annual session in Lucknow
as provocative. This was the moment when the League was
going to consider how to respond to the new situation of
Congress power. Such was its importance that the senior
League leaders in the province, Choudhry Khaliquzzaman
and Nawab Ismail Khan, had decided that it must be presided
over by the League's permanent president, Mr Jinnah.[2]

The atmosphere in Lucknow was febrile. Ahrars, the radical
lower-middle class group from the Punjab, had arrived in
the city wearing their red shirts. They were making speeches
criticising the League's policy of opposing the Congress in the
UP Assembly.[3] There was such fear about how the Congress
government might respond that initially, the League had
difficulty persuading the city's young Muslims to become
volunteers to line the route along which the President would
pass and to keep order in and around the pandal.

On 13 October at Charbagh station, Mr Jinnah,
accompanied by his sister Miss Jinnah, was met by a large car,
from the Mahmudabad estate, with a Sikh driver. The young
Raja of Mahmudabad, no doubt mindful that Mr Jinnah was
a trustee of his estate, stood postilion-fashion, holding a sword
on one side at the back of the car. On the other side, also
riding postilion, was a seventeen-year old madrasah student,
Jamal Mian. As the car moved off slowly, a man was to be
seen trotting beside Jamal Mian. He was Sulaiman, a jeweller

---

1. Choudhry Khaliquzzaman, *Pathway to Pakistan* (Karachi: Longman's
    Pakistan Branch, 1961), 161.
2. Ibid. 171.
3. Ibid. 169–70.

from the Chauk and a follower of Jamal Mian's family; he was there to protect Jamal Mian, not Mr Jinnah. When the car reached Aminabad Park, there were shouts of 'Jinnah go back' and 'Muslim League Murdabad' from a small group of Azad Muslim Leaguers led by Zahur ul-Mulk Kakorvi—some of Jamal Mian's fellow madrasah students pulled down their flags and dispersed them. After this, Mr Jinnah was able to drive to Mahmudabad House in the Qaiserbagh in peace.[4]

The following day in Mahmudabad House, an hour before the first League meeting, the Raja, Khaliquzzaman, and Hassan Ispahani were going over the day's agenda when Nawab Ismail Khan joined them. 'He was, as usual,' Ispahani remembers, 'immaculately dressed and wore a black "samur" cap.' Jinnah was attracted to the cap and asked if the Nawab would part with it for a moment. The Nawab suggested that he put it on, just to see how it looked. Jinnah looked at himself in a full-length mirror and liked what he saw. He was urged to keep it on. He did so and left for his meeting. By the end of the League sessions, many samur caps were being worn.[5]

Later this day at the Muslim League Council, two agreements which were to lie at the heart of Jinnah's power, and also the effectiveness of the Muslim League in the politics of the final years of British India, were finalized. First, a proposed pact with Sir Sikander Hayat was announced. The League would not interfere with the Unionist Party in the Punjab providing the League could represent the interests of Punjabi Muslims at the Centre. This was 'unanimously approved,' Khaliquzzaman tells us, 'with thunderous cheers'.

4. Jamal Mian Tape 5A, Jamal Mian Papers, Karachi, henceforth JMP.
5. M. A. H. Ispahani, *Quaid-e-Azam Jinnah As I Knew Him*, second ed., (Karachi: Forward Publications Trust, 1966), 40–1.

A similar arrangement was reached with Fazlul Huq, the Bengal leader. Thus, at a stroke on 14 October, Jinnah gained the right to represent the interests of India's two most populous Muslim provinces; he had made himself into a man that neither the Congress nor the Government of India could ignore.[6]

On 15 October the League met in full session, in a pandal seating 5,000 delegates, in Lal Bagh. Manzur Mahmud, the father of Talat Mahmud, the Bombay recording star and a relative of Jamal Mian's mother, launched proceedings by singing Iqbal's *Tarana-i Milli*. The Raja of Mahmudabad gave the welcome address, emphasising in particular the injustices being done to Arabs in Palestine and the need to organize the League as a mass organization.[7] He asked Mr Jinnah if Jamal Mian, who had acted as convener of the pandal committee might speak. 'Jinnah Sahib looked at me,' Jamal Mian recalled, 'and seeing my age said, "No, he is too young".'[8] Jinnah gave his presidential speech, translated into Urdu by Hakim Shamsuddin, in which he stressed: how critical the moment was for the League; the need for the League to organize; the problems of dealing with the Congress; the injustices being done to the Palestinian Arabs; and the need for the League to engage hundreds of thousands of Muslims in its work.[9]

6. Khaliquzzaman, *Pathway*, 170–1; Stanley Wolpert, *Jinnah of Pakistan* (New York: Oxford University Press, 1984), 151–2; Ayesha Jalal, *The Sole Spokesman: Jinnah, the Muslim League and the Demand for Pakistan* (Cambridge: Cambridge University Press, 1985), 35–40.

7. Syed Sharifuddin Pirzada, *Foundations of Pakistan: All-India Muslim League Documents: 1906–1947. Vol. II,* (Karachi: National Publishing House Ltd., 1970), 264–5.

8. 18 was the minimum age for Muslim League membership. Jamal Mian Tape 5A, JMP.

9. Pirzada, *Foundations II*, 265–73.

Towards the end of the proceedings an appeal for donations was launched to help the League to fight the forthcoming Bijnor by-election. Jinnah then relented and permitted Jamal Mian to speak:

> I made a passionate speech and then took off my velvet cap … and took a few rupees, about four or seven rupees, and put them in the cap and presented it to Jinnah Sahib as my donation. The cap was then auctioned and Raja Sahib bought it for five hundred rupees. His manager claims that it is still in Raja Sahib's house.[10]

This was the first speech that Jamal Mian, who delighted in public speaking, was to give at a League session. It was to be followed by many hundreds more in the League cause. Thus, at this most important League session, he announced his arrival on the stage of League politics. Who was this most precocious madrasah student?

---

10. Jamal Mian Tape 5A, JMP.

2

Jamal Mian's heritage

JAMAL MIAN CAME FROM A FAMILY WHOSE PRESENCE IN India reached back to the great days of the Delhi Sultanate. This was a background he shared with several key figures who worked with him in the UP Muslim League. The Raja of Mahmudabad claimed descent from Qazi Nasrullah, a Siddiqi Shaikh of Baghdad who came to India in the time of Shahabuddin Ghori (d. 1206) and settled at Amroha. A descendant was sent to Awadh, by Muhammad bin Tughluq, where he began to carve out a position for his family. Ehsanur Rahman Qidwai's ancestor, Qazi Qidwa, came from Anatolia (Rum) and was received by Shahabuddin Ghori outside Delhi. Between 1202 and 1205 he is said to have subjugated fifty-two villages in Awadh, the essential basis of the Qidwai presence in the region, and to have settled in Ayodhya. Aizaz Rasul's ancestors came from Wasit in Iraq and were disciples of Nasiruddin Chiragh of Delhi (1274–1356). In the fourteenth century, they settled in Sandila in the Hardoi district of Awadh. Khaliquzzaman claimed descent from the first caliph, Abu Bakr Siddiq. His ancestors held a *mansab* under Akbar and left their mark by constructing the Macchi Bhawan, the great fort at the end of the Chauk in Lucknow which was blown up by the British in the Mutiny Uprising. Only Nawab Ismail Khan was of relatively recent provenance in India. Descended from the Bangash Pathans—who were primarily eighteenth century

arrivals in India—his great grandfather, Murtaza Khan, after
being awarded a jagir by Lord Lake, bought the Jehangirabad
estate in Meerut district at auction in 1813. Although some
may question the particulars of these claims of origin and
settlement, what is important is that these men identified
themselves with Muslims who had entered India from outside.
Moreover, they saw themselves as part of a long tradition of
power in the land. Being close to power, or wielding it, was
their birthright.

Jamal Mian's Ancestors

Jamal Mian's ancestors were ulama and Sufis more than
soldiers and administrators. So, in the way of those who
focussed on God's purposes rather than man's desires, their
relationship to Muslim power was rather more complex.
Nevertheless, the existence of Muslim power was a positive
force in their history. Jamal Mian claimed descent from the
noted companion of the Prophet, Abu Ayub Ansari, also
known as Khalid ibn Zaid from the Banu Ghanim sub-branch
of the Khazrah branch of the Ansar tribe. Ansari presented
himself to the Prophet in Mecca before the *hijra* and was
his host in Medina. Between 674 and 678 CE he was part of
the Muslim army which besieged Constantinople, where he
died and was buried under the walls.[1] The Ottoman historian,
Evliya Celebi, wrote somewhat ironically of the 'discovery' of
his tomb after the conquest of the city in 1453 CE. Mehmet the
Conqueror and his companions spent seven days searching

---

1. Mawlana Mawlawi Muhammad `Inayat Allah, *Tadhkirah-yi `Ulama-i
   Farangi Mahall,* (Lucknow: Ishaat ul-Ulum, 1928), 8.

for the tomb until the Shaikh ul-Islam, after being in a trance, said it is under my prayer carpet:

> Upon this, three of his attendants together with the Seyh and the Sultan began to dig up the ground, when at a depth of three yards they found a square stone of verd antique on which was written in Cufic letters: "This is the tomb of Eba Eyup." They lifted up the stone and found below it the body of Eyup wrapped up in a saffron-colored shroud, with a brazen play ball in his hand, fresh and well-preserved.[2]

The mausoleum subsequently built at Eyup on the Golden Horn has been a sacred place in Ottoman history. Here, early Ottoman Sultans were crowned. Here, Ottoman armies, leaving on their annual campaigns, would halt to pay their respects. It was hardly surprising that this shrine was an important focus for Jamal Mian and his family in the first half of the twentieth century, certainly symbolically, and perhaps psychologically. Without success, Jamal Mian's father, Abdul Bari, applied to the British for permission to visit it when he went on Hajj in 1912–13.[3] Jamal Mian, however, did succeed in visiting it when he was on the Indian Delegation to the Middle East in 1947.[4]

Jamal Mian's line came from Abu Ayub Ansari through his

---

2. Passage from Evliya Celebi, *Book of Travels*, c. 1670 quoted in Hilary Sumner-Boyd & John Freely, *Strolling Through Istanbul* (Istanbul: Redhouse Press, 1972), 397.

3. 1912 is the only logical date for this application. Abdul Bari to Commissioner of Lucknow, incomplete copy, no date, Abdul Bari Papers, Karachi, henceforth ABP.

4. Jamal Mian Notebooks of Delegation to the Middle East, 25 April 1947, JMP.

son, Abu Mansur, who fought in Khurasan at the behest of the
Caliph Umar and then through a further seven generations to
the great Sufi saint, Abdullah Ansari of Herat (1006–88). He
received titles and robes of honour from the Abbasid caliphs
but was also persecuted by local rulers for his rigid adherence
to the Hanbali school. Nevertheless, he left a substantial
body of work, in particular on devotional themes which have
inspired Muslims down to the present. He died in poverty
and was buried in Gazargah near his Khanqah. On this site
between 1425 and 1427 the Timurid ruler, Shah Rukh, built
a fine mausoleum.[5]

It is not clear whether Abdullah Ansari's line descended
through his daughter, who married his nephew, or not. In
Jamal Mian's family tradition his great grandson, Jalaluddin,
in a direct male line of descent came to India for jihad—the
timing would suggest that he came as part of the Ghorid
invasions—and settled at Sarsali close to Delhi where he built
a Khanqah and a mosque.[6] No evidence of Sarsali has been
discovered in recent attempts to map the region historically,
but sixteenth century records have identified Sirsa on the edge
of the desert some hundred miles west of Panipat.[7]

The great grandson of Jalaluddin, Makhdum Badruddin,
moved into Delhi, settling near the Qutb Minar, founding a
madrasah, and becoming a disciple of Nasiruddin Chiragh-i
Delhi (1274–1356). In old age he moved to Banarwa
northeast of Delhi, where he married and died in 1351. His

5. `Inayat Allah, *Tadhkirah*, 8.
6. Ibid.
7. Irfan Habib, *An Atlas of the Mughal Empire* (Delhi: Oxford University
   Press, 1982), Map 4A, 29+:79+. I am grateful to Megan Robb of the
   Oxford Centre for Islamic Studies Atlas Project for the comment on
   Sarsali and Sirsa.

son, Nasiruddin, died in 1445, and his son, Alauddin, in 1471; they were both buried in Shaikhpur. Alauddin's son, Makhdum Nizamuddin, was the first to come to Awadh where he settled in Qasbah Sehali.[8] It is with his great grandson, Mulla Hafiz, that we enter formally-documented history. In 1559 Mulla Hafiz received, as a scholar, a revenue-free grant (*madad-i ma`ash*) from Akbar in one of the emperor's first known farmans.[9] Farmans and *parwana*s in the Farangi Mahall archive demonstrate the regular renewal of Mughal support for this scholarly family down to the point when the Mulla's great grandson, Mulla Qutbuddin, was attacked by local zamindars who were increasingly coming to resent the privileges which Mughal grant-holders had in the region.[10] On 9 April 1691, Mulla Qutbuddin was killed by the zamindars of Sehali and Fatehpur. The *mahzarnama*, or witness statement, which was taken to the emperor Aurangzeb by two of Qutbuddin's four sons, must be one of the most dramatic documents of seventeenth-century Awadh history. In matter-of-fact language it recounts how relatives, students, and government officials were injured; how two students, Shaikh Ghulam Muhammad, a maternal grandson of the great Shaikh Nizamuddin of Amethi, and Shaikh Izzatullah of Sandila were killed; how Qutbuddin died after receiving wounds from an axe, a musket ball, and seven sword-cuts across the face; how his women folk were humiliated; and how his library of about

8. In earlier works I have identified Alauddin as the first of the family to settle in Sihali. This was wrong.

9. Mufti Raza Ansari, 'A Very Early Farman of Akbar', cyclostyled paper, Centre of Advanced Study, Aligarh Muslim University.

10. Muzaffar Alam, *The Crisis of Empire in Mughal North India: Awadh and the Punjab 1707–1748* (Delhi: Oxford University Press, 1986), 117–22.

900 books, including copies of the Quran and Hadiths, were set on fire.[11]

Out of this tragedy there came imperial support for Jamal Mian's ancestors which was to help make them the leading family of Islamic learning in South Asia down to the twentieth century. Aurangzeb bestowed on the four sons of Mulla Qutbuddin the sequestered property of a European indigo merchant in Lucknow, known as Farangi Mahall. In 1695, the family moved there. Jamal Mian's line, descended from Qutbuddin's second son, Mulla Said, was to play a leading role in managing the property.

The Farangi Mahallis and the Maʻqulat Revolution

Mulla Qutbuddin had been at the centre of the most important intellectual development in Mughal India, the growth of the rational sciences. Traditionally, Islamic education had been divided into two main categories, *manqulat*, the transmitted sciences, such as *tafsir* (exegesis), *hadith* (tradition) and *fiqh* (jurisprudence), and *maʻqulat*, the rational sciences such as *mantiq* (logic), *hikmat* (philosophy), and *kalam* (theology).[12] Under the Delhi Sultanate *maʻqulat*

---

11. *Mahzarnama* in the name of Muhammad Said, Nizamuddin and Muhammad Raza, dated 35 R.Y. of Aurangzeb. I am grateful to Dr Iqbal Husain of Aligarh Muslim University for providing a translation; Mufti Rada Ansari, *Bani-yi Dars-i Nizami* (Lucknow: Nami Press, 1973) 120.
12. Francis Robinson, 'Education' in Robert Irwin ed., *New Cambridge History of Islam, Volume 4, Islamic Cultures and Societies to the End of the Eighteenth Century* (Cambridge: Cambridge University Press, 2010), 497–531.

subjects had not been favoured, but from the time of Sikander Lodi they began receiving attention. The key moment was the arrival of the brilliant Iranian, Fazlullah Shirazi, at Akbar's court in 1573. Fazlullah introduced the works of the great Iranian scholars of *ma'qulat* studies, Jalaluddin Dawwani and Ghiyasuddin Mansur Shirazi, which led to the study of the contemporary scholars, Mir Baqr Damad (d. 1631) and his brilliant pupil and son-in-law, Sadruddin Shirazi (d. 1640). In making these introductions, Fazlullah stimulated Indian work, notably that of Mulla Mahmud Jaunpuri (d. 1652), the foremost philosopher of Shah Jahan's time and the author of the much-valued commentary *Shams al-Bazighah*, and Abdul Hakim Sialkoti (d. 1656) who wrote notable commentaries on logic and philosophy. However, the transmission of the tradition of *ma'qulat* scholarship was particularly important. This went most directly from Fazlullah Shirazi to Mulla Abdul Salam Lahauri (d. 1627), and then to his pupil Abdul Salam of Deva, chief mufti of the Mughal army, and then from him, through Shaikh Danial of Chaurasa, to Mulla Qutbuddin.[13]

The eighteenth century saw an explosion of *ma'qulat* scholarship in Awadh and the surrounding regions. The eighteenth century historian, Ghulam Ali Azad Bilgrami, explained why: 'villages five to ten miles apart in which noblemen dwell supported in scholarship by kings; mosques, madrasahs and khanqahs whose doors are always open; crowds of students come; learning is active'.[14] Bilgrami also pointed out that all the *silsila*s (chains of transmission of learning from

13. Francis Robinson, *The 'Ulama of Farangi Mahall and Islamic Culture in South Asia* (Delhi: Permanent Black, 2001), 42–3.
14. Ghulam 'Ali Azad Bilgrami's *Ma'athir al-Kiram quoted in S.A.H. Nadwi, Hindustan ki Qadim Islami Darsgahain* (Azamgarh: Ma'arif, 1971), p. 37.

teacher to pupil) went back to Mulla Qutbuddin.[15] By the beginning of the nineteenth century, Shaikh Hasan al-Attar, the Shaikh al-Azhar, was commenting on the superiority of Indian scholarship in *ma`qulat* to that in Egypt and the Ottoman Empire. He also noted, amongst others, the work of Abdul Ali Bahrul Ulum of Farangi Mahall.[16]

The Dars-i Nizami

The explosion of *ma`qulat* scholarship, in which Jamal Mian's family was central, lay behind the development of their best-known legacy to Muslim India, the *Dars-i Nizami* madrasah curriculum. This had begun to take shape in the late-seventeenth century, in particular in the practice of Mulla Qutbuddin. However, it was given particular form by his third son, Mulla Nizamuddin. After his brothers, Mulla Asad and Mulla Said, died fighting with Aurangzeb's army in the Deccan, he was the first to preside in Farangi Mahall. His curriculum gave new emphasis to logic and philosophy, and the achievements of Iranian and Central Asian scholarship, especially the dominant figures at the court of Timur, Saaduddin al-Taftazani, and Saiyid Sharif al-Jurjani. But, as is often not understood today, the *Dars-i Nizami* was less a new balance of subjects than a new method of teaching which student skills in the *ma`qulat* subjects would support. Mulla Nizamuddin's method was to teach the two most difficult books in each subject on the grounds that once they had been

---

15. Robinson, *Farangi Mahall*, 53.
16. Robinson, *Farangi Mahall*, 226; for the explosion of Awadh *ma`qulat* scholarship see *Ibid.*, pp. 42–56.

mastered, the rest would present few problems. The student was also expected to show understanding of the text; mere rote learning was not enough.[17]

The *Dars-i Nizami* quickly spread throughout South Asia where it was firmly installed in madrasahs down to the present, although its content and teaching does not always represent the ideas of its originator. It spread with success, in part because its emphasis on understanding and reasoning skills enabled the able student to finish it by the age of sixteen or seventeen, but in part too because its emphasis on *ma'qulat* subjects formed good minds and good judgement for the business of government.[18] Jamal Mian was always conscious of how the *Dars-i Nizami*, when properly taught, helped form a questioning and balanced mind.

The Heritage of Sufism

At least from the time of Abdullah Ansari, Jamal Mian's ancestors had been Sufis. Certainly from the time of their engagement with Nasiruddin Chiragh-i Delhi they had been Chishti. The central figure in the seventeenth-century Sufi life of the Awadh region was Shah Muhibullah of Allahabad (1587–1648), the spiritual confidant of Shah Jahan's son, Dara Shikoh. Muhibullah found his spiritual vocation at the feet of Abu Said Gangohi, grandson of Abdul Quddus Gangohi (1456–1537), the Chishti-Sabiri saint who gave Ibn Arabi's so-called pantheistic ideas wide circulation in India. Then, after time at the Khanqah of Ahmad Abdul Haq of

---

17. Ibid. 213–15.
18. Ibid. 53.

Rudauli (d. 1434) he settled in Allahabad. Here, he produced
a powerful defence of Ibn Arabi's concept of *wahdat ul-wujud*
(the oneness of being) against the arguments of Shaikh Ahmad
Sirhindi (d. 1624). Sirhindi argued that *wahdat ul-wujud*,
which involves a total rejection of the external and acceptance
only of the reality of the One Being, went against reason and
the *shari`a*. In the twentieth century, Jamal Mian's father
declared that the Shah's great achievement was to resolve the
differences between the supporters of Ibn Arabi's *wahdat ul-
wujud* and Sirhindi's *wahdat ul-shuhud* (Unity of Perception).[19]

Mulla Qutbuddin was in the direct line of spiritual
succession from this great Chishti Sufi; his *pir* was Qazi
Sadruddin Ghasi of Allahabad who was a *khalifa* (successor)
of Shah Muhibullah. But the Mulla's descendants, while
maintaining their Chishti affiliation, were swept away by vital
spiritual leadership from another order, the Qadiri. The source
was Saiyid Shah Abdul Razzaq (1636–1724), the grandson
of a soldier from Badakhshan who had been given a *mansab*
by the Mughals and had played a part in putting down the
zamindars of Daryabad and Rudauli. His family, however, fell
on hard times and he was forced to serve as a common soldier.
While doing so in Gujarat, he was initiated into the Qadiriya
by Mir Saiyid Abdul Samad Khudanuma. Eventually he
returned to the region around Bansa in Bara Banki where his
mother's relatives, the Qidwais, lived. Here he led a powerful
Qadiri initiative and, in the subsequent three centuries, his
successors embraced a sizeable chunk of the Sufi life of India.[20]

Jamal Mian's ancestors were closely involved in this

---

19. Mawlana Mawlawi Muhammad Qiyam al-Din `Abd al-Bari, *Malfuz-i
    Razzaqi* (Cawnpur: Ahmad Press, 1926), 53.
20. Robinson, *Farangi Mahall*, 58.

development. There was a passionate relationship between Mulla Nizamuddin and Shah Abdul Razzaq; the Mulla would walk barefoot some thirty miles to visit him in Bansa and the Shah would sense him coming.[21] The Farangi Mahallis honoured the Shah by asking him to inaugurate their mosque and reserving the top step of its minbar for him to preach. In turn, the Shah's family gave them pride of place at the `Urs. Mulla Nizamuddin himself wrote the authoritative text on the Shah's life and sayings, the *Manaqib-i Razzaqiyya*. Among the themes that emerged were: the Shah's respect for the Chishti environment in which he found himself and in particular for the shrine of Ahmad Abdul Haq at Rudauli; his elevation of spiritual concerns over material matters; his following of *wahdat ul-wujud*; and his fundamental respect for the *shari`a*.[22] This said, we should note that later developments of the Bansa tradition were less *shari`a*-minded.[23]

The relationship with Bansa lay at the heart of the Farangi Mahall tradition down to the twentieth century. When Jamal Mian's father re-launched the family madrasah in 1905, it was Shah Mumtaz Ahmad Razzaqi, the *sajjadanashin* at Bansa, who presided. It was the Shah, too, who presided at its prize-giving ceremonies. In 1917 when Jamal Mian's father reflected on the `Urs at Bansa, he declared that for all Farangi Mahalli ulama, however learned they had been, 'attendance at this `urs has been a means of reinforcing faith.'[24]

---

21. Mulla Nizam al-Din, *Manaqib-i Razzaqiyya*, Urdu trans. Sibghat Allah Shahid Farangi Mahalli (Lucknow, n.d.) 30.
22. Robinson, *Farangi Mahall*, 60–5.
23. Ibid.
24. Ibid. 168; `Abd al-Bari, `*Urs-i Hadrat-i Bansa* (Lucknow: n.d.) 10. The original article was published in the Farangi Mahall journal, *Al-Nizamiyya*. It was subsequently republished, as its introduction indicates, immediately after Abdul Bari's death so the actual date of the Lucknow edition was 1926.

The history of Jamal Mian's family's spiritual devotion did not end with the Shah of Bansa. In the nineteenth century, Mulla Qutbuddin's great grandson through Mulla Said, Maulana Anwar ul Haq, had established a burial ground, Bagh Maulana Anwar, about a mile from Farangi Mahall at Rekabganj. Here, in the nineteenth century, family saints began to be acknowledged and regular `Urs celebrations started taking place. Indeed, in the mid-twentieth century, Hasrat Mohani, who was to be buried in the Bagh, recorded in his diary how much he had benefited from celebrating an `Urs there.[25]

From the mid-nineteenth century, Ajmer became accessible by rail. Attendance at the `Urs of Muinuddin Chishti came to be a real possibility for Sufis from all over India. It was then included in the annual round of Farangi Mahalli devotions. It was here, on 12 May 1916, that Jamal Mian's father took the lead in founding the Bazm-i Sufia-i Hind with an organizing committee of fifty-seven, mostly *sajjadanashin*s, who represented the leading Indian lines of spiritual succession. The aim was to make arrangements 'for the teaching of Sufis so that they can conform to the principles of Islam'.[26] Jamal Mian inherited an extraordinary legacy both of spiritual devotion and of spiritual leadership.

Farangi Mahallis under Shia Rule

The experience of Shia rule in Awadh had a significant impact on Jamal Mian's forefathers. Initially, Farangi Mahallis had no

---

25. Hasrat Mohani, 'Roznama', 28 December 1948, JMP.
26. Nur al-Hasan Ajmiri, *Khadimana Guzarish* (Lucknow, 1923), 39.

difficulty as Nawab Burhan ul-Mulk established his power in Awadh from 1722. Moreover, Safdar Jang, his successor from 1739, put such trust in the education that Farangi Mahall provided that he even required Shias to present a diploma from their teachers to be able to work in his bureaucracy.[27] Indeed, for most of Shia rule, Shias, including members of the great Shia learned family of Saiyid Dildar Ali Nasirabadi, continued to sit at the feet of Farangi Mahalli ulama for instruction in *ma`qulat* subjects.[28] The Farangi Mahallis also played a part in state administration, in particular in the administration of justice.[29]

The growth, however, of an increasingly self-confident Shia dimension to the Nawabi state, alongside the usual squabbles that take place when power is at stake, meant that at regular intervals prominent Farangi Mahallis had to leave Lucknow and seek their fortunes elsewhere, a process which helped spread both their influence and their potential sources of support. And so, towards the end of the 1750s, Mulla Nizamuddin's son, the great scholar, Maulana Abdul Ali Bahr ul-Ulum, found that Shia-Sunni tension was putting his life in danger. He left Lucknow for the court of the Nawab of Farrukhabad, Hafiz Rahmat Khan. He left there for Bauhar in Burdwan, Bengal, and finally served at the court of Nawab Wallajah in Arcot, Madras, where he was received with great honour. His tomb in the Wallajahi Mosque is next to that of the Nawab and is the focus of an annual `Urs.* The succession

---

27. J. R. I Cole, *Roots of North Indian Shi`ism in Iran and Iraq: Religion and State in Awadh, 1722–1859* (Berkeley & Los Angeles: University of California Press, 1988), 45.
28. Justin Jones, *Shi`a Islam in Colonial India: Religion, Community and Sectarianism* (Cambridge: Cambridge University Press, 2012), 54–5.
29. Cole, *Roots,* 139–41.

to Bahr ul-Ulum in Arcot was to be a source of grievance
which divided Farangi Mahall down to Jamal Mian's time.
Bahr ul-Ulum favoured his son-in-law, Alauddin, Jamal Mian's
direct ancestor, over his son, Abdul Rab, as his successor.
This led to continuing animosity which the British made
use of when they wanted to counter the political activities of
Jamal Mian's father.[30] But it was also, as we shall see, to be a
source of no small difficulty for Jamal Mian himself. Like his
grandfather, Alauddin's son, Jamaluddin, was forced to leave
Lucknow because of a religious dispute. He succeeded his
father as *sajjadanashin* in Madras, where he is buried in the
Wallajahi Mosque.[31]

Tension between the Farangi Mahallis and the Shia
government of Awadh forced others to leave. After two
Farangi Mahall students were killed in Shia-Sunni rioting
in Lucknow, the great logician, Mulla Hasan (d. 1795),
sometime after 1766, led a deputation of teachers in protest
to the Nawab's Court in Faizabad. When he had no success,
Mulla Hasan decided that it would be wiser to leave Lucknow
for the court of Hafiz Rahmat Khan. He later moved to
Rampur, establishing a madrasah and a connection between
the Nawab of Rampur and Farangi Mahall which lasted into
the twentieth century.[32]

A second outbreak of tension between a Farangi Mahalli
and the Nawabi government had an even more beneficial
outcome. In this case, Mulla Haidar (d. 1840) who was a
richly rewarded servant of the Nawabi government got into

---

30. Francis Robinson, *Separatism Among Indian Muslims: The Politics of
    the United Provinces' Muslims, 1860–1923* (Cambridge: Cambridge
    University Press, 1974), 261 and 161 note 4.
31. `Inayat Allah, *Tadhkirah*, 46.
32. Ibid. 46–8; Robinson, *Farangi Mahall*, 71 note 7.

a dispute with the chief minister. He left Lucknow, finally ending up in Hyderabad, where the Nizam gave him a *mansab* worth Rs 1000 per month and the titles of Afzal ul-Daulah and Malik ul-Ulama. He was able to teach and write in several scholarly areas. Mulla Haider and his descendants were able to offer patronage to Farangi Mahallis and to live at a standard unknown to their relatives in Lucknow. One granddaughter became the mother of Abdul Hai (d. 1886), the greatest Farangi Mahalli scholar of the nineteenth century. Another granddaughter became the mother of Jamal Mian's father.[33]

The final Farangi Mahalli engagement with the Shia government of Awadh arguably came to an end with the first round of the Ayodhya dispute which rocked India in 1992. On this occasion it was Muslim zealots who made the running. In 1855, one Shah Ghulam Husain started a campaign against a Hanuman temple in Faizabad that he claimed was on a site originally occupied by a mosque. The immediate outcome was that Ghulam Husain's followers were massacred by thousands of Hindus at Ayodhya, a suburb of Faizabad. One Maulvi Amir Ali of Amethi declared a jihad with the aim of removing the Hindus from the Hanumangarhi and restoring the mosque. The Farangi Mahallis were divided over the issue: Mufti Muhammad Yusuf, who worked for the Awadh government as a mufti in the civil and criminal court, supported the government's attempts to achieve a negotiated settlement, debating with Amir Ali at Daryabad.[34] Jamal Mian's great grandfather, Abdul Razzaq, along with other relatives without government posts, supported the jihad.

---

33. `Inayat Allah, *Tadhkirah*, 49–52, 76–7.
34. Cole, *Roots*, 210, 249.

Because the Awadh government blocked the exits from the city, Abdul Razzaq escaped the fate of most of the jihadis which was to be slaughtered by government and taluqdari troops near Rudauli.[35]

The Farangi Mahallis under the British

With Abdul Razzaq (d. 1889–90) we engage with the responses of the Farangi Mahallis to the British. Not all were opposed but Abdul Razzaq maintained an approach of hostility throughout his life. After he finished his education in Farangi Mahall, he stayed with his father, Jamaluddin, in Madras for five years. On his way back he noted how much better-governed Hindu-ruled territories seemed to be than the British-ruled ones.[36] During the Mutiny Uprising, he was engaged on the Sepoy side in the siege of Lucknow, his turban used as a banner of defiance.[37] He made it clear to his family that serving the British was an act of *kufr* and he refused to use any ice, sugar, or English paper.[38] When he was awarded the title of *Shams ul-Ulama* by the British, he exclaimed 'What have I done that such a calamity should befall me?', shut himself away in his house, and instructed his son to return the title forthwith.[39] He was very much the activist in defending

35. Ibid. 200; 'Inayat Allah, *Tadhkirah,* p. 98–99.
36. Altaf al-Rahman Qidwai, *Anwar-i Razzaqiyya* (Lucknow, n.d.), 61.
37. Ibid. 29–30.
38. 'Inayat Allah, *Tadhkirah,* 98.
39. Qidwai, *Anwar,* 21; but it was not returned because it was felt that the government would regard it as an insult and his son, Abdul Wahhab, kept it hidden, 'Inayat Allah, *Tadhkirah,* 99–100; in fact, Abdul Razzaq's sanad of *Shams ul-Ulama* still exists in Jamal Mian's papers.

Muslim interests. During the Russo-Turkish war (1878–80) he founded the *Majlis Muid ul-Islam* and toured northern India seeking contributions for the Turkish cause.[40]

Abdul Razzaq's role as an activist in defence of Muslim interests was taken up by his grandson, Jamal Mian's father, Abdul Bari (1878–1926); his son Abdul Wahhab focussed his energies almost entirely on teaching, spiritual leadership, and the management of Farangi Mahall. We have noted Abdul Bari's attempts to give leadership to India's Sufis. He was also a leading scholar of his time. The family historian, perhaps stretching a point, regarded him as the equal of his first cousin, Maulana Abdul Hai, and wrote of the two as shining like the sun and the moon in fame. 'After Bahr ul-Ulum no one amongst the learned men of Farangi Mahall enjoyed such reputations, both amongst their fellow learned men and amongst the people in general.'[41] Abdul Bari wrote 111 books. In noting this figure we should remember that some would now be considered separately published articles or essays. Among them were books on philosophy, logic, jurisprudence (his most important field), principles of jurisprudence, Quran commentary, tradition, Sufism, and literary criticism. On his death, he was writing a Quran commentary in Urdu which was unfinished.[42]

As a teacher, Abdul Bari created the first formal madrasah in Farangi Mahall in 1905. Up to this time, Farangi Mahallis had taught in their homes. He required the madrasah to teach 'modern' subjects, as in government schools, such as arithmetic, algebra, geometry, and geography. He also required that it use

40. Qidwai, *Anwar*, 30.
41. `Inayat Allah, *Tadhkirah*, 106.
42. Ibid. 116; Mawlawi Muhmmad `Inayat Allah, *Risala-yi Hadrat al-Afaq ba Wafat Majmu`at al-Akhlaq* (Lucknow,1929), 12.

up-to-date systems such as timetables, regular examinations, and regular inspections by distinguished teachers from outside. Abdul Bari himself taught as many as 300 pupils. Twenty-two came from Farangi Mahall. There were students from Lucknow, including the odd Shia and members of the High Court Bar who came for Quran lessons. There were Qidwais from Bara Banki and Mohanis from Mohan. Many came from the qasbahs of the UP and Bihar, and also from the shrine families of northern India—Ajmer, Kakori, Kichaucha, Rudauli, Kursi, and so on. There were some, too, from further afield—Bengal, Sind, Peshawar, Afghanistan, and Madras. Given the power of the student-teacher relationship, the spread of his pupils meant that he had potential supporters and helpers all over northern India and further afield.[43]

From 1909, Abdul Bari began to emerge as one of the leading Muslims of his time. He supported the Muslim League's great campaign to establish separate electorates with extra seats for Muslims in the Morley-Minto Council reforms. In 1910, he refounded his grandfather's Majlis Muid ul-Islam to enable the ulama of Farangi Mahall to work with other ulama 'to help Muslims attain progress in worldly matters, while keeping in mind the injunctions of the shariat'. Contacts with both Enver Pasha's Young Turk movement and with Sharif Husain of Mecca, as well as a long visit to the Middle East in 1912–13, meant that he had a real sense of developments in the Ottoman world. So it was not surprising that in 1913, with the help of his spiritual disciple, Mushir Husain Qidwai (1878–1937), he should found the Anjuman-i Khuddam-i Kaaba to work to defend the holy places of Islam in Arabia. At the same time, he became involved with the

---

43. Ibid. 8–10.

political campaigns driven by the 'Young Party' faction of the Muslim League—the Red Crescent Mission to Turkey and the Cawnpore Mosque protest. In the context of this involvement, the greatest popular Muslim leaders of the day, Mahomed and Shaukat Ali, became his spiritual disciples.[44]

From 1913, Abdul Bari became a national figure. In 1914, with the Raja Muhammad Ali Muhammad of Mahmudabad (1878–1931) he tried to dissuade the Ottoman Sultan from entering World War One on the side of Germany. In 1915, he strongly endorsed the principle that the fate of the Ottoman Empire was a religious concern of the Muslims. In 1916, he condemned his friend, Sharif Husain, for raising the flag of Arab revolt against the Ottomans. In 1917, he led the Majlis Muid ul-Islam in making an address to the Secretary of State Montagu and the Viceroy Chelmsford, who were gathering evidence for the preparation of the next stage of reform to the legislative councils, which government described as 'a nakedly impracticable demand for the predomination of priestly influence'. In 1918, he led a group of ulama to the Delhi sessions of the Muslim League where, for the very first time, ulama sat with Western-educated politicians. He and his ulama colleagues were there to bring weight to the League's resolutions on the fate of the Ottoman Empire.[45]

The years 1919 and 1920 saw the height of Abdul Bari's political influence. Soon after the Delhi Muslim League conference, he issued a fatwa enjoining jihad if there was any danger of infidels controlling either the Turkish caliphate or the holy places of Islam. At the same time, he set about raising support in the UP countryside and established a newspaper,

---

44. Robinson, *Farangi Mahall*, 152–5.
45. Ibid. 155.

Akhuwat, to focus on Islamic issues. More important, in terms of the growth of his influence, he set about wooing Gandhi, who came to stay in Farangi Mahall in March 1919, to the Khilafat cause. Within six months he had succeeded. In September 1919, he held an all-India conference in Lucknow which led to the foundation of the All-India Central Khilafat Committee. With his Farangi Mahall relatives, and the lawyer Choudhry Khaliquzzaman, a constitution was drawn up. The Khilafat organization came to be based in Bombay because that was where the Muslim merchants who funded it were based. In November, at the Delhi Khilafat Conference, he took the first steps towards getting non-cooperation with the British adopted as a policy and began the process of doing a deal with Gandhi. In December, at Amritsar, he presided over the first sessions of the Jamiat ul-Ulama-i Hind. In founding this organization, which exists in India, Pakistan, and Bangladesh to this day, he brought to fulfilment what he and his family had been trying to do through the Majlis Muid ul-Islam—the fashioning of an all-India organization of ulama to make their views heard in public affairs. During the months of 1919, Abdul Bari demonstrated a remarkable capacity to make the running in Muslim politics.[46]

The first test for Abdul Bari as a leader of the Khilafat Movement was to make sure that the organization reflected the urgent concerns of most Muslims about developments in West Asia rather than the caution of merchants who did not wish to flout imperial will. He was helped in this by the release from internment of Abul Kalam Azad (1888–1958), who was to bring intellectual leadership to the formation of policies of non-cooperation, and the Ali Brothers, who

---

46. Ibid. 155–6.

were able to bring their gifts in organizing popular protest to the campaign between February and June 1920. Abdul Bari devoted enormous effort to persuading the Khilafat Committee to adopt non-cooperation as a policy and second, at the Allahabad meetings in June, to accept Gandhi as the chair of the group that would put non-cooperation into action. From then until September, Abdul Bari devoted his energies to ensuring that, along with other radical Khilafatists, there was a vast Muslim presence at the Calcutta Special Congress. This enabled Gandhi, with his non-cooperation agenda, to capture the organization of Indian nationalism. Abdul Bari did not attend the Congress because of the death of a daughter. Nevertheless, his contribution to driving forward the strategy which led to the capture of the Congress for a primarily Muslim purpose is demonstrated in his dynamic activity and in the hundreds of letters and telegrams from this period in his private papers.[47]

★ ★ ★

Jamal Mian would have been aware of the extraordinary history of scholarship, of spiritual devotion, and, on occasion, of political activism which had occupied the lives of his forefathers over hundreds of years. In the way of a society which was still powerfully oral in its habits, he would have often heard these achievements narrated. But, should he forget, which was unlikely, this was also a time when family members were increasingly coming to write down and publish their history. The headmaster of the family madrasah, Maulana Inayatullah, (1888–1941) published the family history in

---

47. Ibid. 156.

1928, *Tadhkhira-yi `Ulama-i Farangi Mahall*, and Abdul Bari's biography in 1929, *Risala-yi Hadrat al-Afaq ba Wafat Majmu`at al-Akhlaq*. In the late 1920s, Jamal Mian's effective guardian—his father's close aide, Altafur Rahman Qidwai—produced his biography of Jamal Mian's great grandfather, Abdul Razzaq, *Anwar-i Razzaqiyya*. Then, in either the 1930s or 1940s, Inayatullah's brother, Sibghatullah, published an Urdu translation of the Persian manuscript of Mulla Nizamuddin's *malfuzat* of Saiyid Shah Abdul Razzaq of Bansa, *Manaqib-i Razzaqiyya*. That Farangi Mahallis should have chosen this moment to publish their past raises interesting issues: Did they feel that, with the rise of Islamic Reform and the popularity of Western, as opposed to madrasah, education, the times were moving against them? Did they feel an increasing need to assert their past to bolster their contemporary authority? Did they feel, after the death of Abdul Bari, increasingly exposed to an unsympathetic world? We do not know the answer; they have left us no explanation for this flurry of historical writing. This said, there is no doubt that there was a considerable weight of memory that Jamal Mian had to bear. It was a weight of memory which, in the eyes of others, could bring him prestige and advantages. But it was also, potentially, a psychological burden as he faced the vicissitudes of his rapidly changing world.

The Inner Section of the Farangi Mahall Muhalla in the Early Twentieth Century

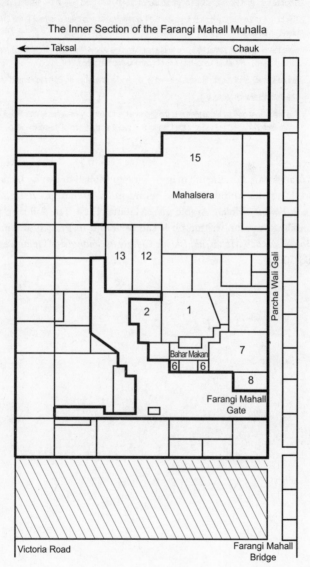

The Inner Section of the Farangi Mahall Muhalla

KEY:

1.   This is the original haveli given by Aurangzeb which was occupied by Maulana Sharafatullah's family. We do not know for sure but it is likely that Sharafatullah's grandchildren, that is Maulanas Salamatullah, Sibghatullah, and Inayatullah, all of whom taught Jamal Mian lived here in the 1920s and 1930s.

2.   The house of Mulla Nizamuddin in which the Farangi Mahall madrasa was held in the first half of the twentieth century.

6,7,8. were the property of Jamal Mian's grandfather, Maulana Abdul Wahhab, which would probably have passed down to Maulana Abdul Bari and Maulana Qutbuddin Abdul Wali.

12.   House known as Walagarh Mosque where Gandhi would stay when he came to Farangi Mahall.

13.   The Farangi Mahall Mosque

15.   The Mahalsera built by Mulla Haider in the mid-nineteenth century. In Jamal Mian's time it was a place where receptions and feasts were held. Abdul Bari had a study in one of the rooms which led off it.

Source:

This map is based on the full map of Farangi Mahall drawn by Jamal Mian's uncle, Maulana Abdul Baqi and found in his *Barkat al-'Ilm wal amal fi Dukkan Farangi Mahall* Arabic mss. Medina, 1324. The full map plus the copious information written on it can be found in Francis Robinson *The 'Ulama of Farangi Mahal and Islamic Culture in South Asia* (Delhi: Permanent Black, 2001).

3

Jamal Mian's early life

JAMAL MIAN WAS BORN ON 5 DECEMBER 1919 WHICH WAS also 12 Rabiulawwal 1335 AH, the Prophet's birthday. It is not recorded that his family saw a good omen in the timing of his entry into the world. But it surely had to be so for a family for whom respect for the Prophet was a central part of their devotional life. Moreover, it was wholly appropriate for someone for whom the performance of *milad* on 12 Rabiulawwal was always an important spiritual exercise; and for whom Medina became the physical focus of spiritual life, after cutting himself off from the holy places of India in 1982.

A photograph of Jamal Mian's father, Abdul Bari, exists, but as there is some doubt regarding its authenticity, we do not refer to it. Instead, we shall rely on the words of those who knew him personally. Recalling Abdul Bari on All-India Radio in 1950, Abdul Majid Daryabadi described him as a 'distinguished scholar and great Indian leader, the spiritual guide of the Ali Brothers and the friend of Gandhiji. He was a very handsome and distinguished personality, a very generous, hospitable and sweet-natured person, who from the beginning showed signs of greatness.'[1] Inayatullah, Abdul Bari's pupil and spiritual disciple, adds to the picture. He agrees with

---

1. Talk by Abdul Majid Daryabadi on All-India Radio, 12 January 1950, Library of Mufti Raza Ansari.

Daryabadi that he was very handsome, of average height,
and had a pale rose complexion. He was broad-shouldered
because he never gave up exercise and walked briskly. He
looked handsome in all clothing—in the summer he wore
a dopalri topi, which by this time had become a distinctive
Lucknow cap, and in the winter he wore a fez, which might
have been an attempt to associate himself with the Young Turk
movement. But, we should also note that by the early twentieth
century, the fez had become the headwear of most respectable
Muslim men. While his father was alive he wore a sherwani,
but after he died he wore a kurta and sometimes an angarkha.
In winter he wore a shaluqa, or full-sleeved buttoned waistcoat,
over which he would wear a cape, or aba, which Abdul Halim
Sharar tells us was introduced to Lucknow by those who had
been to Karbela. On Fridays and on Eid, when he would be
leading prayers, he wore an angarkha with a scarf.[2]

Amongst Abdul Bari's personal characteristics, Inayatullah
lists his management skills, hospitality, bravery, patience, the
fact that he always stood up for truth and justice, that he
never lost his temper, and that he never compromised with
aristocrats or government officials.[3] Part of this assessment
was true, but part as we shall see was challenged by the facts.
Like his ancestors, he was deeply opposed to British rule.
'I can tolerate everything,' he wrote to Dr Syed Mahmud
in 1923, 'but cannot give up my hate of this government of
Satan....'[4] While his relationship with Gandhi was of great

---

2. `Inayat Allah, *Risala*, 30–4; Abdul Halim Sharar, *Lucknow: The Last
    Phase of an Oriental Culture, trans. and ed. by E. S. Harcourt and Fakhir
    Hussain,* (London: Paul Elek, 1975), 176.

3. `Inayat Allah, *Risala*, 30–4.

4. Abdul Bari to Dr Syed Mahmood, 26 Ramadan 1341 (13 May 1923),
    ABP.

importance for the Hindu-Muslim non-cooperation campaign of 1920–22, he was also quick to identify Hindus as the enemy as he did in the Shahabad riots of 1917 and in the rioting and reconversion movements of 1923 onwards.[5] 'Let us kill the most powerful enemy [the British],' he wrote to Abdullah Haroon in 1924, 'then we can deal with the less powerful one [the Hindus].'[6]

Abdul Bari was quick to demand respect for the example of the Prophet and the practices of his faith. When he discovered that the authorities at MAO College, Aligarh, an institution which he supported with donations, did not appear to require students to follow the practice of the Prophet in dress and eating, he engaged them in a vigorous correspondence on the importance of trousers not falling below the ankles and of eating off a mat placed on the ground rather than from a table.[7] During the Balkan Wars, when he was asked at a Red Crescent meeting, attended amongst others by the Nawab of Rampur and government officials, to stand out of sympathy for Viceroy Hardinge who had been seriously wounded during the previous week by a bomb, he refused. Asked by his family friend, the Raja of Jahangirabad, to stand, he replied that he could not 'as an `alim sympathize with a kafir and thus insult Muslims.'[8] When he discovered several prominent Muslims smoking cigars at a crucial Khilafat Committee meeting in early 1920, which was also Ramadan, he lost his temper, chastised them for their kafir-like habits, and stormed out of

---

5. Robinson, *Separatism*, 284–6, 339.
6. Abdul Bari to Abdullah Haroon, 5 Jumada al-Akhira 1342 (12 January 1924), ABP.
7. Correspondence between Abdul Bari and Habibur Rahman Sherwani, 1910, Farangi Mahal, Lucknow.
8. `Inayat Allah, *Risala*, 35.

the meeting.[9] Indeed, given the number of times Abdul Bari
took issue with his fellow Muslims for failing to respect Islam,
it is clear that he took such behaviour as a personal affront.

Despite his biographer's view of Abdul Bari as a patient
man, which stemmed perhaps from his respect for his *pir*,
Abdul Bari had a short temper. 'The fact is,' declared his
pupil Muhammad Shafi, 'the maulana was very hot tempered.'
Political speeches were always risky moments. Shafi recalls
him getting carried away at the Calcutta Khilafat Conference
of 1920 and urging those present to wage war on the British
and to burn down the barracks of their soldiers.[10] Government
recorded his speech as President of the Ajmer session of the
Jamiat ul-Ulama-i Hind on 5 March 1922 as an assault on
the policy of non-violence. The Muslims were not to remain
silent like women but needed action to achieve their aims.
He 'was ready to commit violence by hand, teeth and all the
implements available.'[11] It was not surprising that Mushir
Husain of the Gadia branch of Qidwais, who had worked
closely with him on the Anjuman-i Khuddam-i Kaaba, should
have recommended that he give up making political speeches[12]
and that Harcourt Butler, a governor of the UP well-versed
in Muslim affairs, should have referred to him as his 'diwana'
or 'mad' mulla.[13]

Gandhi, writing in 1924, has left us with an acute
assessment of Abdul Bari's character:

9. Muhammad Shafi Hajjat Allah Ansari, 'Memoir' 15 August 1977, 32,
    ABP.
10. Ibid. 32.
11. Home Poll, File No. 51 of 1920, NAI.
12. Shafi, 'Memoir', 33.
13. Ibid. 43.

He is a simple child of God. I have discovered no guile in him.
He often speaks without thinking and often embarrasses his
best friends. But he is as quick to apologise as he is ready to
say things offensive. He means all he says for the time being.
He is as sincere in his anger as he is in his apology. He once
flared up at Maulana Mahomed Ali without just cause. I was
then his guest. He thought he had said something offensive to
me also. Maulana Mahomed Ali and I were just then leaving
his place to entrain for Cawnpore. After our departure, he felt
he had wronged us. He had certainly wronged Mahomed Ali,
not me. But he sent a deputation to us at Cawnpore asking us
to forgive him. He rose in my estimation by this act. I admit,
however, that the Maulana Saheb can become a dangerous
friend. But my point is that he is a friend. He does not say one
thing and mean another. There are no mental reservations with
him. I would trust such a friend with my life, because I know
he will never stab me in the dark.[14]

★ ★ ★

Abdul Bari was twice married. His first wife was a relative
from Kakori. In 1898, she died in childbirth and her son
a few days later. A year or so later, Abdul Bari married his
second wife, Khurshid un-Nisa—known to her grandchildren
as Ammi Dadi (Dadi meaning paternal grandmother)—who
was from a well-to-do Saiyid family of Dogawan in Lucknow.
Her father was Mahfuz Husain Naqvi and she was connected
through her siblings to several prominent families of Awadh,

---

14. Article by Gandhi in *Young India*, 29 May 1924. *Collected Works of
    Mahatma Gandhi*, XXIV, (Ahmedabad: Director of the Publications
    Division, Government of India, 1967), 146.

amongst them, the taluqdari family of Mahmudabad and the Qidwais of Baragaon and Masauli. The ghazal singer and film actor, Talat Mahmud (1924–98), was also a relative.[15]

Ammi Dadi had a family history of depression. Her granddaughter remembers her telling her about one of her uncles who, during a panic attack, tried to make several of his female family members jump in a well when Lucknow was under threat, probably in the Mutiny Uprising. This illness, which has been identified as a form of bi-polar illness, also affected her daughter Sughra and Jamal Mian.[16]

Ammi Dadi's granddaughter remembers her as being quite tall, with a good physique and a good posture. She was a little darker than her son. Her hair was not completely white but greying, curly, and tied at the back. She wore long loose white kurtas and straight pants (*khara pajama*), usually in darker shades of grey, blue, or brown. As a widow, she always wore a white cotton dupatta which was often finely pleated (*chuna hoa*). She did not wear any jewelry except for a plain gold band with a tiny diamond which had been given to her when she visited the family—that of Maulvi Dada—in Hyderabad. (Maulvi Dada was Nurul Haider, the grandson of Mulla Haidar, who Inayatullah regarded as responsible for the good relations between the Hyderabadi and Lucknow branches of the Farangi Mahall family).[17] She was serious, soft-spoken, and gentle; she did not speak loudly or joke. She moved with dignity and had nothing to do with household management. That was in the hands of Amma, Abdul Bari's sister, the wife of Abdul Baqi, who lived permanently in Medina. On the

---

15. Farida Jamal, Note on the Family, JMP.
16. Ibid.
17. `Inayat Allah, *Tadhkirah*, 188–9.

other hand, she was seriously involved in the upbringing of both her children and her grandchildren.[18]

Ammi Dadi had three children who lived to adulthood. The first was a daughter who was married to Abdul Bari's nephew, Qutbuddin Abdul Wali (known as Qutb Mian). They produced two sons, Muhammad Abdul Razzaq, known as Muhammad Mian, and Nur Abdul Ali, known as Nur Mian. After she died in 1920, Abdul Bari arranged for Qutb Mian to be married to a daughter of Maulana Salamatullah, a marriage which was to produce Jalaluddin Abdul Matin (Matin Mian, 1929–). Matin Mian was to remain close to Jamal Mian and to do his best to sustain the central traditions of his family in Lucknow. The second child was another daughter, Fatima Sughra Haya (born in 1323 AH/1905). She was an able woman and a gifted poet, who also wrote many stories, dramas, and articles. Her *na`t*s are sung in Farangi Mahalli *milad* celebrations to this day; her uncle, Abdul Baqi, thought so highly of them that he placed copies of them in the Prophet's tomb in Medina. She was devoted to Jamal Mian, as he was to her. One letter that she sent to him, which survives, is full of love, as are her poems.[19] Her sufferings from her depressive illness, which at times meant she had to be kept confined to a room under the constant observation of her female relatives, were a source of anguish for him. When recalled in later life, they would bring tears to his eyes.[20] When Sughra died in 1948, Jamal Mian published a small collection of those of her poems which she

---

18. Farida Jamal, 'Recollections of Ammi Dadi' n.d. but sent to the author in 2014.

19. Sughra to Jamal Mian c. 1939. Jamal Mian kept this letter in his 'Personal File' where there were many of the things most precious to him. JMP.

20. Farida Jamal 'Recollections'.

had not destroyed. A tribute to the power of her memory in his life was that nearly twenty years later, in 1967, he published a second edition of her poetry from Karachi. This fragment gives a sense of the sweet and intelligent nature of Jamal Mian's sister:

> Learn from the life of stars O humans.
> How fond they are towards each other, and are happy.
> These tiny little stars with their frail beauty
> How they reflect God's taste and beauty!
> They are the punctuations of the author of eternity.[21]

Throughout Jamal Mian's life, he kept Sughra's pen on his desk.

Ammi Dadi adored Jamal Mian, calling him Bhaiya and he was devoted to her in turn. He copied many of her ways. He did not, following her practice, eat between meals. After eating a meal she would eat a small piece of chappati and then drink water, and so did Jamal Mian until the last days of his life. She would not travel on Wednesdays because she thought it brought bad luck. Jamal Mian was similarly careful about the timing of his travels. Jamal Mian wrote to her when they were apart, always spelling Ammi with an ain. It was, moreover, his desire to see her as she lay dying in Lucknow when he was trapped in Dacca by the Government of India's decision to impound his passport, which led to one of the more fateful decisions in his life.[22]

* * *

21. Muhammad Jamal al-Din ʿAbd al-Wahhab Farangi Mahalli, ed., *Nawa-yi Agahi Kalam-i Sughra,* second Ed. (Karachi: Maktaba Khatoon-i Pakistan, 1967), 44–5.
22. Farida Jamal, 'Recollections'.

The 1906–07 map of Farangi Mahall (see pp. 28–9), which was drawn by Abdul Bari's brother-in-law Abdul Baqi, gives a strong sense of how the young Jamal Mian would have grown up surrounded by his relatives. In the muhalla, there were well over forty separate living units plus several mosques, two madrasah buildings and other teaching areas, a clinic, an entertainment area, and so on. Jamal Mian was raised in the inner quarters of his main home, the Mahalsera and the Bahar Makan; he would have moved easily between the centrally-placed buildings numbered 6, 7, 8, 9, and 15 on the map which would have been occupied by his closest relatives. Close by in the building marked 1 was the family of Maulana Sharafatullah. He had been in British service, retiring as deputy collector of Lucknow. After retirement, he involved himself in the management of the Farangi Mahall madrasah.[23] Many of his descendants contributed to the educational and political projects of Jamal Mian's father. His eldest son, Hidayatullah, after developing a legal career in Hyderabad, retired to teach in the madrasah. His son, Sibghatullah (Illustration 7), had started teaching at the madrasah in 1914. From that year until 1918, he edited *Al-Nizamiyya*, a monthly magazine which expressed the views of Farangi Mahall's younger generation. He was also noted as Farangi Mahall's best orator.[24] Sharafatullah's second son was Maulana Salamatullah, who taught in the madrasah and in political matters operated very much as second-in-command to Jamal Mian's father. He was a major figure in the Anjuman Muid ul-Islam and the Anjuman-i Khuddam-i

23. `Inayat Allah, *Tadhkirah*, 68–71.
24. Ibid.73–4; for a discussion of *al-Nizamiyya* see Robinson, *Farangi Mahall*, 130–44.

Kaaba, and threw himself into the Khilafat protest, going to
jail with Shaukat Ali, Khaliquzzaman, and others.[25] His son,
Maulana Shafi, was seconded by Abdul Bari, at the request
of Abul Kalam Azad, to teach at the Madrasah Islamia in
Calcutta's Zachariah Mosque. He was to return to teach in the
family madrasah. Sharafatullah's third son, Inayatullah, was
the family historian who, while maintaining a vigorous interest
in politics, devoted his life to teaching in the family madrasah
of which he was principal for many years.[26]

Such men were literally on Jamal Mian's doorstep as a child.
But there were other notable figures in his early life. There
was Chaudhuri Azimuddin Ashraf from the taluqdari family
of Paisar, who spend his early days in Abdul Bari's household.
Then, there were two gifted Qidwais of Baragaon, who were
his father's spiritual disciples. There was Ehsanur Rahman
(b. Mohurram 1303/1885) who after an early education at
Farangi Mahall, and then an English education at Canning
College (Lucknow), went to Cambridge. He corresponded
with his *pir* throughout his time in England.[27] On his return,
he developed a successful legal practice and entered politics,
becoming General Secretary of the UP Muslim League.
Ultimately, he was buried in Farangi Mahall's Bagh Maulana
Anwar. The second was Saidur Rahman (1882–1954,
Illustration 3) who, after an early education at Farangi Mahall,
went to Aligarh where he was in the same class as Rafi Ahmed
Kidwai, UP Congress leader and later a minister in the central
government under Nehru. On leaving Aligarh, he became
Shaukat Ali's secretary until the Ali Brothers fell out with

25. `Inayat Allah, *Tadhkirah*, 65–7.

26. For Inayatullah's life see his brother's biography of him Sibghat Allah
    Shahid Ansari, *Sadr al-Mudarrisin* (Lucknow, 1941).

27. This correspondence is to be found in the Abdul Bari Papers ABP.

Abdul Bari over Abdul Aziz ibn Saud's conquest of the Hejaz.
Saidur Rahman followed his *pir*. Throughout his life, he was
to remain devoted to Farangi Mahall in general and Jamal
Mian in particular. Saidur Rahman was notably indulgent to
the young Jamal Mian. He used to take him for rides in the
beautiful horse-drawn carriage he had been given when he was
secretary to the Maharaja of Mahmudabad. He bought him a
child's relaxing chair, a small table, and chairs from an English
shop, probably in Hazratganj. Perhaps most important from
the young Jamal Mian's point of view, Saidur Rahman bought
him a motor car which could be driven manually by a handle.
'It was purple in colour and I used to go around in it within
Farangi Mahall.' This was in addition to the tricycle which his
father had bought him in Bombay and the small cupboard
which the great Memon timber merchant of Bombay and
leading Khilafat supporter, M. M. Chotani, had made for him
in his workshop.[28] From early childhood, Jamal Mian knew,
and was known to, people who were going to be important to
him later in his life.

In addition to these relatives, friends, and devotees of his
father, there were two people particularly attached to Jamal
Mian. The first was Irtiza Husain (Illustration 6), his father's
driver, and his *murid*. Irtiza Husain was from Rudauli and
was employed by Abdul Bari on the recommendation of Shah
Hayat Ahmad, Jamal Mian's future father-in-law. He was
always smartly turned out in a waistcoat, a well-cultivated
moustache, and a small beard. He lived with his wife and
sons in the muhalla adjacent to Jamal Mian's quarters. Later,

---

28. Annotation by Jamal Mian, dated 28.11.92, Choudhry Khaliquzzaman,
    Shah Rah-i Pakistan (Lahore, Anjuman-i Islamiyya, 1967), 489, Jamal
    Mian Catalogue no. 1821.

he became Jamal Mian's driver, driving in his open-top Baby
Austin in Lucknow and looking after his children both in
Lucknow and Dacca. The second was another Qidwai from
Baragaon, Altafur Rahman (b. 10 January 1889, Illustration 2).
He had been educated in Farangi Mahall and never left. He
was Abdul Bari's disciple and personal secretary in whom
he had complete trust. Several of Abdul Bari's major works
were dictated to him and published in his name, for instance
Ahwal-i `Ulama-i Farangi Mahall, Anwar-i Razzaqiyya, and
Altaf al-Rahman ba Tafsir al-Qur`an (4 Volumes). After Abdul
Bari died, he took especial care of Jamal Mian.

It is possible that not all those around the young Jamal Mian
would have treated him indulgently. If he happened to wander
out of Farangi Mahall gate, go up Parcha Wali Gali towards
the Chauk, and then turn left, he would soon find himself in
Taksal Muhalla where his Bahr ul-Ulumi relatives lived. The
two leading figures of the time were Maulanas Abdul Majid
and Abdul Hamid. They were both great-grandsons of Abdul
Rab whose father, Bahr ul-Ulum, had passed over him as his
successor in Madras in favour of Jamal Mian's great great
grandfather, Alauddin. Both Abdul Majid and Abdul Hamid
had worked closely with Abdul Bari in the early years of the
Madrasah Nizamiyya. But in 1912, they had resigned because
of the strong pro-Ottoman line taken by Abdul Bari. From
then on, their relations deteriorated with the Bahr ul-Ulumis
taking a consistent pro-government line. In 1918, in what
was most certainly an unfriendly move, Abdul Hamid had set
up, with the help of a Rs 3,000 grant from the government,
a separate madrasah, the Madrasah Qadima. Throughout
the Khilafat non-cooperation movement the Bahr ul-Ulumis
opposed the activities of Jamal Mian's father, being given

further government recognition for their efforts.[29] We have no record that Bahr ul-Ulumi hostility was visited on the very young Jamal Mian, but it was certainly to be a feature later in his life.

The young Jamal Mian was not just surrounded by relatives and family friends; he was also surrounded by madrasah students and the constant buzz of active young people. There were usually at least fifty students staying at the hostel of which Maulana Salamatullah was a very popular manager. Students would constantly be moving through the muhalla as they went to be taught in the madrasah's main building, which was in Mulla Nizamuddin's old house (Illustration 5), or alternatively went to study in the houses of individual teachers. Abdul Bari, for instance, would give lessons on *tasawwuf* in the mahalsera. Maulana Shafi, who attended these lessons with Qutb Mian and Abdul Qadir, remembers how intense the atmosphere became in these lessons and how Abdul Bari's eyes would become red hot and intoxicated. Once Jamal Mian, aged four, burst into the class in the midst of his play. His father pointed with his eyes that he should go away. Jamal Mian was put out by his father's unusual state and fled.[30]

Jamal Mian's father was renowned for his hospitality and during his early years the boy would have seen many leading figures of Indian politics, and occasionally from beyond, visiting Farangi Mahall, and often staying there. Gandhi would stay in a small room off the Mahalsera with his goat tethered to a papaya tree outside (Illustration 4).[31] Then the

---

29. Robinson, *Separatism*, 270–2.
30. Shafi, 'Memoir', 28–9.
31. The family maintained the practice of cultivating a papaya tree in this position, as I saw in the spring of 1980. I do not know if it was in memory of the Mahatma.

Ali Brothers were also frequent visitors, a notable feast being held in January 1920 when, on their release from internment, Abdul Bari made them his disciples. Congress figures such as Motilal Nehru and Lala Lajpat Rai came, but so too did leading Deobandis such as Mahmud ul-Hasan and Maulana Hafiz Ahmad.[32] Not a week passed when there were not guests in abundance. 'Today that Pir Sahib is coming from Baghdad,' declared Abdul Majid Daryabadi in 1950, 'and tomorrow that alim sahib from Bombay, or from the Hejaz, or from Egypt. Someone or other always used to be coming.'[33]

It is probable that the numbers of Congress and Khilafatist visitors to Jamal Mian's home began to decline in 1923, though often the ties of friendship and respect persisted regardless of the changing political scene The signing of the Treaty of Lausanne with the prospect it offered of the emergence of a viable Turkish state to support the Khilafat took some of the steam out of Muslim protest. This development was hastened by the growth of Hindu-Muslim conflict. The spring of 1923 saw the arrival of a Hindu movement to reconvert Malkana Rajputs to Hinduism, which was immediately countered by a Muslim movement of Tabligh, that is of preaching to raise Islamic standards of behaviour. In the summer of 1923, communal riots broke out across northern India; the energies of the ulama came to be redirected towards defending their community. Then the open political space, in which the ulama had used their capacity to mobilize Muslim protest to such effect was dramatically reduced when the mainstream politicians

---

32. `Inayat Allah, *Risala*, 33–4.
33. Daryabadi, All India Radio, 12 January 1950, library of Mufti Raza Ansari.

decided to drop the politics of popular protest in favour of entering the Montagu-Chelmsford Councils, the political structures created for them by the British.[34]

In this context, Jamal Mian's father had begun to refocus his energies on areas close to his heart as an `alim and a Sufi. He was doing more teaching which would have meant that Jamal Mian would have seen more of his father than in the hyperactive period of the non-cooperation movement. 'I was unable to write to you earlier,' Abdul Bari told Abdullah Haroon in 1924, 'because of my preoccupations with teaching which I enjoy a lot.'[35] He also went on to say that he had been much engaged with the Bazm-i Sufia-i Hind. This was the organization which Abdul Bari had founded in May 1916 to raise the Islamic standards of the Sufi shrines.[36] The lessening of the political tempo had given him time to return to this work. At the Ajmer `Urs in 1923, Muinuddin Chishti's descendant, Maulana Shahabuddin, had been elected Diwan and leader of all the Sufi shaikhs (*Shaikhul Mashaikh*). The work of purification was carried forward by Bazm-i Sufia deputations to shrines in the UP, Punjab, and Sind. But what is of particular interest is the committee formed to advise Maulana Shahabuddin. They were: the Diwan of Baba Farid, Pakpattan, Hamid Mian, *sajjadanashin* of Taunsa, Pir Mehr Ali Shah of Golra, the *sajjadanashin* of Sial Sharif, the *sajjadanashin* of Rudauli Sharif, Shah Sulaiman of Phulwari Sharif, Shah Wilayat Husain of Allahabad, Maulana Abdul Qadir of Badaun, and Maulana Abdul Bari (trustee Dargah Ajmer).[37] All these

---

34. Robinson, *Separatism*, 337–41.
35. Abdul Bari to Abdullah Haroon 5 Jamadi II, 1342 (12 January 1924), ABP.
36. Robinson, *Farangi Mahall*, 169–70.
37. Press Release signed by Abdullah Khan of the *Advocate of India* Rafiq

men, or their successors as *sajjadanashin*s, were to be important supporters of Jamal Mian either as a Muslim League politician or in his subsequent life.

While Abdul Bari was easing himself back into the normal pursuits of an `alim and a leading Sufi, there was trouble brewing. On 1 March 1924, Sharif Husain of Mecca, now that Ataturk had abolished the Turkish caliphate, declared himself Caliph. Abdul Bari, a friend of Husain who had been critical of his alliance with the British in the First World War, sent him a telegram of congratulations. In August 1924, Abdul Aziz Ibn Saud, who in the previous decade had conquered much of Arabia in alliance with the Wahhabi Ikhwan, offended by Husain's bid attacked the Hejaz. On 3 October, Husain abdicated in favour of his son, Ali; ten days later Abdul Aziz captured Mecca. On 5 October, the Khilafat Committee, meeting in Delhi, condemned a statement by the British prime minister which raised the possibility of intervention in the Hejaz. The Committee also passed a resolution welcoming Abdul Aziz's victory which was communicated to him by Shaukat Ali.[38] The scene was set for a serious division between Abdul Bari and the Ali Brothers. For Abdul Bari, the control of the holy places by the Wahhabis with their profoundly anti-Sufi understandings of Islam was a major threat to his beliefs. He would not have forgotten Wahhabi actions when they conquered the Holy Places in the early-nineteenth century, razing many tombs and domes to the ground, including the Prophet's Mosque. For the Ali Brothers and the Khilafat Committee, on the other hand, the issue was a political one. It was about keeping the Holy Places free of British influence.

Manzil, Lucknow, no date but c. March or April 1923, ABP.

38. Khalid Ali, *Ali Brothers: The Life and Times of Maulana Mohamed Ali and Shaukat Ali* (Karachi: Royal Book Company, 2012), 670–1.

Then in August 1925, there came a report from the news agency Reuters which greatly exacerbated relations between Abdul Bari and his famous disciples. The report asserted that Abdul Aziz's troops in their bombardment of Medina had damaged the green dome over the Prophet's Mosque. That the report eventually turned out to be false made little difference to its reception. It was utterly believable given the previous actions of the Wahhabis and their known beliefs. Muslim India divided into two camps, one led by Abdul Bari and the other led by Mahomed Ali.[39] There were protests. The young Jamal Mian found himself in a procession in Lucknow, protesting against the actions of Abdul Aziz, in which he carried a piece of the Kiswah (the cloth which freshly-woven is draped over the Kaaba on the 9th day of the month of Hajj) on a tray on his head. He recalled a protest verse of Zarfi:

What kind of darkness has descended on the Kaaba?
What kind of destruction has been cast upon Medina?
From the wilderness of Najd a Satan has arisen.
In Haram a storm has been raging.[40]

There were rowdy meetings. When Mahomed Ali came to Lucknow to speak on the Hejaz, he was shouted down by Sharifian supporters. There were hurtful misunderstandings between the two sides. Presciently, in January 1924, Abdul Bari had warned Mahomed Ali of the dangers of others trying to cause trouble between them.[41] Nevertheless, when it came to the point, this warning was forgotten and both sides

---

39. Daryabadi, All-India Radio, 12 January 1950.
40. Jamal Mian Tape 8, JMP.
41. Abdul Bari to Mahomed Ali, 11 Jamadi II, 1342 (10 January 1924), ABP.

were hurt by what others writing on their behalf said in their respective newspapers, the *Hamdard* and the *Hamdam*. Yet it seems that harsh words were actually spoken. On 19 October, Maulana Salamatullah noted in his diary that a man had come from Sitapur, where the All-India Congress Committee had been meeting, and reported that Mahomed Ali had been pouring out abuse on Abdul Bari, Hasrat Mohani, Sulaiman Phulwari and himself.[42] At dinner the following day in Farangi Mahall with Hasrat Mohani and Salamatullah, Mahomed Ali denied what had been reported.

On 8 November, when the Ali Brothers came to Farangi Mahall next, Jamal Mian would have been aware of considerable tension. His father refused to see them because Mahomed Ali, during his previous visit, while discussing the green dome over the Prophet's tomb, had told Hasrat Mohani that if it was proved in *shari`a* that a *maqbara* (mausoleum) should not be built then he would remove it with his own hands. They were forced to stay in the Bahar Makan (see Map, pp. 28–9). Eventually, Qutb Mian, Abdul Bari's nephew and son-in-law, and Mumtaz Ahmad Razzaqi, the *sajjadanashin* of Bansa Sharif, intervened and 'on showing his genuine penitence at 11.30 he [Mahomed Ali] was allowed to enter the Mahalsera.'[43] When, after this, he left Farangi Mahall, Mahomed Ali was heard to utter Ghalib's couplet about Adam being cast out of paradise. Nothing untoward took place during the remaining days the Ali Brothers spent in Lucknow.[44]

---

42. The diary of Maulana Salamatullah quoted in Mufti Muhammad Rada Ansari, 'Mawlana Muhammad `Ali aur Mawlana Farangi Mahall' in *Jami`a* Mawlana Muhammad `Ali Numbar, Vol II, 77, February 1980, 119.

43. Ibid. 121.

44. Ibid. 123–4.

The essential differences, however, in the positions of Mahomed Ali and Abdul Bari had not gone away. Matters came to a head in early January 1926. On 13 January, the news came that Abdul Aziz ibn Saud had declared himself King of Arabia. Then, on the same day, Mahomed Ali in the *Hamdard* newspaper publicly renounced his allegiance to Abdul Bari. 'I had established bonds,' he declared, 'with the Ulema and Sufis of India for the sake of Islam and had kept them. But I would not hesitate to break them if truth and God so beckoned.'[45] And so they did in the case of his allegiance to Abdul Bari. Shaukat Ali followed him.

Jamal Mian recalled the moment when the impact of these momentous events hit his father who was deeply hurt by the rejection of his spiritual authority by the Ali Brothers. In the early afternoon of 17 January, he was riding his tricycle round the courtyard of the Mahalsera. He could hear his father pacing back and forth in his study. He was just about to take the train to Ajmer where a conference was to be held in support of Sharif Husain. Suddenly, he heard a groan. His father had collapsed. He had had a stroke and was paralysed down his left side.

The Civil Surgeon of Lucknow, along with allopathic and Western doctors, were summoned. Qutb Mian, who had gone on ahead to Ajmer was recalled by telegram. Qutb Mian returned to find Mumtaz Ahmad Razzaqi sitting by the Maulana's bed. Mumtaz Ahmad said loudly that Qutb Mian had arrived. The Maulana struggled to embrace him, patting him on the back. Then Jamal Mian found himself brought to the bed, along with the other young children of Farangi Mahall, to be made disciples of his father in the presence of

---

45. Ali, *Ali Brothers*, 672.

Qutb Mian, his successor. At 11.20 p.m. on 19 January, Abdul
Bari died.[46]

On the following day, Abdul Bari was buried in Bagh
Maulana Anwar. Thousands of Lucknavis followed the
funeral procession. The vegetable market was closed. Muslims
were excused attendance at the courts. All Shia and Sunni
institutions shut with the one exception of the Madrasah
Qadima of the Baḥr ul-Ulumis, who maintained their enmity
with Abdul Bari even in death. Classes in the madrasahs
of rival schools in Bareilly, Budaun, and Deoband were
closed and readings of the Quran given instead. Messages
of condolence were received from princes, taluqdars, and
nationalist leaders, including Gandhi, as well as from
Muslims abroad. Princes and landowners made donations
in memory of Abdul Bari to support the continuation of his
work of teaching and scholarship.[47] In his obituary in the
Ma`arif of Azamgarh, Abdul Majid Daryabadi quoted the
following couplet:

The death of Qais was not the death of one man only
It was the destruction of the foundations of a qaum.[48]

On 21 January, Mahomed Ali reached Lucknow from
Delhi. Three eyewitness accounts exist from those present at
the time: Raza Ansari (later Mufti), Maulana Hidayatullah's
grandson, who was nine; Abdul Majid Daryabadi's, who was
close both to Farangi Mahall and to Mahomed Ali; and that

---

46. These two paragraphs draw on the personal reflections of Jamal Mian;
    Shafi 'Memoir', 36; and `Inayat Allah, *Risala*, 39–42.
47. `Inayat Allah, *Risala*, 42–7.
48. *Ma`arif*, 1, Vol. 17, January 1926, quoted in `Inayat Allah, *Tadhkirah*,
    114–15.

of Maulana Shafi, Maulana Salamatullah's son, who had been a pupil and close associate of Abdul Bari for ten years. On reaching Lucknow, Mahomed Ali went straight to Bagh Maulana Anwar where, according to Daryabadi, he threw himself on Abdul Bari's grave crying: 'If I cannot come to your funeral, let me come to your grave'. Then he went on to Farangi Mahall, where Raza remembers him entering the gate with a white handkerchief, wiping tears from his eyes. It was 9 a.m. and Abdul Bari's will was being read. The reader, Maulana Salamatullah, who was having difficulty controlling his emotions, had reached the point where the deceased was asking forgiveness from all those to whom unwittingly he might have done wrong. At the end, the disciples of Abdul Bari present were asked to give *nazr*s, gifts of respect, to Qutb Mian, his successor. Mahomed Ali was so overcome that he was unable to stand up; he gave his *nazr* sitting down.[49]

A fine *maqbara* in the Awadhi style was built over Abdul Bari's grave (Illustration 1). An expert craftsman from Ajmer stayed in Lucknow for a year to supervise its construction.

It bore the following verse from Akbar Allahabadi (d. 1921):

Oh heavens let the winds of passion blow
Oh let the springs of action free
Let us work, let us strive,
Let every shaikh like Abdul Bari be.[50]

Jamal Mian had lost a father. In one sense, a huge force had gone out of his life but his father remained a presence.

---

49. Ansari, 'Mawlana Muhammad `Ali' *Jami`a*; the diary of Abdul Majid Daryabadi quoted in Ibid; Maulana Shafi, 'Memoir', 36.
50. Akbar Allahabadi was a great satirist, but in this case he was not being so.

In future, his father's legacy would open many doors and
bring him many contacts throughout India. On the other hand,
there was the weighty legacy of his faith as a Muslim and as
a Sufi to live up to. The first two sentences of his father's will
make this clear:

> All relatives and friends should fear God, obey and love the
> Prophet, his associates and seek their blessing and consider
> this the part of their worship. They should never avoid
> congregational prayers, should never compromise with their
> conscience, they should seek forgiveness of their sins, and
> remember death and the Day of Judgement.[51]

---

51. Abdul Bari's Will, 29 Ramadan 1341 (16 May 1923), ABP.

4

The education of Jamal Mian

THROUGHOUT HIS LIFE, JAMAL MIAN HAD TWO PARTICULAR advantages that sprang from his background: The first was his formal Farangi Mahalli education, which involved the *Dars-i Nizami,* as Farangi Mahallis had come to interpret it by the twentieth century, alongside other subjects such as English language, history, debating, and so on. The second was his exposure to his family's spiritual tradition, which brought a particular focus on the Prophet but also gave a specific pattern to his devotional year. This specific educational experience and the associations which came with his spiritual practices brought him wide respect but also a personal following which was to support him throughout his life.

Jamal Mian was in the last generation to experience the Farangi Mahalli *Dars-i Nizami* in all its glory. His teachers— Maulana Inayatullah, Maulana Sibghatullah, Maulvi Ruhullah, Mufti Abdul Qadir, Altafur Rahman Qidwai—were all students of Farangi Mahall, indeed, of his own father, Abdul Bari. They brought to the task not just the specific lessons they had been taught but also the great respect which existed for Jamal Mian's father throughout the family. Should their memories become hazy, they only had to refer to the specific instructions about the different subjects and books in the *Dars* which Abdul Bari had issued when the madrasah was founded in 1905 and which Altafur Rahman had republished in December 1924.[1]

In the early decades of the twentieth century, Farangi Mahallis had found their educational tradition under growing assault, a process regularly discussed in the annual madrasah reports and other documents.[2] One source of threat came from ulama influenced by the nineteenth-century movement of revival and reform, who wished to bolster the presence of reform in the madrasah curriculum by reducing the emphasis on logic and philosophy, the hallmark of the Farangi Mahalli tradition, and increasing that given to Hadith, the Quran, and Arabic. The issue was brought into the open by the Nadvat ul-Ulama movement which began in 1891. It was brought to a head first by Shah Muhammad Husain of Allahabad's unfavourable report on the curriculum, which he himself had followed as a pupil of Maulana Abdul Hai Farangi Mahalli, and second by the establishment of the madrasah of the Nadvat ul-Ulama to teach a reformed curriculum at Lucknow in 1898.[3] Farangi Mahallis responded to these criticisms by increasing their teaching of Arabic and Hadith. Indeed, in 1916, they founded a *Dar al-Hadith* for the purpose of the latter. Moreover, relations between the two institutions remained civil. Both Abdul Bari and Inayatullah served on the Nadva's governing council.

A rather more serious threat came from the secular system

1. Altaf al-Rahman Qidwai, *Qiyam-i Nizam-i Ta`lim*, (Lucknow: Nami Press, 1924), 3–60.
2. `Abd al-Bari, 'Nisab Ta`lim Nizami', 1328/1910, mss. no pagination, Farangi Mahall; '12th Report of Madrasah-yi Aliya Nizamiyya Farangi Mahall', mss., no pagination, Farangi Mahall.
3. Shah Muhammad Husayn, *Bil Tanzim-i Nizam al-Ta`allum wal Ta`lim*, published at the wish of the Nadwat al-`Ulama (Allahabad, n.d.).

of education and the new routes to material livelihood which developed under British rule. Abdul Bari tells us how he saw the problem:

It is our misfortune that religious teaching amongst Muslims has declined day by day. At this time there are two types of people. One, those who got education from old institutions, and they understand religion on old lines, and follow the old path. The other who do not learn religion through religion, but learn about it from the books of European intellectuals. I want to say that these people get religion not from Muslim ulama but from Spenser or from the translation [of the Quran] of the Reverend Sale. The first group are somewhat superior because having followed the old education they have in themselves the treasure of faith. But there are few of these ... And the other group are totally bad; they have strayed from the right path. I am shocked when I see that these modern educated people for want of Arabic language have to read the Quran through the translation of George Sale in English.[4]

Abdul Bari would have been especially aware of the latter group as he gave special classes to Lucknow's High Court lawyers.

Derived from these differing approaches to religious education, Abdul Bari saw conflicting approaches in Muslim countries as to how the foundations of the further development of Islam should be laid:

One group of thinkers thought Muslims should get educated in the modern way of life because this is the need of the time.

---

4. '12th Report of Madrasah-yi `Aliya Nizamiyya'.

... Their argument is, see how Japan has progressed so far in thirty years by following the European countries ... then the Hindus of our country, how they are going ahead, and how the young Bengalis have gained power and prestige. Apart from this, the progress made by Egypt and Turkey draws us in the same direction ... The second group says our salvation lies in following blindly the earlier generations. They have made it their aim to oppose the modern way of thinking. And just as the first group looks down on all the traditions of the past, so this other group decries this modern thing.[5]

Abdul Bari then offered a typical Farangi Mahalli solution. There should not be the blind following of old tradition because that would lead to stagnation. But equally, change should not be undertaken lightly; if unsuitable changes are made, community ways [qaumi adat] will die and so will community spirit [qaumi ruh]. 'Progress should be made on the following lines. There should be a central core of custom in which no change should be allowed, which should form the nucleus. Ordinary things should change according to the needs of the times. In my opinion this is the only guidance which should be before us in order to find the means to advance.'[6]

This approach was exemplified in the changes made in Farangi Mahalli teaching in their madrasah from 1905. Modern subjects as taught in government schools—arithmetic, algebra, geometry, geography—were introduced and made compulsory. English became part of the syllabus for the higher classes, the teacher who was rather more expensive

---

5. Ibid.
6. Ibid.

than normal being paid for by the taluqdar of Paisar. History was a subject to which Abdul Bari paid particular attention. History had key lessons for being guided in the present. No set book was included in the *Dars*. He admitted that as far as the Prophet was concerned, the *hadith*s were enough, but when it came to the companions, caliphs, and kings, no history was available. For understanding the historical circumstances that led to the rise of the Shia, he recommended Ibn Suyuti's *Tarikh-i Khulafa* and Shaikh Ahmad Dahlan's *Dowala Islamiyya*. For drawing conclusions from history there was nothing to match the *Muqaddimah* of Ibn Khaldun. 'It is a model,' he declared, 'it is a treasure of knowledge. By reading this book you develop the capacity to come to conclusions. For these reasons it should be studied very carefully.'[7] Three decades later, more modern history books were being recommended, including works by Shibli, Sulaiman Nadvi, Amir Ali, and Nazir Ahmad alongside works on Iran and Egypt. There is a real sense of the need to use the works of modern historians to help to make sense of the world. The madrasah report for 1946 also talks of the importance of cultivating an interest in the press and current affairs. Much attention was paid to developing skills in communication, in debating, and in public speaking. 'All possible efforts have been made,' the report declared, 'to enable Muslim students to learn worldly knowledge alongside the religious sciences.'[8] It was in a madrasah with this distinctive approach that Jamal Mian was educated. Moreover, most of those who taught him were also actively involved in public life.

---

7. Altaf al-Rahman, *Qiyam*, 57.
8. Qutb al-Din `Abd al-Wali, *Nisab Nizami*, 1946, mss. Farangi Mahal, no pagination.

The madrasah was established in the old house of Mulla
Nizamuddin in Farangi Mahall (see Illustration 5 and Map,
pp. 28–9). This was rented from a descendant of Bahr
ul-Ulum and the fact that Mulla Nizamuddin had taught in
its front room was felt to give it a special aura. The building
had collapsed in the monsoon of 1916 and there was some
sorrow that the reconstruction, which was paid for by the Rani
of Jahangirabad and Nawab Nasiruddin, had not included
this special place. The building had two storeys: the teaching
of advanced subjects took place on the upper floor and of
primary subjects on the ground floor. Students sat on mats.
The Maulvi course lasted five years; the Maulana course three
years; and the Allama course, a very specialized programme,
two years. All teaching was timetabled after the fashion of
government and mission schools.[9] Students had access to a
library of about 1,000 books and they also had access to the
libraries of their teachers, that of Maulana Inayatullah had
over 3,000 books.[10] The teaching year began on 9 Shawwal
and continued to the middle of Shaban, so there was a long
break of about two months covering Ramadan. Lessons were
for five hours daily—in the summer from 6–11 a.m., and for
six hours daily in the winter from 9 a.m. to 4 p.m. with a one
hour break for *Zuha* prayers and a meal. Examinations were
held after three months, then six months, and then at the end
of the academic year in Shaban. Although they were examined
on particular books in the *Dars,* students no longer received

---

9. In fact, the organization of the Farangi Mahall madrasah as established
    in 1905 mirrored in many ways what was established at Deoband nearly
    forty years earlier. See Barbara Metcalf, 'The Madrasah at Deoband:
    A Model for Religious Education in India', *Modern Asian Studies,* Vol.
    12, Part 1, February 1978, 111–34.
10. Sibghat Allah, *Sadr al-Mudarassin,* 46.

an *'ijaza*, or permission, to teach the book as they would have done in the past. Now, they received *sanad*s, or degree certificates, after successfully completing the requirements for Maulvi, Maulana, and Allama.

In Jamal Mian's time the madrasah normally had 50–60 students, most of whom were supported by scholarships. The madrasah was primarily for the children of the Farangi Mahall family and those of the shrines. Nonetheless, there were also students from families long associated with Farangi Mahall—from the qasbah of Mohan, the Chaudhuris of Paisar, and the Qidwais of Baragaon. Furthermore, there were students from further afield; the 1917 report notes students from Bengal and Goa, but also Burma, South Africa, and Arabia. Students from outside Lucknow stayed in a boarding house. Games and sports were permitted, from marbles and kite-flying to swimming, football, and hockey. Holidays were normally on Fridays and the last Thursday of each month. Holidays were also used to celebrate major religious festivals such as the *'Urs* of saints special to Farangi Mahall. At other times, holidays were decreed by the Majlis Muid ul-Islam, the effective governing body, such as when the monsoon led to the collapse of the madrasah building. The students themselves arranged *milad* celebrations during Rabiulawwal.

To judge from the advice which Abdul Bari gave the teachers of the Farangi Mahall madrasah in 1905, and which was republished in 1924, Jamal Mian's education took place in an unusually civilized and thoughtful environment. He proclaimed himself against the old method of teaching in which a text was memorized but not necessarily understood. Books had to be taught with examples so that students could absorb their lessons with pleasure rather than pain. Furthermore, teaching should move from the simple to the abstract and enable learning to become natural. The manner of delivering a lesson should be cordial and not abrasive. The teacher's manner should not discourage the student from owning up to ignorance. Teachers should always behave in a manner worthy of a person engaged in conveying religious knowledge.[11] Madrasah education throughout the Islamic world had the reputation of being enforced by beating, often savagely so. Abdul Bari made it clear that such behaviour had no place in his madrasah.[12] Maulana Inayatullah, the head teacher of the madrasah in Jamal Mian's time, exemplified many of the ideal qualities set out by Abdul Bari. He treated his pupils as though they were his own children. In turn, they all addressed him as 'Abu', meaning Daddy. He was humane and forgiving in dealing with the shortcomings of the young and never once, it is said, expelled a pupil. There was, however, one occasion in which Jamal Mian irked him beyond endurance. Inayatullah reprimanded him, perhaps with a slap. 'Would you treat me like this if my Bawa Mian [his father] was still alive?' Jamal Mian cried. Inayatullah was mortified and broke down.[13]

11. Altaf al-Rahman, *Qiyam*, 15–17.
12. For a discussion of the beating of children in education see Francis Robinson, 'Education' in Robert Irwin ed., *The New Cambridge History of Islam, 4, Islamic Cultures and Societies to the end of the eighteenth Century* (Cambridge: Cambridge University Press, 2010), especially 220–2; for a graphic Indian example see Lutfullah, *Autobiography of Lutfullah: A Mahomedan Gentleman and his transactions with his fellow creatures*, Edward B. Eastwick ed. (London: Smith, Elder, and Co., 1858), 12–21; and for a graphic example in Indian popular literature see Ghalib Lakhnavi and Abdullah Bilgrami, *The Adventures of Amir Hamza*, introd. Hamid Dabashi (New York: Random House, 2007), 70–83. For Abdul Bari's disapproval see Altaf al-Rahman, *Qiyam*, 96.
13. Sibghat Allah, *Sadr al-Mudarrisin*, 55–6; Communication from Farida Jamal, 5 May 2015.

So central was the transmission of knowledge in Islamic civilisation that it developed the most powerful traditions of respect which the pupil was to show the teacher. In Jamal Mian's educational experience, this tradition seems to have remained undiluted. His father set out the *adab* or etiquette which pupils should adopt in words which substantially mirrored those of the thirteenth-century Arab scholar, Al-Zarnuji:[14]

The student should remain respectful and silent before the teacher. As long as the teacher does not ask a question he should not speak. He should not raise a question without his teacher's permission. If his teacher is angry over any mistake, he should apologise, not make the mistake again and affirm his obedience and loyalty. Whatever the instruction of his teacher, and whatever he may himself think, he should not overtly or indirectly disobey. Indeed not the slightest suspicion should be raised that he regards himself as more able and intelligent than his teacher. Before his teacher he should not make gestures, or whisper, or talk in any way. He should not glance either to the right of the left but pay attention only to his teacher. He should remain seated with his head bowed. When the teacher stands up, he should do so, and when the teacher leaves, he should remain standing silently. He should not walk with the teacher talking much. When the teacher reaches his destination he should leave him unless asked to accompany him ... he should follow several steps behind his teacher and listen respectfully to his talk ... every student

---

14. Burhan al-Din Zarnuji, *Ta`lim al muta`allim-tariq at-ta`allum, Instruction of the student: the method of learning,* trans G. E. Von-Grunebaum and Theodora M. Abel (New York: King's Crown Press, 1947).

should consider it fortunate that he is among the first to obey
his teacher. He should not burden his teacher with thanks,
but should nevertheless remain grateful. He should regard the
instructions of his teacher as the last word and not differ from
them. Indeed they should be carried out even if he disagrees
with them.[15]

Jamal Mian's father followed this classic advice with advice
on how the student should behave with his fellow students:
he should be friendly towards them but discriminating in
choosing close friends; he should favour those who were wise
and of a kindly disposition; he should keep his temper under
control; and he should support those students who stand
up for their rights. On the other hand, he should avoid bad
characters, liars, and the greedy. 'Greediness is a fatal poison.
It is the fountain of all vice.'[16] Students should be willing to
make sacrifices for their fellow students, either physically or
financially as required. Moreover, they should be quiet about
their sins and not condemn them, talking in public only about
their good deeds. They should not boast in anyway about
their relatives, their poetry, or their publications. They should
not exaggerate like females, use hair oil, and frequently comb
their hair. They should not discuss their finances. Although
this advice was addressed to the madrasah students in general,
it was surely typical of the advice which any father might
give a son.[17]

★ ★ ★

15. Altaf al-Rahman, *Qiyam*, 85–7.
16. Ibid. 89.
17. Ibid. 85–96.

Soon after his father died, Jamal Mian began his education. As was usual, he began by memorizing the Quran. His first teacher was Altafur Rahman, who taught him to read using a classic primer, *Qa'ida Baghdadi*, and how to write the Arabic script using a wooden board surfaced with clay. He then went to the madrasah to learn the Quran. If his teachers followed his father's advice, he would have been taught how to recite the Quran using the correct cadences. In memorizing, he would have begun with those passages he would need for prayers. These would be followed by the shorter *surah*s. Then steadily the tempo would be increased so that he would become comfortable reciting *surah* after *surah* from memory. Abdul Bari recommended that translation should be taught alongside the memorization process; others actually found that this interfered with memorization.[18] Eventually, it was decided that Jamal Mian had memorized the whole Quran and there was a celebration. But then in the following Ramadan 'I was asked to recite *Tarawih*. Soon enough it was found out that I remembered very little and some of it was all wrong.'[19] Jamal Mian was then placed in the hands of an able *Hafiz*, Fayyaz Husain, from the Madrasah Furqania close to Farangi Mahall. He took Jamal Mian in hand and made him *Hafiz*, and to ensure that there were no embarrassing lapses in future, Maulvi Ruhullah got him to rehearse each day before reciting *Tarawih*, and stood behind him in the mosque to prompt if necessary. Jamal Mian would have

---

18. Altaf al-Rahman, *Qiyam*, 42. Jamal Mian's nephew, Jalaluddin Abdul Matin (Matin Mian) was one of those who found that knowing the meaning got in the way of memorization, Personal Communication.
19. Jamal Mian Tape 7, Jamal Mian Papers, Karachi.

been twelve, or perhaps a little older, when he completed the Quran.[20]

By the time that Jamal Mian completed the Quran he was more than half way through his madrasah course. We have no comment from him as to how his learning went except that he did not regard himself to be a particularly assiduous scholar. Nevertheless, what we do have is a timetable setting out what subjects were taught and when, over the ten-year period of Maulvi to Allama.[21] We also have his father's guide to the course and how different subjects and books in it should be approached. So we know that his first year would have been taken up doing maths and dictation, learning Persian and engaging with *Panj Ganj*, Nizami's collection of five narrative poems which were used in madrasahs throughout the Persianate world. He was also learning Arabic grammar, particularly tenses and pronouns. At this stage, the teaching was in Urdu and students were expected to translate Urdu and Persian words into Arabic. If his father's advice was followed, he would have had daily tests in grammar.[22]

In the second year there was more maths. This, however, was the year in which Arabic grammar was addressed with a vengeance. The books studied were *Nahw Mir*, *Hidayat un-Nahw*, and *Sharh-i Muatta 'Amil*. Sentences were analysed, the changing shape of words discussed, and Jamal Mian began to learn about the one hundred or so prepositions in Arabic—

---

20. The reason for the doubt over Jamal Mian's precise age when completing the Quran is that an invitation from Altafur Rahman Qidwai, dated 16 July 1932, inviting people to Jamal Mian's Quran completion exists in Jamal Mian's papers, but it is not clear whether it refers to the first or the second completion. Personal File, JMP.
21. Altaf al-Rahman, *Qiyam*, 12–14.
22. Altaf al-Rahman, *Qiyam*, 23–4.

how they should be used and how they might change the shape of a word. Indeed, he was learning how to cross what his father termed the first 'big bridge' in mastering the language.[23] Already in his second year, he was expected to study *Sharh-i Muatta-i ʿAmil* at home with a dictionary and come to class prepared. Some of the teaching was in Arabic alone. For some relatively light relief from his heavy diet of Arabic, he would have also had his first engagement with *mantiq*, logic, in the form of Saiyid Sharif Jurjani's *Sughra* and *Kubra*.

In his third year, Jamal Mian would have had more logic in the form of *Sharh-i Tahzib* which was Najmuddin Qazdi's commentary on Saaduddin Taftazani's *Tahzib*. At this point, if his teachers were following his father's guidance, they would have monitored his progress from *Sughra* to see if 'the desired mental development' had taken place and then taken appropriate action if it had not.[24] At the same time, there was more Arabic grammar in the shape of *Sharh-i Jami* which was Mulla Jami's commentary on the *al-Kafiya* of Ibn Hajib on *Nahw*. This was a book which required some knowledge of logic and philosophy and which the twenty-first century madrasah student is said to find particularly difficult.[25] Alongside this intellectual heavy lifting, Jamal Mian was probably relieved to have one class a day devoted to Arabic literature.

In his fourth year, Jamal Mian engaged with some of the great books in the madrasah curriculum. In logic, there was Qutbuddin Razi's *Qutbi*. Then in Arabic, he was introduced to Taftazani's *Mukhtassar al-Maʿani* which dealt with the niceties

23. Ibid. 24.
24. Ibid. 29.
25. Ibid. 29; Ebrahim Moosa, *What is a Madrasah?* (Edinburgh: Edinburgh University Press, 2015), 117–18.

of language and writing well. His teacher, who in this case was probably Maulana Sibghatullah, would at the same time draw attention to similar issues in the writing of Persian and Urdu.[26] At the same time, he would have had his first introduction to jurisprudence in the form of Ubaidullah ibn Masud's *Sharh-i Viqaya*. Then, with the help of *Rashidiyya*, he would have had the excitement of being introduced to *manazara*, debating. He would have learned how to make propositions and advance arguments and discuss current topics with the class divided into two groups. In the process, he would have also learned the importance of showing courtesy and not displaying anger.[27]

In his fifth year, Jamal Mian began to take on subjects at an advanced level. In logic, he would have been introduced to his ancestor, Mulla Hasan's, commentary on Muhibbullah Bihari's *Sullam al`Ulum*. Doubtless, at the same time, he would have been made aware of other major works in the Awadhi tradition in the field. Works such as, *Qadi* of Qazi Mubarak of Gopa Mau; and *Hamd Allah* of Hamdullah of Sandila alongside the great works of Mir Mahmud Zahid al-Hawari, his *Risala Mir Zahid*, and *Mulla Jalal*. In explaining why Farangi Mahallis paid so much attention to logic, Jamal Mian's father declared that logic was crucial for defending right actions and beliefs and for rejecting those which were wrong. Additionally, 'logic is an instinct; we possess it, it should not possess us. If people allow logic to master them, they are no longer logical.'[28] At the same time, Jamal Mian also addressed advanced mathematics in the form of Bahauddin Amili's *Khulasat al-Hisab* which had been written in Safavid

---

26. Altaf al-Rahman, *Qiyam,* 27.
27. Ibid. 36.
28. Ibid. 30.

Iran in the late sixteenth century. Also in this year, he began to acquire some of the key skills of the maulvi. He began learning *Usul-i Fiqh*, or the Principles of Jurisprudence, beginning with *Nur al-Anwar* which had been written by Aurangzeb's tutor, Mulla Jiwan. 'This is a very important subject in the present day' his father wrote, 'because of the new problems that are continually coming up. It is all the more necessary to find answers to these new problems with the help of *fiqh*.'[29] In the last class of the day, in the fifth year, there was a bit of light relief. Jamal Mian read the *Maqamat*, the entertaining tales written in rhymed Arabic prose by al-Hariri of Basra (1054–1124). He was able to follow the escapades of the rogue, Abu Zaid, through fifty episodes while relatively painlessly absorbing Arabic grammar and rhetoric. Success in the examinations at the end of this year would have given Jamal Mian the title of Maulvi. We have no evidence that he did not succeed.

Jamal Mian now began the three-year Maulana course. The first year was notable for the substantial attention paid first to *Ilm al-Kalam*, theology, in which he studied *Mir Zahid*. This was Mir Muhammad Zahid al-Harawi's gloss on Qazi Adud al-Din of Shiraz's *Mawaqif* and *Sharh-i Aqaid-i Nasafi* which his father declared set out the fundamentals of the Hanafi position and should be fully understood.[30] Beyond this there was a focus on the practices of religious ritual.

In the second year of the Maulana course, serious attention was paid to writing in Arabic and substantial time devoted to poetry in Arabic. The main focus was the *Diwan* of al-Mutanabbi (915–65), 315 poems by the man regarded as

---

29. Ibid. 35.
30. Ibid. 48.

the greatest of all poets in Arabic. Another highlight was
astronomy taught not just through the traditional texts of
Tasrir and *Sharh-i Chaghmini* but also through modern books
bought in Beirut which brought the subject up to date. As
far as possible, Jamal Mian's father urged that the subject
should be taught with a globe and with maps, as he did.[31]
In the third and final year of the Maulana course there was,
as usual, regular practice in writing Arabic. But there were
also two notable high points. There was natural philosophy,
which was approached through Mulla Mahmud Jaunpuri's
Shams-i Bazigha, widely regarded as the most important book
on the subject written by an Indian in Arabic. According to
Jamal Mian's father, the book was not only easy to understand
but would help the student grasp Aristotle, Plato, and Ibn
Sina. Indeed, the student would learn to expound philosophy.
'Time,' he declared, 'is not wasted in teaching this book.'[32] The
second high point came in *Usul-i Fiqh* when *Tawzih Talwih* was
studied, which was Taftazani's commentary on Ubaidullah
ibn Masud's *Talwih*. Jamal Mian's father warned that it was
difficult so it should be taught in full. It showed the student
how to derive conclusions from the Quran, *Hadith*, *ijma*, and
qiyas in the light of *shari`a*. Students were given lots of practice
in using these source to come to conclusions on points of
law.[33] At the end of this year, Jamal Mian sat his Maulana
exams with success. There is no hint in the record that he was
unworthy of the title he bore throughout his life.

As Jamal Mian began the *Dars* in 1926, he would probably
have taken his Maulana exams in 1935. He continued to

---

31. Ibid. 40.
32. Ibid. 39.
33. Ibid. 35.

the programme of the Allama degree, the final two years of the *Dars*. That he was doing this is arguably confirmed by his mother's concerns in autumn 1937 about the impact of his Muslim League involvement on his studies; she was reassured by Maulana Inayatullah that all would be well. Over these two years, Jamal Mian acquired the knowledge and skills of a fully-fledged traditional Muslim scholar. He had substantial teaching in *Tafsir*, Quran commentary. 'Whatever we teach students,' his father declared, 'its aim is to teach them to understand as much of the Quran as possible.'[34] It followed that there was no especially recommended book on the principles of Quran commentary because that was the function of the whole course. However, Jamal Mian was required to read the great texts by Hanafi ulama: *Baydawi*, the *Tafsir Anwar al-Tanzil* of Qazi Nasiruddin Baizawi of Shiraz and *Madarik,* and the *Tafsir al-Madarik,* of Imam Abdullah ibn al-Nasafi. *Baydawi* was taught because it was difficult and mastering it would enable students to understand other commentaries. *Madarik* was taught thoroughly from beginning to end. The only other commentary was from the Shafii school, known through much of the Muslim world as *Jalalayn*, the *tafsir* of the two Jalals, Jalaluddin Mahalli and Jalaluddin Suyuti.[35]

'The purpose of *Hadith*,' Jamal Mian's father reminded his readers, 'is to know about the life of the Prophet and his words in order to enable you to live well in this world and in the next.'[36] Like most of the Farangi Mahallis before him, Jamal Mian would have studied just one book, the *Mishkat al-*

---

34. Ibid. 33.
35. Ibid.
36. Ibid. 43.

Masabih of Muhammad bin Abdullah al-Khatib. While doing
so he would have been told to keep his eye on the six canonical
collections of *Hadith* (Bukhari, Muslim, Tirmizi, Ibn Majah,
Abu Dawud, and Al-Nisai). Nevertheless, because the author
of *Mishkat* was a Shafii, he as a Hanafi should read it alongside
the commentaries of Mulla Ali Qari of Herat (d. 1605) and
Abdul Haq Muhaddis of Delhi (d. 1642) to avoid becoming
a *ghayr muqallid* or non-conformist. Moreover, if there was
any clash between Hanafi understandings and those of the six
canonical collections, they should be resolved by consulting
Aini's commentary on Bukhari.[37]

During this period Jamal Mian would also have been
introduced, in the area of *Usul-i Fiqh,* to one of the great
peaks of Indian scholarship in the early modern period,
Muhibbullah Bihari's *Musallam al-Thubut.* 'In teaching
Musallam al-Thubut,' declared Jamal Mian's father, 'there
should be no miserliness. The beauty of this book is that
points are beautifully made in fine language. There is no book
to compare with it.'[38] To enable Jamal Mian and his fellow
students to gain the skills to make their knowledge socially
useful, the last class of each day, in the final year, was devoted
to learning the art of writing *fatawa.*

While Jamal Mian was studying the *Dars* he was joined in
his class by Ali Husain Mohani. Ali Husain suggested that they

---

37. Ibid. 44; Abdul-Bari was referring to the *Umdat al-kari fi Sharh al-
    Bukhari* of Abu Muhammad Mahmud al-Ayni, a Mamluk scholar born
    21 July 1361 at Ayntab between Antioch and Aleppo. This had been
    published in Cairo in 1890 and in Constantinople in 1891–92 in eleven
    volumes and so would have been readily available in Farangi Mahall;
    W. Marcais, *al-Ayni,* P. Bearman et al. eds, *Encyclopaedia of Islam,* 2nd
    ed., (Leiden: Brill, 1954–2004), 790–1.
38. Ibid. 36.

take the Persian literature course at Lucknow University, an action which was likely to excite the disapproval of many of their elders as it was a government institution. Nevertheless, they went ahead which meant taking the entrance exam. Jamal Mian found himself having to translate out loud the *Anwar-i Sohaili* (commonly known as the *Khalila wa Dimnah,* which was Mulla Husain ibn Ali Waiz al-Kashfi's version of the Fables of Bidpai). His examiner was Ali Naqi Naqvi, the Shia mujtahid and great expounder of the humanity and personal qualities of Imam Husain.[39] When he started following the course, Jamal Mian discovered him to be a great teacher. We might also note that in his own life, Jamal Mian came to be a great admirer of Imam Husain. Ali Husain and Jamal Mian were able to attend the classes at Lucknow University because they were held in the afternoon after madrasah teaching had stopped. Getting there was a problem as it was a good five miles away. Bicycles were the answer, although, Jamal Mian's legs were so short that they did not reach the pedals and blocks of wood had to be added to them. He got a Diploma of Dabir-e-Mahir (second division) in both 1934 and 1935, and a Diploma of Dabir-e-Kamil (second division) in 1936.[40]

At this time, Jamal Mian had also begun to study English. His teacher was Mirza Muhammad Askari, whose grandfather had been a friend of Ghalib and a *shagird* or pupil of Qatil. The Mirza had studied under both Muhammad Siddiq Hasan Khan of Bhopal, the *Ahl-i Hadith* scholar, and at Canning College, Lucknow. He had held a range of posts, including those of Government Translator and of secretary to the Maharaja of Mahmudabad. He was a close friend of Jamal

---

39. Jones, *Shi`a Islam in Colonial India,* 212.
40. Jamal Mian Tape 7c and degree certificates in his Personal File, JMP.

Mian's cousin and known for being a wit and good company—
one of his party pieces was declaiming Antony's 'Friends,
Romans and Countrymen' speech from Shakespeare's *Julius
Caesar*. In his autobiography he remembers Jamal Mian thus:

> A young man compared to me, but beautiful and attractive
> [here he enjoys the play on Jamal] apart from this he has all the
> qualities. He is wise, balanced and modest, but in spite of this
> he makes speeches which set fire to Muslim League meetings.
> He is my favourite English and Farsi student.[41]

Muhammad Askari started Jamal Mian down the road of
English and perhaps gave him the taste for English literature
which was to stay with him throughout his life. It is evident,
however, from Jamal Mian's diary that more work needed
to be done to get his English to the highest levels. But what
was important was that by 1937–38, his command of English
was great enough for him to move easily with the primarily
Anglophone leaders of the All-India Muslim League such as
Jinnah and the Ispahanis.

When Jamal Mian entered politics just before his eighteenth
birthday, he had been fortunate enough to receive the finest
education which the Indian Islamic world could offer. He had
followed the course of great books generated by scholars in
the Arab, Persian, and Timurid worlds which his ancestors
had brought together in the *Dars-i Nizami* and to which they
and their associates had substantially added in the eighteenth
century. He had, moreover, been taught by members of

---

41. Muhammad Askari, *Maan Kestum?* (Lucknow: Uttar Pradesh Urdu
    Academy, 1985) 86. The tenor of the quotation suggests that Askari's
    autobiography was actually written in the 1940s.

his family steeped in the traditions of the *Dars*. Maulana
Inayatullah 'used to tell me,' he recalled, 'please learn these
books from me ... There are only three people in the world
who can teach these books. One is Baqi Bhai ['Abdul Baqi,
the husband of his father's sister who lived in Medina], the
other is Maulana Qaim who was in Jaunpur, and myself, Mufti
Inayatullah. He used to implore me to read ... I did not make
the effort I should have.'[42] In spite of this self-deprecating
statement, Inayatullah saw Jamal Mian as the man to maintain
the scholarly tradition of the family. He was recognized as a
man having the authority of a scholar by his Muslim League
contemporaries and he was also recognized as such by India's
leading `alim of the second half of the twentieth century,
Sayyid Abul Hasan Ali Nadvi.[43] The Saudi Arabians would
appear to have valued his contributions to the annual sessions
of their Rabita al-Alam al-Islami for more than thirty years; in
May 1968 he received a major award for his scholarship from
King Hassan II of Morocco (Illustration 22). That Jamal Mian
maintained scholarly pursuits throughout his life can be seen
from his library which we will analyse later.

---

42. Jamal Mian Tape 5, JMP.
43. Jamal Mian thought that Nadvi played an important role in
    recommending him, as a representative of Pakistan, to the Rabita al-
    Alam al-Islami although, as we note below, he thought Mufti Amin
    al-Husseini played the key role.

5

The devotional world of Farangi Mahall

WHILE JAMAL MIAN WAS ABSORBING THE EDUCATIONAL traditions of his forefathers, he was also, day by day, week by week, absorbing their spiritual traditions. Much of this had been given the shape in which Jamal Mian received it by his great grandfather, Abdul Razzaq. It had then been further developed by his father, Abdul Bari, and by others in Abdul Bari's generation.

Veneration of the Prophet lay right at the heart of Farangi Mahalli devotional life. 'To follow the Prophet,' Abdul Bari declared in the beginning of his last book, his biography of Saiyid Shah Abdul Razzaq of Bansa, 'is the way to come close to God.'[1] He wanted to set out what was for him the basis of *tasawwuf* or Islamic mysticism. It was first that 'those who have received faith (*iman*) love God very much, and we should try to become like them,' and second that 'Muhammad [PBUH] told the people that if they treated God as a friend then he will treat you as a friend.'[2] Those in Jamal Mian's world knew that they must fill their lives with love of the Prophet and try always to come as close to him as possible. Abdul Bari continued:

---

1. Mawlana Mawlawi Muhammad Qiyam al-Din `Abd al-Bari, *Malfuz –i Razzaqi* (Cawnpur: 1926), 2. Abdul Bari wrote this biography at the especial request of Altafur Rahman Qidwai and Mumtaz Ahmad Razzaqi, the *sajjadanashin* at Bansa.

2. Ibid. 4.

To follow the Prophet truly is this: to follow his habits, his behaviour, his manner, his instructions so that the life of the Muslim becomes like the life of the Holy Prophet. ... This is called the true Khilafat, to lose one's identity in the being of the Prophet.[3]

Biographers of Farangi Mahalli ulama were concerned to show how closely their subjects had followed the example of the Prophet. Hence, in Altafur Rahman Qidwai's biography of Jamal Mian's great grandfather, Abdul Razzaq, he portrayed him as following the Prophet in the minutest detail. When he drank water, he did so in three gulps. When he ate, he did so sparingly. He washed three times both before and after eating. He took his food sitting on the ground and put it into his mouth with three fingers. And, before he began, he always said 'Bismillah'. 'He always tried to wear clothes,' Qidwai tells us, 'according to the traditions of the Prophet and his own ancestors, which were in accordance with the traditions of the Prophet.'[4] He then goes on to give a detailed description of his sartorial practices, as well as his praying, his sitting, his standing, and so on. Such was his success in following the Prophet that Qidwai makes his physical appearance close to what must have been the popularly accepted image of the Prophet:

He was a wheatish colour, and of medium size but veering towards tallness. His head was round and large. The forehead was broad and the eyelashes long. He had big eyes and in the white parts there were red lines. ... The mouth was large and

---

3. Ibid.
4. Qidwai, *Anwar-i Razzaqiya*, 36–9.

the teeth set apart. ... His arms and legs were stocky like those of an athlete. His hands and feet below the joints were soft.[5]

Men were struck by his face, used to gaze upon it for pleasure, and at times saw a halo of light about it.[6] Qidwai was too young ever to have seen Abdul Razzaq. He was conveying Farangi Mahalli oral tradition and perhaps, very specifically, the view of Abdul Bari which makes his grandfather very like the image conveyed in the classic collection of *Hadith* the family used for teaching, the *Mishkat al-Masabih*.[7] Whatever the truth of the matter, Jamal Mian would have been in no doubt as to the model he should follow and how closely he should do so.

Then, it was the way of those amongst whom Jamal Mian moved on a daily basis to show their respect for the Prophet. So Maulana Inayatullah, the headmaster of his madrasah, recalling the Prophet's injunction to care for orphans, was known to make clothes for them.[8] He showed especial respect for the Prophet's descendants, excusing one Saiyid several hundred rupees he owed in rent and always using the respectful 'aap' rather than the usual 'tum' when he addressed the Saiyids amongst his pupils.[9] In the same way, he held back from using harsh words about Sharif Husain of Mecca, whose action of rebelling against the Ottoman Caliph he detested.[10]

---

5. Ibid. 35–6.
6. Ibid. 36–7.
7. Al-Hajj Maulana Fazlul Karim, *Al-Hadis: An English Translation and Commentary of Mishkat-ul-Masabih* (Lahore: The Book House, n.d.), book 4, chapter 44, 331–41.
8. Sibghat Allah, *Sadr al-Mudarrisin*, 41.
9. Ibid. 24–5.
10. Ibid. 25.

Of course, his veneration extended to Medina where the Prophet was buried. When people were going there, he would see them off saying 'take my *salaam* to the threshold of the King', and when they returned he would kiss their hands and ask them to pray for him.[11]

The performance of *milad*—readings and lectures about the life of the Prophet—was a major aspect of Farangi Mahalli devotional life. Abdul Razzaq had begun the practice in Madras, although it is not known why—perhaps a response to the activities of Christian missionaries or, alternatively, to the innovations of Muslim reformers. When he returned to Lucknow, he introduced the practice to Farangi Mahall. The process of celebration took place over the first twelve days of Rabiulawwal. On the first eleven days, lectures on different topics relating to the Prophet written by Abdul Razzaq would be read and then there would be a major statement, or *Milad Sharif*, on 12 Rabiulawwal, the Prophet's birthday. *Milad Sharif* might be recited at other times to bring the Prophet's blessing on a new house, perhaps, or a new enterprise. But 12 Rabiulawwal was the key celebration.[12]

The performance of *milad* had been long contested and the process of contestation continued in Jamal Mian's youth. There was good reason for concern as this was an expression of devotion which did not necessarily have the guiding hand of an `alim or a Sufi; it was open to any individual to hold a ceremony. So in some *milad* performances, alcoholic drinks and drugs might be consumed and celebrants would begin to sing and shout in praise of the Prophet, disturbing the

---

11. Ibid. 19.
12. Mawlana Jalal al-Din 'Abd al-Matin, 'The Farangi Mahall Year'; Interview with Mahmood Jamal, 2012 JMP.

neighbours. In others, decorum might be perfect but untrue incidents were sometimes included in the telling of the life of the Prophet. In yet others, the focus might be on the beautiful visage of the central performer.[13] It was such practices that led the great Deobandi Sufi and `alim, Ashraf Ali Thanvi, to issue a fatwa which declared that while the performance of *milad* was permissible, it was better that Muslims did not do so.[14]

Ashraf Ali's criticism and the rather less polite attacks of other reformers persuaded Farangi Mahallis to leap to the defence of *milad*. Maulana Salamatullah published, probably in the 1920s, some guidelines for its correct performance. He was concerned that people should realize that it 'was a very good thing for which we will receive benefit … [moreover] the ignorant should not be misled and they should know what our ancestors have all along been doing is not *bida`*.'[15] We can be sure that the ideal practice he set out will have been that followed in Farangi Mahall in Jamal Mian's time. 'The purpose of *milad*,' declared Salamatullah, 'is to create love for the Prophet in the hearts of people, to induce them to follow in the footsteps of [Prophet] Muhammad [PBUH], and to make them perform good actions and abstain from evil.'[16] After Abdul Bari's death, Qutb Mian was the host. Family members and neighbours would be invited to the ceremony. The place of assembly would be covered with white sheets and incense burned. The *milad* reciter would sit in a slightly elevated position; as time went on, Jamal Mian was to become one of them. The recitation would cover the life of the Prophet,

---

13. Mawlana Salamat Allah, *Islah-yi Tariq-yi Mawlud Sharif* (Lucknow: Mujtaba'i Press, n.d.), 3–4.

14. Ibid. 14–20.

15. Ibid. 2.

16. Ibid. 5.

his qualities, good deeds, and miracles. When at the end of the *milad* the birth of the Prophet was described, some would stand out of respect, others would not.[17] At the end of the ceremony, sweets would be distributed. Later in the day, if it was 12 Rabiulawwal, Farangi Mahallis would go to Muala Khan ki Sara to pay respect to the hair of the Prophet which had been donated by Maulana Abdul Razzaq.[18]

At some stage in Jamal Mian's youth, a *milad* was written for him by Maulana Ruhullah (See Appendix 1). This is a powerful, even stirring statement of the life and virtues of the Prophet, emphasising in particular his courage and capacity to endure, but also his civility, humanity, mercy, love, and forgiveness. It ends with these uplifting words:

> In short, at home, in the mosque, in the bazaar, on the field of battle, in the madrasah in the religious gathering, in the company of friends, in the graveyard, wherever you care to imagine, and see with a discerning eye, the light that emerged from Mecca and found rest in Medina will be a lamp of guidance for you. ...

> Thanks be to Allah that we are the lucky people of this Ummah. This is the blessing and bounty of the enslavement that today, when many great empires of the world are crumbling and civilised and cultured nations are being annihilated, and those more deserving than us are being destroyed, at this time we who are the devotees of Rahmat ul l'il alimin are dwelling in peace and tranquillity and dignity. Everywhere new life is emerging and awakening and progress is being manifested, we

---

17. Ibid. 4.
18. 'Abd al-Matin, 'Farangi Mahall Year'.

stand proudly and say loudly: 'Since I received the stamp of
your slavery, I am king wherever I go.'[19]

Milad was only part of Jamal Mian's devotional life. His
father had indicated that if he wanted to come close to the
Prophet, he needed a spiritual guide, a *pir*. 'Reality,' Abdul
Bari declared:

> is to follow the Holy Prophet. For this purpose the discipline
> of masha'ikh and pirs is needed. The shaikh is the spiritual
> physician who heals the diseases of soul and body. The pir
> is the gateway to absorption in the Holy Prophet. Through
> him we reach the congregation of the Prophet, and to reach
> this congregation is to become close to God. ... Before the
> arrival of the Prophet, these spiritual physicians were Prophets
> themselves, and since the arrival of the Prophet they succeed
> him, wearing his cloak.[20]

'Once a murid has found his *pir*,' Abdul Bari told the Bazm-i
Sufia-i Hind, 'then the laws of God and his Prophet, and the
sayings of his *pir*, are his religion. Then he is neither Hanafi,
Shafii, Maliki, Hanbali ... he is Muhammadi.'[21] Obedience to
the *pir* was necessary after obedience to God, the Holy Quran,
and the Prophet.

Jamal Mian, as we have noted, became a disciple of his
father when the latter was on his death bed and he was only
six years old. This raises the question: from whom or from
where did he receive spiritual guidance in subsequent years?

---

19. 'Milad Written by Maulana Ruhullah for Jamal Mian', JMP.
20. 'Abd al-Bari, *Malfuz-i Razzaqi*, 15.
21. Ajmiri, *Khadimana Guzarish*, 49.

He is not known to have had any other *pir* while he lived in
India. This said, such was the impact of his father on his male
relatives, most of whom were Abdul Bari's disciples, and such
was the continuing power of his memory in Farangi Mahall
after his death, that Jamal Mian would not have been short
of models of correct behaviour, or of a vibrant oral tradition
which would help him follow the example of his dead *pir*.
But such models and such tradition are not the equal of the
person-to-person relationship which lies at the heart of the
care of a Sufi master for his disciple.

There were Sufis and *sajjadanashin*s for whom Jamal Mian
had considerable respect up to his middle age, amongst them:
Shah Mumtaz Ahmad Razzaqi; the *sajjadanashin* of Bansa;
Shah Hayat Ahmad; the *sajjadanashin* of Rudauli, who became
his father-in-law; and Pir Mehr Ali Shah of Golra, with whom
he became friendly in the context of Ajmer and who tried to
look after him in Pakistan. However, he did not make *bai`at*
with any of these. Beyond this, there were older men, almost
of all of whom were of a spiritual disposition who acted as
quasi-father figures, among them: Altafur Rahman Qidwai,
who looked after him after his father died; Saidur Rahman
Qidwai, who used his personal resources to help to keep the
Farangi Mahall madrasah going; Maulana Inayatullah, his
respected head master; Maulana Abdul Baqi, his uncle-in-
law who lived in Medina; Hasrat Mohani, who twice went
with him on Hajj; and Tasadduq Rasul Khan, the Raja of
Jahangirabad, who showed particular concern for his welfare.
Such men were all important in the 1920s, 1930s, and 1940s.
Then, as Jamal Mian developed a business career from the
1940s which eventually took him to Pakistan, Mirza Ahmed
Ispahani and M. A. H. Ispahani moved into the role of father
figures. Yet, not one of these men was a spiritual guide. It was

not until the 1970s, when he lived in Karachi and came to know Pir Gilani, the descendant of Abdul Qadir Gilani, that he found a *pir* again.

Jamal Mian was brought up in, and fashioned by, the rhythms of the Farangi Mahalli devotional year. These were completely focused on the Prophet, his family, and respect for the saints, both from the family and beyond who were known to be close to him. Jamal Mian's nephew (Qutb Mian's son), Matin Mian, has left us a description of the devotional year in Farangi Mahall. This was the year as he remembers it, as a madrasah student in the 1930s and 1940s, a time when Jamal Mian was involved in the madrasah's management. He chooses to begin, not with Muharram—the beginning of the Muslim year—but with Ramadan. We shall follow him.[22]

The last Friday of Ramadan, Matin Mian recalls, 'was special. It was called *Al-Wida* [meaning farewell; that is farewell to a time of heightened religious consciousness and gratitude for God's revelation].' Many came to hear Qutb Mian's emotional address during Friday prayers. It was full of poetry. He often wept while reading the *khutba*; the atmosphere could be electric.[23]

When the new moon was sighted and the month of Shawwal began, it was the end of a period of particular privation for the select group of Farangi Mahallis who had chosen to be in *I'tikaf*, that is to spend the last ten days of Ramadan in meditation in one of the muhalla's mosques, forbidden to leave the place during the period, their food being sent from Qutb Mian's house. But for everyone, of course, it was a time of celebration. Up to midnight, there were many visits from

---

22. 'Abd al-Matin, 'Farangi Mahall Year'.
23. Ibid.

family members and neighbours and the preparation of food for the following day. Many well-known people from the city came for early-morning prayers at the mosque and then assembled in the *Bahar Makan* [the big place] outside Qutb Mian's house for mutual greeting and congratulation. Then, breakfast would be taken and afterwards the family would go to Bagh Maulana Anwar.[24]

At this point, we must note the importance of the Bagh, the family graveyard in Rekabganj, to the family's devotional life. From his youth, Anwar ul-Haq, who had established the graveyard, used to go to the tomb of his father, Ahmad Abdul Haq, to meditate. 'Whatever you need,' he used to say, 'you can get at the tomb of your forefather. God willing, your desires will be met'[25] Jamal Mian's father would go to the Bagh every Thursday and Friday to say *Fateha*. On leaving Lucknow, he would first say *Fateha* at the shrine of Shah Mina (d. 1479), the Sufi who is said to have persuaded the Sunni Shaikhs to settle in Lucknow), then at the Bagh, and go on to the railway station, and then on his return follow this ritual in reverse order. His secretary, Altafur Rahman Qidwai, would spend part of each day meditating in the Bagh. It was the family *adab* to seek the presence of their ancestors and to give thanks in their company.

There was another event on this day. Close to the Bagh they would visit Kashmiri families who lived nearby and take Kashmiri tea (a rich, pink tea made from green tea leaves, milk, and salt which may also contain pistachios, almonds, cardamom, and cinnamon). Returning home, they would

---

24. Ibid.
25. Wali Allah Farangi Mahalli, *al-Aghsan al-Arba'a* (Lucknow: Nadwa ms., n.d.), 43–4.

go to Maulana Inayatullah's house where there would be a short *qawwali* session on the subject of Eid. After afternoon prayers there would be a lunch at Mufti Abdul Qadir's house. In the summer, this would be followed by rest. Then, until late in the evening, there would be much visiting and being visited which would include relatives from the qasbah Kakori settled in Lucknow. Such activities continued on 2 Shawwal, including, amongst other events, a visit to Jamal Mian's English teacher, Mirza Askari, where there would be a cultural event. Then in the afternoon, there would be a visit to Dogawan, the home of Jamal Mian's mother. During this season, the Farangi Mahallis took those acts of civility and neighbourliness, which were themselves a form of worship, seriously.[26]

Eid had barely finished and on 5 Shawwal there was the `Urs of Saiyid Shah Abdul Razzaq of Bansa. Abdul Bari had impressed on his family the importance of attendance at this `Urs for their ancestors. 'They considered it to be a place for treatment of their spiritual and worldly problems.' This was the case, he said, even for the most learned amongst them, Maulana Abdul Hai (d. 1886).[27] Everyone, including the women, went to Bansa for the `Urs. They went by bus, by train, and, in the case of Qutb Mian and Jamal Mian, by car. The ceremonies at the `Urs emphasized the respect of the saint's family for the Farangi Mahallis. They stayed apart from the rest of the pilgrims; they were placed immediately behind the *sajjadnashin* in the procession to the shrine; they sat on either side of him in the Khanqah; it was Farangi Mahallis who recited the *Fateha* for Saiyid Shah Abdul

---

26. 'Abd al-Matin, 'Farangi Mahall Year'.
27. 'Abd al-Bari, *'Urs-i Hadrat-i Bansa* (Lucknow: n.d.), 10.

Razzaq after Maghreb. On the 6th everyone would make their way back to Lucknow, although Jamal Mian, Qutb Mian, Altafur Rahman and other senior folk would break their journey to visit their friends and relatives amongst the Qidwais of Baragaon.[28]

Nothing special happened in the month of Zilqada. The next event was on 9 Zilhijja when the `Urs of Ahmad Abdul Haq, son of Mulla Said and father of Anwarul Haq was celebrated with a fast, a *Fateha* was read at the Bagh, and the fast broken afterwards. The following day was Eid *al-Adha* which Matin Mian did not find nearly as exciting as the Ramadan Eid. Sheep were sent down from the family's orchards in Kakori and slaughtered early on the morning of the 10th. Then, on 18 Zilhijja, there was a commemoration of Hazrat Usman. After *Asr* prayers, his qualities were enumerated in the Bahar Makan by the reading out of an address written by Maulana Abdul Razzaq. Then, on the 29th of the month, there was a similar event for Hazrat Umar.[29]

The first ten days of Muhurram saw a particular focus on the Prophet and his family. On 1 Muharram, after *Maghreb* prayers, the death of the Prophet was discussed and commemorated. This was followed on the 2nd by a talk, and a formal address written by Maulana Abdul Razzaq on Abu Bakr Siddiq. 3–6 Muhurram saw similar events with addresses by Maulana Abdul Razzaq for Hazrat Umar, Hazrat Usman, Hazrat Ali, and Imam Husain. On 7, 8, and 9 Muhurram the events of Karbala were remembered with a commemoration of the life of Imam Husain on the 9th with the usual address written by Maulana Abdul Razzaq. On 10 Muharram there

---

28. 'Abd al-Matin 'Farangi Mahall Year'.
29. Ibid.

was a *Fateha* for Imam Husain. Matin Mian tells us that the
purpose of these ceremonies was to draw a direct line from the
Prophet to Karbala and to counter Shia influence. Jamal Mian
was amongst those who took part in reading the addresses.[30]

Jamal Mian, in fact, has left us a particular record of his
respect and love for Imam Husain. It is an address dated
6 Muhurram, probably in 1942, written for a majlis at
Jahangirabad.[31] He tells us of the love of the Prophet for his
grandchildren, of how they had the reverence and respect of
the Prophet's companions and heirs long before the tragic
events of Karbala.

Then, speaking specifically of Husain he declares:

He was loved because of his ancestry; he was elevated and
worthy of respect because of his position, because of his beauty
and attraction, because of his manners and character, because
of his awesomeness and dignity ... It was not Karbala which
made Imam Husain but Imam Husain who made Karbala.
Even if this event had never occurred, there would have been
no diminishing of our love for him.[32]

Jamal Mian moves to his climax making a point which
followed from the heart of his religious understanding:

Of all the good and eternal marks that this story of truth
and [a] heart-rending event has left on the heart and soul

---

30. Ibid.
31. In January 1942, Jamal Mian noted in his diary that he had given a
    bayan on Husain at Jahangirabad; 2, Jamal Mian Diary, 27 January
    1942, JMP.
32. Maulana Jamal Mian, 'Address at Jahangirabad on Imam Husain'
    6 Muhurram, JMP.

of the Islamic world is that it provided the foundations of
the grand and fruitful mansion of *tasawwuf*. Hazrat Imam
Husain, leaving to one side worldly power and glory, opened
that trail of knowledge to spread Islam, following which those
robed fakirs spread far and wide across the world, whose
glittering foreheads move more than the flashing swords of
conquerors, and whose pure and exemplary lives, more than
the fat books of the ulama, and whose love and chastity and
open-heartedness spread Islam in a far better way than others,
and millions followed them in the footsteps of the Prophet's
true message. In brief the light of Islam spread to India and
Ajam through these very Sufis. This light came from the sun
of East and West, the heir of the Prophet, that very Husain.
On this basis Khwaja Muinuddin Chishti Rahmatullah Ilayhe
has uttered:

> Husain is the Shah, Husain is the King,
> Husain is the Din, Husain is the protection of Din.
> He gave his head, but not his heart to Yazid,
> Truly he is the basis of La Illah [ie the *Kalima*].[33]

The second half of Safar was a time of quite intense activity.
This began on the 20th with the `Urs of Shaikh Qawamuddin
(d.1436) in the compound of the Dargah of Shah Mina, close
to the Medical College. Qawamuddin came from Kara, a
qasbah near Allahabad, and was famed for having made the
Hajj, on foot, seven times. Qawamuddin adopted Mina, who
was a relative, on his deathbed and made him his successor.
A powerful cult built up around Shah Mina (d. 1479) who
was renowned for his miracles. On 21 Safar, after `Isha prayer,

---

33. Ibid.

there was a *Milad* which was customarily read by a Farangi Mahalli. This inaugurated the 'Urs of Shah Mina which saw the washing of the grave or *ghusl* on the 22nd. Everybody was expected to attend *Asr* prayer at the Dargah.[34] Qawamuddin and Shah Mina were amongst the first Sufis to establish themselves in Lucknow. In attending the 'Urs, the Farangi Mahallis were acknowledging, consciously or unconsciously, the establishment of the spiritual tradition in their city which guided Muslims towards the example of the Prophet.

Two days later the major Farangi Mahalli 'Urs began—that of Maulana Abdul Razzaq on the 25th, of Maulana Abdul Wahhab on the 26th, and of Maulana Abdul Bari on the 27th. On each day the *Fateha* was read in Farangi Mahall, that of Maulana Abdul Bari's death, at 11.15 p.m. precisely. Afterwards, Kashmiri tea, *shirmal* (a saffron-flavoured flat bread, a delicacy of Lucknow), and *balai* (cream) was distributed. On each day, there would be *qawwali* in the Bagh. This had been introduced in the mid-nineteenth century by Abdul Wali and Abdul Wahhab, Jamal Mian's grandfather, who had built the pavilion in which it took place. *Qawwali* was very important to Jamal Mian who loved it less for the music than for the poetry. In the 1930s, the master of ceremonies was Mumtaz Ahmad Razzaqi, the *sajjadanashin* of Bansa. The *qawwal*s, or singers, traditionally came from the family's old qasbah of Sehali, amongst them Ghulam Hazrat, Muhammad Umar, and Usman. Jamal Mian also brought the great performer, Murli, from Rudauli, who became a distinguished performer on All-India Radio and after Partition was invited to perform in Dacca and Karachi. In the Bagh, proceedings would usually begin, not with the *hamd*, a hymn in praise of

---

34. 'Abd al-Matin: Farangi Mahall Year'.

God, but with a *na`t*, a poem in praise of the Prophet. This
emphasized the Prophet-centred nature of Farangi Mahalli
devotionalism. The *na`t*s might be by Abdul Rahman Jami,
Hasan Dehlavi, or Muinuddin Chishti, but they might equally
be by a contemporary poet like Hasrat Mohani. This would
be followed by a *manqabat* in praise of a great saint of the past,
Abdul Qadir Gilani or Muinuddin Chishti. Then there would
be a *manqabat* in praise of the saint whose `Urs it was. This
would be followed by ghazals focusing on mystical love from
Hafiz, Rumi, Saadi, Khusrau, Nizami, Jami, Bedil, and so on.
Jamal Mian was particularly fond of a couplet of Hafiz:

> You have spent so much time sitting in the madrasah,
> Now try your luck in the tavern.

After this, the *qawwal*s would perform the *rang* in which
the descent of mystical knowledge from Abdul Qadir Gilani,
through Muinuddin Chishti, down to the saints whose `Urs
was being celebratedwas recited. This was followed by the *Qul*
when the four *sura*s of the Quran beginning with *Qaf* were
recited, the task being shared amongst those present. The
ceremonies would conclude with the *Fateha* recited back in
Farangi Mahal. The month ended with a reading on Hazrat
Imam Hasan on the 29th, after *Asr* prayer.

'Then Rabiulawwal begins', declares Matin Mian, 'the
most important 12 days are upon us.'[35] Thus he confirms,
specifically in the discussion of *Milad* above, and more
generally in the whole emphasis of the devotional year, the
centrality of the family's veneration of the Prophet. We should
also note that while the men were listening to *Milad* sermons

---

35. 'Abd al-Matin, 'The Farangi Mahall Year'.

and addresses, the women were also holding their own *Milad* ceremonies indoors.[36]

There now began Rabiussani, the month of Abdul Qadir Gilani (1088–1166), the greatest of the Muslim saints. He himself claimed: 'My foot is on the neck of every saint', a statement which no one seemed to contest.[37] The founder of the Qadiriyya order, hewas also known as *Ghaus-e A`zam* (The Greatest Help) and *Pir-i Dastgir* (the *pir* who holds one's hand). A *Fateha* was said for him in Farangi Mahall on the 11th of the month, both in the mosque after Maghreb and indoors. On this day, Altafur Rahman Qidwai had a pulao made and distributed. During the first eleven days of Rabiussani, addresses on the qualities of Abdul Qadir Gilani, written by Maulana Abdul Razzaq, would be read out by Qutb Mian after *Maghreb* prayer each day. In later life, Jamal Mian was to travel to the shrine of *Ghaus-e A`zam* in Baghdad whenever he could. Of course, it was one of the mercies of his later life in Karachi that he was able to become a disciple of a descendant of Abdul Qadir Jilani. There was a supplication to Abdul Qadir Gilani by Hasrat Mohani, which was sung by the *qawwal*s in Farangi Mahall, and which Jamal Mian would frequently recite:

> I need your guidance my lord
> O Amir of Baghdad I am helpless
> Though I am not deserving of special favour
> I am one of your slaves
> You will get whatever you ask from Ghausul A`zam, O Hasrat
> Just say 'I am a supplicant at your door!'[38]

---

36. Ibid.
37. Annemarie Schimmel, *Mystical Dimensions of Islam* (Chapel Hill: University of North Carolina Press, 1975), 247.
38. Note by Mahmood Jamal, 26 June 201, JMP.

On the 13th of the following month, Jamadussani,
everyone went to the `Urs of Ahmad Abdul Haq in Rudauli.
This Chishti-Sabiri saint had given birth to arguably the
most influential Sufi tradition in the province.[39] Maulana
Salamatullah, as one of the organizers of the event, went
ahead of the rest of the family. The occasion attracted *pirs*,
*sajjadanashin*s and *qawwal*s from far and wide; there was also
a large popular attendance. On the 14th, after `Isha prayer,
there was a major *qawwali* performance which many felt was
the best aspect of the occasion. Some present would fall into
a trance. In the morning of the following day, the grave would
be washed and then after *Zuhr* prayer, the *sajjadanashin* would
go into the women's section of his house. There he would sit
on the floor, be dressed in a much-repaired *khirqah* or cloak—
symbolic of his humility which was said to have belonged to
Ahmad Abdul Haq and to have been repaired by the ladies
of the family down the generations—and then have a *pugri* or
turban placed on his head. Once he was dressed, a group of
strong men would carry him to the Dargah, all the while those
present were struggling to touch his *khirqah*. He was then
taken into the Dargah around which they would walk several
times, and then he would be carried up into the Khanqah
which commanded the highest position in the premises. From
here he would lead the *Asr* prayer, which was a mass prayer
followed by hundreds of people around the complex. After
prayers, the *sajjadanashin* was brought back into the house
where his *khirqah* was removed, folded, and put back in a
wooden trunk. It was an inclusive event in which everyone

39. For the vitality of the Rudauli tradition in the age of Islamic reform
    see Moin Ahmad Nizami, 'Reform and Renewal in South Asian Islam:
    The Chishti-Sabiris in 18th and 19th c. North India' (Cambridge: PhD
    thesis, 2010).

wore the same items of clothing, a kurta or a shawl, in a
brownish orange colour, which was referred to as the 'sabri
colour', after Alauddin Sabir of Kaliyar. The *sajjadnashin,* as
we shall see, was to be most important in the life of Jamal
Mian. One particular contribution Jamal Mian made to the
'Urs was introducing Urdu *qawwali*s to a menu which was
usually in Purbi and Persian.

At the beginning of Rajab, all Farangi Mahallis went to the
'Urs of Muinuddin Chishti at Ajmer, which extended over the
first six days of the month. Muinuddin (d. 1236) had arrived
in the Delhi region from Sistan around the very same time
that ancestors of the Farangi Mahallis arrived from Herat.
He settled at Ajmer around the beginning of the thirteenth
century. His dargah grew into the premier Sufi shrine of
India. Muhammad bin Tughluq (d. 1351) was the first Delhi
Sultan to visit. Under the Mughals, it became a major focus of
imperial devotion—the emperor Akbar making his pilgrimage
from Agra on foot. Imperial and local rulers contributed to its
rich built environment. Its finest mosque and one of its two
gateways were contributed by Shah Jahan (d. 1666); in 1888,
Sir Asman Jha of Hyderabad began the construction of the
Sama` Khana* where *sama` took place every night throughout
the 'Urs; in December 1911, the Queen Empress Mary visited
the shrine and gave Rs 1,500 for the repair and roofing of the
tank in front of the *Sama` Khana.*[40]

Jamal Mian's father would go to Ajmer every year. It was
here, according to his *murid,* Maulana Shafi, that he would
sketch out his programme for the year. Shafi recalls two
specific visits with Abdul Bari to the 'Urs. Apparently, it was

---

40. P. M. Currie, *The Shrine and Cult of Mu'in al-din Chishti of Ajmer* (Delhi:
Oxford University Press, 1989), 97–116.

not the practice of Farangi Mahallis to enter the mausoleum. Nevertheless, Shafi asked Abdul Bari's permission to do so. He went in. Abdul Bari then asked him what he had seen. Shafi said: 'What could I see except marquetry and arabesques?' The Maulana asked him to go in again. 'When I went inside I saw the whole place irradiated with light.' Shafi left the mausoleum in a state of high agitation. The Maulana did not ask him what he had seen, nor did Shafi tell him.[41] On another occasion, Shafi kissed the threshhold of the shrine and touched it with his hands and kissed them. Abdul Bari asked him why he did this. He said that he had seen his uncle, Maulana Inayatullah, doing it and so he thought it was part of the etiquette of the shrine. 'When you become Maulana Inayatullah,' Abdul Bari said, 'you will have the right to do this. But it is not among the *adab*s of the shrine. Have you ever seen me doing this?'[42] This said, Maulana Shafi tells us that while he was in the Shah Jahan mosque in Ajmer or the Begumi Dalan, which Shah Jahan's daughter, Jahanara, had had constructed, he saw Abdul Bari talking to people 'but his sight never moved from the dome of the mausoleum'.[43]

Jamal Mian will have been in no doubt about the importance of attendance at the Ajmer ʿUrs for his father and his family.

41. Shafi, 'Memoir', 24.
42. Regardless of the intrinsic interest of this statement, there was a specific reason for Shafi including it in his memoir. At the time when relations between the Ali Brothers and Abdul Bari broke down over the Saudi/Wahhabi invasion of the Hejaz, with the consequent damage to the holy places, Abd al-Majid Daryabadi had apparently written a biographical piece on Abdul Bari claiming that he prostrated himself before the shrine and kissed the threshold. Shafi, writing nearly fifty years later, clearly thought it important to rebut the propaganda which had been uttered during that bitter quarrel. Ibid. 24–5.
43. Ibid. 25.

In addition to its significance in personal devotion, it was also the occasion at which the spiritual elite of northern India came together, which was why his father had used it in 1916 as the occasion on which he founded the Bazm-i Sufia-i Hind. When he began to attend in the 1930s, the numbers of pilgrims were between 50,000 and 70,000.[44] The most important event was the *qawwali* performance which took place each evening in the *Sama` Khana* each evening after `Isha prayer. The most important of these were on 5 and 6 Rajab. In the *Sama` Khana*, the *sajjadanashin* sat at one end under a silken canopy, the *qawwals* at the other end. The most privileged members of the audience sat cross-legged in rows in between. Beadles (*chobdars*) wearing white angarkhas and carrying silver staffs of office controlled the audience. By this time, music had come to be relayed by loudspeaker to all parts of the dargah. Some amongst those present achieved a state of ecstasy at which point the *sajjadanashin* and the whole audience rose to honour the state of the devotee. The proceedings were brought to an end with the reading of the *Fateha*. Bowls containing rosewater which had been used to wash Muinuddin's tomb were passed around, the fortunate being able to drink some, the remainder content with being sprinkled with it. The *sajjadanashin* then left with a general scramble to touch him as he did so. Thus, the *Sama`* finished. On the morning of the final day of the `Urs, all pilgrims gathered in and around the dargah to pray before they returned home. On 9 Rajab, the whole dargah was ceremonially washed with rose water.[45]

In Shaban, Farangi Mahallis fasted on the 14th and 15th. After `Isha on the 14th, they paid respect to the graves of

---

44. Currie, *Ajmer*, 118.
45. Currie, *Ajmer*, 126–9.

their ancestors in the Bagh. There was also a *Fateha* in which all of the important personages of Islam were remembered, beginning with the Prophet. 22 and 26 Shaban saw the *'Urs* of Maulana Abdul Wali and Maulana Abdul Haq. Then there was Ramadan. Every household, as one would expect, had a *hafiz*. *Tarawih* was recited by Jamal Mian in the Mahalsera and by his nephews, Nur Mian, in the mosque, and Muhammad Mian, in the Bahar Makan. The *sahur* meal, taken before dawn, was a very sociable time with many gathered in the Bahar Makan, discussing a wide range of subjects until daybreak when all dispersed and went off to sleep. People would generally wake at 11 a.m. and carry on with their daily activities until sundown when the fast was broken with a light meal, which was followed by an evening meal and *Tarawih* prayers. Such was the pattern of the day up to *Eid ul-Fitr*.[46]

This family devotional year, built on the pattern of the Islamic year, set a basic devotional framework for the life of Jamal Mian. This is not to suggest that he followed every element in later life but he most certainly followed, for as long as he was able, the basic structure. It would seem that there had been an incremental development steadily fashioned by his forefathers, from the establishment of the family Bagh by Maulana Anwar ul-Haq, followed by the introduction of *qawwali* in the Bagh by Maulana Abdul Wali, and the introduction of *Milad* to the family by his great grandfather Maulana Abdul Razzaq, and also other elements of remembrance embracing the Prophet's family and the saints. His father's example as a Sufi and his overall leadership in family matters helped consolidate family practices. Right at the heart of the family's devotional life was the Prophet,

---

46. 'Abd al-Matin, *Farangi Mahall Year*.

his family, and those Sufi saints, whose spiritual achievement and Abdul Qadir Gilani apart, whose presence for centuries in northern India could bring the individual closer to the Prophet. In all of this *qawwali*, the verses sung rather than the music itself, opened the doors of emotion, and set free the flow of love for the Prophet.

1. The Tomb of Maulana Abdul Bari, Bagh Maulana Anwar, Lucknow.

2. Altafur Rahman Qidwai

3. Saidur Rahman Qidwai

4. The Mahalsera Farangi Mahall. Matin Mian, wearing a turban, on his way to lead Friday Prayers in the Farangi Mahall mosque with Jamil Mian Razzaqi. Gandhi's room can be seen to the right with a papaya tree outside.

5. The entrance to Mulla Nizamuddin's house, the place of the madrasa in the twentieth century.

6. The young Jamal Mian in the mid-1930s, with Irtiza his driver (left) and an unknown man.

7. Maulvi Sibghatullah, one of Jamal Mian's teachers and a renowned orator.

6

Jamal Mian's rise to the front rank of Muslim Politics, 1936–43

IN THE SEVEN YEARS FROM 1936, JAMAL MIAN ROSE TO THE forefront of Muslim politics in India. A range of factors made this possible. One, most certainly, was his gift as an orator at a time when much campaigning needed to be done to spread the Muslim League message throughout India. Second, was the reputation of his family across India which meant, for instance, that his name was recognized by crowds in Hyderabad and Calcutta and that he might stay with key figures like Abdullah Haroon in Karachi or Pir Ibrahim or Shaukat Ali in Bombay. Third, there were his excellent relationships with the leadership of the UP Muslim League, many known to him for years, among them Choudhry Khaliquzzaman, Ehsanur Rahman Qidwai, and the Raja of Mahmudabad. There were also the good relations he established with Jinnah without whose support he most certainly would not have been able to join the Muslim League High Command. In addition, there were his relationships with the Ispahani family of Calcutta, one of the leading Muslim business families of India and most important supporters of the Muslim League. Important, too, of course was his willingness to sacrifice time and energy to the Muslim cause and his acknowledged integrity.

In one sense, Jamal Mian had been involved with politics

through the many politicians whom he met in Farangi Mahall
during his young life. But his first engagement, when he
was almost a sentient adult, came in early 1936. Maulana
Shaukat Ali was going from Simla, where he was a member
of the Central Assembly, to Calcutta to attend a Palestine
Conference—Arab resistance to British rule had won much
support amongst Indian Muslims. Jamal Mian's aunt had
sent him with the driver, Irtiza Husain, bearing snacks for
Shaukat Ali as the train stopped at Lucknow. The Maulana
asked him if he had seen Calcutta. When Jamal Mian said no,
the Maulana arranged a ticket and carried him off to Calcutta.
There, they went to Shahid Suhrawardy's house where they
found the Bengal statesman in vest and pyjamas, lying on a
bed surrounded by telephones and visitors. Jamal Mian was
put in the charge of Suhrawardy's son, Abid Bhai, given some
new clothes and taken off to the Palestine Conference. To
begin with, he seems to have been more excited by eating ice
cream at Magnolia Ice Cream and seeing the Metro Cinema
for the first time. However, when Jamal Mian actually began
seriously to engage with the conference he found it very
exciting with Zafar Ali Khan, Hasrat Mohani, and others
making emotional speeches. When I arrived, 'Shaukat Sahib
saw me and introduced me and mentioned my father and said
I would speak. The subject was Palestine and the role of youth.
As I spoke a few sentences the Maulana would ask the public
to shout Allah-o-Akbar to encourage and egg me on.'[1] This
was an extraordinary experience for a young man who was not
yet 17. 'That was my first exposure to political speaking ... I
started going to public meetings.'[2]

---

1. Jamal Mian, Tape 8, JMP.
2. Ibid.

A little later, in April 1936, the Congress annual session came to Lucknow. Qutb Mian invited Jawaharlal Nehru, the Congress President, and some of his co-workers to tea in Farangi Mahall. Jamal Mian recalled that he was wearing a sherwani of white khaddar, which could have been interpreted as a gesture of support for the nationalist cause. As Nehru left the tea party to chair the next Congress session he said to Jamal Mian:

"Come along. I will show you Congress." I said OK and got into the car. All the shopkeepers started garlanding him; as the garlands got too many he would put one or two on me. We finally arrived at Moti Nagar. There, there was a huge procession and Jawaharlal joined in and held my hand. I saw many big Congress leaders, including Pandit Malaviya, Mukhtar Ahmad Ansari and also Abul Kalam Azad. We finally arrived on the stage which had straw mats on it.[3]

Of the speeches he heard that day, Jamal Mian was most impressed by the South Indian, Satyamurti, who spoke in English, and the Hindu Mahasabha leader, Pandit Malaviya, who spoke in 'eloquent Urdu' and quoted Hafiz. When the time came for Maghreb prayers, he asked Maulana Azad what they should do. He was told that they would pray on the stage. Jamal Mian gave the call for prayer and Maulana Azad led the prayers.[4]

It is worth reflecting on Nehru's actions. The Lucknow Congress of 1936 was one at which his radicalism was placing him well ahead of most Congressmen. There was little support

---

3. Ibid.
4. Ibid.

for his line that the Congress should not accept office in the provincial governments which were to be formed after the first elections under the 1935 Government of India Act. He preferred direct action. His Presidential address, moreover, had been full of socialist militancy, which was anathema to many. In these circumstances, when there were more tensions than usual amongst the Congress leaders, it was a tribute to the longstanding relations between the Nehrus and the Farangi Mahallis that Jawaharlal should have accepted Qutb Mian's invitation to tea. Arguably, it was even more of a tribute that he should have taken the brightest scion of that family with him to the Congress platform. In the years up to Independence, Jamal Mian was to be a frequent critic of Nehru. But in the years after Independence he came to realize that Jawaharlal was one of the few true friends of the Indian Muslims in the Congress leadership. He had a special place in Jamal Mian's mind.[5]

We have already noted in Chapter One how Jamal Mian announced himself in All-India Muslim politics at the Lucknow League session in October 1937. This was immediately followed by bye-election campaigns in which there was bitter competition between the Congress and the League as Nehru put his Muslim Mass contact Programme into operation. The first bye-election campaign was for the Bijnor-Garhwal seat. It was occasioned when Hafiz Mohammad Ibrahim, who had won the seat for the Muslim League in the general elections of 1937, had gone over to the Congress, becoming a minister in its government. He was now seeking fresh mandate as a Congressman. His Muslim League

---

5. Jamal Mian, 'Note on Jawahahrurlal Ne's Death' no date but probably 1964, JMP.

opponent was a local lawyer, Abdul Sami. Shaukat Ali led the
Muslim League campaign. He was assisted by major figures
from other parts of India—Maulana Zafar Ali Khan, the editor
of the *Zamindar* of Lahore; Khwaja Hasan Nizami of Dargah
Nizamuddin Aulia in Delhi; Saiyid Zakir Ali of Agra; and
Hasrat Mohani, poet and Muslim leader of Cawnpore. Every
dirty trick was played from declaring that a vote for Congress
was *kufr* to accusations that Nehru was aiming to ban *namaz*
and *adhan*. On the other side, Ibrahim had the support of
the Congress machine and the majority group at Deoband
under the leadership of Husain Ahmad Madani.[6] Jinnah was
also involved in the campaign and it was in this context that
Jamal Mian came to know the great man better. They both
gave speeches in Bijnor, Jinnah doing so in Urdu. They then
left Bijnor by car for Najibabad. It was an old convertible and
the roof was down. Shaukat Ali, a massive man, sat in front
while Jamal Mian sat between Jinnah and Zafar Ali Khan at
the back. As they drove into the countryside they became
covered with dust. Jamal Mian had to use an abaya, given to
him by Pir Ibrahim, a descendant of Abdul Qadir Gilani who
lived in Bombay and had been close to his father, to protect
those in the back seat from dust. Jamal Mian recalled the
conversations they had on this trip and in the dak bungalow
at Najibabad. 'He [Jinnah] said to me: "Every man must have
an ambition. What is yours?" I said my idea is of a university
or institution where religious sciences and modern sciences
could be taught together. He said "All this is only possible
when you have political power."' Jinnah asked Jamal Mian to

---

6. Venkat Dhulipala, *Creating a New Medina: State Power, Islam, and the
   Quest for Pakistan in Late Colonial North India* (New Delhi: Cambridge
   University Press, 2015), 90–2.

see him the following day. 'When I went next day, he gave me three books, two were compilations of his speeches and the other his Fourteen Points. He then said: "You are a very good orator, but do not make politics your means of livelihood or profession."'[7] Jinnah was subsequently to act, as we shall see, to try to make sure that Jamal Mian had independent means. But the involvement of these men in the League campaign was not fruitful. Abdul Sami lost.

This defeat was followed by three further bye-elections in Muslim seats—Amroha-Moradabad, Saharanpur, and Bulandshahr on 9, 13, and 18 December. Nehru campaigned vigorously for the Congress in all constituencies. Jinnah stepped back from this campaign and responsibility for it was undertaken by the UP Muslim League leadership with Shaukat Ali in charge. We know that Jamal Mian was involved in the Saharanpur campaign and the odds are, as the constituencies were all in the same region, that he was involved in the other two. A significant feature of these elections was that the minority faction in Deoband, under the leadership of Ashraf Ali Thanvi, was coming to throw its weight behind the Muslim League which won all three elections decisively.[8]

During 1938, although not yet formally a member of the Muslim League, Jamal Mian became increasingly involved in League activities. He spent much time in Bombay, speaking at meetings. When he was there he stayed either with his father's friend, Pir Ibrahim, or with Shaukat Ali in Khilafat House. His close friend, the Raja of Mahmudabad, stayed

7. Jamal Mian, Tape 5A, JMP.
8. Dhulipala, *New Medina*, 93–6; Khaliquzzaman, *Pathway*, 177; Khalid Ali, *Ali Brothers*, 878–82.

in Juhu. Both men enjoyed Bombay society.[9] In this period, Jamal Mian's reputation as an orator grew. He recalled a speech at a big meeting on Mohamed Ali Road over which Jinnah presided. After Shaukat Ali and Mahmudabad spoke, Jamal Mian launched into a major address. In one of its key passages, urging the need for unity and national organization, he declared:

> And now things have reached such a low point that our enemies have begun to say openly that there are only two forces in India, the Congress and the British. [He referred to recent statements by Jawaharlal Nehru] And seven crores of Muslims are merely ... their slaves. It is a law of nature that the more powerful the tyrant, the more insignificant the creature or force that destroys him—something or someone he never imagines would do that job. Those who attacked the Kaba could never have imagined that they would be destroyed by starlings. Nimrod had no idea that a mere mosquito would lead to his death. Gandhi and Nehru could never have imagine[d] that to counter the Jamiat ul-Ulama and the Ahrars, that nature would choose a sinful and profligate man of Malabar Hill, a hard working, honest lawyer to come alive and find strength in his weak hands to mobilize his nation. He stood up and said: "NO, MUSLIMS ARE ALSO SOMETHING" ... And what an effect his words have had. The Ummah awoke. Hearts were alive; each of us began to feel the danger. They who understand now know that without a party, without uniting together as one force, we will not succeed.[10]

---

9. The two young men enjoyed the company of society figures, on one occasion Mrs Currimbhoy. Raja of Mahmudabad to Jamal Mian, 17 November 1942, Mahmudabad correspondence, JMP.

10. 'Speeches at Muslim League Jalsas', and also Jamal Mian, Tape 3, JMP.

Jamal Mian recalled that when he and Maulana Inayatullah had gone to see Ashraf Ali Thanvi, who was undergoing medical treatment in Lucknow, the Deobandi had said how much he had enjoyed this speech which had been reported in the *Khilafat* newspaper.[11] But so too did Jinnah, himself. When he gave a garden party for the Raja of Mahmudabad as he left Bombay—an occasion which included Lord Lothian, the Aga Khan, and several Congress leaders—Jinnah declared as Jamal Mian left, on being reminded by Shaukat Ali that Abdul Bari had been Jamal Mian's father: 'A Lion's son is a lion' [Sher ka bachha, sher hota hai].[12] Nevertheless, Jinnah still felt that Jamal Mian had lessons to learn about public speaking. 'When you stand up to speak,' he told him, 'One gets the feeling of a mail train. It is not proper to move with such haste. You should use words that your audience understands and pause after each sentence. You should watch the reaction of your listeners, and if they are unable to understand your discourse, you should explain to them once again.'[13]

At this stage, Jinnah was working to build up the Muslim League's organization and authority throughout India, but especially in the Muslim majority provinces. He had already done deals with the leaders of the Punjab and Bengal, giving them a free hand in their provincial politics provided they supported him as their representative voice at the centre. This meant that he turned his attention to those minority provinces whose politics left openings for the League, namely the NWFP and Sind. Jamal Mian was heavily involved in this campaign. In late August and early September 1938, there

11. Jamal Mian, Tape 3, Ibid.
12. Jamal Mian, Tape 4-1, Ibid.
13. Substantial typed document in English on Jinnah 'Writings on Jinnah Saheb in Urdu and English', Ibid.

was a bye-election which the League needed to win in the NWFP. The Congress had launched a major campaign against the League. Jamal Mian, along with Zafar Ali Khan, Maulana Abdul Hamid Budauni, the Raja of Mahmudabad, Hasrat Mohani, Haji Abdullah Haroon, and Abdul Majid Sindhi went on a speaking tour to bolster League resistance. The League candidate won and after the victory, Jamal Mian was present at a Provincial Muslim League conference at Abbottabad over which Choudhry Khaliquzzaman presided. A photograph taken at the time indicates the close relationship between Jamal Mian and the old Lucknow political master (Illustration 8).[14]

At this point, Jamal Mian formally became a member of the All-India Muslim League; he had recently reached the qualifying age of eighteen. In his public statement, he said he did so to counter the impression that all the ulama were with the Congress.[15] This was followed by the first Sindh Provincial Muslim League Conference at Karachi on 8–12 October 1938. Jamal Mian and the Raja of Mahmudabad stayed with Abdullah Haroon, his father's old friend and very much the driving force behind the occasion. The conference report describes an occasion of considerable grandeur. Jamal Mian was in the thick of it, seconding one of the major resolutions, but more notably being amongst those to address the opening session along with Fazlul Huq, chief minister of Bengal, Sikander Hayat, chief minister of the Punjab, and Shaukat Ali.[16]

---

14. M. Rafique Afzal, *A History of the All-India Muslim League 1906–1947*, (Karachi: Oxford University Press, 2013), 413.

15. Ibid. 330; *Times of India*, 9 October 1938, Ibid. 330.

16. *Report of the General Secretary, The First Sindh Provincial Muslim League Conference 8th, 9th, 10th, 11th, 12th of October 1938, Karachi Sindh*, <http://gulhayat.com/sindhmuslimleagueconference.asp>.

Jamal Mian recalled a fascinating, and perhaps slightly competitive exchange, between Jinnah and Abdullah Haroon at dinner during this Conference. Both men were talking about their early lives. Abdullah Haroon said that there had been a time when he was destitute; he used to sleep with the porters at Karachi Railway Station. Then he got a job at Rs 4 per month. Later, he opened a small provision store. His aim was to earn enough to set up a sugar mill; eventually he came to own a sugar factory. Jinnah said that when he returned to Karachi from London as a barrister, his family's finances were a mess. His relatives wanted him to start practice in Karachi. But his ambition was greater than this; he began practice in Bombay with just Rs 40. Then his ambition was tested. He was appointed a temporary magistrate and did so well that a British High Court judge offered him a permanent post. Jinnah declined it. Explaining the offer, the judge said that the job would lead to the rank of High Court Judge and a large salary. Jinnah replied that it was his ambition to earn a High Court judge's salary each day. Much later, when the judge returned to visit Bombay after retirement, he asked Jinnah if his income had reached the level he had set himself. Jinnah said, yes.[17]

Jinnah followed this Provincial Muslim League Conference by visiting Jacobabad, Shikarpur, and Larkana, amongst other places, in the Sindh interior. Jamal Mian went with him.[18] Although he claimed that he attended most Muslim League meetings, there is no evidence that Jamal Mian attended the annual session at Patna in December 1938. Arguably,

---

17. Note by Jamal Mian on Jinnah in English. 'Writings on Jinnah Saheb in Urdu and English', JMP.
18. Illustration 11, Jamal Mian in group with Jinnah at Jacobabad.

his first period of League activity was nicely rounded off when he wrote his first letter in English, in February 1939, to Mahmud Haroon, the son of Abdullah Haroon, whom he had got to know in the previous year.[19]

In August of 1939, Hasrat Mohani, regardless of the threat of war, decided to visit Europe. Jamal Mian went with him as far as Damascus. As he was leaving his sister, Sughra, gave him a poem, instinct with her love for him. It was published in the Urdu daily, *Haqiqat*, under the title 'A Sister's Letter to her Brother'.

Listen to what Sughra has to tell you.
Amma's favourite and Ammi's beloved.

Brother, you are going in search of knowledge.
But you already have enough knowledge for your age.
You are searching for religious knowledge and are going to Arabia.
Courageous youth. God is with you.
Please look after yourself.
Amma's favourite and Ammi's beloved.

You are a very intelligent person
But you look like a child.
Times are very bad and I am frightened
As it is a perilous journey you engage on.
But on this journey you must present the goodness of your way.
Amma's favourite and Ammi's beloved.

When you come back you have a lot to do.
You have to fight the enemies of religion.

---

19. Jamal Mian Diary 14 February 1939, JMP.

You have to enter the battle against the unbeliever.
You will have to carry the sword of truth in your hand.
Come back in the form of Khalid.
Amma's favourite and Ammi's beloved.

The adhans that echoed in Medina.
Those adhans are still echoing in our heart.
They still cause terror amongst the unbelievers.
The lovers of the adhan are still gathering in the mosque.
Go and learn the style of Bilal in singing the adhan.
Amma's favourite and Ammi's beloved.

As long as Allah keeps you in this world.
May He keep you in the Milky Way of happiness.
Whether He keeps you in Arabia or in Hindustan,
Sughra prays that He keeps you under His protection.
I am very sad that you are going away
Amma's favourite and Ammi's beloved.[20]

In addition to her love for her brother, Sughra's poem also makes clear that he was the favourite of the senior women in the household and that much was expected of him on his return. By the time Jamal Mian and Hasrat Mohani reached Damascus, war had broken out in Europe. Hasrat Mohani was determined to go to London to talk to the British government about Palestine and Indian freedom, even if he had to swim there! He eventually got there by boat and by train, but also by prison, because he did not have a visa. His *ghazal*s tell us that he was entranced by the jasmine-skinned beauties of Beirut, Cyprus, Greece, Rome, Paris, and London. Jamal

---

20. Jamal al-Din `Abd al-Wahhab ed., *Nawa-yi Agahi*, 34–5.

Mian returned quickly to India. Hasrat Mohani did not do so until the mid-1940s.[21]

Jamal Mian was present at the Lahore session of the Muslim League in March 1940 when the famous resolution was passed setting out the League's requirements for the Constitutional future of India. It was the resolution which the *Tribune* of Amritsar was to call the 'Pakistan Resolution' although it had not been given that name at Lahore. But Jamal Mian did not speak at the session; he was ill.[22] But soon afterwards, he was working with the Raja of Mahmudabad on a speaking tour to explain the Resolution to the people of Bihar.

In February 1941 a crisis blew up around the Raja of Mahmudabad. The Raja had become tired of the problems of his estate, which was the largest Muslim estate in the UP. He was also tired of the demands which, on account of the war, the government was making of the large landlords. Moreover, he was uneasy about the contributions his estate was making to the British war effort. 'Now how can I make speeches,' he wrote to Jamal Mian, 'when my estate has contributed money to the British to defend India? What right have I now got to advise the Muslims?'[23] He told the Governor, Sir Maurice Hallett, that he was going to abdicate from his estate. Hallett was worried about the impact of the Raja's decision on the war effort; he asked Khaliquzzaman to intervene and Khaliquzzaman asked Jamal Mian to take a letter to Jinnah, who had been the Raja's guardian and to whom he referred as 'uncle':

---

21. K. H. Qadiri, *Hasrat Mohani* (Delhi: Idarah-i Adabiyat-i Delli, 1985), 272–6.
22. Jamal Mian Tape 4-2, JMP.
23. Raja of Mahmudabad to Jamal Mian, undated, Mahmudabad correspondence, JMP.

So I took a letter from Khaliq Saheb and went to Bombay to
see Mr Jinnah. He used to live on Little Gibbs Road. When I
gave him the letter he was very moved and almost tearful. He
at once started looking at legal books to establish the legal
aspects of it all. Then Miss Jinnah came and started criticising
Raja Saheb's action and Mr Jinnah reprimanded her for this.
Then he asked me 'when are you going back'? I said I am
planning to take the next train back. He said his tailor was
coming to take some measurements and he would be dropped
back in his car and the same car would drop you to the station.
I said fine. He asked me to rest for a while and also asked me
to eat lunch with him. He had pomfret fish with parathas, and
we were joined by Miss Jinnah. After that I rested and the tailor
(RANKIN) came and I was dropped by car to the station. I
arrived in Lucknow and went to Raja Saheb's place by car. It
was 8th Muharram and no one was about, but I persisted and
met Raja Saheb and handed him Jinnah's letter.[24]

On 18 February, Jamal Mian was able to tell Jinnah that
his letter had had the desired effect. 'The Raja Saheb has seen
... HE today, and has told him that he had changed his mind.
Thereafter he met us and assured us that he would do nothing
in future which may give any cause for anxiety.'[25]

By 1941, although the histories of the All-India Muslim
League give him no official position, Jamal Mian was,
according to his diary, regularly attending meetings of the
League's Council and Working Committee. He was also a
member of the Council of the UP Muslim League. In all

---

24. Jamal Mian Tape 4-1, Ibid.
25. Maulana Jamal Mian to Jinnah, Lucknow, 18 February 1941. Shamsul
     Hasan Papers, United Provinces, Vol. 30, Sind Archives, Karachi.

probability, he spent the period from 25 February to 5 March taking the League case to the Muslims of the northern Bombay Presidency.[26] In April, he was attending the Madras session of the League. At this session, the Chairman of the Reception Committee, Abdul Hamid Khan, graciously referred to the way in which Jamal Mian's ancestor, Maulana Abdul Ali Bahr ul-Ulum, had come from Lucknow 'and was responsible for a great intellectual awakening in the South'.[27] After this, Jamal Mian and the Raja of Mahmudabad toured southern India to promote the League's case (Illustration 12). The rest of 1941 saw much Muslim League promotional activity but we have no specific mention of Jamal Mian until the League Conference which Khaliquzzaman held in Lucknow in November 1941.[28]

Around this time, the Ispahani business family temporarily moved from Calcutta to Lucknow to be in a safer place as the Japanese advance through SE Asia threatened eastern India. The Ispahanis were amongst the foremost Muslim businessmen in India. Their firm had been established in 1820 in Bombay. By the twentieth century, the firm had branches in, amongst other places, Rangoon, Madras, and Calcutta, where the head office was placed. Mirza Ahmed (1898–1986, Illustration 10) was the eldest of the three brothers who came to Lucknow. The others were M. A. H. (Hassan) Ispahani (1902–81), who had been educated at Cambridge and was a barrister, and the youngest, Mahmud, who had

---

26. The Raja of Mahmudabad had invited him to do this. Raja of Mahmudabad to Jamal Mian 8 February 1941, Mahmudabad correspondence, JMP.

27. Syed Sharifuddin Pirzada ed., *Foundations of Pakistan: All India Muslim League Documents: 1906–1947*, Vol. II (Karachi: National Publishing House, 1970), 351

28. Khaliquzzaman, *Pathway*, 260.

been educated at Aligarh. Mirza Ahmed had joined the family firm in 1921. By 1927, he had doubled the firm's business with the Middle East, Europe, and the Americas. By skilful dealing when Britain left the Gold Standard in 1931, he made his firm the top shipper of hessian. His firm was also the biggest shipper of gunny bags used for Cuban sugar.[29] By the time the Ispahanis came to Lucknow, Jamal Mian had already developed a business relationship with them, which we shall address in subsequent chapters. What was important about their establishment of a temporary base in Lucknow, where they stayed in the Raja of Mahmudabad's Butler Palace, was that it helped to foster a deep and lasting relationship between Jamal Mian, Mirza Ahmed, his younger brother, Hassan, and Mirza Ahmed's son, Mirza Mehdi known as Sadri (1923–2004). These relationships were to help to shape Jamal Mian's life. On the other hand, the Ispahanis, Mirza Ahmed in particular, were not slow, especially after independence, to make use of Jamal Mian's political access.

With this developing relationship the concerns, political and otherwise, of the Ispahanis came to be added to Jamal Mian's. Hassan was the most political of the three brothers. He was the leader of the Muslim League group in the Calcutta Corporation. In 1941, he had been made a member of the All-India Muslim League Working Committee, occupying the slot of Fazlul Huq, the Bengali politician whom Jinnah had expelled for ignoring League discipline. He was a frequent correspondent of Jinnah and a key figure in winning Bengal for the League.[30] On 22 January 1942, Hassan asked Jamal Mian

---

29. Nafiseh Ispahani, 'Edited Memoirs of Mirza Ahmad Ispahani: 5.8.1898—12.3.1986', 1–9, JMP.

30. See Z. H. Zaidi ed., *M.A. Jinnah—Ispahani Correspondence 1936–1948* (Karachi: Forward Publications Trust, 1976).

to attend the Bengal Provincial Muslim League conference on 14/15 February: 'Jinnah will be presiding and we need you to help in the political annihilation of Fazlul Huq.'[31] After touring in Meerut, Delhi, Allahabad, and Lucknow in the earlier part of the month, Jamal Mian spent four days at the conference in Sirajgunj.[32] In the following months, Jamal Mian continued his regular travelling on behalf of the League. The next major event was the meeting of the Working Committee of the All-India Muslim League at Bombay on 16 August to consider how to respond to the 'offer' of the Cripps Mission in the light of the Congress's response of mass civil disobedience to drive the British out of India. The Raja of Mahmudabad, Hassan, and Jamal Mian met Jinnah in his Mount Pleasant house two days before the meeting, putting the view that the League should align itself with the Congress. Jinnah took the view that it was not the time to take sides; the League had to be wary of handing power over to Hindu domination. 'The result of this discussion was similar to that of any other previous session,' Jamal Mian recalled, 'the majority of the Working Committee had to accept the weakness of their stand and bow to the will and logic of the Quaid-e-Azam'.[33] The outcome was not well-received in the Ispahani household. 'You are my Guru in this walk of life,' Sadri Ispahani wrote, 'Mr Jinnah should have joined hands with the Congress. All this "Hindu Raj Congress" and fighting on two fronts will not take one too far. I am ashamed of

---

31. M. A. H. Ispahani to Jamal Mian, 22 January 1942, Ispahani Correspondence, JMP.
32. Jamal Mian Diary, 4–16 February 1942, Ibid.
33. Jamal Mian 'Writings on Jinnah Saheb' JMP; All-India Muslim League Working Committee Meeting, Bombay, 16–20, 1942; Pirzada, *Foundations II*, 395–8.

myself for being a Leaguer.'[34] Mirza Ahmed sent three letters
of disapproval to Jamal Mian.[35]

There was one further development in 1942 which indicated
the authority which Jamal Mian had come to have amongst
the Ispahanis. On 22 September, Sadri told him that Mirza
Ahmed and Hassan had had a huge row over the proportions
of the Company, i.e. M. M. Ispahani, each owned. There was
a danger of the Company breaking up.[36] Mirza Ahmed was
travelling back from Bombay by train. Jamal Mian and Sadri
went to intercept him at Kharagpur. Jamal Mian succeeded
in resolving the quarrel. 'Return in triumph,' Jamal Mian
confided to his diary on 25 September. 'Sadri and I are in
the train, happy and relaxed.'[37]

In April 1943, Jamal Mian's rising status in the All-
India Muslim League was officially recognized when he
was appointed Honorary Joint Secretary.[38] On 31 August,
after an energetic political tour of the Punjab, he joined
the Ispahanis in Camac Street, Calcutta. He found the
family beleaguered by accusations in the Bengal Legislative
Assembly, and widespread in the press, that the firm of M.
M. Ispahani had been profiteering in rice. The background
to this situation was the famine that had developed in Bengal,
one of the most severe experienced in British India, in which
approximately three million people were to die. Calcutta was
full of men, women, and children, driven by hunger from
the villages to search for food. The state government did

---

34. Sadri Ispahani to Jamal Mian, no date but the context is clear, Ispahani
    Correspondence, JMP.
35. 22 August 1942, 28 August 1942, and 3 September 1942, Ibid.
36. Jamal Mian Diary, 22 September 1942, Ibid.
37. 25 September 1942, Ibid.
38. Resolution XIV, Delhi Session April 1942; Pirzada, *Foundations II*, 440.

not have the machinery to purchase rice in the surplus areas
of Bengal, Orissa, and Bihar. In these circumstances, the
Muslim League government had turned to M. M. Ispahani
Ltd., who for years had been Bengal's leading rice merchants,
to do the job for them. This created the opening for the
opposition in the Assembly, the Hindu Mahasabha, led by
Dr Shyamprasad Mukerjee, and the Forward Block, led by
Sarat Chandra Bose, to launch attack after attack, making
statements which were far from the truth. Amongst the
accusations was the statement that the greed of the Ispahanis
was actually causing the famine. The aim was, far from
establishing the truth, to bring down the Muslim League
government and, by damaging the Ispahanis, to weaken the
Muslim League in India in general.[39] Jamal Mian noted that
Mirza Ahmed was keen to continue rice trading while Hassan
was worried by newspaper criticism and wanted to abandon
it.[40] Jamal Mian told Hassan that to leave the rice trade now
would be an admission of guilt which would lead to victory
for their enemies. Hassan accepted this advice but it did
not prevent him from being made ill by the experience. A
month later, he noted that the Ispahanis were very upset that
Jinnah had not come to Calcutta to support them.[41] Jinnah
had, however, written to Hassan saying, in effect, that this
is politics and one had to put up with it.[42] Still, Jamal Mian
did what he could for his friends, publishing an article in
Asr-i Jadid, lauding the firm of M. M. Ispahani, its modern

39. Mirza Abol Hassan Ispahani, *Qaid-e-Azam Jinnah as I Knew Him*
    (Karachi: Forward Publication Trust, 1967), 91–6.
40. Jamal Mian Diary, 1 September 1943, JMP.
41. 1 October 1943, Ibid.
42. Jinnah to M. A. H. Ispahani, 10 September 1943, Zaidi ed., *Jinnah-
    Ispahani Correspondence*, 373–4.

methods, and the great services of the Ispahani family to the Muslim cause.[43]

On 7 September 1943, Jamal Mian received a great tribute which indicated the extent to which he had become established as a public figure. He was invited to lead the Eid prayers at the end of Ramadan on the Maidan in Calcutta.[44] We do not know for certain but it seems that the invitation came from Khwaja Nazimuddin, the Chief Minister of Bengal, who was much involved with the proceedings. Jamal Mian was replacing Abul Kalam Azad, who was in jail; Azad traditionally gave the sermon. Arriving in Calcutta a week before Eid, Jamal Mian tried out his *khutba* on Nazimuddin, who apparently liked it.[45] He went on to see the relief kitchens which were being run by the Muslim judges.[46] On 2 October, he recorded in his diary: 'Went to Maidan with Nazim Sahib. I had never before seen such a large crowd.'[47] 'In Calcutta in the morning,' *The Statesman* reported the following day, 'all roads led to the Maidan where thousands of Muslims, rich and poor, from different parts of the city assembled round the Ochterlony Monument and, led by Maulana Jamaluddin Mohomed Abdul Wahhab of Ferangi Mahal, Lucknow, offered congregational prayers.'[48] Jamal Mian's *khutba* fell into two parts. The first, after discussing the obligatory duties of Muslims, stressed the importance of unity for Muslims:

43. An undated draft of this article is in his diary for 1943, Jamal Mian Diary, JMP.
44. 17 September 1943, Ibid.
45. 25 September 1943, Ibid.
46. 30 September 1943, Ibid.
47. 2 October 1943, Ibid.
48. *The Statesman*, Calcutta, 3 October 1943.

Today's great and wonderful gathering is an awesome expression of the unity and brotherhood of Muslims. In this vast Maidan we, the rich and the poor, the great and the small, are calling God with one heart and one voice. All our worldly differences and our ranks are hidden away. This lesson of unity and organization is not just for Eid grounds and mosques, but is a lesson for homes, bazaars and societies.

The Quran states unambiguously that all Muslims are brothers and should make peace and unity amongst them. And the Prophet has said that creating friendship and peace amongst Muslims is a greater form of worship than *namaz*, *roza* or giving alms. The truth is that all the ills and decline of our Ummah are because we have forgotten this lesson. Muslims progressed and prospered while they remained united. But once they divided into sects, classes and occupations, they were dishonoured, dispersed, and they declined.[49]

Jamal Mian went on to talk of how wrong it was for Muslims to see themselves as separate nationalities and follow the example of the Western countries. He talks of the welcome signs of the growing desire for unity in the Muslim world, for instance, the current campaign for an Arab Federation. He then moved on to make precise points about the Muslim politics of Bengal and of India:

Most encouraging is the truth that today Indian Muslims have made great gains in political unity and organization. They have a strong party and a separate identity. And,

---

49. *Khutba 1*, reproduced in Jamal Mian Diary 1943, JMP, for *Khutba*s 1 and 2, that is the full sermon, see Appendix 2.

thank God that the Muslims have freed themselves from
the greatest political folly of power-sharing .... Now they
are neither interested in forming a partnership government
with non-Muslims nor are they willing or desirous to accept
the guarantees of foreign powers protecting their rights and
interests. Their hearts are alive with the desire to be vice
regents of God on earth and a free independent Muslim
nation has become their central objective.[50]

After this comment on the contemporary scene, Jamal Mian
launched into the second part of the *khutba* designed to use the
occasion for social and humanitarian purposes. He reminded
his audience of the temporary nature of the things of this
world. He said how ironic it was that we do not heed this and
proceeded to use the image of the contemporary blackout in
Calcutta, enforced against the bombing raids of the Japanese.
'We hide our light from these enemies in the skies but we
are not willing to extinguish the raging fire of our sins.'[51] He
warned the audience that the evidence of God's wrath existed
in the bombs that fell from the skies and the current problems
of the city on the ground. In these circumstances, the best way
to please God 'is to make honest repentance for your sins and
to give alms.'[52] He drew their attention to an Eid in the time
of the Prophet when the women of Medina handed over their
jewelry to Bilal for the purposes of charity:

From this incident we conclude that today the most cherished
act is the act of charity and the greatest Sunnah is to alleviate

50. Ibid.
51. *Khutba 2,* Ibid.
52. Ibid.

the needs of humanity. Come Fellow Muslims. Let us celebrate as that Eid was celebrated in Medina and, despite our straitened circumstances, give a part of our wealth to our poorer brothers so that we can be called true slaves and servants of the Prophet. The Prophet has said that they are incomplete in their religion who have filled their stomachs and spent their lives in comfort while their brothers lie starving.[53]

Jamal Mian then goes straight to the point:

Is there anyone in this city who can donate to the poor and afflicted here and by doing so earn the *ziarat* of the Prophet's shining face in the hereafter?...Today in your city and province how many are there that are homeless and destitute? How many young are exhausted with starvation. How many mothers and widows are driven by hunger? How many innocent infants are an unbearable weight of suffering and pain for parents to bear? On the streets and alleys of Calcutta, in Bengal and other cities and villages, the calamity-stricken family of God lies helpless. Is there anyone amongst you who will go forward and look after them?[54]

Jamal Mian's sermon seems to have been well-received. 'They said,' he noted in his diary, 'they had never before heard a *khutba* like that,'[55] which was probably a reference to its style and eloquence. Two days later, *The Statesman*'s leading article declared: 'We do not exaggerate when we say never was more readiness shown [than] after these prayers to help

53. Ibid.
54. Ibid.
55. 2 October 1943, Ibid.

those in need.'[56] One response seems to have been particularly special to Jamal Mian because he kept the letter, with those he treasured most, for the rest of his life. It was from an inmate of Alipur Jail close to the Maidan. He had been able to hear the sermon as it was transmitted by loudspeaker and wrote: 'I hope you get the same respect as Maulana Abdul Bari got and continue his tradition.'[57]

The year 1943 saw the emergence of Jamal Mian at the forefront of Muslim politics. There is a pleasing circularity in the way in which the adolescent, who had enjoyed ice cream at Magnolia Ice Cream and made his first speech at the Calcutta Palestine Conference in 1936, should have set the seal on his rise with his Eid sermon on the Maidan in 1943. In his diary, Jamal Mian summed this year with endearing honesty:

- As is my habit I travelled a lot and every journey was a [business] failure. From a commercial point of view it was incredibly disappointing. Every day income fell and expenditure grew. But the most important thing is that I am paying less attention to this. Although I did not suffer a financial worry, things are looking precarious.
- Health OK.
- I increased my friendships.
- In total terms this year has been a good one. There were several important events: my marriage 11 Oct. in Rudauli with the youngest daughter of Shah Hayat Ahmad; ... in the month of April I was appointed Jt. Asst. Sec. of the all-India Muslim League—I went on several delegations and presided

---

56. *The Statesman*, Calcutta, 4 October 1943.
57. Ansar Hai to Jamal Mian, Alipur Jail, censored letter, 4 October 1943, 'Personal File', JMP.

over some; I led Eid prayers on the Calcutta Maidan; my
Urdu *khutba* was considered a great success by everyone.[58]

Jamal Mian took action on the basis of this financial
analysis. On 31 December, he wrote to Jinnah saying that he
was thinking of asking to be relieved of the Joint Secretaryship,
not because of any dissatisfaction but because of his financial
condition. His business was suffering because of many long
journeys and absences from Lucknow; he was finding it
difficult to meet the travel expenses from his own pocket. 'I
wanted to explain my difficulties to you personally but my
courage failed. Now I have decided to perform my duties till
the next election.'[59] Jinnah replied saying that he understood
the situation well and would consider it carefully at the next
Council meeting.[60]

58. Summary of 1943, Jamal Mian Diary 1943, Ibid.
59. Jamal Mian to Jinnah, 31 December 1943, Shamsul Hasan Papers,
    United Provinces, Vol. 30, Sind Archives, Karachi.
60. Jinnah to Jamal Mian, 14 January 1944, Ibid

7

Business, marriage, and friendships

DURING THE YEARS DOWN TO INDEPENDENCE IN 1947, alongside his political activities, there were other significant developments in Jamal Mian's life: he became a businessman; he got married; and he developed important friendships.

Business

Jamal Mian did not become a businessman because it was a calling; indeed, Mirza Ahmed Ispahani said he was most unsuited to it—he did not love money enough. He did so because he needed to support himself, his family, and the family madrasah. He recalled how it happened. Probably in 1941, he had been asked by the Raja of Mahmudabad to go to Calcutta for some meetings. There he stayed with the son-in-law of Mumtaz Mian, the *sajjadanashin* of Bansa. The Raja stayed with the Ispahanis at Camac Street. The two would meet at the Ispahani office in Ezra Street and spend time together. While he was there, Maulana Ruhullah asked him to approach some people who had promised to donate funds to the madrasah. The first name on the list was Adamjee Haji Dawood. Hassan Ispahani said his office was nearby:

So I arrived at Sir Adamjee's office in the early evening. Most

125

of the workers had left and I saw him sitting behind a glass partition. I sent my card in and he invited me to his desk. He asked the purpose of my visit. So I said there is a madrasah in Lucknow for which you promised a donation for the construction of a hostel ... He said: 'I am not an architect nor a construction man, so I cannot help you.' Then he added; 'We are traders; our time is very precious.' I was very annoyed and left his office ... I thought to myself that these people think their commercial activity is more important than what we were trying to do, that is scholarship and promoting religion. How dare they![1]

This rejection spurred Jamal Mian into thinking what he could do about it. The next day he went to the Ispahani office and told Hassan that he wanted to get into the tea business. What Jamal Mian did not know was that there were at least two reasons why Hassan and his brother were pleased to hear this. The first reason he only discovered much later, in London in the 1970s. Jinnah had asked Mirza Ahmed to help Jamal Mian. He said, according to Mirza Ahmed: 'the maulvis and ulama of the Jamiatul Ulama are causing me a lot of problems ... but I have met one young MAULVI who is equal to all of them and he is a great orator. I want him to stand on his feet so he does not have any financial problems.'[2] The second reason was that the Ispahanis were at a stage when they wanted to expand their tea business into the rest of India. Hassan sent

1. Jamal Mian, Tape 3-2, JMP. Sir Adamjee Haji Dawood (1880–1948) was a major businessman and philanthropist in British India. Both a rival and a collaborator of the Ispahanis, he established the third jute mill to be established by an Indian and the first Muslim public company. For his services to his countrymen he was knighted in 1938.

2. Jamal Mian, Tape 4-1, JMP.

Jamal Mian upstairs to meet his manager, Arakie. He bought some tea and samples for Rs 65 and all fitted into one suitcase. He then saw the Raja and surprised him with the news that he was going to sell tea. He went back to Lucknow the next day.[3]

On reaching Lucknow, Jamal Mian immediately set out to sell tea, going from shop to shop in his Baby Austin. Not all were pleased with his new activity. Hakim Abdul Haseeb, for instance, said: 'Look Mian, this does not suit you. Your ancestors never indulged in such things.' Others were more helpful, suggesting that he focus on the cantonment where there were many Britons and a big demand for tea. When he got there and went to the canteen, the first person he met was a disciple of Pir Mehr Ali Shah of Golra. He asked: 'What on earth are you doing here? Is everything alright?' Jamal Mian told him that he had just taken up a tea agency. 'Tea', he said, 'we will buy any amount of that.' Jamal Mian gave him all the tea he had and was told 'we will buy whatever you can get hold of.' 'I returned', Jamal Mian recalled, 'and wired Ispahanis to send me chests by parcel mail. Ten to twelve were sent, and then more arrived. The tea business took off.'[4] Jamal Mian established his Ispahani Tea Agency in Hazratganj, modern Lucknow's main shopping street, as opposed to the Chauk. He appointed Ali Husain Mohani, his friend at the madrasah and at Lucknow University, his accountant. A key piece of office furniture was Jamal Mian's hookah. When the Ispahanis made their wartime evacuation from Calcutta to Lucknow, the office became a place of resort for the young. The Baby Austin parked outside was the sign he was in residence.

Jamal Mian's tea business did not continue with quite the

---

3. Ibid.
4. Jamal Mian Tape 3-2, JMP.

zest with which it began. In February 1942, he noted that he had had an order from Liaquat Ali Khan, the secretary of the All-India Muslim League, and from the Nawab of Rampur for 'Special Brand Orange Pekoe'.[5] During this year, he seems to have tried to combine his presence in Bombay on League business with tea sales, but with no success. One idea seems to have been tea export but by March 1942, he was being asked to return his export licence for 343 chests of tea to the Ispahanis as he had decided to sell the tea locally.[6] However, by 17 July he noted in his diary: 'have spent much time in Bombay. And since the first day have not sold a single pack of tea. I am trying, but not succeeding. God help me!'[7] The following day he wrote to Mirza Ahmed explaining the situation and saying that he was returning to Lucknow. He was instructed to hand over his Bombay stock to a Mr Mahmood for sale.[8] We should note that, despite this business reversal, Jamal Mian's reputation with the Ispahanis remained equal to resolving the dangerous quarrel between Mirza Ahmed and Hassan in September of this year. Nevertheless, financial facts were facts. Jamal Mian's end-of-year visit to the Ispahani office in Calcutta left him depressed. 'I really wish you had stayed another few days', Sadri wrote, 'but I could see that the sale of tea and that accursed hour in the Tea Dept. discussing about accounts were playing on your mind and you were fed up.'[9]

5. Jamal Mian Diary, 16, 22 February 1942, JMP.
6. Sadri Ispahani to Jamal Mian, 28 March 1942, Ispahani Correspondence, Ibid.
7. Jamal Mian Diary, 17 July 1942, Ibid.
8. Mirza Ahmed Ispahani to Jamal Mian, 21 July 1942, Ispahani Correspondence, Ibid.
9. Sadri Ispahani to Jamal Mian, 11 December 1942, Ispahani Correspondence, Ibid.

Business in 1943 was not much better. In January, Jamal Mian was expanding the Ispahani agency network into the great industrial city of Cawnpore.[10] A little later he would appear to have been trying to do the same in the Punjab, but with no success. This led to an interesting reflection on the part of Mirza Ahmed on the obstacles to Muslims expanding their trade:

[In the Punjab] Hindus monopolise trade. This is entirely communal. They have no objection to agencies for Lipton or Brooke Bond. Muslims will have to organize economically and fight tooth and nail to get into the trade. [Turning to Bengal and the Japanese bombing of Calcutta he declared:] Most of the Bengalis are serving in the Government offices and as clerks in the mercantile firms where the Banias from all over India are fleeing together with the Scotchmen. India's population is being strangled[,] one side of the rope being held by the British and the other by the Banias.[11]

The Ispahanis followed their own advice. They launched a drive to establish Muslim Chambers of Commerce. In April 1943, Hassan sent the Report of the Committee of Muslim Chambers of Commerce, with details of how to form one, to Jamal Mian. 'Please get on with the job without delay,' he wrote, 'and get as many Muslim merchants and industrialists [as possible] to join the Chamber. I know you can do it.'[12]

10. Mirza Ahmed Ispahani to Jamal Mian, 8 March 1943, Ispahani Correspondence, Ibid.
11. Mirza Ahmed Ispahani to Jamal Mian, 12 March 1943, Ispahani Correspondence, Ibid.
12. Hassan Ispahani to Jamal Mian, 24 April 1943. Ispahani Correspondence, Ibid.

Another response to competition in the tea market was to trade in another commodity. From 1943, the Ispahanis were encouraging Jamal Mian to trade in gunny bags, as well as tea, and telling him how to do it. 'There is no difficulty in selling gunnies,' Mirza Ahmed assured him.[13] Moreover, the best plan was to get a government contract, which Jamal Mian did. 'This should not end your career in the Gunny business,' Mirza Ahmed told Jamal Mian, 'but it should be a prelude to establishing a regular business in Gunnies in the whole of UP.'[14] But, Mirza Ahmed knew that Jamal Mian did not think like a businessman and easily took fright at changes in price and the market:

> I again repeat to you my advice that you should be patient and everything will turn out all right in the long run. Even when you held tea last year you were very agitated but there was a time when you had no tea for sale. Large stocks at the moment should not worry [sic]. A time may come when you will be sorry for not having more in stock. By this I do not mean that you should not use every endeavour in the furtherance of your sales but just to have confidence in the move we are making from this end for the sale of commodities in the UP.[15]

The following month, the value of Jamal Mian's tea stock fell by half.[16] Understandably, he became cast down by his

13. Mirza Ahmed Ispahani to Jamal Mian, 5 May 1943, Ispahani Correspondence, Ibid.
14. Mirza Ahmed Ispahani to Jamal Mian 8 May 1943, Ispahani Correspondence, Ibid.
15. Ibid.
16. Sadri Ispahani to Jamal Mian, 3 June 1943, Ispahani Correspondence, Ibid.

business performance just when everything else was going so well. But, he was learning to cope as his diary summary for 1943 quoted at the end of Chapter Six suggests. The key passage was: 'From a commercial point of view it [the year] was incredibly disappointing. Every day income fell and expenditure grew. But the most important thing is that I am paying less attention to this.'[17]

Jamal Mian's diary for 1944 does not exist so we do not have his observations on the progress of his business. Nevertheless, it is clear from his correspondence with the Ispahanis that early in the year the tea market was still weak.[18] But towards the end of the year, things were looking better. In November, he was able to receive eighty or so chests of tea and have wagon space reserved on the railway for 400 more.[19] Moreover, the Cawnpore agency was firmly established and there was talk of opening further agencies in Rampur, Gorakhpur, and Aligarh.[20] Jamal Mian had also been talking to the Ispahanis about teaching commerce to young Muslims. 'What happened to your mercantile training class?' Mirza Ahmed asked in February 1944, 'You should not give up; I am willing to pay all the expenses in this direction because Muslim youths must be trained to eke out an existence as traders which is the lifeblood of our economy. Kindly let me know what the cost is so that I may contribute the amount.'[21] By the autumn, he was able

17. Summary of 1943, Jamal Mian diary, 1943, Ibid.
18. Sadri Ispahani to Jamal Mian, 7 February 1944, Ispahani Correspondence, Ibid.
19. Hassan Ispahani to Jamal Mian, 9 November 1944, Ispahani Correspondence, Ibid.
20. Sadri Ispahani to Jamal Mian, 3 November 1944, Ispahani Correspondence, Ibid.
21. Mirza Ahmed Ispahani to Jamal Mian, 24 February 1944, Ispahani Correspondence, Ibid.

to report that he had begun night classes in commerce at the Farangi Mahall madrasah.[22] By this time Jamal Mian had also begun to recommend family members for jobs in the Ispahani organization, a process which had mixed success. Youths from Lucknow seemed to treat a job with the Ispahanis in a cavalier way. 'Abdul Hai is the rarest chap I have ever seen,' Sadri told Jamal Mian, 'He is not to be found. I have reports that he does not attend regularly and spins "yarns", and what is more has applied to the Air Force. Will be speaking to him seriously.'[23] A little later, Mirza Ahmed told Jamal Mian he had had to get rid of two of his recommendations who had 'bluffed and cheated' him.[24]

In 1945, Jamal Mian's time was, once again, increasingly taken up by politics. Nevertheless, he still kept a sharp eye on his tea business. This meant that he bridled somewhat when Mirza Ahmed suggested sending one of his men from Calcutta to improve the performance of his UP agencies. He told Mirza Ahmed that, if his end of the operation was to work well, then the men at the top must be able to run:

the whole organization on systematic lines as Brooke Bonds and Liptons do, so it is necessary to strengthen staff at head office. As long as it is not possible new salesmen at the agency cannot serve any useful purpose. If you could spare some time to review the files, you could find that I have constantly been stressing the need of reorganization of tea department for

22. Sadri Ispahani to Jamal Mian, 3 November 1944, Ispahani Correspondence, Ibid.
23. Sadri Ispahani to Jamal Mian, 18 December 1944, Ispahani Correspondence, Ibid.
24. Mirza Ahmed Ispahani to Jamal Mian, 18 June 1945, Ispahani Correspondence, Ibid.

better quality, better packing and regular supply, competitive price and advertisement. After settings things right at the centre, the next step should be to overhaul agencies and meet their needs. Our present workers are disappointed with the low salaries and deficient staff. [For instance, two men in Moradabad have been doing their best] but find it to be impossible to pull along with [their] present salary of 50?- per month. ... Qamar Raza's arrival on a higher salary [would upset their morale].[25]

This letter, which is the only letter we have from Jamal Mian to Mirza Ahmed, was typed in English, indicating its importance from Jamal Mian's point of view. It was a courageous, even a headstrong, thing for Jamal Mian to do to criticize the running of the Ispahani business when Mirza Ahmed knew that he did not give himself heart and soul to selling tea. Mirza Ahmed's response came in June 1946. It was, in effect, an Ispahani takeover of Jamal Mian's UP agency organization. He was sent a scheme of reorganization, which incorporated all the suggestions Jamal Mian had made from time to time as well as some ideas of their own. M. M. Ispahani was going to send him a trained officer to help in the reorganization. Jamal Mian was asked to retain his tea depots throughout the province but in future they would be manned by Ispahani staff. Jamal Mian's commission was to be reduced because he would no longer have to pay commission to sub-agents. 'We will be sending you 5 chests of each of our brands by passenger train on 5th instant,' Mirza Ahmed wrote in finishing his letter, 'and on receipt of same you are

25. Jamal Mian to Mirza Ahmed Ispahani, 23 December 1945, Ispahani Correspondence, Ibid.

requested to place your monthly order for the agency.'[26] This
letter was typical of Mirza Ahmed's dispassionate and ruthless
efficiency. Brutal though it was, Mirza Ahmed's reorganization
certainly resulted in Jamal Mian's best sales year. In 1947 he
sold 1,11,000 pounds of tea for Rs 2,18,902.[27]

As Independence neared, both the Ispahanis and Jamal
Mian were expanding their business interests. On 23 October
1946, the Ispahanis along with Sir Adamjee and the Arag
Group founded Orient Airways. Mirza Ahmed was the first
Chairman, and tried to get Jamal Mian to invest.[28] On 4 June
1947 the airline began operations and on 11 March 1955,
with several other airlines, was merged to form Pakistan
International Airlines. In July 1947, Hassan told Jamal
Mian that the Ispahani head office had been transferred
provisionally to Chittagong.[29] At the same time as Mirza
Ahmed was getting Orient Airways off the ground, Jamal
Mian took over the management of the old Urdu newspaper,
The Daily Hamdam. It had been very popular in the past, he
told Jinnah, and he was trying to give it new life to serve
the League.[30] Jinnah was very appreciative of Jamal Mian's
initiative.[31] His friends were more wary. 'You want to take out

---

26. Mirza Ahmed Ispahani to Jamal Mian, 3 June 1946, Ispahani Corre-
    spondence, Ibid.
27. Mirza Ahmed Ispahani to Jamal Mian, 9 January 1949, Ispahani
    Correspondence, Ibid.
28. Mirza Ahmed Ispahani to Jamal Mian, 30 November 1946, Ispahani
    Correspondence, Ibid.
29. Hassan Ispahani to Jamal Mian, 16 July 1947, Ispahani Correspondence,
    Ibid.
30. Jamal Mian to Jinnah, 6 October 1946, Shamsul Hasan Papers, United
    Provinces, Vol. 30, Sind Archives, Karachi.
31. Jinnah to Jamal Mian, 16 October 1946, Shamul Hasan Papers, United
    Provinces, Vol. 30, Ibid.

a daily newspaper,' the Raja of Mahmudabad wrote, 'This is important for leaders. May it succeed. But tell us who is going to take control of the editing of this newspaper; it is a very difficult job. The person must be someone of similar views. Also we don't need to publish many lies. ... Do you want to drive me mad? Please give me a clear answer.'[32] Mirza Ahmed, on being told of Jamal Mian's plans, was supportive but did not think there was money to be made in newspapers, which of course was not Jamal Mian's purpose.[33]

Marriage

Through much of their recorded history, Farangi Mahallis practised cousin marriage. Those who married an outsider, *ajnabiyya* was the term used by Inayatullah in the family *Tadhkirah*, found that their children were not recorded in the family history. By the twentieth century, marriage practices began to change. Jamal Mian's father was amongst the first to marry outside the family with no apparent disadvantage in the family record. By the middle of the century, the granddaughter of Maulana Salamatullah had married a Hindu.[34] Jamal Mian was to follow in his father's footsteps.

The process happened at breakneck pace. It would

---

32. Raja of Mahmudabad to Jamal Mian, n.d. but probably 1946. Mahmudabad Correspondence, JMP.

33. Mirza Ahmed Ispahani to Jamal Mian, 22 November 1946, 9 January 1949, Ispahani Correspondence, Ibid.

34. Francis Robinson, 'Living Together Separately: The Ulama of Farangi Mahall c. 1700–1950' in Mushirul Hasan and Asim Roy eds., *Living Together Separately: Cultural India in History and Politics* (New Delhi: Oxford University Press, 2005), especially 164.

appear that in October 1943, Jamal Mian's family decided
that he should marry the youngest daughter of Shah Hayat
Ahmad, a former pupil of his father and the *sajjadanashin*
at the Dargah of Ahmad Abdul Haq at Rudauli. In terms of
religious leadership in Awadh, it was the unification of two
great lines. When on 8 October 1943 Jamal Mian got back
to Lucknow after the triumph of his Eid sermon in Calcutta,
Qutb Mian came to see him in Mall Avenue where he was
with the Ispahanis. Qutb Mian put the idea to him, saying
that the marriage had to take place before his nephew, Nur
Mian, left for a job. Jamal Mian discussed the idea with Mirza
Ahmed, but probably also with the Baragaon Qidwais, Saidur
Rahman, Altafur Rahman, and Ehsanur Rahman, whom he
saw that afternoon. 'My idea,' he told his diary, 'is to get it
all over in 2–4 days.'[35] On 9 October, Qutb Mian went off to
make the proposal to Shah Hayat Ahmad, who agreed saying
that the *nikah* should take place in two days; the arrangements
were finalized over the telephone.[36] On 10 October Jamal
Man told his friends, Choudhry Khaliquzzaman and
Chaudhuri Azimuddin Ashraf of Paisar. He also saw the Raja
of Jahangirabad (Illustration 16) to ask for the use of his car:
Jamal Mian's Baby Austin, romantic though it might have
been, was not going to be large enough to accommodate the
numbers travelling to and from Rudauli. The Raja agreed
and 'was ready to do much more but I did not want any more
favours in this matter.'[37] So Jamal Mian went to Rudauli in
the Raja's car, driven by Irtiza Husain and accompanied by
Qutb Mian and Altafur Rahman Qidwai. Then it appeared

---

35. Jamal Mian Diary, 8 October 1943, JMP.
36. 9, 10 October 1943, Ibid.
37. 10 October 1943, Ibid.

that Jamal Mian had a moment of doubt, which was not unreasonable given the speed of events; 'I wasn't sure of this marriage as it was not according to my wishes. But I decided to accept it as one accepts a lot of things for family and relatives.'[38]

The *nikah* took place on the 11th. The Rajas of Pirpur and Jahangirabad came to give congratulations. 'Pirpur wanted to have a big party but I avoided it. Raja Jahangirabad gave a necklace and other jewelry. He was very hurt he could not do more.'[39] After meeting his bride, Asar, Jamal Mian confided to his diary: 'I liked her. She is innocent and intelligent.'[40] After meeting her again, later in the day, he wrote: 'This time I liked her even more.'[41] Five days later he wrote: 'Had a long chat with her. And with other ladies in the house [in Rudauli]. Had a less than formal meeting with her—getting on very well.'[42]

For the next few days, Jamal Mian spent his time between Lucknow and Rudauli, but with a real desire to be in Rudauli, as his diary indicates.[43] In Lucknow there were the respects he needed to pay to his ancestors in the Bagh. There was a Sunni Waqf Board meeting to attend. There were alterations to oversee in Farangi Mahall in the light of his wife's forthcoming arrival. There were friends and acquaintances to see: Mirza Askari, Hakim Shamsuddin, the Raja of Mahmudabad (often), Mirza Ahmed and Sadri Ispahani, the Raja of Jahangirabad, and Altafur Rahman. In Rudauli there was the company of his wife and new duties to perform such as the *nikah* for his

---

38. Ibid.
39. 11 October 1943, Ibid.
40. Ibid.
41. Ibid.
42. 16 October 1943, Ibid.
43. 18 October 1943, Ibid.

wife's sister.[44] On 25 October, with his bride, Jamal Mian left
Rudauli for Lucknow, accompanied by her nephews, Akhlaq
Mian and Iqbal Mian, and a female attendant.[45] In family oral
tradition, Khaliquzzaman used to say to Jamal Mian: 'You just
went to Rudauli and kidnapped her.'[46]

Friendships

When Jamal Mian noted in his end-of-year summary diary
entry in 1943 that 'I increased my friendships', among
those he had in mind were those with Dr Faridi, the Raja of
Mahmudabad, Mirza Ahmed, Hassan, and Sadri Ispahani.
Their relationships probably deepened when the Ispahanis
evacuated from Calcutta to Lucknow in 1942 and 1943
and they began to see each other as a group. It is to these
friendships that we now turn.

Dr Muhammad Abdul Jalil was descended from Baba
Fariduddin Ganj Shakar, and hence came to be known as
Dr Faridi. His father had been a judge in Jaipur and his
mother came from the Qidwais of Baragaon. On retirement
his father had built an imposing house in the Machli Mahal
area of Lucknow; the family also owned an office building of
several storeys in Hazratganj. Dr Faridi had been educated at
the Medical College in Lucknow and then did further studies
in England before returning to practise in Lucknow.

Jamal Mian first met Dr Faridi before the outbreak of World
War Two, when he was travelling widely for the All-India

---

44. 17, 18, 19, 20, 21, 22, 23, 24 October 1943, Ibid.
45. 25 October 1943, Ibid.
46. This is in part a reference to the fact that no great celebrations
    accompanied the marriage. Recollection of Mahmood Jamal.

Muslim League and suffering from stomach ailments. Ehsanur Rahman Qidwai, who was Secretary to the UP Muslim League, told him that he had a young relative, a doctor, who had just returned from London. He should consult him. Jamal Mian did and was given medicine which worked. Dr Faridi's fame spread beyond Lucknow; his practice grew rapidly and soon there were long queues for his clinic in Faridi Buildings.[47]

Jamal Mian's Ispahani Tea Agency in Hazratganj was close to Dr Faridi's clinic. The two used to have lunch together almost every day. One afternoon, he recalled, Dr Faridi came to my office looking very worried. His first marriage had been to a relative who was a very good lady but Dr Faridi was unhappy in the marriage. He said that there was a Christian lady, whom he had known since his student days, who was willing to become a Muslim and marry him. What should he do? Jamal Mian advised him not to go ahead as he would cause great pain to his father and his wife. But Faridi's mind was made up. The marriage took place in Faridi Buildings and Jamal Mian performed the *nikah*.[48]

'In this period', Jamal Mian wrote, 'my friendship with Dr Faridi became very close.' He was not directly involved in politics but his sympathies were with the Muslim League. From time to time he took action. On one occasion, just before the Simla Conference, he tipped off Jamal Mian that the deputy leader of the Congress, Abdul Qayyum Khan, who was in Lucknow for a health consultation with him, was unhappy with the Hindu orientation of the Congress. Dr Faridi suggested that we should try to persuade him to leave the Congress. Jamal Mian met Qayyum Khan in Dr Faridi's

47. Jamal Mian 'Note on Dr Faridi at his passing away, 20 May 1974', JMP.
48. Ibid.

office. A few days later he resigned from the Congress and joined the League. Jamal Mian made no claim that his intervention made a difference. The second occasion was the inauguration of Pakistan on 14 August 1947 when Jamal Mian travelled to Karachi with Dr Faridi for the occasion.[49] When in April 1949 Jamal Mian became very ill:

> Dr Faridi was distraught. He was with me 24 hours a day, watched me deteriorate, but was helpless to do anything about it. This was a time when I got proof of his true devotion and love for me. He would tolerate my reasonable and unreasonable demands and tried in every way to help me to recover.[50]

After this Jamal Mian lived in Dacca more and more, but he still saw Dr Faridi at least once a year. Dr Faridi and many members of his family were especially devoted to Nawab Khadim Hussain of Ajmer. He always attended the `Urs at Ajmer and the two men tried to coordinate their travel plans every year. In later years Dr Faridi became a member of the Upper House in the UP, a great campaigner for Muslim interests and the driving force behind the All-India Muslim Majlis. 'Truthfulness, forbearance, diligence, courage, resilience were hallmarks of his character', Jamal Mian declared in his note on Dr Faridi's death, 'in personal terms, an irreplaceable friend has parted from me.'[51]

The Raja Muhammad Amir Ahmad Khan of Mahmudabad (Illustration 9) was arguably an even closer friend of Jamal Mian than Dr Faridi. The two were distantly related. But

---

49. Ibid.
50. Ibid.
51. Ibid.

the Raja, as the largest Muslim landholder in the UP, lived a different life with different responsibilities. Nevertheless, they shared a love of Urdu and Persian poetry (the Raja's *takhullus* was 'Mahboob' or 'Beloved'). They were both particularly devout. This said, that the Raja was a Shia, indeed a prominent supporter of a Shia missionary College, the Madrasat ul-Waizeen[52] and Jamal Mian was a devout Sunni seemed to make no difference to their personal closeness.

The Raja was born in 1914 and was, therefore, five years older than Jamal Mian. Although the two young men must have known each other before 1937, the first intimation we have of their alliance is their joint work for the 1937 Muslim League conference in Lucknow which we observed in Chapter One. This was followed by ten years of political work for the League, at times very intense, in which they often toured India together. When they were apart they wrote to each other. Nearly two hundred letters exist, all from the Raja to Jamal Mian; it has not been possible to locate any of Jamal Mian's to the Raja. The letters divide into two groups. Those mainly in English which deal with Muslim League business and those in Urdu of a more personal nature, revealing their close friendship.

Several letters of the 1940s were notably playful. On 27 August 1940, the Raja wrote:

Maulvi Hazrat Hujjatul Islam, Faqih ul Mominin, Moin ul-Millet, Qari o Hafiz ul-Quran, Maulvi, Allama Jamaluddin Abdul Wahab Saheb, Sullamahu. I give my respects to your

52. See, Amir Ahmad Khan 'Local Nodes of a Transnational Network: a case study of a Shi'i family in Awadh 1900–1950' in Justin Jones and Ali Usman Qasmi eds., *The Shi'a in Modern South Asia: Religious History and Politics* (Delhi: Cambridge University Press, 2015) 57–79.

letter, affection, truthfulness and wisdom—the eye of affection which you have bestowed on this poor, wretch faqir, Amir.

The Raja then goes on to say that we got the lawyer, sought an omen (*istikhara*), and turned this lawyer into Quaid-i-Azam. He ends mysteriously, saying that the beguiling beauty you mentioned in your letter is now seven seas away.[53] On 7 December 1940 the Raja wrote: "Sarkar Maulana I wish you Salaams. The Mulla runs to the Masjid and I run to you." He then asked Jamal Mian for his commentry on a surah of the Quran.[54]

On 30 May 1943 the Raja wrote indicating how he had looked for signs of Jamal Mian's presence in Lucknow:

> Rev. Maulana and My Dearest Brother, Salaam and Dua. I am very sad that I could not meet you in Lucknow. I was passing through Hazratganj in the intensity of the afternoon heat when I noticed that there was a lock on the door of the shop [ie the Ispahani Tea Agency], which stood like a silent guard. And the Baby Austin was nowhere to be seen, and there was no signboard to be seen. Surprised and saddened I decided to go on to Mahmudabad and spend the summer.[55]

A few days later the Raja wrote a letter which suggested that he might have been aware of the discussions about

---

53. Raja of Mahmudabad to Jamal Mian, 27 August 1940, Mahmudabad Correspondence, JMP.
54. Raja of Mahmudabad to Jamal Mian 7 December 1940, Mahmudabad Correspondence, Ibid.
55. Raja of Mahmudabad to Jamal Mian, 30 May 1943, Mahmudabad Correspondence, Ibid.

Jamal Mian's marriage which were taking place amongst the Farangi Mahallis:

> We have by unanimous decision decided that the best way to 'imprison' you would be immediately to have you married, and I have heard that there is a respectable lady of the Punjab, who having returned from a trip to Europe is looking for a husband.[56]

We do not know who the 'respectable lady of the Punjab' was, if she existed at all. The importance of these letters is that they reveal the humour and closeness of the relationship.

In other letters the Raja shares his personal problems with Jamal Mian. In 1943 he seems to have gone through an intense religious phase, which may have meant that he did not have as much time to offer the Muslim League as before. 'I want you to relax', he told Jamal Mian in February 1943, 'and not worry that I am reading the Quran all the time. I do other things. You are criticising me because you have always been suspicious of this part of me.'[57] In September 1943, he wrote explaining why he could not go on a Muslim League visit to Aligarh. He was ill after being stung by bees and the annual management budget of the estate still had to be finished. Not going to Aligarh had nothing to do with his religious concerns. 'I can assure you that the suspicion which you and other gentlemen have about me [is wrong]—My fasting is not really fasting nor my prayers, prayers.' He ends

---

56. Raja of Mahmudabad to Jamal Mian, 11 June 1943, Mahmudabad Correspondence, Ibid.
57. Raja of Mahmudabad to Jamal Mian, 27 February 1943, Mahmudabad Correspondence, Ibid.

rather charmingly: 'I wish to spend many Eids in the company
of you and my mother.'[58]

In other letters, the Raja shared his concerns over Shia-
Sunni tension on his estate which required his presence as a
mediator, and also his concerns about Shia-Sunni tension in
Lucknow.[59] Even this problem could be the subject of humour.
'I give my heart and soul to you in devotion,' he wrote in June
1939, 'every Muslim should have four wives so that they fight
each other rather than as Shia and Sunni—Maulvis would
benefit from extra *nikah*s.'[60] This friendship was sustained in
affection and mutual support in India, Pakistan, and London,
until the Raja died in 1973.

Probably the most important friendships for Jamal Mian
were with the Ispahani family, that is Mirza Ahmed, Mirza
Abol Hassan, and Mirza Mehdi who was known as Sadri.
These brought him not only much affection and moral
support but also for nearly thirty years the means of sustaining
himself and his family economically. Mirza Ahmed, the eldest
Ispahani, was the leading figure in the family business and
known as 'Bara Saheb'. His correspondence with Jamal
Mian shows him to be a businessman to his fingertips. His
assessments of business performance were cool and rational.
His assessment of Jamal Mian as a businessman was no
less so; he would never be much good because he was not
interested enough in money. His tone in correspondence
could be brutal. Yet, Jamal Mian developed affection as well

58. Raja of Mahmudabad to Jamal Mian, 4 September 1943, Mahmudabad
    Correspondence, Ibid.

59. Raja of Mahmudabad to Jamal Mian, two undated letters, and a third
    dated 1939, Mahmudabad Correspondence, Ibid.

60. Raja of Mahmudabad to Jamal Mian, 6 June 1939, Mahmudabad
    Correspondence, Ibid.

as respect for Mirza Ahmed. 'I am developing a strange connection with Bara Saheb', he told his diary in September 1943. 'I had certain suspicions in my heart but now I feel that his affection is fatherly and his friendship is true.'[61] Jamal Mian certainly showed Mirza Ahmed the respect of a son, later in September postponing a visit to Rudauli to see his bride when he heard that Mirza Ahmed was about to arrive in Lucknow from Calcutta, and sending him gifts of *shirmal* and mangoes.[62] Mirza Ahmed on the other hand congratulated him on his election success in 1946, condoled him on the death of Sarojini Naidu, Governor of the UP in 1949—'Very sad at Mrs Naidu's death. You were her supporter and she was your friend, and was willing to persist in supporting Jamal Mian in business in spite of his sceptical appraisal of his interest and desire.'[63] This relationship was sustained in Pakistan and in London for the rest of Mirza Ahmed's life.

Jamal Mian's relationship with Hassan Ispahani, to judge by their correspondence, involved less business and more politics than that with Mirza Ahmed. But the striking difference was its greater intimacy. In January 1943, Jamal Mian had written to Hassan a letter clearly full of his worries about money and life, and the fact that the Japanese were bombing Calcutta. Hassan replied with a letter that establishes the tone of their relationship:

Your love and affection for me are worth much more than loads of gold and wealth. Do not worry about me. Work hard

61. Jamal Mian Diary, 3 September 1943, Ibid.
62. Mirza Ahmed Ispahani to Jamal Mian, 11 January 1943, 25 January 1943, 30 June 1946, Ispahani Correspondence, Ibid.
63. Mirza Ahmad Ispahani to Jamal Mian, 6 March 1946, 4 March 1949, 14 August 1949, Ispahani Correspondence, Ibid.

and become a No 1 trader. You are and will be my pride and
your success in life will become a fountainhead of joy for me.
Give up sulking and brooding. Give up imagining that you are
not well. Give up wandering aimlessly. Settle down to work
and build yourself a sound future.

The moon is up and so the bombs may come down again.—do
not worry. We shall do our best to dodge them.[64]

Later in the year, on 11 October in fact, he was wondering
if Jamal Mian was married yet,[65] and two years later he was
asking after Miss Jamal Mian.[66] Hassan valued Jamal Mian
highly enough, both as a friend and as an individual to invite
him to join the delegation he was leading to the Middle East
in 1947 as his personal secretary. Later in the year, he wrote
from New York to share with Jamal Mian his pleasure at the
success of the Pakistan Delegation to the United Nations of
which he was a member. 'Sir Mohamed Zafrullah is a brilliant
man and it is a treat to be associated with him'.[67]

Towards the end of his life, Jamal Mian described Sadri
Ispahani as his 'closest friend'. The relationship seems to have
begun in 1941 as Jamal Mian started his tea business and
intensified as they were together, or apart, in Lucknow and
Calcutta between 1942 and 1944. Unfortunately, for the most

64. Hassan Ispahani to Jamal Mian, 9 January 1943, Ispahani Correspond-
    ence, Ibid.
65. Hassan Ispahani to Jamal Mian, 11 October 1943, Ispahani Corre-
    spondence, Ibid.
66. Hassan Ispahani to Jamal Mian, 19 February 1945, Ispahani Corre-
    spondence, Ibid.
67. Hassan Ispahani to Jamal Mian 3 November 1947, Ispahani Corre-
    sponence, Ibid.

part, we only have Sadri's letters to Jamal Mian which make clear the strength of feeling which this young man of 18–21 years had for the Maulana who was four years his senior. This said, the frequency and nature of the correspondence suggest that these feelings were reciprocated.

In March 1942, Sadri had exams and like many young people was fixing his mind on post-exam pleasure. 'I really do not think we should plan' he told Jamal Mian. 'Remember how we went to Cawnpore. No plan ... and what we got.' He then goes into a reverie about their Cawnpore escapade which included a Chinese restaurant, tea in the Musafir Khana, Maulvi Ali Husain's [Mohani] fear when the horse refused, and 'your melodious laughter'. He then moves on to other japes. 'Do you remember the party at Dr Faridi's place with the Dye checking that day. Oh I could go on for days and nights and yet would not end. Our going to Jehangirabad and Mahmudabad –histerical [sic]. I wish you were here—Me—You- and your hukka.'[68]

Over the rest of the year, Sadri writes in lovelorn fashion, tracing Jamal Mian's movements throughout India, hoping that they might be able to travel together, pleased that Jamal Mian might be coming at the end of the month and cast down when he does not.[69] 'I hope you will not disappoint me by making false and uncertain promising of coming to Cal', he wrote on 20 August, and then went into a comparison of sleepy Lucknow and high-pressure Calcutta before begging him to come to Calcutta:

68. Sadri Ispahani to Jamal Mian, 8 March 1942, Ispahani Correspondence, Ibid.
69. Sadri Ispahani to Jamal Mian, 11, 14, 18 March, 30 July, 3 August 1942, Ispahani Correspondence, Ibid.

Slothful Lucknow has its charms. Can you imagine walking
on Chowringhee looking at the sky, or talking old news in
Calcutta. Well all that one can do in Lucknow. I laugh when I
think of our Agency there with the Hukka and pan and dear
Irtiza and one or two letters a week. Here on my word. No
time for lunch and no lock or key to the office.[70]

The rest of the year was taken up with further wondering
about when Jamal Mian was coming to Calcutta.[71] But then
on 11 December Sadri writes overwhelmed by the gifts Jamal
Mian has given him: 'You really do not know what sense of
love and affection and kind thoughts they encouraged in me.'[72]
Then seven days later he bared his heart at the thought that
Jamal Mian might be with him very soon:

Another week and I will be feeling your bearded cheek and
hearing your musical voice. I am eagerly looking forward to
your arrival ... If you do not come within this week, I shall be
very disappointed and will accept no excuse.[73]

The first eight months of 1943 saw more of the same. In
February, Sadri was hoping that Jamal Mian had made up his
mind to come to Calcutta.[74] In March, he was again looking

---

70. Sadri Ispahani to Jamal Mian 20 August 1942, Ispahani Correspondence,
    Ibid.
71. Sadri Ispahani to Jamal Mian, 16 October, 18 October, 15 November
    1942, Ispahani Correspondence, Ibid.
72. Sadri Ispahani to Jamal Mian 11 December 1942, Ispahani Corre-
    spondence, Ibid.
73. Sadri Ispahani to Jamal Mian, 18 December 1942, Ispahani Corre-
    spondence, Ibid.
74. Sadri Ispahani to Jamal Mian, 11 February 1943, Ispahani Correspond-
    ence, Ibid.

forward to the end of his exams and hoping that the two could go to Mussoorie together.[75] In May, he was regretting having stayed in Lucknow for so long because he missed the celebration of his father's silver jubilee in business.[76] Later in the month he wrote triumphantly to say that he had passed his exams with a first-class mark in Physics.[77] Letters in June suggest that Sadri was becoming increasingly involved in working for the Ispahani business.[78] Then in August 1943, they had a 'tiff'. Sadri objected to the business like tone of Jamal Mian's letters. His objection speaks loudly of the emotions caught up in the relationship:

It is heart rendering [*sic*] to see you write business like letters to my personal letters and just after that a second letter accusing me of writing short curt letters. Please bear no misapprehension against my ways and means. They are done to the best of intentions. If my only dear chummy and that is you, will be annoyed with me what is there left to do. Please reply lengthily and in Urdu to prove that you are not annoyed. You have started mis-construing my affectionate sentiments for you—just as you did before I left Lucknow. ... I will always be thankful to you for everything you have done for me during my stay in the UP and even outside it. Do you remember our Kashmir tour and our Punjab tour and

75. Sadri Ispahani to Jamal Mian, 14 March 1943, Ispahani Correspondence, Ibid.
76. Sadri Ispahani to Jamal Mian, 12 May 1943, Ispahani Correspondence, Ibid.
77. Sadri Ispahani to Jamal Mian, 24 May 1943, Ispahani Correspondence, Ibid.
78. Sadri Ispahani to Jamal Mian, 9 and 23 June 1943, Ispahani Correspondence, Ibid.

Cawnpore Musafirkhana[?] How could you forget all these
pillars of companionship and accuse me of writing shortly
and other things.[79]

Then, there was an event which substantially altered the
dynamics of their relationship, as such an event does to bachelor
relationships in much of the world. It was Jamal Mian's
marriage. Sadri began to get suspicious and alarmed in July:

I think there is something fishy in these trips that you attend.
Is there any chance that you get married in one of these? I am
not sure that you are not already married ... because you are
one to keep mum about all this. Please do not do anything
in my absence[,] especially do not marry—I will be terribly
disheartened if you do.[80]

Sadri, as we know, was not far from the truth. In
acknowledgement of their relationship, Jamal Mian did send
Sadri a note both before and after his marriage, for which
Sadri was deeply grateful.[81] This was followed by a telegram
of congratulations from the whole Ispahani family.[82] This
said, Sadri could not completely conceal his bitterness at the
change in their relations. In December 1943 there was another
slight 'tiff':

79. Sadri Ispahani to Jamal Mian, 21 August 1943, Ispahani Correspond-
    ence, Ibid.
80. Sadri Ispahani to Jamal Mian, 11 July 1943, Ispahani Correspondence,
    Ibid.
81. Sadri Ispahani to Jamal Mian, 17 October 1943, Ispahani Correspond-
    ence, Ibid.
82. Telegram, Sadri Ispahani to Jamal Mian, 20 October 1943, Ispahani
    Correspondence, Ibid.

Your accusation that I do not write to you is baseless and further to your letter I have replied and written again. Besides I have sent you the Registered Parcel of the medicine last week. When you receive it you will know that I am still a <u>bachelor</u> and hence have friends ... I wish you had accepted to lead the [1944 Eid] prayers here. Well last time was different I suppose as you were then a bachelor.[83]

In the following year, Sadri was still looking for ways in which they might live the old life together. In February he proposed a tour to Simla, Madras, Mysore, Hyderabad, and Bombay.[84] He continued to mourn the bachelor times that were past. 'Sometimes I think of the time when I used to sit in your office and chat away with you ... sometimes I [would] recite poems etc ... These were good old days whose value we then did not know of. Now of course you are married and your old friends are forgotten.'[85] Then Sadri's attention turned to the fact that Asar was pregnant. He referred frequently to this, almost obsessively, and to the fact that Jamal Mian was about to become a father.[86] By September he was eager to see the baby girl, called Farida. 'Is she fair?', he asked. 'Can you describe her to me or send a photograph of father and daughter?'[87] In the midst of all this baby concern, Sadri was

83. Sadri Ispahani to Jamal Mian, 1 December 1943, Ispahani Correspondence, Ibid.
84. Sadri Ispahani to Jamal Mian, 7 February 1944, Ispahani Correspondence, Ibid.
85. Sadri Ispahani to Jamal Mian, 15 March 1944, Ispahani Correspondence, Ibid.
86. Sadri Ispahani to Jamal Mian, 14, 23 June and early July 1944, Ispahani Correspondence, Ibid.
87. Sadri Ispahani to Jamal Mian, 14 September 1944, Ispahani Correspondence, Ibid.

still trying to engineer meetings between the two of them. 'Sometimes I miss Lucknow—of course with you in it. I do want you to come to Calcutta but here you are different and busy seeing ministers and all others who sit on the laps of the Gods.'[88] Jamal Mian replied immediately, offering a meeting if Sadri could join him on a trip to Lahore. This was 'not at all possible much as I want to see you.'[89] Both men were now having to set aside youthful pleasures in favour of business, politics, and marriage for Jamal Mian and for the demands of M. M. Ispahani Ltd., in which Sadri was now fully engaged.

This intense period of youthful emotional engagement between Sadri and Jamal Mian from 1941 to 1944 was the foundation of their lifelong friendship. A new level of maturity was evident in correspondence from 1945. For instance, when Sadri congratulated Jamal Mian in December on the likelihood of his election to the UP Legislative Assembly[90] or on his All-India Radio talk on the assassinated Gandhi in February 1948, which he thought was much more generous in spirit than Jinnah's response to the tragedy.[91] In 1949, at the extraordinarily young age of twenty-six, Sadri became Chairman of M. M. Ispahani Ltd. This did not prevent him, as we shall see, from being closely involved in the life of Jamal Mian and his family from their move to Dacca in the 1950s and beyond.

---

88. Sadri Ispahani to Jamal Mian, 12 July 1944, Ispahani Correspondence, Ibid.

89. Sadri Ispahani to Jamal Mian, 14 July 1944, Ispahani Correspondence, Ibid.

90. Sadri Ispahani to Jamal Mian, 14 December 1945, Ispahani Correspondence, Ibid.

91. Sadri Ispahani to Jamal Mian, 14 February 1948, Ispahani Correspondence, Ibid

If the 1920s and 1930s saw the key frameworks of Jamal Mian's life established in his learning, his spiritual life, and his public engagement for Indian Muslims, the 1940s saw three further pillars established which were also to help sustain him through his life. They were: his business relationship with the Ispahani family; his marriage to Asar who, his children declare, held things together while Jamal Mian lived his business and public life; and his male friendships, which brought an especial warmth and affection into his being.

8. Expanding the writ of the Muslim League: Jamal Mian with Choudhry Khaliquzzaman, President of the Muslim League Conference, Abbotabad, NWFP, July 1938, and others.

9. Jamal Mian with his close friend, Amir Ahmad Khan, Raja of Mahmudabad, in the 1940s.

10. Mirza Ahmed Ispahani.

11. Spreading the [Muslim League message: Jinnah at Jacobabad, Sindh, 1938; Jamal Mian is sitting on the far left of the picture.

12. Spreading the Muslim League message: Jamal Mian and the Raja of Mahmudabad with Hyderabad nobility.

8

The Simla Conference, fighting the 1945–46 elections, and membership of the UP Legislative Assembly, 1946–47

THE NEXT STAGE OF JAMAL MIAN'S POLITICAL LIFE WAS dominated by preparations for the 1945–46 elections, the elections themselves, and their outcome. This meant that he had to think, perhaps more seriously than before, about what the demand for Pakistan might really mean. Jinnah, for excellent political reasons, left definitions vague. But increasingly those who followed him were having to work out the following: Did it mean the achievement of Pakistan within a federal India? Or did it mean a completely separate sovereign state? And would this separate sovereign state embrace all of the designated Pakistan provinces? Or would they be partitioned? And would the new state of Muslims also be an Islamic state, whatever that might mean?

This period of, at times, intense political activity for Jamal Mian began with the Conference which Viceroy Wavell called at Simla in June 1945. His aim, as he told the Conference on opening it, was not to produce a formal settlement between the Congress and the League but to pave the way towards one by getting agreement on how his Executive Council was to be composed. It was quickly agreed that there should be equal numbers of Muslims and Hindus on the Council of

fourteen. But negotiations collapsed when Jinnah insisted that
all Muslims on the Council had to be Muslim Leaguers. He
would not, for instance, tolerate a separate Muslim Unionist
presence on the Council from the Punjab, as there had been
for years.[1]

Jamal Mian was in Simla as a member of the League
Working Committee. Often in later life, he recalled an
exchange he had had with Jinnah over the Punjab Unionist
Minister representation issue. The exchange happened thus.
Sir Maharaj Singh[2] had invited to tea:

Jawaharlal Nehru, Mrs Naidu, Pandit Govind Ballabh Pant,
Nawab Ismail Khan, Choudhry Khaliquzzaman, Raja Saheb
of Mahmudabad and Hassan Ispahani. I was also invited.
Jawaharlal Nehru had lost weight considerably in jail. The
black sherwani he was wearing was so loose that it appeared
to be a borrowed garment. Seeing this condition of Jawaharlal
we were moved. I asked him whether he had written any new
book while in jail. He answered in the affirmative and perhaps
he referred to his book *The Discovery of India*.

Through his jokes and conciliatory talk, Sir Maharaj Singh was
trying to unite the two parties and on that day when we parted
every heart was filled with the sentiments of Congress-League

1. Ayesha Jalal, *The Sole Spokesman: Jinnah, the Muslim League and the
   Demand for Pakistan* (Cambridge: Cambridge University Press, 1985),
   128–31.
2. Sir Maharaj Singh, 1878–1959. From the Kapurthala royal family, he
   was educated at Harrow and Balliol, Oxford. Called to the Bar in 1902
   he entered the ICS serving in the UP. He was elected Chancellor of
   Lucknow University in 1941 and served as the first Indian Governor
   of Bombay, 1948–52.

amity. By chance the following day at ten I was due to meet Qaid-e-Azam at Cecil Hotel. Nawab Ismail Khan said to me that I should speak to Mr Jinnah that it was not justifiable to fight over one single seat of the Punjab. The Congress was willing that out of the Muslim seats in the proposed Viceroy Council one should be represented by the Unionist Party and the rest by the Muslim League.

The next day I went to see Qaid-e-Azam. Right at the outset he shook me with the unaccustomed remark in Urdu, 'Kiya Hukum hai', 'What is your order[?]' I replied 'It is your order which prevails. I just want to put to you that the Muslims are in no way organized, and even the Muslim League is a non-entity. This whole show emanates from no one other than you. Therefore, in your own lifetime it would be better if you solve the Hindu-Muslim problem so nobody can say what will be our fate'.

I uttered these words with such force and conviction that Mr Jinnah was much moved and enquired what my intention was. I recounted my meeting with Nawab Ismail Saheb and gave his message. For some time Mr Jinnah went on talking about the fair stand of the League as opposed to the obstinacy of the Congress. He then addressed me directly and said that the substance of my suggestion amounted to this: that 'since the Muslims are weak they should commit suicide'. After this he dilated on the Pakistan demand and finally warned me that when we talk about the Hindu-Muslim problem, we always looked at what Gandhi had said and what Nehru had written[,] and what resolutions were passed by the Congress Working Committee[,] and on their strength tried to solve our problem. But when he,

Qaid-e-Azam, thought over the problem[,] he was always
conscious of the reactions of the Hindu nation as a whole,
ignoring Gandhi, Nehru and their Congress. At the time,
I was much chagrined and a number of my friends who
came to know about the details of this interview were very
disappointed and everybody held that Jinnah's attitude was
adamant and obdurate.

But after Partition I witnessed the fate of the promises made
by Congress to the states. I also witnessed the apathy of Pandit
Nehru and Gandhiji over the issues of Urdu and cow slaughter
in the United Provinces and I was all the more reminded of
the justifiable stand taken by Qaid-e-Azam.[3]

★ ★ ★

Two months after the Simla Conference, the Viceroy
announced that elections to the Central and Provincial
Assemblies would be held in the near future. One of the tasks
of these Assemblies would be to elect representatives to a
Constituent Assembly which was to frame a new constitution
for British India. The Muslim League quite rightly interpreted
these elections in Dhulipala's words as a 'Referendum on
Pakistan'. Muslim Leaguers would fight them on the platform
of Pakistan. Substantial victories in the reserved Muslim seats
would establish the popular demand for Pakistan.[4]

  It is appropriate at this stage to ask what ideas about

---

  3. Essay by Jamal Mian in English. File entitled 'Writings on Jinnah Saheb
      in Urdu and English, JMP. NB Jamal Mian's typed text actually has
      Jinnah saying 'Kiye Hukum Irlai'; I have taken the liberty of correcting
      the Urdu.
  4. Venkat Dhulipala, *New Medina*, 389–461.

Pakistan, what interpretations of the Lahore Resolution of 1940, existed in those circles in which Jamal Mian moved, as a prelude to identifying his views. Discussing the Lahore Resolution at a UP Muslim League Conference at Allahabad in December 1940, Nawab Ismail Khan, the President of the Provincial League, declared that all the Resolution did was to group the provinces in which Muslims were a majority into zones 'which would be sovereign'. These zones would retain their character; there would be no exchanges of population. Moreover, the fact that they were to be sovereign would not prevent them from federating with other states, the implication being, perhaps, that the states of Pakistan and Hindustan could form a confederation within India.[5]

Khaliquzzaman had a largely similar view. British India would be partitioned along the lines set out in the Resolution. He was adamant that this meant whole provinces. He was unhappy with the phrase 'such territorial readjustments as may be necessary' and strongly supported the 'hostage theory', the idea that good treatment of the Muslim and Hindu minorities in Hindustan and Pakistan would act as a mutual guarantee of their security. To this basic position he added the vision, flowing perhaps from his Khilafatist past, that Pakistan would emerge as a leader of the Muslim world and play a powerful role in bringing about its unification.[6]

In his speech to the Madras session of the League in April 1941, Jinnah gave his clarification of the Lahore Resolution:

Let me clarify our position with regard to our goal. What is the goal of the Muslim League? What is the ideology of the

5. Ibid. 205–6.
6. Ibid. 217–27.

Muslim League? Let me tell you as clearly as possible ... the goal of the All-India Muslim League is as follows: we want the establishment of completely Independent States in the North-Western and Eastern Zones of India with full control of Defence, Foreign Affairs, Communications, Customs, Currency, Exchange etc.; and we do not want under the circumstances a Constitution of an All-India character, with one Government at the Centre. We will never agree to that. If you once agree, let me tell you, the Muslims will be absolutely wiped out of existence.[7]

Later in this year, Liaquat Ali Khan was talking of Pakistan as an independent state and, for a moment, seems to have gone off message in being willing to consider territorial readjustments which might lead to a truncated Pakistan.[8] By 1943, the territorial coverage of Pakistan was beginning to be represented in more concrete forms. Maps of Pakistan decorated the Pandal at League sessions. In Haroonabad, moreover, a Karachi beauty spot, a Mughal garden had been laid out. At its centre there was a fountain playing around a map of Pakistan which marked the two groupings of provinces in the northwest and the northeast.[9]

There was a second issue which flowed from the Lahore Resolution—what was to be the constitution of this state of Muslims? How Islamic would it be? And, if it was to be Islamic, what did that mean? Soon after the Lahore Resolution, Nawab

---

7. Jinnah, Presidential Address to the All-India Muslim League Madras session, April 1941, S. S. Pirzada ed., *Foundations of Pakistan: All-India Muslim League Documents: 1906–1947*, Vol. II (Karachi: National Publishing House Ltd., 1970), 361.
8. Dhulipala, *New Medina*, 227–32.
9. *Dawn*, 20 December 1943.

Ismail Khan convened a conference of ulama and intellectuals to draft a blueprint for an Islamic constitution for Pakistan. Amongst those present were: Ismail Khan; Khaliquzzaman; Abdul Majid Daryabadi; Saiyid Abul Ala Maududi, who had founded the Jamaat-e Islami in 1941; Azad Subhani, a leading `alim from Cawnpore; and Saiyid Sulaiman Nadvi, pupil of Shibli and recognized as one of the most learned ulama of the day. The conference was held at the Nadvat ul-Ulama, Lucknow; Nadvi was appointed convener of the committee which was set up to do the work. A first draft of the deliberations of the Conference was put together by one Muhammad Ishaq Sandelvi, but then matters seemed to rest. Perhaps Jinnah had got wind of what was happening and, fearing the disruptive impact of its proposals, had instructed the notably obedient Nawab Ismail Khan to close things down. The content of what was discussed was not publicly aired until Sandelvi published his record of the Conference in 1957. This said, a connection was made between this group and the making of the Pakistani Constitution when, after Partition, Sulaiman Nadvi was invited to head the Islamic Teaching Committee to advise the Constituent Assembly on an Islamic Constitution for Pakistan.[10]

However, there was one direction from which Jamal Mian was very aware of a demand for an Islamic state in Pakistan; it was from his close friend the Raja of Mahmudabad. He had made his views plain when he addressed the Bombay Provincial Muslim League just a month after the Lahore Resolution. Pakistan was going to be a laboratory. In a great experiment, the government of Islam would be re-established. 'The creation of an Islamic state...,' he declared '- I say Islamic not Muslim—

---

10. Dhulipala, *New Medina*, 232–43.

is our ideal.'[11] Subsequently, he was not to put too much flesh
on what he meant by an Islamic state, which may have been
because Jinnah asked him not to air his views from the Muslim
League platform.[12]

There does not seem to have been much public discussion
of Pakistan as an Islamic state until 1945 when Shabbir
Ahmad Usmani, a disciple of Ashraf Ali Thanvi (d. 1943)
and a member of his group at Deoband, formed the Jamiat
ul-Ulama-i Islam. His aim was to oppose the ideology of
composite nationalism (*muttahida qaumiyyat*) espoused by
the Jamiat ul-Ulama-i Hind under the leadership of Husain
Ahmad Madani, and in the process, support the All-India
Muslim League in the forthcoming elections. Jamal Mian was
made a member of the Working Committee of the Jamiat ul-
Ulama-i Islam. But, as we shall see, it would be surprising if he
fully endorsed their vision for Pakistan. For Usmani, Pakistan
was the 'new Medina', the 'first Islamic state in history that
would attempt to reconstruct the Islamic utopia created by the
Prophet in Medina'. Moreover, just as the first Muslims spread
from Medina to conquer Arabia, Pakistan would be a step on
the way to the Islamic conquest of the subcontinent. Such
somewhat impractical idealism apart, Usmani was adamant
that Pakistan was only the first stage in the establishment of
an Islamic state, which would be a gradual process.[13]

It was in the context of the airing of these, and other views
about the nature of Pakistan, and whether it should be an
Islamic state or not, amongst friends and colleagues that Jamal

11. Ibid. 210.
12. Raja of Mahmudabad, 'Some Memories', in C. H. Philips and M.
    Wainwright eds., *The Partition of India: Politics and Perspectives, 1935–
    1947* (London: Geo. Allen & Unwin, 1970), 388.
13. Ibid. 354–67.

Mian formed his own opinion. He started from the position of his father and his branch of the Farangi Mahall family; he sought the best way of protecting Muslim interests. In his view, Pakistan was necessary to protect the interests of Muslim minorities in India. He was well aware of how under the previous Congress Ministries of 1937–39, Muslims in many areas, and particularly in the UP, had felt oppressed by Hindu assertiveness.[14] Pakistan was needed to protect the interest of Muslim minorities. On 20 October 1945, addressing a large gathering of peasants at Sitapur during his election campaign, he said:

> The Lahore Resolution explicitly envisaged the conclusion of a treaty between Hindustan and Pakistan by which the rights of Muslims, where they were in a minority, will be properly safeguarded. It will not be a mere verbal understanding but will be incorporated in statutes etc. Presuming Hindustan does not abide by the agreement, a free Pakistan will exert diplomatic pressure.

> What guarantees are there in a United India that the Muslim rights will not be trampled down? Are the Muslims of the UP, whose sympathies are with the Muslims of the whole world, prepared to let down 61/2 crores of their brethren in North-Western and North-Eastern India by voting against the League and Pakistan?[15]

Thus, in trying to reassure his audience of Muslim peasants,

---

14. See William Gould, Hindu Nationalism: The Congress in North India (Cambridge: Cambridge University Press, 2004).
15. *Dawn*, 22 October 1945.

Jamal Mian implicitly endorsed both the first and second paragraph of the Lahore Resolution.

When it came to whether the Pakistan Constitution should be Islamic or not, there is nothing that he is recorded as saying in public on the matter before Independence. We are forced to deduce his views from what he said afterwards. He was, for instance, sceptical of the Objectives Resolution of 1949 which was to guide the development of the Pakistani Constitution. Substantially influenced by Shabbir Ahmad Usmani, it created the opening for those who wished to develop an Islamic, as opposed to a secular, state. Jamal Mian's view, in spite of his friendship with Mahmudabad and other League leaders who favoured an Islamic direction, was that it was a bad idea. He joked that the Objectives Resolution 'Qarardad-e Muqassid' was the 'Qarardad-e Mufassid' or Disorder Resolution.[16] For the rest of his life, as we demonstrate below, he continued to object to the introduction of Islamic measures into the Constitution and the workings of the state.

★ ★ ★

On 21 September 1945, the Muslim League launched its election campaign at a well-attended meeting in Amiruddaulah Park in Lucknow. Nawab Ismail Khan, as President of the Provincial League, appealed for funds to support the campaign. 'We are poor people', Jamal Mian declared in supporting the Nawab's appeal, 'unlike Hindus we don't have Birlas, Dalmias and Tatas. But we value a poor man's gift, however small, more than that of a millionaire.' Jamal Mian then sent his cap round

_____

16. Mahmood Jamal, oral tradition in Jamal Mian's family.

and a total of 123 Rupees 12 Annas and 9 Pies was collected. Then, in an auction reminiscent of the response to his speech at the Lucknow session of the Muslim League in September 1937, his cap was auctioned raising Rs 2000.[17]

The elections were for two bodies. The first was for the Central Legislative Assembly and involved six reserved seats for Muslims from the UP. The second was for the Provincial Legislative Assembly and involved sixty reserved Muslim seats. The UP Muslim League Parliamentary Board planned the campaign like a major military exercise. Z. H. Lari, the Board Secretary from Gorakhpur, led the campaign. Beneath him there was a tier of bosses responsible for divisions of the province. Under these were sixty-six party candidates who were promised a personal secretary and an advisory council. Given the likelihood of election malpractice, booth leaders with twenty-one assistants were appointed for each of the 1,372 polling stations. Ten publicity vans with microphones and loudspeakers were made available to each divisional boss. Training camps were set up for election workers. Every town and village was to have placards, charts, and maps explaining the League programme. To help carry the campaign forward, there was to be a volunteer force of 15,000. The students of Aligarh and the ulama of the Jamiat ul-Ulama-i Islam were shock forces to be applied at sensitive points.[18]

Jamal Mian now launched into a period of intense electioneering activity, although quite how intense it was is difficult to judge as we must depend, for the most part, on newspaper reports. On 25 September, he was vigorously attacking the Congress at a meeting of Lucknow Muslims.

---

17. *Pioneer*, 22 September 1945.
18. Dhulipala, *New Medina*, 438–9.

Instead of relying on groups like the Jamiat ul-Ulama-i Hind
for its election candidates, he said, the Congress should put
up its own Muslim candidates: 'I can guarantee that these
Congress Muslims would not only lose the elections but also
their deposits.[19] In late September and early November, Jamal
Mian was leading an electioneering deputation to Moradabad
along with his old schoolteacher, Maulana Sibghatullah. At
the beginning of October, he was back in Lucknow addressing
a student audience in the Ganga Prasad Memorial Hall. After
they had been regaled with poetry by 'Majaz' and 'Majruh'
glorifying the Muslim demand, he told them that Jawaharlal
Nehru's statement that Pakistan meant the division of the
Punjab and Bengal was 'sheer nonsense'.[20] On 20 October, as
we have seen, he made a major speech at Sitapur.

On 25 October, Jamal Mian, along with the Maharajkumar
of Mahmudabad, Ehsanur Rahman Qidwai, and Maulana
Sibghatullah were given a major popular reception at
Rudauli. Five decorated arches heralded their arrival and
Chaudhuri Muhammad Ali, a leading zamindar of the
qasbah, gave the welcoming address. It is hard to believe
that Shah Hayat Ahmad, Jamal Mian's father-in-law and the
sajjadanashin at Rudauli, who always took a close interest
in Jamal Mian's progress, was not also involved. Before a
'mammoth' gathering these League figures resolved to take
the League campaign to every village in Awadh. Jamal Mian
attacked Congress maulvis who issued fatwas against the
League. By referring to the injunctions of the Quran, they
were doing a disservice to Islam.[21] On 6 November, along

---

19. *Dawn*, 26 September 1945.
20. Ibid. 5 October 1945.
21. Ibid. 27 October 1945.

with Hasrat Mohani and the Maharajkumar of Mahmudabad, Jamal Mian was speaking at Rae Bareli.[22] On 23 November, he was supporting a house-to-house canvassing campaign in Lucknow, addressing street corner meetings from one of the loudspeaker vans which the Parliamentary Board had provided. Then, at the end of November, he was with Nawab Ismail Khan, Nawab Sir Muhammad Yusuf, and Maulana Abdul Qayum on a ten-day tour, embracing Meerut, Shahjahanpur, Moradabad, and Bijnor.[23]

This was a lot of time given to politics for a man who also had a business to run. Jamal Mian stepped away from politics in December 1945. One reason was his business. Unfortunately, we do not have his diary for the second half of 1945, a document which is usually informative about his business worries. But we do know, as we have seen, that in December 1945, Mirza Ahmed Ispahani decided that the progress of Jamal Mian's business was unsatisfactory and it needed restructuring. A second likely reason was that he wanted to spend more time with his family to which a boy, Bari Mian, had recently been added. But then he was also getting ill. On 19 November, Sadri Ispahani wrote saying he was sorry that Jamal Mian was still unwell. 'I suspect that this is due to your excessive travelling and irregularity of diet. Do look after your health as you have to serve the nation many years more.'[24] He was still ill towards the end of December; he told Mirza Ahmad Ispahani that illness had prevented him from going on a League campaigning tour.[25] This said, it is arguable that the political pressure lifted slightly at the end of

22. *Pioneer*, 8 November 1945.
23. *Dawn*, 1 December 1945.
24. Sadri Ispahani to Jamal Mian, 19 November 1945, JMP.
25. Mirza Ahmed Ispahani to Jamal Mian, 27 December 1945, Ibid.

November when it was announced that the Muslim League had won every reserved Muslim seat in the Central Assembly.

At the beginning of January 1946, the Muslim League Parliamentary Board met to decide who its candidates would be for the sixty reserved Muslim seats in the Provincial Legislative Assembly. In this context, Jamal Mian had a major row with his friend, Hasrat Mohani. It occurred over the League nomination for the Lucknow women's seat. Begum Habibullah, the wife of Sheikh Mohammad Habibullah, the manager of the Mahmudabad estate who came from the taluqdari family of Saidanpur, was the sitting member. She had Hasrat's support. Jamal Mian, probably unaware that the Begum wished to stand again, nominated Begum Mohamed Ali, the wife of the great Khilafatist and disciple of his father. He sent his relative, Maulana Hashim, to fetch her from Bhopal where she lived, so that she could be interviewed by the Board. 'Maulana Hasrat', he recalled, 'was livid. He said this is a kind of deceit, a fraud an act of *bayimani* [bad faith]. After that we came to Raja Saheb's [Mahmudabad's] place and were sitting when Hasrat Saheb continued... and kept saying "*bayimani ... bayimani*". I lost my temper and said: "If you use such words, this *gupti* [meaning swordstick although he was probably wielding his umbrella] I will plunge it into your stomach." Anyway all calmed down and Hasrat Mohani recited a very beautiful ghazal and the storm subsided.'[26]

Begum Mahomed Ali received the nomination. At the beginning of February, Begum Habibullah issued a press statement explaining how the muddle had occurred. Apparently, it went thus. In October 1945, Begum Waseem, Khaliquzzaman's sister, had tried to persuade her to stand

26. Jamal Mian, Tape 1, JMP.

for the seat again. She had said no, and did not change her mind until Khaliquzzaman sent her a message through her husband that she had Khaliquzzaman's full support. So she applied for a ticket. Clearly, the statement said, if people had talked to each other, this mix-up could have been avoided. Begum Mahomed Ali would have her full support. Having rapped her Muslim League colleagues over the knuckles, she retreated with dignity.[27]

On 10 January 1946, Jamal Mian's candidacy for the Bara Banki Muslim seat was announced.[28] The Parliamentary Board endorsed the candidature of sitting members. Khaliquzzaman, however, was concerned that this rising figure in the League should have a chance of entering the Legislative Assembly. He went with Jamal Mian to see the sitting member, the Raja of Jahangirabad, a Qidwai sheikh and as we have seen a patron of Jamal Mian. The Raja said he would be very happy for Jamal Mian to be a candidate for his seat.[29] The matter, however, was not quite so simple. Jamal Mian's candidature was challenged on the grounds that he was not twenty-five and, therefore, did not qualify for the position of MLA. Of course, he was twenty-five but the misapprehension had arisen because Ali Husain Mohani had made out their ages to be younger than they were when they applied to Lucknow University. The Deputy Commissioner decided the challenge in Jamal Mian's favour.[30]

Jamal Mian was assisted in his campaign by an intriguing range of people. There was: Maulvi Ghulam Mustafa Rahman 'who sacrificed most in my election [and]... never took a penny of expenses'; his brother-in-law Afaq Mian of Rudauli who

---

27. *Pioneer*, 2 February 1946.
28. Ibid. 10 January 1946.
29. Jamal Mian Tape 1, JMP.
30. Ibid.

'went round in an ekka to drum up support'; and Maulana
Karam Ali of Malihabad. There were Hindus of Malihabad
who supported him; 'one of the reasons for this was that they
were devotees of Shah Abdul Razzaq Banswi'. He was also
supported by a key opposition figure, the President of the Bara
Banki Congress Committee. 'The reason for this was that he
did not like Baragaon (from where Jamal Mian's opponent
came); he was a Masauli Qidwai and there was some tension
between the two.'[31] He also had the support of the Raja of
Mahmudabad's mother who had the reputation of being an
extremely efficient administrator of her Bilehra estate.[32] 'I have
advised all workers on the estate of Bilehra to get busy with
your campaign,' she wrote to him, 'God grant you success and
make the Muslims proud.'[33]

Jamal Mian had started campaigning before the
announcement of the 10th. On 1 January, he was in Rudauli,
Bara Banki, and Lucknow meeting Muslim League workers.
On the 2nd, he left Lucknow for Barauli with Afaq Mian and
Maulana Hashim Mian where he spoke to a public meeting
at 5 p.m.[34] On the 3rd, he left Barauli at 8 a.m., had lunch
with the Qidwais of Baragaon and then reached Bansa at
1:30 p.m. It is clear that the people of Bansa Sharif were
not going to be outdone by those of Rudauli Sharif in their
welcome for Jamal Mian. In procession, the young gentlemen
of Bansa came to meet him outside the village and then
conveyed him to the Dargah. 'I went to Saiyid Sahib's grave',

31. Ibid.

32. Nurul Hasan Siddiqui, *Landlords of Agra & Avadh* (Lucknow: Pioneer
    Press, 1950), 99

33. Mother of Muhammad Amir Muhammad to Jamal Mian, no date,
    Mahmudabad Correspondence, JMP.

34. 1, 2 January 1946 Jamal Mian Diary Ibid.

he recorded in his diary, 'and wept a lot. Then the meeting began outside the Dargah. Raja Sahib Mahmudabad arrived unexpectedly and made a passionate speech. I also made a very hardline speech.'[35]

On 4 January, he and the Raja went to Bara Banki to address a major public meeting. From 6 to 8 January he was laid up with fever which prevented him from going to campaign in Sindh, but he was able to receive Muslim Leaguers from Bara Banki on the 6th and Muslim League workers on the 7th.[36] On 11 January in response to a local request, Jamal Mian went with Ehsanur Rahman Qidwai and raised the Muslim League flag in Bagh Maulana Anwar. Perhaps this was seen as a way of attaching the aura of the family saints to the Muslim League cause. On 3 February, after evening prayers, there was a public meeting in Bagh Maulana Anwar.[37] However, as election day approached, we do not sense that Jamal Mian, for reasons we shall see below, felt he had to campaign with great intensity. On 20 January, he addressed a major public meeting at Rudauli, which was followed by a party hosted by Chaudhuri Muhammad Ali.[38] On 23 January, along with Maulana Sibghatullah, Maulana Shafi's son, Nasim Ansari, who had just won a speaking prize at Aligarh, and several others, he addressed a Muslim Students Federation meeting of 5,000 at Bara Banki.[39] And then to judge from the Press—his diary entries fizzle out—there was little activity. Polling took place on 4

---

35. 3 January 1946, Ibid.
36. 4, 5, 6, 7 January 1946, Ibid.
37. 9, 11, January, 3 February 1946, Ibid.
38. 20 January 1946, Ibid.
39. *Pioneer,* 25 January 1946.

March and his victory by 10,006 to 4,390 was announced
on 12 March.[40]

★ ★ ★

C. M. Naim, who was a boy of eleven at the time, has left us
a charming vignette of the Bara Banki election which may
explain why Jamal Mian did not feel he had to campaign
too intensively. Naim, who later became a Professor of Urdu
literature at the University of Chicago, was an enthusiastic
member of the Muslim Students Federation which had
opened a branch in Bara Banki recently. Federation members,
all boys, used to manage Muslim League processions with
banners and flags and raised slogans of which 'the most potent'
was 'What does Pakistan mean? There is no God but Allah'.
He particularly valued the small library in the Federation's
'dingy office' where, coming from a home which only took the
English-language *Pioneer*, he could read the League's Urdu
newspapers, the weekly *Manshur* from Delhi, and *Tanwir* from
Lucknow which the UP League had established to fight the
elections. He recalls in particular the popularity of the hostage
argument in 1946.[41]

Naim makes it clear that Jamal Mian 'was the perfect choice
for Bara Banki. His father, Maulana Abdul Bari of Firangi
Mahal—we called him Bari Miyan—had gained national
fame as the leader of the Khilafat movement. The famous
Ali Brothers had once declared him their spiritual mentor.'[42]
Naim's family were Chaudharis, long prominent in the district.

---

40. *Dawn*, 14 March 1946.
41. C. M. Naim, *The Muslim League in Bara Banki: A Suite of five Sentimental
    Scenes*, (Shimla: Indian Institute of Advanced Study, 2010), 6–8.
42. Ibid. 9.

His great uncle, Raja Naushad Ali Khan, had been one of the founders of the All-India Muslim League at Dhaka in 1906. 'In our *jawar*', he continues:

> That hard-to-define landscape of kinships and marriages but also of emotional affinity and cultural one-ness that cut across religious and sectarian divides, Bari Miyan has been the most revered Sunni figure during his life. Probably no Sunni Muslim elite family in our *jawar* was without someone who was Bari Miyan's spiritual disciple. My late grandfather must have been one, since he had sent my father to study at Firangi Mahal; my grandmother,certainly, was—though at a second remove. She was a disciple of Qutub Miyan, Bari Miyan's *Khalifa*. I had seen Jamal Miyan at our house; he called my grandmother *'chachi'*(aunt), and she, in turn, did not observe *purdah* with him.[43]

The Farangi Mahallis, as they came from Sehali in Bara Banki district, were all considered men of Naim's *jawar*.

Naim suggests, probably rightly, that before 1945 the Muslim League did not have much presence in Bara Banki, although he overlooks the fact that his Qidwai relative, Raja Ejaz Rasul of Jahangirabad, one of the largest landowners in the district, had been the Muslim League member since 1937. This said, his point is that the Congress had a powerful presence in Rafi Ahmad Kidwai of Masauli. He had been Revenue Minister in the UP in the 1937 Congress government and was a key figure in the central government after independence. The Bara Banki seat would have been an obvious one for him to contest but he chose to stand for three

---

43. Ibid. 9–10.

seats elsewhere. This left the way free for his distant cousin, Jamilur Rahman Qidwai of Baragaon, who was President of the District Congress Committee. Naim enjoys the fact that the battle for Bara Banki was fought between a Jamal and a Jamil, 'a rather confusing manifestation of the truth in the Prophet's axiom, *Allahu-j-jamil wa yuhibbu-j-jamal,* "God is Beautiful, and Loves Beauty".'[44]

The contest produced some telling conflicts of loyalty. Naim's father was a friend and distant relative of Jamil, and would normally have worked for his campaign. But Jamal Mian was the son of his grandmother's spiritual guide and he addressed his father as 'Masud Bhai'. 'Clearly when it came to Father's loyalties, Jamal Miyan had a higher claim— not on account of his politics, but in his own person.'[45] So he 'energetically' supported Jamal Mian, hosting visitors, discussing how to influence voters on polling day, and lending his car and driver to get women voters to the polling booths. In the matter of *jawar* loyalties the balance fell in Jamal Mian's favour; no matter what political belief was involved. 'I honestly do not recall,' Naim states, 'ever hearing him discuss any *qaumi* (national) issue or attending an election meeting.'[46]

In the case of another conflict of loyalty, Jamil's elder brother, Ehsanur Rahman Qidwai, the secretary of the UP Muslim League, would normally have been expected to support him. But here, political commitment trumped the ties of blood. After troublemakers tried to implicate him in some distasteful spoiling action in his brother's campaign, he felt compelled to issue a statement:

---

44. Ibid. 10–11.
45. Ibid. 11.
46. Ibid.

So far as the UP Assembly elections in Bara Banki are concerned, I am opposing my brother Mr Jamilur Rahman Kidwai but my opposition is not based on personal reasons. I am a Muslim Leaguer and consider it my religious and political obligation to oppose every candidate who is fighting a Muslim Leaguer, even if the opponent be my own brother.[47]

Naim takes pleasure in the gentlemanly manners, the *sharif* values, of those involved in the election campaign. When the Provincial Congress Committee offered to send some Maulvis from the Jamiat ul-Ulama-i Hind to counter the League's Islamic rhetoric with their own, Jamilur Rahman refused to have them saying that: 'if the voters wished to elect a person who prayed more often than he did they were welcome to do so.' When his supporters wished to publish allegations that Jamal Mian had improperly earned income from property belonging to a mosque, he stopped them. Naim is in no doubt that Jamal Mian would have done exactly the same:

No *sharif* person in those days ever did certain things. When the campaign manager of the League's candidate against Rafi Ahmad Kidwai needed a car—'since his own was out of order'—he telephoned his good friend Rafi; the latter immediately sent him his own car with a full tank of petrol.[48]

Finally, Naim takes us to the League's election rallies. They were usually held between *maghreb* and `*isha* prayers; the town's open air grain market, with its impressive backdrop of the Jubilee Clock Tower, was the favoured site. People

---

47. *Pioneer*, 3 March 1946.
48. Naim, *Muslim League in Bara Banki*, pp. 20–21.

would slowly trickle into the venue, looking for something to sit on, or perhaps bring with them a cot. 'Only the humble and meek—or the senior boys seeking to be close to the girls in the *purdah* section—happily sat on dusty dhurries spread before the speakers' platform.' Before the speakers arrived, the microphone and platform were open to local poets and orators. The better-known poets from outside only came to the microphone after the speakers had arrived. The most popular of these in Bara Banki was a young poet called 'Dil Lakhnavi'. He was not much of a poet but the force of his recitation was extraordinary. 'Tall and fair, dressed in a black sherwani and a Jinnah cap', Naim recalls, 'Dil was a hit with everyone, particularly with some of those in the curtained area. As a volunteer in that section I had to get his autograph for many an ecstatic girl.' Naim is grateful that only two of his 'awful' verses have stuck in his memory:

> The community's boat
> With Jinnah's support
> Merrily floats
> From shore to shore.

And,

> Jinnah is shaded by Muhammad and Ali
> God's favours to him are manifold.[49]

Naim concludes his discussion of the Bara Banki public meetings saying:

---

49. Ibid. 14–15.

Poetry, particularly bad poetry, is of course more memorable than prose. That's why I could quote Dil but have no memory now of what Jamal Miyan and others said in the speeches I enthusiastically applauded that winter. Doubtless they were heart-warming and mind-boggling in equal measure. The one name that still lingers is that of Maulana Sibghatullah 'Shaheed' of Firangi Mahal, but neither his words nor Jamal Miyan's are recorded in the sources I have access to.[50]

Naim's vignette gives us insight into the style of campaigning in this elite world, and what could and could not be done. But most importantly, it gives us a sense of why Jamal Mian might have come to feel almost complacent about his election campaign. Once Rafi Ahmed Kidwai was out of the running, the great weight of his family reputation in the district, the alliance of influential landed families, and the support of the major Sufi shrines suggested that he was well-placed to win. If illness kept him from the fray, as it seems to have done in December, it did not matter.

★ ★ ★

'The U.P. Legislature Meets After Nearly 7 Years' was the headline in the *Pioneer* newspaper on 26 April 1946.[51] The Muslim League formed the opposition to the Congress government. Khaliquzzaman was the leader and Z. H. Lari the deputy leader. Rafi Ahmad Kidwai was the Home Member in the Congress government. Jamal Mian used to go to the Assembly in his Baby Austin, driven by Irtiza Husain, with

---

50. Ibid. 17.
51. *Pioneer*, 26 April 1946.

Hasrat Mohani sitting in front while he and Begum Mahomed Ali sat in the back.[52] Jamal Mian made a big impact on the first debate which took place on the following day. 'On the first day,' he recollected, 'a bill was presented relating to the salaries of ministers. I knew nothing of the rules. I stood up and started addressing everyone as I used to do in public meetings. Lari quietly admonished me and said: "Here you address the Speaker, not everyone".'[53] Jamal Mian was soon into his stride attacking the proposal to raise ministerial salaries to Rs 1,500 pm:

Mr President. This is the first day of our new Assembly and on the first day one was hoping that our first bill would be to end Monarchism [ie the rule of the British Crown] and Capitalism. Our policies would show that we have come here to help the poor and serve their interests and progress. Instead, on the very first day we are putting forward measures which will increase the standard of living of our ministers, instead of helping the public.

Honourable Sir! To pass such a bill on the very first day of the Assembly would be deeply disappointing to the people of this province.

Honourable Sir. This ministry which raised the slogan of QUIT INDIA for serving the poor and the progress of the workers ... as soon as they sit in their [Assembly] seats, their very first thought is to increase their salaries and fill their pockets. My party, and in particular I myself, are determined to oppose

52. Jamal Mian Tape 1, JMP.
53. Ibid.

a bill which wants to increase the pay of the ministers and increase their comforts and lifestyles. Today there are many in the province who are destitute, search for a decent set of clothes and are unable to find them. Are there not enough people in this province who earn 500 rupees a month. Is this not enough for them? At least you could have shown some patience over the salary for a few days. Why was it necessary to immediately to try to increase your standard of living?

Honourable Sir. It should be a practice for every government that claims to serve the people to show the way by its own actions and policies to those whom it represents such as the poorer officers under it, and not become like foreign rulers who care first for their own interests and then worry about the public. In this very building there are clerks, there are security officers, who are asking for an increase. Is the administration not worried about their welfare? On this occasion I would also like to add this, that when last time the Congress left government, people thought that when Congress returns again, it would have loftier ideals and aims ... however it seems that the people thought wrongly. The people never thought that the Congress would behave in this way on its return. But what is this spectacle before them? On the very first day the people of this province are being told that we are not the same as they thought we might be ... We have come only to enjoy the luxuries and benefits of power. First we will look after ourselves then worry about the rest. This approach, whether in politics or any other arena of life, is not to be praised. The need is first to look after the weak, then the strong.[54]

54. UP Legislative Assembly, 27 April 1946, Vol. XXII, No 2, 28, in Urdu, British Library.

As Jamal Mian sat down, there were Opposition cheers.[55] He was personally congratulated by Parshotam Das Tandon, a senior Congress figure. Jamal Mian also noted that, as he spoke, the doors to the Assembly chamber opened and ordinary workers, peons, and security men all crowded there to listen to him.[56]

Jamal Mian, however, had more to offer on 27 April. The Government followed the Ministers' emoluments bill with the Members' Emoluments (Amendment) Bill in which members' salaries were to rise to Rs 200pm and their per diem to Rs 10. In opposing the bill, Jamal Mian, somewhat self-righteously, compared the sacrifices which the League was prepared to make with the approach of the capitalists who supported the Congress, and then linked the issue with that of zamindari abolition which was in the air:

Honourable Sir. People who have spoken before me have asked us why we are opposing this bill as well as the Ministers' salaries bill. They should know that this is the way we behave: when we ask for sacrifices from others, we are ourselves ready to make those sacrifices. If we had only opposed the Minister's bill, then all accusations and allegations made against us would be justified. If we are opposed to increasing emoluments for ministers, then in order to prove our own honesty and integrity, we are also ready not to increase our own salaries.

(One voice: Why are you worried? You can return your salary if you like.)

---

55. *Pioneer*, 28 April 1946.
56. Jamal Mian Tape 1, JMP.

This is our way and we have entered a new era, and a new path lies before us. At this time, whichever provinces have Muslim League ministries, and wherever the Muslim League is in the Assembly, the League has exhibited this same attitude and belief. They will tell you what sacrifice and steadfastness is all about and how capitalism can really be fought. All the members of this Assembly know who has provided the funds for the Congress and how the election was fought. Did the poor fight the elections? Did not money from the MAHAJANS flow like water? You say you will finish off Zamindari and Taluqdari. You accuse us of supporting the Zamindars and Taluqdars. I would like to inform you that all the Zamindars and Taluqdars who are members of this party—if you can abolish from this province, and from the country, capitalism and the Mahajans, each and every one of them will be ready to be abolished.

(Hear! Hear! From the Muslim League Benches)

... If you are willing to serve the poor, and tour the villages, and want to struggle for the downtrodden, then remember that only they can work hard who go into villages in poverty, struggle and modesty, and not those who want 2–300 rupees allowance and ride about in cars with orderlies and private secretaries. Only he who is prepared to eat dust and walk on foot can serve the villages.

Jamal Mian then quoted Hafiz:

Those brought up in comfort and luxury cannot tread the Beloved's path

Love's path requires those who are intensely drunk (with devotion).[57]

Jamal Mian's speeches made no difference to the outcome. There was a large government majority and both emoluments bills were passed.[58]

Jamal Mian remained active in the Assembly, concerned in particular with defending Muslim interests. In early July, somewhat illogically after his earlier attacks on capitalism, he gave notice of a resolution to be moved in the forthcoming budget session of the Assembly opposing a 'Socialist State' for the UP.[59] He was referring to the Zamindari Abolition Bill on which the Muslim League position remained that the abolition of zamindari could only go hand in hand with the abolition of capitalism. At the same time, he proposed another resolution, rather more directly focussed on protecting Muslim interests. He called upon those members who had just recently been elected by the UP Assembly to the Constituent Assembly of India to see that in the future constitution of India, central control should not be binding on the United Provinces and 'that all controversial questions relating to minorities may be decided by a majority vote of the minority community concerned'.[60] A week later, he was attacking the Congress in the UP for the way in which politics had been brought into the provision of food grains and the rationing of necessities such as kerosene, cooking oil, and sugar. 'I have received shocking reports from Bara

---

57. UP Legislative Assembly, 27 April 1946, Vol. XXII, No 2., 48, in Urdu, British Library
58. *Pioneer*, 30 April 1946.
59. *Dawn*, 7 July 1946.
60. *Ibid.*

Banki,' he declared in a press statement, 'which show that in the district it is the Congress and not the administration which rules. Permits have Congress and not government seals. They are only obtainable if individuals subscribe to Congress funds. Muslims are being discriminated against.'[61] On 7 August, he was intervening in the debate on the zamindari abolition bill to remind the government that Muslim zamindars supported *waqf*s (charitable endowments) which yielded Rs 50 lakhs per annum. If the government was willing to finance the *waqf*s, he would support the abolition of zamindari.[62] In the issues taken up over these few months of Congress dominance, it is not difficult to see how Muslims, not just elite Muslims, felt threatened by Congress power.

The next matter to attract Jamal Mian's attention in the Assembly made the matter of Muslim fears more clear, indeed, it underlined the reasons why some felt Pakistan was the answer to their problems. In the autumn of 1946 there had been the Calcutta disturbances, on which Jamal Mian reported to the League High Command,[63] and severe communal riots in Bihar and Naukhali (Bengal). Moreover, there had been a general increase in communal feeling in the UP. In this context, Rafi Ahmad Kidwai moved in the Assembly the UP Maintenance of Public Order Bill. This made provision for preventive detention, the imposition of collective fines, control of public meetings and processions etc. In opposing this strengthening of the government's coercive powers in relation to society Jamal Mian said:

61. Ibid. 16 July 1946.
62. Ibid. 9 August 1946.
63. Ibid. 18 September 1946.

You forget one thing that the law and ordinance is not
your invention. It is the bastard child of the old [British]
government. These remnants are the gift of a foreigner which
are now being embraced by your government. The Defence
of India Act, which many big leaders of the Congress have
condemned and opposed a hundred times in the streets
and bazaars and in their speeches. The Government needed
this Act and to increase its power it wants to add a further
ordinance to this act to make it even more draconian. Please
don't be misleading in this debate by saying these laws are
necessary to stop communal violence. Don't put a veil on
the truth by mixing Muslim League and Congress issues
with it. The old government has used this weapon to attack
you. Congress members of the house tell us this law is
necessary to protect Muslims. If this is the case, then just
add an amendment which will help to banish our fears. But
I think this is not the case. Our clever home minister has
cunningly misled his own party members. He has made the
debate all about communal violence. In the debate we heard
mention about Naukhali and Bihar etc ... I feel nobody
has carefully considered what hardships it can bring to the
general public.[64]

When the Bill was passed a week later, Jamal Mian warned
that the very powers which government had been determined
to give police officers would be used against the Congress
before long.[65]

Later in life when Jamal Mian reflected on the speeches

64. UP Legislative Assembly, 11 January 1947, Vol. XXVII, No 1., 57–9,
   in Urdu, British Library.
65. *Dawn*, 20 January 1947.

made in the Assembly he noted that, although Hindi was the official language, only a few spoke good Hindi. On the other hand, the atmosphere was very friendly and relations between opponents were civilized.[66]

66. Jamal Mian Tape 1, JMP

9

Middle East Delegation, Independence, the end of the All-India Muslim League, and the death of Gandhi, March 1947–January 1948

GIVEN THE MOMENTOUS EVENTS OF 1947, ONE WOULD expect their enormity to be reflected in the life, or at least the thoughts, of Jamal Mian in that year. It may be because we only have his diary covering three months of that year, and these were months when he was out of India. Beyond this, it may be because we only have his reflections recorded decades later, that his responses seem relatively low key. On the other hand, we do have the very detailed diary of his close friend, Hasrat Mohani, in which Jamal Mian is often mentioned. But Hasrat's diary focuses much more on the quotidian and the ordinary rather than the great events of the day. This leads one to think that it is historians and politicians with the advantage of hindsight who have turned moments such as the 3 June agreement over Partition, or Independence itself (on 14 and 15 August), into the notable events they now seem to be. Hasrat, for instance, makes no mention of Indian independence in his diary entry for 15 August. However, what does emerge very clearly from Hasrat's diaries for the second half of 1947 is that life was quickly becoming more and more harsh for Indian Muslims. For Jamal Mian, the period March 1947 to January 1948 is marked by his membership of the Indian Trade Delegation to the Middle East from March to May; his attendance at the inauguration of Pakistan in Karachi on 14 August; his attendance at the All-India Muslim League Council meeting in Karachi in December; and his meeting with Gandhi on the day before his death, which was followed by his tribute to the Mahatma on All-India Radio.

The Middle East Delegation

On 5 February 1947, Hassan Ispahani wrote to Jamal Mian to say that he had been at the Delhi Air Conference 'watching out for Muslim interests', and second, that he was being sent on a tour of the Middle East for eight to ten weeks.[1] Soon afterwards, he may have indicated that he was to lead this delegation. Then, Jamal Mian received two official telegrams. The first told him that he had been selected to accompany the Indian Trade Delegation to the Middle East as private secretary to its leader. There was a long list of vaccinations he was to have. He should also acquire a passport and visas for Iran, Turkey, Syria, Lebanon, Egypt, Sudan, Hejaz, Palestine, Jordan, and Greece. He was to report to Karachi no later than 6 March. The second official telegram said cryptically 'Take warm clothes and dinner jacket'.[2]

Jamal Mian found it difficult to come to a decision about the offer. On the one hand, there was the excitement of travel

1. Hassan Ispahani to Jamal Mian, 5 February 1947, Ispahani Correspondence, JMP.
2. Middle East Delegation File, Ibid.

and the pleasure of working closely with Hassan Ispahani. On the other, his wife was about to give birth to their third child and he may have thought that he should not be too far away. Moreover, as a man of a valetudinarian disposition he may not have fancied the long list of injections. This said, we do not know for sure. What we do know is that he communicated his indecision to Hassan Ispahani who was 'very disappointed' by Jamal Mian's response and told him to make up his mind.[3] This seemed to have forced Jamal Mian to a decision. Soon afterwards, he received an official letter of invitation which told him that the trip would last thirty-eight days going by Karachi-Basra-Baghdad-Tehran-Damascus-Beirut-Ankara-Izmir-Istanbul-Cairo plus the possibility of Jeddah and Khartoum.

Members of the Delegation:

1. Mr M. A. H. Ispahani, leader, of Ispahani Co.
2. Mr Har Das Zeljee, Hon. Secy. member, Buyers and Shippers Chamber, Karachi
3. Mr Haji Dawood Bhej Habib, member, of Messrs Habib & Sons, Bombay
4. Mr Chinobai C. Jare, Hon Secy, All India Export Assoc;, member, Bombay
5. Mr Ibrahim Yousuf Zainul Alireza of Bombay, adviser*

Mr M. Ayub ICS will go as secy of the Delegation.
Mr Jamaluddin Abdul Wahhab MLA UP will act as secy to the Leader.
Mr Qamran Ali will be stenographer.[4]

---

3. Sadri to Jamal Mian, 25 February 1947, Ispahani Correspondence, Ibid.
4. Official Notification, 3 March 1947, Middle East Trade Delegation File, JMP.

*Ebrahim Yusuf Zainal spelled his name thus, and so shall we.

The delegation left by air for Basra on 11 March, stayed there for two days and then went on to Najaf, Karbala, and Baghdad. In Baghdad, they were hosted by the Commerce Ministry and met members of the government. They also met many journalists and Jamal Mian gave a lengthy interview to the *Al-Sharq* newspaper. In addition, they met various politicians, in particular, Muhammad Mahdi Kubba, the leader of the Istiqlal or Independence party which carried the standard of Arab nationalism and opposition to British rule. They were given a dinner by Amir Abdullah of Jordan, to whom they presented a message from Jinnah. Particularly important from Jamal Mian's point of view were his meetings with the family of Abdul Qadir Gilani and the visits he was able to make to his shrine.[5] It seems that in these early stages of the trip Jamal Mian was unwell. Qutb Mian pursued the delegation for news about his health; Pir Saifuddin Ibrahim of Baghdad and the Raja of Jahangirabad sent telegrams praying for his welfare.[6]

As the delegation journeyed from Karbala to Najaf where they paid their respects to the tomb of Hazrat Ali, Jamal Mian sought the help of the fourth Caliph. With memory of the previous autumn's massacres of Muslims in Bihar weighing heavily upon him, and his general concern about the fate of India's Muslims, he wrote thus, beseeching Hazrat Ali, the most active amongst the warriors of the early Muslim community, to come to their aid:

---

5. Jamal Mian, Middle East notebooks 7 March 1947–20 Mary 1947, entries for 11–18 March, JMP.
6. Middle East Trade Delegation File, JMP.

You are the leader of the Aulias [friends of God]
You are the strength of the Prophet's arm
Devotion to you is the sign of belief
You, the conqueror of Khaibar, Amir of believers
At your abode is this insignificant slave
On his lips Salaams and your praises!
Your threshold's magnetism brought me here
And the burning of my sins brought me here
I have come for forgiveness to you
I have come with a plea to you
Your devotees, Muhammad's slaves
Say this after respectful Salaams
We depend on your durbar
We have trust in your power
Though we are all crying helplessly
Especially wounded are the dwellers of Bihar
Whose dwellings have been destroyed
Whose green fields have been ravaged
The Muslim of India is very helpless
His heart is broken and wounded
We are besieged by *kufr* from all sides
The enemies of our Deen are flanking us
Our nation, our wealth, our homes are in danger
Our respect, our belief, our lives are in danger
In short we are in a miserable state
Our Deen is trodden over by *shirk*
This is the condition of Muhammad's devotees
This is the condition of 10 crores of Indian Muslims
The *Millat* of the King of Prophets is without a crown
It is begging for the power of your sword!
Oh Conqueror of Khaibar, in Allah's name
Have pity on us for Muhammad's sake

Help us help us oh king of the world
Oh you, who are protector, protect us![7]

On the 19 March, the delegation proceeded to Iran where they stayed until 4 April. Some time was spent in Isfahan but most of the stay was in Tehran. As in Iraq, the delegation met many politicians and journalists, visits were also made to factories and Jamal Mian was impressed by the signs of industrial progress. This said, he was clearly not as comfortable in Iran as in Iraq: there were no Sunni mosques for offering prayers; alcohol was freely available; and society had marked inequalities. 'On the one hand there are huge palatial houses, and on the other so many shacks and huts where the poor dwell. On the one hand there are well-dressed and fashionable young men and women and on the other there are half-naked beggars who roam the streets.'[8] After meeting a large number of people, Jamal Mian concludes that 'the negligence of the Abbasid Sultans has left Iranis quite indifferent to Islam'.[9]

On 29 March, the delegation met the Minister of Finance, who first of all complained about the relationship between the centre and the provinces; the latter all wanted investment in schools and hospitals but were prepared to give nothing in return. He then observed that Iranians were obsessed with becoming Westernized. They wanted to ape the West in dress, in manners, and in every other way, but were ignoring basic aspects such as the economic well-being of the people. Jamal Mian was struck by what the Minister had to say and

---

7. 'I wrote this between Karbala and Najaf' Jamal Mian recorded in his notebook; the poem is dated 17 March 1947. Jamal Mian, Middle East Notebooks, 19 March–4 April, JMP.

8. Ibid.

9. Ibid. 29 March 1947.

concluded that the Iranians were at last becoming aware of their domination by the West and were beginning to think in the right direction. Later in the day, Jamal Mian received his first letter from Lucknow since the trip began in which Altafur Rahman Qidwai told him that Asar had given him a son, Mahmood Jamal.[10]

On 4 April, the delegation left Tehran by air for Damascus (Illustration 15). After meeting businessmen and visiting Saladin's tomb, they went on by road to Beirut where, after meeting businessmen and government officials, they met Amir Abdullah again and Shaikh Abdullah Sarraj, the Qazi al-Quzzat of Mecca. There followed a tour of over two weeks to Turkey where they were official guests and had their own plane for their travels (Illustration 13). The visit began in Ankara where Jamal Mian noticed that 'wine flowed' at a dinner in the Ankara Club hosted by the Turkish Minister of Commerce and that the Turks like the sound of Urdu. After a visit to Ataturk's vast mausoleum Jamal Mian noted 'May God forgive this man's sins. Where he has served Turkey well, he has also harmed Islam greatly.' The delegation then met a group of Indians who had been settled in Turkey since World War One. We do not know for certain but they could well have come from the joint Indian-Turkish colony at Erzine in the Adana district on the south coast. It had been established as a Pan-Islamic project by the Ottoman Ministry of the Interior and which Mahomed Ali, as editor of the *Comrade*, had supported.[11] After this, they went to a girls' college where they were impressed by the progress that women were making in education and Jamal Mian was pleased to discover that the students seemed

---

10. Ibid.
11. Ibid. 4–17 April 1947 and Robinson, *Separatism*, 207–8.

to enjoy listening to him making a speech in Urdu (Illustration
14). The delegation, in particular Ebrahim Zainal Alireza,
became much disturbed when they were given gifts, including
wine. Jamal Mian noted with pleasure that Ankara was a clean
city in which he had not seen any beggars. He noted with
considerable perceptiveness, given future developments, that
'Turks have an Islamic heart despite Europeanisation. They
were indifferent to religion initially but now seem to have a
better balance, and are returning to religion.'[12]

On 19 April, the delegation flew to Izmir where, amongst
other things, they noted one aspect of the return of Islam; on
going to a mosque they discovered that the call to prayer was
in Turkish but the prayer and sermon was in Arabic. Then
they went to Istanbul where a great deal of sight-seeing took
place and they discovered that many Turks regarded Indian
visitors as British spies. There were two aspects of specific
importance for Jamal Mian. The first was a meeting with the
Turkish literary figure and feminist, Halide Edib (1884–1964).
She had visited India for some months in 1935 and left a
fascinating description in her book *Inside India*. Amongst the
places she visited was Lucknow, although Jamal Mian would
have been too young to have met her on that occasion. She
stayed in the house of Choudhry Khaliquzzaman's sister,
Begum Waseem, Dolly Bagh, of whose life and atmosphere
she left an excellent picture.[13] More important for Jamal Mian
would have been his visit to the tomb of his ancestor, Ayub
Ansari at Eyup on the Golden Horn.[14]

On 30 April, the delegation reached Cairo, having travelled

---

12. Jamal Mian, Middle East Notebooks, 17 April, JMP.
13. Halide Edib, Mushirul Hasan ed. and introd., *Inside India* (Delhi:
    Oxford University Press, 2002), especially 100–6.
14. Jamal Mian, Middle East Notebooks, April 17 1947, JMP.

from Istanbul via Cyprus. There they met the Minister of
Commerce who hosted a reception for them in the Muhammad
Ali Club (Illustration 17). On 1 May, they met Mufti Amin
al-Husseini (1897–1974), the Mufti of Palestine who was
living under house arrest. The Mufti had visited Lucknow in
the 1930s and made many enquiries about Farangi Mahall.
Jamal Mian described the Mufti as 'a true friend of Pakistan
and a standard bearer of Muslim Brotherhood'. He was to
be a good friend to Jamal Mian in later life. Later, there were
visits to Al-Azhar, to Alexandria, and many meetings with
businessmen, journalists, and officials. One of Jamal Mian's
last meetings was with Hasan al-Banna (1903–49), the leader
of the Muslim Brotherhood. He noted that the rise of Jinnah
had substantially enhanced Arab awareness of Muslim affairs
in India.[15]

After Cairo, Saudi Arabia was the delegation's last stop.
They arrived at Jeddah on 11 May where they were received
by Yusuf Zainal Alireza, the brother of Ebrahim Zainal, the
delegation member who, apart from Hassan Ispahani, was
closest to Jamal Mian. There was the usual meeting with
the Chamber of Commerce but on this occasion there was
also one with the British Ambassador. The delegation then
went on to Mecca where Jamal Mian performed *tawaf* of
the Kaaba and prayed for the Muslims. The group also went
to meet King Abdul Aziz in Riyadh. But the high point of
Jamal Mian's stay in the region was the visit to Medina. Here
he had the pleasure of staying in the house of Abdul Baqi,
whose Lucknow wife, Amma, managed the Farangi Mahall
household. Abdul Baqi had died and Jamal Mian was looked
after by Abdul Baqi's Medina widow and other relatives. The

---

15. Ibid. 30 April–9 May.

notebooks give a sense of a man who experienced a spiritual
'high'; many poems in praise of the Prophet were recited. On
the other hand, Jamal Mian was very unhappy about the
impact of Saudi rule on the city. Its condition had been so
much better under the Turks. Now nepotism and bribery
were very common Because the Saudi rulers were focussing
attention on their homeland of the Najd, the population of
the city which had been c. 100,000 under the Turks had sunk
to 30,000, of whom 10,000 were Indians.[16]

The delegation got back to Karachi on 21 May. One
impression with which Jamal Mian returned was the
unhappiness of Middle Easterners about Indian businessmen.
'Wherever we went', he said in an interview, 'we met with a
common twin reaction, namely, a desire for Indian goods and
complaints about the integrity of Indian businessmen. The
same, sorry and humiliating tale was heard by us from Shiraz
to Constantinople and it filled us with shame and sadness.'[17]
He gave examples of sharp practice. Turkish importers of
pepper had received consignments full of black stones; Saudi
importers of cloth complained that most of the goods were
torn and unusable; Iranians found a consignment of shoes
which contained a disconcerting quantity of cardboard.[18] A
second impression is given by a letter Jamal Mian wrote from
Jeddah (on Zainal Alireza notepaper), which was probably to
be published in his newspaper *Hamdam*. He writes of a lot of
Congress propaganda in the Middle East, of Congress' agents
touring Middle Eastern countries. The impact he wrote could
be deduced from the failure of the Asian Conference of the

16. Ibid. 11–14 May 1947.
17. A clipping from the *Statesman*, 31 May 1949, Middle East Trade
    Delegation file, JMP.
18. Ibid.

Congress because the Arabs refused to participate: in Baghdad, Congress agents worked hard but no one would commit to the conference if there was not an Indian Muslim presence; Syria was agreeable to the conference but then its Prime Minister refused to attend because Jinnah was not attending; the editor of the *Beirut* newspaper refused to go without Jinnah being present; the Arab League was present but only as an observer.[19]

From this letter we can deduce that under the Interim Government the Congress and the League were already conducting separate foreign initiatives. The Indian Delegation to the Middle East originated in the Ministry of Commerce where I. I. Chundrigar (1897–1968) was in charge. It might have been paid for by Government of India funds, have been supported by an ICS man, and have been assisted from time to time by British diplomats across the Middle East, but it was clearly a Muslim League show, staffed by Muslims amongst whom there were two senior Muslim League figures. In participating in this operation, Jamal Mian would appear to have been engaged in a form of partition before the Partition. His pleasure in the Arab rejection of the blandishments of the Congress would seem to reinforce this view.

Attends the Inauguration of Pakistan

Less than three months after he returned from the Middle East, Jamal Mian was faced by the Independence and Partition of India. He decided with this friend, Dr Faridi, that they would attend the inauguration celebrations in Karachi on 14 August. They were to be joined by the Raja of Mahmudabad

---

19. Undated letter, probably a copy, Ibid.

and Faridi's friend, Ehsan Kirmani. As they gathered in Delhi, it turned out that while the Raja and Jamal Mian were going to go by rail, Dr Faridi and his friend, perhaps deterred by the news of the appalling killings which were taking place on trains to and from what was to be Pakistani and Indian Punjab, wanted to go by air. There was a big row as Jamal Mian wanted them to go by rail. 'But he was a stubborn man', Jamal Mian reflected later, 'and once he decided on a plan he would not change it. I, on the other hand, even when I had made a programme would often not execute it.'[20] So Dr Faridi and his friend went by air and Jamal Mian and the Raja went by rail. They travelled by Ajmer and Marwar. But when they got to Rorhi junction, the Raja suddenly decided that he would not go to Karachi but instead would travel to Mashshad in Iran by Quetta. Jamal Mian went to Karachi alone. After leaving his luggage in Bhopal House where Choudhry Khaliquzzaman's son was staying, he went in search of Dr Faridi. Together, they attended the inauguration on the 14th, which also happened to be 27 Ramadan 1366 AH, the Lailat al-Qadr, the 'Night of Power' or the 'Night of Destiny' when Muslims believe that the first verses of the Quran were revealed. It is also a night on which Muslims believe that the blessings and mercy of Allah are abundant. We do not know if Jamal Mian reflected on the coincidence of this holy day with the inauguration of Pakistan. Nevertheless, we do know that while attending a firework display on the evening of the 14th, the Prime Minister, Liaquat Ali Khan, asked him if he had enjoyed himself. Jamal Mian replied with a couplet from Hasrat Mohani:

---

20. Jamal Mian, 'Note on Dr Faridi', JMP.

I saw the beauty of your celebrations.

I destroyed my home and saw it go up like fireworks.[21]

During the visit, Ikramullah, who was Secretary to the Ministry of Foreign Affairs, offered Jamal Mian an ambassadorship. He turned it down on the grounds that he had not been an employee before and did not know the work of diplomacy.[22]

A period of uncertainty and fear

On 17 August, Jamal Mian, with Dr Faridi and his friend, flew back to Delhi. They found the atmosphere very tense. When they reached Delhi railway station to take the train to Lucknow, there was a crowd of young people carrying banners, shouting 'Jai Hind' and forcing travellers to donate money to their cause. They had just bought their tickets and were walking towards the Lucknow train when one of the youths tried to pin a small flag with 'Jai Hind' written on it to the lapel of Dr Faridi's sherwani. 'Dr Faridi slapped the boy's face', Jamal Mian recalled. 'There was pandemonium. We started running towards the train chased by the crowd. Thank God we got onto the moving train and locked the doors and the windows from the inside. I told Dr Faridi "You nearly had us all killed today".'[23]

---

21. Jamal al-Din `Abd al-Wahhab, 'Awraq-i Parishan' or 'Scattered Leaves' mss. no pagination, copied August 1950 by Jamaluddin Abdul Wahhab and written on paper headed UP Muslim League, JMP.

22. Annotation by Jamal Mian 12.10.94 in Stanley Wolpert, *Jinnah of Pakistan* (New York: Oxford University Press, 1984), Jamal Mian Catalogue no. 1905.

23. Jamal Mian, 'Note on Dr Faridi', JMP.

This life-threatening fracas at Delhi Railway Station was
Jamal Mian's introduction to the madness which was sweeping
through northern India. Choudhry Khaliquzzaman writes
with authority:

> The period between August and September 1947 was the
> blackest period in Indian history—a period of woe, misery and
> suffering for the unprotected and the unwary. Neighbours were
> killing neighbours, friends friends, and human life had lost all
> significance. Areas which had been their homes for generations
> and generations were denuded of people. Cities and towns lost
> their character, for properties and men changed overnight, the
> old faces disappeared as if they had never existed.[24]

Jamal Mian, a keen reader of newspapers and listener to
the wireless, would have been well aware of the development
of what has been called a 'national crisis' in both India and
Pakistan, whose borders were finally defined on 17 August
1947. He would have had an idea of the vast movement across
the new borders, which has been estimated as being as many
as 8 million people by November 1947.[25] At this stage, he
would have known much more regarding the slaughter of
Hindus, Sikhs, and Muslims as they travelled on foot and by
rail than when he travelled to Karachi; the news of the trains
that turned up at Lahore or Delhi full of dead bodies could
not be concealed. He would certainly have known that life in
many of the towns of northern India had become unsafe for
Muslims. For weeks, Delhi was out of control as armed gangs

24. Khaliquzzaman, *Pathway*, 396.
25. Yasmin Khan, *The Great Partition: The Making of India and Pakistan*
(New Haven and London: Yale University Press, 2007), 156.

hunted down Muslims, seeking their lives and their property. Curfews were imposed in many towns and cities. Hasrat Mohani's diary gives a good sense of what this meant day by day in Cawnpore as well as the considerable efforts he had to make to try to get Muslims, who felt they had been unjustly imprisoned, released. His diary also tells us of the stratagem he adopted to avoid the dangers of Delhi railway station as he travelled there to attend the Constituent Assembly; he would get off the train from Cawnpore at Ghaziabad and take a lorry with a Muslim driver into the city.[26] Nothing brought home the dangers of the situation more effectively than the violent death of friends and acquaintances. On 18 October 1947, Shafi, the brother of Rafi Ahmad Kidwai and a civil servant in Mussoorie, was stabbed to death as he walked to work at the Municipal offices. That he was, like his brother, a dedicated nationalist did not save him. It was enough that he was a Muslim.[27]

Two particular events in October would have impressed on Jamal Mian how his world was changing. The first took place on 8 October 1947 when, by an administrative order which was followed up by the UP Official Language Act of 1951, Hindi in the Devanagari script was declared to be the state language. From 1953 onwards, Hindi became the sole medium for writing High School examinations.[28] This brought to an end a process of displacing Urdu written in the Persian script with Hindi in the Devanagari script which had

---

26. Hasrat Mohani, 'Roznama', 8, 12, 13, 17, 19 August 1947, 15, 16, 26, 27, 28, 29, 30 September 1947, 3, 4, 13, 15, 16, 17 September 1947, 17 November 1947 etc., JMP.

27. Khan, *Great Partition*, 164-x66.

28. Mushirul Hasan, *Legacy of a Divided Nation: India's Muslims since Independence* (Delhi: Oxford University Press, 1997), 148–60.

been going on since the 1860s. It had been driven forward
by Hindu revivalists and had been helped from time to time
by well-meaning British administrators, who wanted the
language of government and education to be congruent with
the preferences of the majority of the province's population.[29]
What it meant was that a language and a cultural heritage
that Muslims shared with many elite Hindus became just a
Muslim language and a symbol of Muslim rule and culture. It
also meant a further marginalisation of the shared persianate
culture of the elites who had once served the Mughals
and subsequently served, and opposed, the British. Jamal
Mian would have known that this development was likely.
Nonetheless, it would also have reinforced his sense of the
beleaguered position, particularly of north Indian Muslims,
now that Pakistan had been established.

The second event, which came a little later, was the sudden
move of Khaliquzzaman, who had long been Lucknow's
leading Muslim politician, to Pakistan. Up to this point,
Khaliquzzaman had always insisted on his determination
to stay in India. Moreover, he was one of the eight UP
Muslim members of the Constituent Assembly. Earlier in
the year, Jinnah had asked him to lead the Indian Muslims.
Khaliquzzaman had demurred, saying that Nawab Ismail
Khan would be more acceptable to Hindu India than him
in the light of his desertion of the Congress for the League
in 1937. But then, he accepted Jinnah's request. When on 11
June 1947 the time came to elect the Muslim League leader
in the Assembly, Khaliquzzaman supported Nawab Ismail
Khan, but the message came from Jinnah that Khaliquzzaman
should have the role, which was logical given that he had been

---

29. Robinson, *Separatism*, 69–77.

made overall leader of India's Muslims. Thus, Khaliquzzaman
was elected. Nawab Ismail Khan was not pleased.[30] In his
leadership role, Khaliquzzaman had clearly followed Jinnah's
advice that 'the minorities should be loyal to the State to
which they belong'. When the time came on 27 July to
approve the new Indian flag with Asoka's *chakra* or wheel on
it, he spoke firmly in support of Nehru's proposal. When five
minutes after midnight on 14 August Jawaharlal Nehru, in the
presence of the Viceroy spoke in the Constituent Assembly to
welcome Indian independence, Khaliquzzaman immediately
followed him with similar sentiments. On both occasions,
Nehru showed a warm appreciation of Khaliquzzaman's
statesmanlike approach.[31]

Khaliquzzaman spent August and September 1947 doing
what he could to ameliorate the attempts of Hindus to avenge
themselves on Muslims for the creation of Pakistan; it led to
a temporary nervous breakdown.[32] Then, Sir Zafrullah Khan,
the leader of the Pakistan delegation to the United Nations,
although he admitted that this was only his personal view,
issued a public threat to the Government of India, warning
that unless it took steps:

> to end the slaughter of Muslims a formal complaint would be
> filed with the United Nations. If satisfaction is not obtained
> the Government of Pakistan may have to resort to direct
> measures.[33]

Khaliquzzaman, rightly concerned that statements of this

---

30. Khaliquzzaman, *Pathway*, 388–90; Jamal Mian Tape 6a, JMP.
31. Khaliquzzaman, *Pathway*, 393–5.
32. Ibid. 396–400.
33. Ibid. 401.

kind would make the situation of India's Muslims worse, produced an immediate rejoinder, dated 20 September 1947, in the *National Herald* in which he noted: that non-Muslim minorities had also suffered in the West Punjab; that given the way power had been handed over by the British, the state, both in India and Pakistan, had found itself helpless in the face of popular violence; that neither the Congress government nor the Congress organization could be regarded as complicit in the violence; and that Mahatma Gandhi was 'straining every nerve' to bring peace to troubled regions.[34]

Towards the end of September, Gandhi asked Khaliquzzaman to come and see him in Delhi. Rafi Ahmad Kidwai had to make special arrangements to receive him at the airport as conditions were still not safe for Muslims. Gandhi asked Khaliquzzaman to go to Karachi and work with the Pakistan government to dissuade Sindhi Hindus from migrating to India. This would, he said, make his work of trying to bring peace to India much easier.[35] Khaliquzzaman went to Karachi and met Jinnah on 5 October. Jinnah gave him a dressing down for his response to Sir Zafrullah Khan's statement saying: 'It has hurt us very much'. Jinnah was dissatisfied with his response that a statement from a Muslim of India could not be regarded as binding, or having any effect on, the Government of Pakistan. Khaliquzzaman replied to Jinnah saying that he would resign as the leader of India's Muslims to enable someone who had Jinnah's confidence to hold the position. He then made the decision to stay in Pakistan.[36] What is striking about this incident is that Jinnah, as the ruler of

---

34. Ibid. 402–3.
35. Ibid. 404.
36. Ibid. 410–13.

a separate state, still felt that he had authority over Indian Muslims, and that Khaliquzzaman was willing to acquiesce in this. It says much for Jinnah's authority over India's Muslims.

There was a particular reason why Jamal Mian should have been shocked by this development. Before Khaliquzzaman went to see Gandhi, he contacted Jamal Mian to say that it had been decided that he should go on a peace mission to Karachi and that he wanted Jamal Mian to join him. Khaliquzzaman would let him know when he should come to Delhi to join the mission. Jamal Mian was still waiting for Khaliquzzaman's call when, after Eid on 25 October, the son of Mushir Husain Qidwai came to see him and said:

> Jamal Mian I have heard something rather strange. I had gone to see Rafi Sahib for Eid. He said: 'Khaliq Sahib is not coming back now. He is calling his whole family over by chartered plane and taking all his household goods and he will not return from Karachi.' I said; 'What are you talking about? Khaliq Sahib has said he is going on a peace mission and was going to take me, and has asked me to be ready.' He said: 'No, no, Rafi Sahib does not lie. What he said is true'.[37]

The desertion of the Indian Muslims by their designated leader was followed by a more acute issue which increasingly agitated them as they confronted the realities of survival in a Congress-ruled India. How should they be represented politically? The Muslim League was now seen, by some at least, as a provocation to the Hindus and, therefore, an incubus. On 6 October, a group of UP Muslims urged their fellow Muslims to join the Congress 'because it is, as it always

---

37. Jamal Mian Tape 6A, JMP.

has been, the one political party that can establish a stable, truly democratic government and ensure that prosperity and progress of all citizens without any distinction of caste or creed.'[38] On 10 October, a group of Delhi Muslims observed an 'Anti-Pakistan Day', and a 'Dissolve Muslim League Day' a fortnight later.[39] Hasrat Mohani's diary gives a good sense of how Muslims were thinking about alternative representation at the time. Moreover, we should remember that while he was doing this he was simultaenously a Muslim League member of the Constituent Assembly, a Muslim League member of the UP Legislative Assembly, and a member of the Muslim League Council. On 25 August, he was pleased to have persuaded one Aziz Ahmad to have joined Sarat Bhose's Socialist Republic Party. On 12 September, he noted that Muslims must stop being a religious party and become a socialist party. On 9 October, he noted that a new political formation which was being discussed, the Azad Hind Party, must not have any religious affiliation. On 4 November, he told himself that the Muslim League should stay on as an Opposition party but change is name to 'Independent Socialist Party'. On 15 November, Hasrat argued at the Provincial Muslim League Council in Lucknow that the League should become an Independent Socialist Party. Then on 4 December, he noted that he had persuaded Sardar Ali Sabri to become a member of the Socialist Republican Party.[40] Hasrat Mohani may have been a senior Muslim Leaguer but in these difficult months, when it was increasingly becoming clear that a dominant

---

38. Statement of Syed Abdullah Brelvi, M. Y. Nurie, K. A. Hamied, and Moinuddin Harris in Hasan, *Legacy*, 189, fn. 82.
39. Ibid. 189.
40. Hasrat Mohani, 'Roznama', 28 August, 12 September, 9 October, 4, 15 November, 4 December 1947, JMP.

Congress needed opposition, he was trying to put together
a Socialist opposition of some kind which might embrace
elements of the old Muslim League.

Jamal Mian would have been very aware of how North
Indian Muslim ideas were moving in general, and of those
of Hasrat Mohani in particular who often stayed in Farangi
Mahall, when in December 1947 he went to attend the All-
India Muslim League Council meeting in Karachi. The
meeting had been called to consider the fate of the All-India
Muslim League in the new circumstances of two separate
sovereign states. Three hundred members of the Council
attended the sessions in Karachi's Khaliqdina Hall on 14–15
December of whom 160 came from India. 'When I arrived in
Karachi', Jamal Mian recalled:

> Lakhs of refugees from different provinces of India were
> dotting [sic] about uprooted. Thousands of old Muslim
> League workers had become victims of untold suffering and
> helplessness. On the other hand, the leaders of the Muslim
> League who had now attained their status as Ministers
> were so much engrossed in official duties and governmental
> responsibilities that they had no time to attend to the misery
> of their brothers. Apart from this, I observed that people who
> held high posts were oblivious of the conditions of the Muslims
> who were left across the border in India.[41]

This comment of support for the poor and needy against
those who enriched themselves at the hands of the state flowed
from the same world view as his attack in the UP Assembly in

41. Essay by Jamal Mian on Jinnah in English. File entitled 'Writings on
    Jinnah Saheb in Urdu and English', Ibid.

the previous year on the emoluments which UP ministers were preparing to award themselves.[42] Jamal Mian noted, critically, the pomp and circumstance with which Jinnah entered the Hall, a Governor-General with ADCs trailing in his wake; the fact that ministers of the new state sat on the platform and not members of the League Working Committee; and the lordly way in which Jinnah dismissed justifiable objections from the floor that the League constitution could not be changed by the League Council but only in an annual or open session.[43]

The main resolution which was to divide the All-India Muslim League into two Leagues, independent and separate from each other, was proposed by Liaquat Ali Khan and seconded by Abdur Rab Nishtar. The preamble to the resolution spoke of the League's 'ultimate triumph in the birth of the largest Muslim State and the fifth largest of all States in the world.'[44] This use of the term 'Muslim State' led Jamal Mian to propose an amendment that the words 'Muslim State' should be dropped from the text of the resolution. 'I said', he recalled 'that Islamic History had witnessed a number of bad rulers who in the name of Islam had committed all sorts of sins and cruelties. Then turning to Quaid-e-Azam, I remarked "Now Your Honour should not open a new chapter." After this I turned towards the Ministers and described them thus: "If one visits their houses, one fails to observe the glory of the Muslim rulers."' In winding up his speech, he attacked Jinnah directly for having declared in his speech that the Indian Muslims should boycott the Azad Muslim Conference and that they should organize themselves on new lines and

---

42. See Chapter Six.
43. Essay by Jamal Mian on Jinnah in English, JMP.
44. Pirzada, *Foundations* 2, 575.

bring forth new leadership. He criticized Khaliquzzaman for deserting India for Pakistan. He criticized Liaquat Ali Khan for not working to keep the League organization going in India at Partition, and now it was withering away in the provinces. As Jamal Mian sat down there was uproar. Jinnah adjourned the session.[45]

When the discussion on the resolution resumed the following day, Jinnah addressed the Council and said:

Let it be clear that Pakistan is going to be a Muslim State based on Islamic ideals. It was not going to be an ecclesiastical State. In Islam there is no discrimination as far as citizenship is concerned. The whole world even UNO, has characterized Pakistan as a 'Muslim State'.

There must be a Muslim League in Hindustan. If you are thinking of anything else you are finished. If you want to wind up the League you can do so; but I think it would be a great mistake. I know there is an attempt by Maulana Azad and others are trying to break the identity of Muslims of India. Do not allow it. Do not do it.[46]

Jinnah then asked those who had proposed amendments to withdraw them. According to Pirzada's record, which is as near as we can get to an official record of this occasion, Jamal Mian withdrew his amendment. But, according to Jamal Mian's record, the amendment was put to the vote and lost.[47] The resolution was then put to the vote and carried

---

45. Essay by Jamal Mian on Jinnah in English JMP.

46. Pirzada, *Foundations*, 2, 571–2.

47. Ibid. 572; Essay by Jamal Mian on Jinnah in English, JMP.

with just ten votes against. Liaquat Ali Khan was elected
the convenor of the new Pakistan Muslim League and
Mohammad Ismail (1896–1972), President of the Madras
Provincial Muslim League, was elected convenor of the new
Indian Muslim League. Their sessions were to be held soon
in Karachi and Madras.[48]

The following evening, Jinnah invited the members of the
League Council to tea in the Governor-General's house. It did
not take Jamal Mian long to realize that most of the ministers
and politicians were annoyed with him, which was hardly
surprising, given what he had said about them. But Jinnah
was not:

> Qaid-e-Azam was sitting on a sofa alone and as I passed him,
> he beckoned to me and asked me to sit down by his side.
> He appeared ill at that time and was very calm. Turning to
> me he said that he was not displeased with my speech, that
> I had done right in speaking as I did, and that it was very
> necessary for someone to remind his Ministers of their duties
> and responsibilities. ... This reaction of Qaid-e-Azam to my
> scathing attack the previous day bears ample testimony to
> his true greatness. I little realised that this was to be my last
> meeting with him.[49]

Jamal Mian and the assassination of Gandhi

After returning to Lucknow from Karachi, Jamal Mian went

---

48. Pirzada, *Foundations*, 2, 572.
49. Essay by Jamal Mian on Jinnah in English JMP.

to Calcutta, amongst other things, to see the Ispahanis. He returned to Lucknow in time for the Farangi Mahall `Urs on 8 and 9 January. Here he met Hasrat Mohani as he was to do on several occasions around League and Assembly business.[50] They will most certainly have discussed Jinnah's insistence that the Muslims should keep the Muslim League, or some form of communal representation going, as against Abul Kalam Azad's insistence, when he met a group of five UP Muslim League leaders at a Lucknow hotel on 27 December, that they must abandon Muslim institutions.[51]

Around 28 January, Jamal Mian went to Delhi where he met Mahatma Gandhi on the 29th. Gandhi was a supporter of Sufism and a regular visitor to saints' shrines. Gandhi had discovered that because of the current communal difficulties, the `Urs of Hazrat Bakhtiar Kaki was not being celebrated. He made sure that the `Urs did take place in safety and security and joined its celebrations.[52] The day after his meeting with the Jamal Mian, the Mahatma was assassinated. Jamal Mian was asked to make a tribute to him on All-India Radio. Early on in his talk he mentioned that his father had likened Gandhi to Sarmad, a free-thinking Sufi and an apostle of love, who had greatly impressed Dara Shikoh, Shah Jahan's designated successor. After Aurangzeb won the battle for the succession to his father, he had Sarmad executed. Jamal Mian told his audience that he had heard that some Delhi Muslims were planning to take some flowers from Gandhi's cortege and bury them near the grave of Sarmad by the Juma Masjid.

---

50. Hasrat Mohani, 'Roznama', 8, 9, 11, 14, 15, 16, 17, 24 January 1948, Ibid.
51. Hasrat Mohani, 'Roznama', 27 December 1947, Ibid.
52. Jamal Mian, Talk on All-India Radio in Urdu on the death of Gandhi, February 1948, Ibid.

Thus, the lives of two lovers of God and humankind would be symbolically united.[53] Jamal Mian continued:

> Gandhiji was always a friend of the Muslims. Those who are familiar with recent politics will know how hard Gandhi had struggled for reconciliation and understanding. It was his personality that made all agree on the June 3rd plan and the nation achieved freedom. And it is because of him that Hindus and Muslims are as close to each other as they were before British rule.
>
> It is because of his Muslim-friendly attitude that when anyone says that he was a leader for only Hindus that Muslims feel aggrieved. Gandhiji was everybody's. But Muslims believe that he was theirs. Gandhiji trusted us and loved us. He gave his life for us and left us the responsibility to spread his message of peace and truth and to fulfil those wishes of his that remained unfulfilled in his life. Thanks be to God that Muslims are able to recognise and respect his qualities and are today mourning his death as they have not done for any other leader. And it is not only Indian Muslims for whom he gave his life, but also in Pakistan, and in other countries, we learn from newspapers and broadcasts that his sacrifice and favours are duly recognised. ...

---

53. Sarmad the Martyr was also a central figure in the religious understanding of Abul Kalam Azad; he was a man who through love rose above the surface elements of Hinduism and Islam to reach the greater truth, the understanding of the 'oneness of religion' which was the ultimate goal of true believers. Ian Henderson Douglas, Gail Minault, and Christian W. Troll, eds., *Abul Kalam Azad: An Intellectual and Religious Biography* (Delhi: Oxford University Press, 1988), 286–90.

From the day of this fateful event in Delhi, the whole world is expressing praise of Gandhiji's qualities and goodness. Some are calling him the Himalaya of greatness, others refer to him as an ocean of love and a sun of leadership. In my opinion, he was a human being and an example of humanity in front of which the mountains of greatness, the force of oceans and the brightness of suns seems inadequate.

What was his message? That is also being related in different ways. I feel his message was as simple as it was attractive: when the poison of intolerance and prejudice had made our hearts immune to brutality and violence, when the fervour of our enmities prevented us from hearing the cries of the innocent, when the intoxication of self-preservation and opportunism had made us oblivious to the needs of mankind, it was Gandhiji who awakened us by removing the curtain [of one sidedness] from our eyes, and by filling our hearts with the need for love, forgiveness and tolerance, honesty, truthfulness and the struggle for truth. And his blood flowed to teach us how to become human. The truth is that to die for the truth has that glory, that greatness, that devotion and that steadfastness which is the essence and heart of humanity.[54]

Jamal Mian seems to be doing at least three things in this talk. First, he was providing a well-judged assessment of Gandhi's greatness, not just as an Indian but also as a citizen of the world. Second, he was saying how much this Hindu, who was assassinated by another Hindu, meant to India's Muslims. Therefore trying, trying thus, in a small way, to alleviate some of their problems of the moment. Third, in

---

54. Jamal Mian, Talk on All-India Radio on the death of Gandhi, JMP.

setting out his understanding of Gandhi's greatness, he was
also, as we all do when we express ourselves, revealing much
about himself. Thus, the period of momentous events came to
a close. Jamal Mian did not know it at the time, but in the six
weeks from the end of the All-India Muslim League Council
meeting to the assassination of Gandhi, he had seen for the
last time, and at first hand experienced, the greatness of both
Jinnah and Gandhi.

13. The Middle East Delegation with its aeroplane supplied by the Turkish government.

14. Turkish audiences, and particularly women, loved to hear Jamal Mian speak Urdu.

حديثه بإخوانه العلميه ة سوريا الى مولانا جمال الدين كلبرلوي

دتشق ٢٢/٥/ ١٢٦٦ الوافق ٧/٤/ ١٩٤٧

15. The Middle East Delegation in Syria; Jamal Mian sits next to his leader
M. A. H. Ispahani in the centre.

16. The Raja of Jahangirabad, a key supporter of the young Jamal Mian.

17. The Middle East Delegation in Cairo.

10

Things fall apart, 1949–50

AFTER ATTENDING THE LAST MEETING OF THE ALL-INDIA
Muslim League in December 1947 and coming to terms with
the death of Gandhi in January 1948, Jamal Mian returned to
his old life in Lucknow. Here, he focussed on his tea business,
on trying to keep his *Hamdam* newspaper going, on his
service for the Sunni Waqf Board, on his service for the Ajmer
Dargah Committee of Management, and on his trusteeship
of the Jahangirabad estate. All of this took place alongside his
membership of the UP Legislative Assembly, his general care
for the Farangi Mahall madrasah, and his observance of the
established pattern of the Farangi Mahall spiritual year.

However, it soon became apparent that the old pattern of life,
the old certainties, might be difficult to sustain. For the months
and years that followed Partition, the Indian Muslims in
general, and those of the UP in particular, were a beleaguered
people. They were treated as being personally responsible for
the emergence of Pakistan. Many Muslim government officials
who had opted to stay in India found themselves punished
by the loss of their jobs. There were arbitrary arrests, as the
diaries of Hasrat Mohani, a vigorous worker for his local
community, reveal.[1] Muslims were harassed. Muslim travellers
on the railways, even though they had bought their tickets,

---

1. Hasrat Mohani, 'Roznama', 14, 17, 19, 20, April 11–12 May 1948, JMP.

were forced to pay extra sums to railway officials and the
police if they wanted to travel.[2] Muslims and their houses were
searched for arms. It did not matter if the Muslims concerned
were senior officials or even, as in the case of Syed Mahmud
(a spiritual follower of Jamal Mian's father) a member of the
Bihar government.[3] In the UP, Hindus took advantage of the
new Muslim weakness to impose their cultural preferences
and deepen their political advantage. We have already noted
how in October 1947, Hindi was made the sole language of
administration, an action which was soon followed by the
banning of cow slaughter.[4] Muslims continued to migrate to
Pakistan. If in 1947, 200,000 left Delhi for Karachi, between
1947 and 1950, a further 300,000 more did. 'The atmosphere
was so bad for Muslims' recalled one Aligarh citizen, 'that
everybody wanted to migrate from here.'[5]

Jamal Mian Experiences Blow after Blow

1948 was an utterly depressing year for Jamal Mian both in
his public life and in his personal affairs. In the public arena,
the consequences of Pakistan and overwhelming Congress
dominance, sustaining a vengeful Hindu element, came to
be worked out. The marginalising of Urdu, or indeed of
any language which, like Hindustani, maintained elements

2. Ibid. 5 February 1948.
3. Syed Mahmud to S. K. Sinha c. 1948, V. N. Datta and H. Cleghorne
    eds., *A Nationalist Muslim and Indian Politics* (Delhi: The Macmillan
    Company of India Ltd., 1974), 263–4.
4. Hasan, *Legacy*, 147.
5. E. S. Mann, *Boundaries and Identities: Muslims, Work and Status in Aligarh*
    (Delhi: Sage, 1992), 60 quoted in Ibid. 173.

of Persian, Arabic, and Chaghatai Turki, continued. The impact of the UP official language decision was quickly felt as, for instance, Urdu teachers began to lose their jobs in schools.[6] The discussion on official language policy in the Constituent Assembly, which continued for most of the year, made clear the future dominance of Hindi as Hindi in the Devanagari script was made the official national language of India. Hindustani had some support in the early Constituent Assembly discussions as it was a language which was widely shared by the peoples of northern India. But its claims were undermined by Partition and by the determination of the supporters of Hindi, a large group in the Constituent Assembly, that their language should triumph and should do so in the most sankritized form they could persuade people to accept.[7] Hasrat Mohani was a strong supporter of Urdu, in particular for education in UP schools, a stubborn position in the face of the political facts, like so many in his life. He made his point by refusing to use a single Hindi word in his speeches in Parliament.[8] Towards the end of the year, Jamal Mian was publicly protesting against the marginalising of his culture. In his Eid sermon on 14 October 1948 in Lucknow he inveighed against those 'people who think they can change our language merely through enactment of laws, or eradicate all cultures, replacing them with one homogenous culture, by fiery speeches, or stop *Qurbani* [cow sacrifice] through use of the powers of a District Board or municipal orders.'[9] Four

---

6. Hasrat Mohani, 'Roznama', 24 February 1948, JMP.
7. Granville Austin, *The Indian Constitution: Cornerstone of a Nation* (London: Oxford University Press, 1966), 274–85.
8. Hasrat Mohani, 'Roznama', 15 June 1948, JMP.
9. Khutba on Eid ul Azha, 1948, Lucknow, File 'Old Personal Essay and Speeches', Ibid.

days later, he will have noted how the new session of the UP
Legislative Assembly was dominated by plans to promote
sanskritized Hindi. He will also have noted how the Persian
couplets which decorated the Assembly chamber had been
removed, an act which led Hasrat Mohani to tell his diary
that 'such a narrow-minded government will not last long.'[10]
Arguably, Jamal Mian expressed his opposition most effectively
in sarcastic poetry, published in his *Hamdam* newspaper:

> Having studied the desire of the national leaders, the great
> poet, Sharir Banbasi writes a

National Poem

Reason demands my friends that you start studying Hindi
If you want to live, then friends you must study Hindi
If you want to earn a living, friends, you must study Hindi
If you want to live in Hindustan, then Hindi is compulsory
Don't intrigue any more, friends, you must study Hindi!
We ask from our hearts, study Hindi at once.

Reason demands my friends that you start studying Hindi
If you want to live, then friends you must study Hindi
Move forward from *kufr* and *Iman*, and become a philosopher
Leave sectarianism and become human!
Become an enemy of Urdu and an opponent of Persian
Instead from head to toe become a DEVANAGARI man.[11]

---

10. Hasrat Mohani, 'Roznama', 16 October 1948, Ibid.
11. Poem published in *Hamdam* but no date given. File, Old Personal
    Essays and Speeches, Ibid.

Running alongside the language and script issues was the fate of the Muslim League in particular and how Muslim interests should be protected in general. Abul Kalam Azad, the leading Indian Muslim political figure of the moment, continued the line he had put to the UP Muslim League leaders at Lucknow the previous December that Muslims should abandon communal organizations. In meetings in Delhi and Lucknow in April and May 1948 he set out to convert the Jamiat ul-Ulama-i Hind into a non-political body, indeed a purely religious body, devoted to the community's interest.[12] In February and March 1948, Hasrat Mohani spent much energy trying to organize Muslim Leaguers, Socialists, and other political elements into a 'Left Front' opposition to the Congress.[13] After one of his meetings trying to build Muslims and others into an opposition front he had a fascinating psychological reaction as he attended the 'Urs of Hazrat Nizamuddin in Delhi, 'I felt clearly while I was there' he told his diary, 'that no power could remove Muslim history and culture from Delhi.'[14] On 10 March, the meeting of the Indian Muslim League under Muhammad Ismail's chairmanship, which had been prefigured at the last meeting of the All-India Muslim League in Karachi in December, took place in Madras. Muhammad Ismail wanted to keep the Muslim League going, but the majority of those present, in deference to the mood of the times, would only support its continuance as a party of social and cultural struggle.[15]

---

12. Hasan, *Legacy*, 211–12.
13. Hasrat Mohani, 'Roznama', 16, 20, 21, 27, 29 February and 3, 4, 5, 7, 8 March 1948, JMP.
14. 24 Februry 1948, Ibid.
15. 10 March 1948, Ibid.

These developments set Jamal Mian thinking about how best, as a devout follower of the Prophet, he could serve the people. On 29 March 1948, he wrote thus to Nawab Ismail Khan:

I had, after the last meeting, decided to resign from the Council, but the letter was never posted. However, an incident took place recently which quite unsettled me, and increased my anxiety. And I have begun to feel that staying in present political parties is a waste of time and that we are not really serving humanity or any real service to Muslims either. The details of this crisis in my thought are as follows. I had gone to Rudauli *Sharif* and there was a young boy who used to operate the fan in the afternoon, and I used to have conversations from time to time and ask him questions. I found out that he was the son of a dhobi. His name is Qaisar. He works all day and gets 4 annas for his labour with which he looks after his blind brother, sister and mother. I asked him if his father was alive. In answering my question he just burst into tears. I asked him: 'Do you want to go to school?' He replied 'yes, but can I study? If I stop working we would have nothing to eat.' This young lad's honesty and his character was further proved when I tried to give him some money as a gift and he refused to take it.

From that day I have been troubled by thoughts of how many millions of boys and humans like these are in this country who have no support for food, who have no shelter or home, who have no opportunity for education or to gain wealth. In such conditions Pakistan, Freedom, Muslim Nation, Hindu Majority and many other political issues seem so irrelevant!

I do not want to join the Congress, Communist Party, or any

other organization. But I do feel that I want to separate myself from the political toing and froing, and think seriously about whether in fact I can, in the light of Islamic injunctions, and the example of the Prophet, do some service for the people or not, and to act upon what conclusion I can reach, and to present to the leadership of the nation some of my ideas.

It is a strange coincidence that my original desire to resign was purely on a personal basis, but then things happened which opened my eyes to new issues. [Jamal Mian then put his ideas into verse ending with the lines: 'May there be a caravan led by the Prophet's example/You have spent your life screaming and shouting O JAMAL/Do something that will please the Prophet now!] I can assure you that I do not want to create any trouble either in the Muslim League nor am I capable of doing so. I want to steer clear of elections, party politics, and other disputes. If I have any anxiety or want to do something, then I will make sure I consult you before embarking on any course of action. I hope that, despite my withdrawal from the scene, I will not be deprived of your kindness and blessings.[16]

We do not know if this letter was actually sent to Nawab Ismail Khan, or perhaps it is just a copy; it is not clear from the evidence in the file. Nevertheless, it does give us excellent insight into Jamal Mian's state of mind and his concerns about how best he might serve the people after Independence and Partition. However, despite his doubts and his desire to leave the scene, Jamal Mian did not. Later in the year, all the old leadership of the provincial Muslim League, with of course the

16. Jamal Mian to Nawab Ismail Khan, 29 March 1948. File 'Old Personal Essays and Speeches', JMP.

exception of Khaliquzzaman who was now in Pakistan, met at Farangi Mahall. Taking their lead from the majority at the Madras meeting, they agreed that the League should refrain from Parliamentary activities and limit itself to the 'struggle for Muslim rights and their protection'. It was resolved that there should be only one organization representing Muslim interests. Z. H. Lari was to be the leader, Nawab Aizaz Rasul the General Secretary and Jamal Mian Secretary. Z. H. Lari set out to bring all Muslims onto their platform. The Jamiat ul-Ulama-i Hind was at the same time indicating that all Muslims should join their organization.[17]

The second half of 1948 saw a third blow for many Indian Muslims in general and to the world of Jamal Mian in particular. This was the so-called 'police action' of September 1948 by which the Government of India forcibly brought the largest princely state of the former British India under its control. For at least 150 years, Hyderabad had been a source of employment for north Indian Muslims and, more recently, it had become an important source of subsidy for Muslim institutions. Hasrat Mohani's diary gives a sense of the horror with which from northern India he observed the unfolding tragedy in the Deccan.[18]

In June he was praying to God that the independence of Hyderabad would be respected.[19] When he heard of the declaration of emergency in Hyderabad on 26 July, he exclaimed 'Is there no limit to this man's [Patel] enmity? Does he want to destroy the Indian Muslims?'[20] When on

---

17. Jamal Mian to G. B. Pant, Chief Minister, UP, 24 February 1949, Ibid.
18. Hasrat Mohani 'Roznama', 15 June, Ibid.
19. 26 July, 8, 18, 27, 31 August, 3, 17, 18, 19, 21 September, 18 October 1948, Ibid.
20. Ibid. 26 July, 1948.

17 September he learned that the Nizam had accepted his defeat, he was clearly upset. He wondered if events had taken this turn because the Nizam had flirted with Shiism, or perhaps it was the revenge of Tipu Sultan! It was most certainly 'an example of English perfidy and failure to protect their friends.'[21] The crowning insult, from the Muslim point of view, was the resolution passed by the UP government in the Assembly congratulating the Government of India on its action in Hyderabad.[22]

During the period of the 'police action', between one in ten and one in five of all Muslim males in Hyderabad city were killed, while up to 40,000 Muslims were killed in the state as a whole.[23] As the Government of India sought to re-balance the Hyderabad administration in communal terms, at least 10,000 Muslims lost their jobs in the Police, Military, and Bureaucracy.[24] Jamal Mian would not have known the scale and detail of these events; Pandit Sunderlal's report on the massacres was, until recently, suppressed by the Government of India.[25] Nevertheless, his relatives and spiritual followers in the state would have kept him informed of the nature of events. Moreover, he would have been acutely aware of one outcome of the demise of Hyderabad; Farangi Mahall lost the institutional grant which had long been paid to it by the Nizam. After some lobbying by Qutb Mian in late 1948,

21. Ibid. 17 September 1948.
22. Ibid. 18 October 1948.
23. A.G. Noorani, *The Destruction of Hyderabad* (New Delhi: Tulika Books, 2013), pp. 238–39.
24. Taylor C. Sherman, *Muslim Belonging in Secular India: Negotiating Citizenship in Post-Colonial Hyderabad* (Cambridge: Cambridge University Press, 2015), pp 92–109.
25. Noorani, *Destruction*, p. *xxii*.

Jawaharlal Nehru achieved a stay of execution but the grant was stopped in 1950.[26] Things seemed so bad in the autumn of 1948 that Hasrat Mohani planned to give two months of his stipend as a member of the Legislative Assembly, Rs 1,300, to Qutb Mian 'so that his troubles may be lessened'.[27]

Throughout this period, Jamal Mian was producing the *Hamdam*, the daily newspaper which he had restarted in 1946. Jamal Mian had installed the *Hamdam* press in a part of his property which was next to one owned by the Bahr ul-Ulumis. This gave them an opportunity to stir up the old family enmity which went back through the non co-operation movement to the time when Jamal Mian's ancestor, Alauddin, succeeded the great Bahr ul-Ulum in Madras rather than their ancestor, Abdul Rab. In July 1947, Muhammad Kamil Bahr ul-Ulum's lawyer had notified Jamal Mian that they expected to receive damages for the mental and physical stress they had endured on account of the press at the rate of Rs 10 per diem.[28] Jamal Mian won the case. But the friction did not disappear. It was probably responsible for the stones which were being lobbed into the Farangi Mahall courtyards at this time and, as we shall see, the enmity continued in other ways into the 1950s.

Hasrat Mohani's diary, as with so many things at this time, keeps us informed about *Hamdam* and developments concerning it. Hasrat was a regular reader of *Hamdam* along with English language papers such as the *Pioneer* and *Statesman*. In February 1948, Jamal Mian was trying to buy a new press for *Hamdam*—perhaps one which might disturb his neighbours less, and Hasrat was working to get it removed

---

26. Sherman, *Muslim Belonging*, p. 81.
27. Hasrat Mohani, 'Roznama' 23 October 1948, JMP.
28. R. F. Mathur, Vakil, to Muhammad Jamaluddin Abdul Wahab, Proprietor, *Hamdam* Press, Lucknow, 5 July 1947, Personal File, Ibid.

from some form of blacklist.[29] In March 1948, Jamal Mian's ambitions were growing as he wanted to start an English language paper to run alongside *Hamdam*.[30] In late October 1948, just at the time when Jamal Mian and Qutb Mian were deeply worried about the impact of the ending of the Hyderabad subsidy to the Farangi Mahall madrasah, Jamal Mian was working to turn *Hamdam* into a limited company. Hasrat was one of the directors, paying for Rs 2,000 worth of shares; others were also persuaded to invest.[31] Mirza Ahmed Ispahani thought this development a good move.[32]

No file of *Hamdam* of this period can be found in Jamal Mian's library. Jamal Mian's complete set disappeared when his property in Dacca was ransacked in the troubles surrounding the emergence of Bangladesh. Amongst the pieces of his writing for *Hamdam* that have survived is an elegy on the dire straits of Lucknow which suggests the depressed state in which his experiences since Independence and Partition had left him. Entitled *Shahr-e Ashob,* after the classical genre mourning lost cities, it consisted of forty stanzas of which the following are typical.

> How can I describe what state Lucknow is in?
> This city which was called the city of gardens,
> Which was considered the centre of fine things,
> Which was the envy of heaven,
> Alas! Fate and the heavens have been unkind to it.

---

29. Hasrat Mohani, 'Roznama', 23 February 1948, Ibid.
30. 20 March 1948, Ibid.
31. 23, 26 October, 2, 23 November 1948, Ibid.
32. Mirza Ahmed Ispahani to Jamal Mian, 9 January 1949, Ispahani Correspondence, Ibid.

Knowledge is no more, nor wisdom here
Goodness gone, beauty lost, love no more!
Adornment lost, attraction gone, allurement disappeared!
Festivity gone, spring and freshness no more!
Each thing is in lament at its helplessness!

Those protectors of peoples rights are no more
Those decent folk, those kind humans are no more
Those loyal friends and companions all gone
Those gracious Hindus gone, Muslims disappeared.
All replaced by vicious wolves and gangsters.[33]

At this low point, Jamal Mian was hit by two further blows. On 25 November, Sughra, his elder sister to whom he was deeply attached, as she was to him, died. As a tribute he published a collection of her poems which had survived. Condolences from friends made it clear that they knew how much Sughra meant to him.[34]

The second blow was the decline of Jamal Mian's tea business, the income from which, as other sources disappeared, had become more important. Among the reasons for the decline were the problems of selling tea branded with the Ispahani name, which was strongly associated with the movement for Pakistan, in a virulently anti-Muslim atmosphere, and the fact that Jamal Mian had not committed himself, heart and soul, to the business of selling. On 30 December 1948, Mirza Ahmed Ispahani's assessment was brutal:

---

33. Jamal Mian, 'Old Personal Essays and Speeches', Ibid.
34. Hasrat Mohani, 'Roznama', 29 November 1948, Ibid; Sadri Ispahani to Jamal Mian, 1 December 1948; Mirza Ahmed Ispahani to Jamal Mian, 30 December 1948, Ispahani Correspondence, Ibid.

With regard to the tea business, there is absolutely no justification for my office here to continue this business in the UP. I was shocked to see that expenses in 1948 have been Rs. 16,000/- against sales of Rs. 35,000/-. As you have always suggested that this business is of no interest to you, and that for the past 5 or 6 years that you have been handling the business you have not been able to put it on a profitable basis for the Company here it is best that the whole thing is shut down unless you have some arrangement by which you can meet the terms which are being offered to all Indian agents.[35]

A few days later, after Jamal Mian's accounts had been thoroughly inspected, Mirza Ahmed declared them 'most unsatisfactory'.[36] These were hard messages to receive from a man who had set him up in business and who had treated him like a son. Matters were not helped when an 'Ansari boy' whom Jamal Mian had recommended, had had to be dismissed for trying to organize the workers.[37]

The Crisis

Battered by these blows, Jamal Mian then had to face a crisis for the Muslim League in the UP Legislative Assembly. The Jamiat ul-Ulama-i Hind, doubtlessly feeling that its record in the Independence struggle gave it the upper hand, decided to take on the League. Their struggle was conducted at the

---

35. Mirza Ahmed Ispahani to Jamal Mian, 30 December 1948, Ispahani Correspondence, Ibid.
36. Mirza Ahmed Ispahani to Jamal Mian, 9 January 1949, Ibid.
37. Mirza Ahmed Ispahani to Jamal Mian 2 February 1949; Jamal Mian to Mirza Ahmed Ispahani, 25 February 1949, Ibid.

pettiest of levels. It happened thus. For a long time, the Muslim
League had rented offices in Laurence Mansion in Aminabad,
Lucknow, whose owner lived in Karachi. In December 1948,
the Parliamentary Secretary to the UP Government asked
Aizaz Rasul to allow members of the Jamiat to use a room
in the building on a temporary basis. Unwisely, he gave
permission. The League soon found this civility repaid with
hostility. The Jamiat used its influence to persuade the Rent
Control and Eviction Officer of Lucknow to allot the building
to its secretary, Muhammad Qasim.[38] The Jamiat then removed
the Muslim League sign from the building and set out to
expand its occupation of it. On 22 February, Jamal Mian made
a formal complaint to the District Magistrate on the basis that
the Rent Control and Eviction Office had no power to allot the
property, and on the District Magistrate's instructions sealed
the building, giving him the key. At the same time he told his
League leader that he was determined to throw the Jamiatis
out.[39] The matter then went into limbo as the government
decided what to do.[40] During this period of waiting, it would
appear that Jamal Mian had an altercation with the Jamiatis
which required a formal apology. On 2 April, probably before
the District Magistrate, Harpal Singh, he declared: 'I do
hereby solemnly and sincerely apologise to all. I do agree that
a curtain should be dropped on past. I most humbly declare
"Thy people will be my people and thy God is my God."'[41]

---

38. Order, 15 February 1949, under the Control of Rent and Eviction Act,
    Ibid.
39. Jamal Mian to Z. H. Lari, 22 February 1949, Ibid.
40. Jamal Mian to Harpal Singh, District Magistrate, 9 March 1949, 26
    March 1949, on both occasions pressing for a decision, Ibid.
41. The quotation is from The Bible, Ruth 1:16. Formal apology drafted
    on *Hamdam* notepaper, Ibid.

The episode for which Jamal Mian had to apologize, coming after a year of strain, was in all likelihood a symptom of the bi-polar illness that afflicted him from time to time. Looking back over his life in 1983, he identified this period as the first in which he experienced '"mental imbalance", "nervous breakdown" whatever name one might give it; anxiety of spirit, talking too much, becoming mentally restless in sleep; becoming oversensitive....'[42] On 24 February, he was up at 3 a.m. writing a letter of over 4,000 words to G. B. Pant, the Chief Minister, setting out the quarrel with the Jamiat people which he admitted had 'wrecked his peace of mind'.[43] On 18 March, he tried to resign from the Legislative Assembly by thrusting a letter into the hands of fellow Muslim Leaguer, Nafisul Hasan, in the debating Chamber. Hasan returned the letter saying that he did not think that Jamal Mian was well and that anyway resignations had to be submitted to the Governor[44] On 30 March, Hasrat Mohani was at Farangi Mahall in the morning:

There Dr Abdul Hamid was attending to Jamal Mian. Jamal Mian has become increasingly oversensitive. I am convinced that this has affected his health. His conversation is disconnected [ukhri ukhri bate]. The attack seems to have disturbed his equilibrium. ... I was very pained to see this.[45]

Around this time, Jamal moved into a period of frenzied activity typical of his illness, involving a wholesale tidying up of his affairs in a mixture of decisiveness and indecisiveness.

42. Jamal Mian 'Reflections' 25 May 1983, Ibid.
43. Jamal Mian to G. B. Pant, 24 February 1949, Ibid.
44. Nafisul Hasan to Jamal Mian, 19 March 1949, Ibid.
45. Hasrat Mohani, 'Roznama', 30 March 1949, Ibid.

In late March he told his father-in-law that he was resigning from the UP Legislative Assembly.[46] But then he wavered as he came under pressure from leading Congress figures, Jawaharlal Nehru, G. B. Pant, and Rafi Ahmed Kidwai, to withdraw his resignation.[47] He sent in his formal resignation to the Governor on 26 April and at the same time withdrew his opposition to the allotment of the Muslim League offices to the Jamiat.[48] Around this time he must have resigned as Secretary of the Province Muslim League as he planned the transfer of all his official papers to Aizaz Rasul, the General Secretary.[49] At the same time he set matters in train to close down his *Hamdam* newspaper. Sadri Ispahani sent him Rs 2,000 to cover the costs of closure plus his medical and travel expenses, but this was returned immediately with the statement that all expenses were covered.[50] Dr Faridi was to be asked to travel with him to the `Urs at Rudauli on 14 April and then go on with him to Ranchi.[51] He resigned from the Board of Guardians of the Jahangirabad estate.[52] He even found time to write a letter of apology to the Bahr ul-Ulumis: 'I from the bottom of my heart beg for forgiveness of my sins and for any pain that I may have caused your household.'[53]

With these actions, Jamal Mian freed himself to focus on

46. Jamal Mian to Shah Hayat Ahmed, 26 March 1948, Ibid.
47. Jamal Mian to G. B. Pant 29 March 1949 and Jamal Mian, 'Note on Nehru', 1963, Ibid.
48. Jamal Mian to Harpal Singh, 26 April 1949, Ibid.
49. Yardasht, 8 April 1949, Ibid.
50. Sadri Ispahani to Qutb Mian, 7 April 1949; Jamal Mian to Sadri Ispahani, 12 April 1949, Ispahani Correspondence, Ibid.
51. Yardasht, 8 April 1949, Ibid.
52. Jamal Mian to District Judge, Bara Banki, 8 May 1949, Ibid.
53. Jamal Mian to Maulana Muhammad Aslam Bahr ul-Ulumi, 2 Jamadus Sani 1368 (1 April 1949), Ibid.

the recovery of his health and on resurrecting his tea business for which he had been offered new terms by the Ispahanis. Correspondence with Hassan Ispahani, who by this time was Pakistan's ambassador to the USA, makes it clear that Jamal Mian was taking time to recover.[54] In September, he was still under doctor's orders and thinking of going to the School of Tropical Medicine in London.[55] After this, concerns about his health seemed to subside. Business worries returned. In August 1949, he admitted to Mirza Ahmed Ispahani that he could not make the business work in Lucknow. Mirza Ahmed responded by inviting him to start again in Calcutta or East Pakistan.[56]

By the end of 1949, news of Jamal Mian's failure to make a living, of the economic threat to Farangi Mahall, and that he might have to work for the Ispahanis in East Pakistan had begun to spread. Muhammad Ali Zainal Alireza, the Bombay businessman with whose brother, Ebrahim, he had travelled on the Indian Delegation to the Middle East in 1947 was shocked by the thought of the Farangi Mahall madrasah closing. He was even more shocked by a misheard rumour that Jamal Mian was working in a jute factory. 'When Muhammad Ali Zainal heard about your illness', Saidur Rahman Qidwai wrote to him, 'he started crying. When he recovered from his weeping he said that "Jamal Mian is a kind of person who only appears rarely. It is a tragedy of the Muslims that a man like

54. Hassan Ispahani to Qutb Mian, 21 April 1949, to Jamal Mian, 4 May, 27 May and 24 June 1949, Ispahani Correspondence, Ibid.
55. Sadri Ispahani to Jamal Mian, 9 September 1949, Ispahani Correspondence, Ibid.
56. Mirza Ahmed Ispahani to Jamal Mian, 14 August 1949, Ispahani Correspondence, Ibid.

him whom I love more than anyone else should be working in a jute factory".'[57]

Taking Stock

It was clearly time for Jamal Mian to take stock, to consider how he might be able to earn a living to support his family, and to help to support the madrasah. He made a tour of West Pakistan, something he had long discussed with Mirza Ahmed Ispahani. We know something of what he did and felt on his visit, not because he kept a diary but because on his return he set out to write Saidur Rahman Qidwai a long letter describing his experiences. But rather than sending it, he decided to publish it. 'Not many books have been published about Pakistan in India', he declared in his Preface dated 13 July 1950. 'I am writing this so that people can be better-informed about Pakistan.' As far as we know, the manuscript was not published; given the general suspicion attached to any Indian Muslim with Pakistani connections, he may have thought this to be the wiser course.[58]

His first comments are about all the things that have changed in making the journey from Lucknow to Karachi. He notes how the technologies of the modern state now control movement between India and Pakistan. 'Before partition this journey was not even worth mentioning but now because of the problem of no objection certificates and permits this journey has become a very difficult one. With the help of

---

57. Saidur Rahman Qidwai to Jamal Mian, Bombay, 2 January 1950, Ibid.
58. Jamal al-Din `Abd al-Wahhab, 'Awraq-i Parishan', copied 29 August 1950, unpaginated and on old Muslim League notepaper, Ibid.

Mahbub Alam, Secretary of the Sunni Waqf Board, and Deputy Commissioner, Harpal Singh Sahib, I had no problem in getting the no objection certificate... on the afternoon of 15 May I left for Delhi.'[59]

He then reflects on how Delhi has changed. 'Since the revolution of 1947 staying in Delhi has become an issue. Before 1947 there were hundreds of people I knew in Delhi, and a long time spent there would seem short, but now new faces and strange visions greet the eye.'[60] He sees Rafi Ahmed Kidwai as is now his custom on going to Delhi; 'since he became a federal minister the UP Muslims have suffered because he was not around.'[61] He was full of praise for the way Rafi Ahmed would entertain people without distinction of religion, race or creed, friend or enemy. On going to the Pakistan High Commission, which was in Gul-e Rana, the former house of Liaquat Ali Khan, 'I remembered all those meetings which used to happen in the Muslim League days which are haunting the building.'[62] When he took the Orient Airways plane from Delhi, he found Abdur Rahman Siddiqui, Bengali businessman and formerly a co-worker with Maulana Mahomed Ali, with him. Siddiqui pointed out that there were several English people on the plane who could not find work in Bengal and were going to Karachi. 'They had only their clothes with them.'[63]

As the plane flew to Karachi, Jamal Mian goes over his previous visits since the Muslim League Provincial Conference of October 1938. 'At that time', he says of his 1938 visit, 'one

---

59. Ibid.
60. Ibid.
61. Ibid
62. Ibid.
63. Ibid.

could not imagine that in this desert place the Muslims of Hind might find a home.'[64] Referring to a visit in the following year, he writes: 'I never thought then that this place would become a commercial centre of any importance.'[65] This time, on reaching Karachi on 27 May 1950 he notes how different it is from 1938: 'nature changes, people change, ideas change, everything has changed.'[66]

As usual, Jamal Mian stayed at the Raja of Mahmudabad's house, 2 Framroze Road. Mirza Ahmed Ispahani's brother, Mahmud, made a car available to him, a Cadillac. On arriving he made a list of those he wanted to see; he was very concerned that they should know that he had not come with an ulterior motive. 'I have not come to settle here and partake of their good fortune. I have just come for a few days to spend time.'[67] The first person he contacted was the Governor-General, Khwaja Nazimuddin, whom he had known for many years. The Khwaja Sahib replied saying come and have dinner next evening. This was the first of three meals that Jamal Mian was to have with Nazimuddin during his brief stay. He was very impressed by the warmth of his welcome. He was also impressed by the simplicity of life in Government House and by the way in which during prayer time, all of the staff from the Governor General to the chaukidars lined up together in prayer.

By the evening of 28 May, the word had got round that Jamal Mian was in Karachi and invitations were flowing in. 'In nearly two days', he declared, 'I realised that I had not just arrived in Karachi but also encountered Hyderabad, Bombay,

---

64. Ibid.
65. Ibid.
66. Ibid.
67. Ibid.

Calcutta, Jaipur and God knows how many other cities, friends, relatives, connections. They seemed to have been assembled from all over the place.'[68] The following day, after dinner with the Pakistani ambassador to Moscow, he strikes the same note: 'in every house I felt that I had arrived at my own home where stories from Bombay, Lucknow and so on are being recited all the time.'[69]

On 1 June, Jamal Mian went to pay his respects to Miss Jinnah. It was the first time he had done so since Jinnah's death. He noted that she had no official position, but was respected by all the officials, and that 'although she is the epitome of modern education, she does not display the uninhibited gestures of the modern women.'[70] A little later he went to Jinnah's grave which had a shamiana over it. The place was always crowded, especially so on Thursdays. Indeed, it had become a place of pilgrimage and was treated like a saint's shrine with *qawwali*s being sung. But the Government of Pakistan had banned this behaviour. 'When I arrived, there was a soldier and a bit of the *Ghilaf* over it. When I saw the grave the thought came into my head that a man who would not allow one crease in his clothes was now lying under a heap of dust.'[71]

In reflecting on Pakistani officialdom he notes that there are former UP bureaucrats everywhere. For instance, Hashim Raza and Ali Raza, his brother, and Madani, the son of Nawab Ismail Khan, were all playing a leading role in the Karachi administration. Nevertheless, what Jamal Mian found refreshing was that:

---

68. Ibid.
69. Ibid.
70. Ibid.
71. Ibid.

People seem to love their ministers. It is natural to be critical and to have complaints but most people think the ministers are deserving of their positions. No one thinks there could be a better PM than Liaquat Ali Khan, and no better Foreign Minister than Zafarullah Khan. Ghulam Muhammad's knowledge of Finance is also considered to be solid.[72]

Moreover, after meeting Ghulam Muhammad, Jamal Mian thought he was genuine about improving relations with India. Indeed, one of his final thoughts was that 'most of the people here are friendly towards India and seek a peaceful resolution to any problem. They think Nehru a good thing for Pakistan-India relations.'[73]

Jamal Mian notes the varying fortunes of those who have come to Karachi. The family of Mr Justice Qadiruddin of Delhi, for instance, were all doing very well, but there were many talented people in difficulties. Some had to commute to Karachi from the island of Menara because there was nowhere to live in the city. When he paid a visit to Menara he found two members of the family of Shah Abdul Razzaq of Bansa as well as members of his own family. Then, after noting that the grandson of the Hyderabadi aristocrat, Nasir Yar Jang, was working for Orient Airways, he declared that:

One outcome of Partition and the events in Hyderabad is that many young middle class men have had to go in search of a livelihood. Up to this point our young people have wasted their lives in laziness. There were families where mothers looked after their middle-aged children as children. My view is that

72. Ibid.
73. Ibid.

our problems come from his laziness. Partition has brought a change in attitudes.'[74]

Jamal Mian then comments on political and socio-educational issues. In terms of foreign relations he notes that Pakistan under the leadership of Zafarullah Khan has developed a distinct foreign policy of its own. Indeed, Muslim countries were beginning to regard it as one of their leaders. But the bulk of his political comment was reserved for internal matters. Pakistan's Constituent Assembly was at work. On the issue of Pakistan as an Islamic state he declared:

As soon as the foundation stone was laid, it was announced that it would have an Islamic government. So long as this was just a slogan, this was no difficulty, but now the question is should we try to alter this objective or try to realise it?[75]

He continues saying that 'the leaders of Pakistan interpreted Islamic government as meaning Parliamentary democratic government but there did seem to be much restlessness amongst the people about this.'[76] He notes that some ulama want to run the state according to the laws of *fiqh*, and that Maududi and his party have a precise idea of how this should be done. The Muslim League, on the other hand, although promising the objective of an Islamic state, is also trying to consider the requirements of a modern society. 'Several people I talked to seemed confused.'[77] The Muslim League leader, Choudhry Khaliquzzaman, perhaps reflecting the Pan-

74. Ibid.
75. Ibid.
76. Ibid.
77. Ibid.

Islamic strand in his thinking, which had existed since his
youth, took the position that an Islamic society cannot be
created in one country. All Muslim countries need to become
one. 'Only then can we have an Islamistan.'[78] It may be telling
that in two of the quotations in this paragraph, Jamal Mian
used the first person plural. It is as though during his stay
among old friends he had slipped back into being a League
leader again.

Another major issue which concerned the constitution
makers was should the government be centralized or federal,
and in the latter case how much authority should the
provinces have? This was closely tied up with the problem
of the relationship between Bengal (East Pakistan) and West
Pakistan. Jamal Mian's view was 'that government should keep
a strong centre while giving as much power to the provinces as
possible.'[79] Related to this issue was that of Urdu, which Jinnah
had said should become the national language. But there was
also the problem of powerful provincial languages,although
Jamal Mian does not mention Bengali specifically, which was
soon to be a major issue, and the fact that government business
was transacted in English. Apparently, there was concern
regarding the government's lack of support for Urdu. Some
pointed to what India was doing for Hindi as an example of
what Pakistan should do for Urdu. Nevertheless, Urdu seemed
to be looking after itself quite well. 'Urdu is progressing day
by day,' he noted. 'It has reached cities and rural areas; the
muhajir press is very important in carrying it forward. No other
language has the publications of Urdu at present.'[80]

---

78. Ibid.
79. Ibid.
80. Ibid.

On the socio-educational side, Jamal Mian observed that
Karachi was a multicultural city. 'A dark side of this picture
is the new freedom of women in dress and behaviour. This is
hurting the feelings of the common man. Whether we have
veils or not, what are the limits of unveiling? Those limits have
not been decided yet.'[81] Jamal Mian also refers to the '*muhajir*
problem'; the clash of interests between *muhajir*s and local
inhabitants, between 'old *muhajir*s' and 'new *muhajir*s' and so
on. 'My view,' he concludes, 'is that most *muhajir* problems
derive from irresponsible elements in their own community.'[82]
On the educational front he notes that there are very few
madrasahs in West Pakistan but 'in East Pakistan there is a lot
of Islamic education. Every city has a madrasah. The province
has 5,000 madrasahs.'[83]

Jamal Mian does offer a brief section on East Pakistan,
despite not travelling there on this occasion; we must assume
that it was included to strengthen the work as a publication.
He says that on the basis of population and gross domestic
product, East Pakistan is the stronger part of Pakistan.
Most industrial progress has taken place in East Pakistan.
Seventy-five per cent of the world's jute is grown there and it
produces most of Pakistan's foreign exchange. After Partition,
there was major investment in the industrial processing of
jute. Dacca, which had no daily newspapers before Partition,
now has two in English, two in Urdu, and two in Bengali.
Chittagong is the most beautiful city in the region and some
say it might become one of the great ports of Asia. He makes
one striking comment:

81. Ibid.
82. Ibid.
83. Ibid.

Of all the people of Pakistan these people [the Bengalis] seem most to adhere to their religion. There are many mosques, madrasahs—prayer times respected—but not many women veiled. Where in the rest of Pakistan the Muslim League was run by the upper class, in Bengal the drive came from the poor.[84]

'Leaving Karachi was sad', Jamal Mian wrote, 'I had been there so long.' In fact he extended his stay by fourteen days, which meant he had to extend his 'No Objection Certificate' at the Indian High Commission, which proved to be an 'awful experience until Sir Sita Rana's secretary, Kapoor, helped me.'[85] At the airport he noted many of the 'clan of Khaliq' to see him off, and how it took everyone a long time to say good bye because of the uncertainty of being able to get the necessary permission to travel back and forth across the frontier again.

As he marked the barriers which the modern state was throwing up between India and Pakistan, Jamal Mian also marked real differences which were developing. He marvelled at the fact that the Rupee had a different value in each country; the Pakistani rupee was markedly stronger against the pound sterling than the Indian. Moreover, he felt that Pakistanis were travelling on a different road from Indian Muslims:

Pakistan has all the roads of worldly success open to it. But in this success-story there is a danger that Pakistanis will lose their way in their desire for comfort and pleasure. The Indian Muslims, if they have a fault, it is that they do not have the

---

84. Ibid.
85. Ibid.

doors of comfort and pleasure open to them. Only those can
live here in India who have the conviction and courage to make
a place for themselves and to have the courage to engage in
this struggle.[86]

In this passage, Jamal Mian seems to be rationalizing a
decision firmly to stay in India and perhaps also a decision
to earn his living in East Pakistan where he would escape, so
he thought, many of the pressures of his old life, particularly
the political pressures which had helped to make him ill. In
September 1950, he went on Hajj with his wife and four
children—Farida, Bari Mian, Mahmood, and Alauddin
who was still a baby—plus Hasrat Mohani, the Raja of
Mahmudabad, and the Raja of Salempur. They set off from
Bombay on 8 September in a boat called Mohammadi.
Jawaharlal Nehru helped to smooth his passage by making the
services of the Indian consulate in Jeddah available to him.[87]
As it turned out, the Hajj was uneventful, although Mahmood
does remember baby Alauddin being hit by a hailstone.

On 13 November, the party without Hasrat Mohani, who
had made a detour to see relations in Karachi, returned to
Lucknow. Hasrat followed a little later and it was clear that he
was dying. For some years, Jamal Mian had been arranging for
him to have medical attention, but then his health deteriorated
markedly while on Hajj. On returning to Cawnpore in the
autumn of 1950, he quickly moved to Lucknow, sending
Jamal Mian the message: 'I am here and it weighs upon my
mind that you are not here.'[88] On the first of January 1951, he

86. Ibid.
87. Jamal Mian, 'Note on Jawaharlal Nehru', JMP: K. H. Qadiri, *Hasrat
    Mohani* (Delhi: Idara-i-Adabiyat-i Delli, 1985), 290–1.
88. Qadiri, *Hasrat Mohani*, 291.

noted in his diary that Jamal Mian had sent him two novels. One he did not like but the other—*The Good Earth*, Pearl Buck's story of peasant life in China before the revolution—he enjoyed.[89] On 11 April, Jamal Mian took him from his hospital in Lucknow to Farangi Mahall.[90] As on 13 May, surrounded by weeping relatives, he was breathing his last, he saw Jamal Mian and with great effort asked him to tell them that 'this is no new thing which is happening.'[91] He was buried in the Farangi Mahall Bagh, close to the grave of his pir, Maulana Abdul Wahhab.

89. Ibid. 292.
90. Jamal Mian Diary, 11 April 1951, JMP.
91. Qadiri, *Hasrat Mohani*, 293

11

Life in Dacca, 1951–1957

IN HIS *LEGACY OF A DIVIDED NATION* THE INDIAN MUSLIM
scholar, Mushirul Hasan, writing of Partition declares:
'Overnight educational institutions were depleted of students
and teachers. Maulana Jamal Mian's departure from Lucknow
was a blow for the Firangi Mahal seminary.'[1] We have already
noted that Jamal Mian remained firmly in India after Partition.
Moreover, even after he developed a successful business
in Dacca, he remained firmly an Indian citizen until the
government of India forced him to take the idea of Pakistani
citizenship seriously.

Jamal Mian establishes his business and family in Dacca

February 1951 saw Jamal Mian trying to establish his
business in Dacca. Two men were crucial; his old patron,
Mirza Ahmed Ispahani, whom he saw almost every day, and
Ghulam Faruque, Chairman of the Jute Board, and one of
British India and Pakistan's most distinguished civil servants.[2]

---

1. Hasan, *Legacy*, 176.
2. Ghulam Faruque Khan Khattak, 1899–1992. Pakistani bureaucrat,
   politician, economist, and industrialist. He as the son of a landlord,
   social worker, and civil contractor of Nagpur. In 1921, he joined the

243

Indeed, jute was to be his prime business; matches and tea
were to follow later in the decade. Mirza Ahmed showed
him the ropes. Jamal Mian began to make regular visits to
Narayanganj, the jute-dealing area of Dacca; he presented
himself at the Jute Board; he went with Mirza Ahmed to a
political meeting held by Fazlul Huq, the veteran Bengali
politician, and met Mirza Ahmed and Ghulam Faruque at
the airport, who regaled him with tales of their successful trip
to Delhi and Lucknow.[3]

Jamal Mian, however, was uneasy in Dacca. His wife
was not well. 'Poor thing', he noted in his diary, 'she must
have got tired of waiting for me. I feel that even staying a
minute longer would be unbearable, but when I consider my
problems I must stay.'[4] The following day he spoke to Asar on
the phone—Partition had not brought an end to the ability to
book telephone calls between the two regions—and tried to
persuade her to come with the family to Dacca, but she was
unwilling to do so. Then, he received two letters from Altafur
Rahman Qidwai which made him anxious about his children,
but which may also have raised issues of shortages of money
and the impact of Qutb Mian's illness on the Farangi Mahall

Bengal-Nagpur Railway and rose to become the first Indian Muslim
General Manager of East Indian railways. In 1949, after moving
to Pakistan, he was made Chairman of the Cotton and Jute Board
and from then until the 1980s he led a wide range of organizations
involved in the development of Pakistan. In the 1980s, he was also
elected twice to the Senate of Pakistan. Alongside his administrative
and political career, he also established a major business conglomerate,
Ghulam Faruque Group. Under the British he was appointed OBE
(1944) and CIE (1946) and in Pakistan Hilal-e Pakistan (1958)

3. Jamal Mian Diary, 17 February, 2, 7, 8 March 195, JMP.
4. Ibid. 3 March 1951.

community. So, after little more than five weeks in Dacca, Jamal Mian returned to India.[5]

Several matters occupied Jamal Mian on his return. There was, of course, the devotional round which he rarely missed. On 21 March, he was at the `Urs at Rudauli which would also have been a welcome family occasion for his wife and children.[6] In the middle of April he was at the `Urs at Ajmer with Dr Faridi. Around this visit, he also went to Delhi where he saw his devoted supporter, Saidur Rahman Qidwai, and visited Parliament with Nawab Ismail Khan, seeing many old friends.[7] But, most important about this Delhi trip was that he was staying with Rafi Ahmed Kidwai, by now Minister for Communications, and seeing him frequently. Apart from the pleasure which the two clearly had in each other's company, Jamal Mian had been commissioned to talk business with Rafi Sahib. The Ispahanis wanted the return of an Orient Airways plane which the Government of India had impounded; they also wanted to sort out their tax affairs. Jamal Mian did not make much progress on this occasion except that through Rafi Ahmed's good offices, the appropriate ministries were alerted to the issues.[8] On 21 April, he returned to Lucknow to look after Hasrat Mohani who was close to death. He also took stock of Qutb Mian's illness, its impact on the running of the madrasah, and the family finances in Lucknow. In all likelihood, he also pressed the case again for his family to join him in Dacca.

On 19 June, Jamal Mian returned to Dacca. Clearly he

5. Ibid. 8, 14, 17 March 1951.
6. Ibid. 22 March 1951.
7. Ibid. 12, 13, 14, 15 April 1951.
8. Ibid., 17, 18, 19, 20 April 1951; Jamal Mian to Mirza Raza Sahib, 24 December 1949, Personal File, JMP.

had decided to persevere in developing his business. Even
though it was Ramadan and it was very hot, he got himself
a jute licence, warehousing and export privileges. He also
bought a car (up to now he had been travelling in Dacca by
bicycle), got himself a Pakistani driving licence, and opened a
bank account with credit facilities.[9] Mirza Ahmed made him
an agent; his contract guaranteed him Rs 1 per bale of jute
delivered.[10] His firm was established with Ali Husain Mohani,
his friend from Madrasah and Lucknow University days, as
manager. Because Jamal Mian was not a Pakistani citizen, the
business was registered as Ansari Ltd. in the name of Habib
Mian, the son of Maulana Sibghatullah Farangi Mahalli, a
move which would later cause grief.

On 5 July, before the setting up of his business was finished,
with Mirza Ahmed's permission, Jamal Mian returned to
Lucknow for Eid. He found that many Lucknavis, who had
sought work in Pakistan, had returned for the festival. Jamal
Mian met old friends and attended two meetings of the Sunni
Waqf Board.[11] On 16 and 17 July, he was in Delhi, seeing
Rafi Ahmed and pressing forward Ispahani interests.[12] On
the 19th, he was back in Lucknow where he again addressed
the problems created by Qutb Mian's illness, among them
deteriorating relations with other members of the family.[13] By
the 23rd, via Calcutta, he had returned to Dacca where he
was met by Muhammad Azfar.[14] He stayed with Asar's elder

   9. Jamal Mian Diary, 20, 23, 24, 25 June, 1951, Ibid.
  10. Ibid. 12 August 1951.
  11. Ibid. 5, 7, 8, 13 July 1951.
  12. Ibid. 16, 17 July 1951.
  13. Ibid. 19, 20 July 1951.
  14. Muhammad Azfar, ICS, OBE, (1909–2001). Youngest son of
      Khan Sahib Akbar Ali, Deputy Inspector of Schools, UP. Educated,

brother. Around this time, he found work for her younger brother, Usman, as he did for three of her siblings. More importantly, he had found a house to rent, No. 110 Agha Sadek Road, and identified a plot of land in Magh Bazaar where he could build a house.

On 12 August, Jamal Mian achieved his objective of bringing his family together in Dacca. His daughter, Farida, remembers how they travelled from Lucknow to Calcutta by train, accompanied by piles of baggage and several family members to see them off. From Calcutta, they went by train and then by river steamer until they reached Dacca. Jamal Mian's mother, Ammi Dadi, was one of the party. She had insisted on bringing lots of baggage, including her *sil*, a large stone for grinding spices and cutting vegetables. Grandmother took granddaughter in hand, teaching her *saleeqa*, good housekeeping, but also regaling her with stories of her visits to Damascus, Baghdad, Mecca, and Medina in the company of Maulana Abdul Bari. She also taught her Persian by reading Saadi's *Gulistan*. Of course, lessons were learned from the great poet and humane thinker of Shiraz. The young Farida would sometimes look scruffy which led Ammi Dadi to tell the story of how Saadi turned up without his official dress for a function in his honour and was refused entrance by the palace guards despite his protestations that he was the guest of honour. He returned in his official robes and was admitted. At

---

universities of Allahabad and Oxford; 1940–45 Depy Commr Sambalpur, Orissa; 1945–57 Secy of Finance, Govt. of Orissa; 1948–54 Home Secy, Govt of East Pakistan; 1954–57 Jt Secy in charge of Kashmir Affairs; 1958–61, Chief Secy, East Pakistan1961–63 UN Special Representative in Somalia; 1963–65 Establishment Secy, Govt of Pakistan; 1965–66 Secy National Assembly;1966 retired by Ayub Khan; 1966–76 Chairman of the Urdu Dictionary Board.

the feast he poured each of the dishes served over his clothes saying 'eat you robes, this is for you'. When he was asked why he did this, he said it was because it was his clothes which were being honoured and not him. People apologized and begged forgiveness. 'Ammi Dadi thought Shaikh Saadi was right', Farida recalls, 'people are very superficial and go for appearances. But she emphasized the importance of being well-groomed and suitably-dressed. The world judges by what one appears to be, so better be presentable.'[15]

Soon after the family was established in Dacca, Jamal Mian was back in Calcutta. He wanted to see Rafi Ahmed indeed he saw him several times over a few days. He also took Mirza Ahmed to see him.[16] Jamal Mian then returned with Mirza Ahmed and Ghulam Faruque to Dacca. Faruque offered Jamal Mian a post in the central government as a Liaison Officer with pay of Rs 1500 pm and expenses of Rs 500 pm. Three houses were attached to the position in Karachi, Lahore, and Lyallpur. The handsome salary, with the extras that came with it, would have made life easier for Jamal Mian. But, as he had just set up his business and brought his family to Dacca, the offer came at the wrong psychological moment. Moreover, Jamal Mian did not like to be an employee, particularly of government.[17]

On 16 October, there came the news of the assassination of Liaquat Ali Khan, Pakistan's Prime Minister. Jamal Mian noted that he had first met Liaquat in the Royal Hotel in Lucknow. He had just returned from Europe and was beginning to work for the Muslim League. 'After I was

---

15. Farida Jamal, 'Recollections of Ammi Daddi', 2014, JMP.

16. Jamal Mian Diary, 29 September and 1 October 1951, Ibid.

17. Jamal Mian Diary, 2 October 1951, Ibid.

appointed Joint Secretary of the Muslim League, I saw much of him. Whenever he met me he did so with great warmth ... As compared with Jinnah he was warm and liked a joke. He taught me how to light a cigarette in a moving car.'[18]

As he did on several occasions Jamal Mian wrote a summary of the year in his diary:

> This has been a good year. Good health. And in terms of general well-being I have established my business, and as far as financial matters are concerned, I have never had so much income. I have moved my family to Dacca and spent Rs. 1,500 in the process. Significantly my relationship with the Ispahani family deepened considerably. Among the painful matters are the incidents with Qutb Mian. .... These matters helped me to be away from Lucknow. People who are close to me, among them Hasrat Mohani, died. When I cast eye over my own faults, I find there is no diminishing of them. A very important thing in this year is that I have insured my life with two companies.[19]

For the next six years down to 1957, Jamal Mian continued the pattern of movement and engagement with his old friends across the Indo-Pakistan border. He kept up the family devotional round as far as he could. He never missed attendance at the Ajmer `Urs. In 1952, he was there with Dr Faridi and Saidur Rahman Qidwai. He also made the acquaintance, for the first time, of Pir Mohiuddin Gilani of Golra, whose father had supported his father, and who was to be an important supporter during his life in Pakistan.[20] In

---

18. Ibid. autumn 1951 but no precise date.
19. Ibid. end of year note, 1951.
20. Pir Mohiuddin Gilani of Golra (1888–1974), son of Pir Mehr Ali Shah. Golra Sharif is a leading shrine of the Punjab in the Margalla

1953, he records meeting many of his relatives: Muhammad Mian, Hashim Mian, Raza Mian, Sibghatullah Shahid, Hamid Mian, and Matin Mian.[21] In 1954, he saw his relatives again but also records weeping at the `Urs for Shah Muhammad Husain of Phulwari Sharif, the descendant of Shah Sulaiman, long associated with Farangi Mahall.[22] He also met Aijaz Mian of the Ajmer Dargah family who made it clear that he was 'really upset at my leaving Lucknow'.[23] In 1955, Jamal Mian met, amongst others, Dr Syed Mahmud, whom we have already noted was a disciple of his father, and people associated with Rafi Ahmed. He emphasizes that the Diwan Sahib's *mahfil* and the *Sama` Khana mahfil* were the high points of the occasion for him.[24] During this period, when possible, Jamal Mian also attended the `Urs at Rudauli, Bansa, and the family Bagh, but did not manage to do so on an annual basis.

Moving with the political elites of India and Pakistan

Jamal Mian's political associations in both India and Pakistan set out the extraordinary nature of his connections. It is unlikely that anyone else in the early 1950s had such access at the top of both countries. In 1952, after a meeting with the Pakistan Prime Minister, Khwaja Nazimuddin, whom he

---

Hills, close to modern Islamabad; Jamal Mian Diary, 30 March 1952, JMP.

21. Ibid. 21 March 1953.
22. Ibid. 14 March 1954.
23. Ibid.
24. Ibid. 1 March 1955.

was helping to improve his speech-making,[25] his encounters were entirely with leading Indian politicians. He was in India for the country's first general elections, declaring himself a supporter of the Congress but also saying that he had finished with politics.[26] He then moved from Lucknow to Delhi where he stayed with Rafi Ahmed Kidwai who was about to become Minister for Food and Agriculture in Nehru's new administration. With Rafi Ahmed he saw Feroze Gandhi, Nehru's son-in-law, and a rising politician, and Bal Krishan Sinha. Then later, he met Abul Kalam Azad, now Education Minister, and Dr Syed Mahmud.[27] He also met briefly, and was impressed by, Abdul Ghaffar Khan, the 'Frontier Gandhi'.[28] While in Delhi, he noted that the Jama Masjid was improved. 'Anyone who had seen Delhi in 1947 would be relieved and happy at this sight.'[29] Over the next three months, from March to May, Jamal Mian saw Rafi Ahmed frequently, joining him at a Congress meeting in Calcutta,[30] throwing a party for him at Farangi Mahall,[31] and then meeting him in Delhi in June along with Abul Kalam Azad, Dr Syed Mahmud, and a new ICS acquaintance, Ahmed Mohyuddin.[32] On 22 May, he went to Parliament to listen to Jawaharlal Nehru give an 'hour-long well-argued speech' and was enthralled by a speech made from the opposition benches by Shyam Prasad Mukherjee. Later that day he had tea with Nehru in South Block. 'When

25. Ibid. 27 January 1952.
26. Ibid. 4 March 1952.
27. Ibid. 8 March 1952.
28. Ibid.
29. Ibid.
30. Ibid. 22 March 1952.
31. Ibid. 11 April 1952.
32. Ibid. 19 May 1952.

I talked to Jawaharlal about my Dacca experiences he bowed
his head in concentration. I said nothing about my personal
difficulties.'[33] In June and July, Jamal Mian continued to see
Rafi Ahmed both in Calcutta and Delhi. In July, he held a big
party for Ahmed Mohyuddin in Lucknow.[34] Then there is a
gap in his diary. When it starts again, he is seeing Rafi Ahmed
in Delhi, but on this occasion staying with his new friend,
Ahmed Mohyuddin.[35]

After being particularly engaged with leading figures in
India's politics in 1952, subsequently, Jamal Mian was
much more involved with the leaders of Pakistan. From 11
December 1952, he was in Karachi having a very sociable
time. By 1 January 1953, he thought he had been there too
long but was reluctant to leave because Mirza Ahmed was
unwell. The following day, he went with Hassan Ispahani to
meet Ghulam Mohamed,[36] the Governor-General.[37] He also
saw Miss Jinnah, Iskander Mirza,[38] whom he knew from his

---

33. Ibid. 22 May 1952.
34. Ibid. 9 July 1952.
35. Ibid. 7, 10 December 1952.
36. Malik Ghulam Mohamed, CIE (1941), KCIE (1946). Pathan brought
    up in the old walled city of Lahore and educated at Aligarh Muslim
    University where he read accountancy; co-founder of Mahindra
    & Mahomed Steel Co.; Controller of Supplies and Purchases for
    the Indian Railways Board; 1946, Ministry of Finance; 1949 Prime
    Minister of Pakistan; 1951–55 Governor-General.
37. Jamal Mian Diary 1, 2 January 1953, JMP.
38. Iskander Mirza, CIE, OBE (1899–1969), great grandson of Mir
    Jafar whose treachery helped the British win the battle of Plassey
    in 1757; officer in the British Indian Army who joined the Indian
    Political Service; 1946 Joint Defence Secretary of India; 1947 Defence
    Secretary of Pakistan; 1954 Governor of East Pakistan; 1954 Minister
    for Commonwealth and Kashmir Affairs, Federal Government; 1955
    Governor-General; 1956–58 President.

political campaigning in the North West Frontier in the 1930s, and learned that Khwaja Nazimuddin was put out because he had not already called upon him.[39] Before returning to Dacca on 6 January, he managed a one-to-one meeting with Iskander Mirza and also saw I. I. Chundrigar, the Governor of the West Punjab.[40] In late March 1953, Jamal Mian's connections to the political elite were strengthened when Khaliquzzaman, his former political boss, was appointed Governor of East Pakistan. He began to see him almost every day. Mahmood Jamal, Jamal Mian's second son, remembers Khaliquzzaman teaching him chess at this time. In June, Jamal Mian held a party for Khaliquzzaman. Among the guests were Muhammad Azfar, now Chief Secretary of East Pakistan, Mirza Ahmed, Sadri, Dr Faridi, and Nawab Ismail Khan, the former President of the UP Muslim League who was visiting from India.[41] Two of his sons, G. A. Madani[42] and I. A. Khan[43] rose to senior positions in the East Pakistan administration.

---

39. Jamal Mian Diary, 2 January 1953, JMP.
40. Ibid., 3, 5, 6 January 1953.
41. Ibid. 12 June 1953.
42. G. A. Madani, ICS (1913–79) Eldest son of Nawab Ismail Khan q.v. Educated Aligarh Muslim University and Cambridge; 1937–39 posted in the Basti, Bareilly and Hardoi districts of the UP; 1939–47 posts in Gonda, Bahraich, Faizabad, Lucknow, Jaunpur, and Delhi; 3 October 1947 travelled with his family from Meerut to Karachi in the last military train;1947–50 Ministry of Education Govt. of Pakistan; 1952–54 Secy Ministry of Education East Pakistan;1954–62 Commr. Dacca Division; 1961–62 Commr Karachi Division; 1962–64 Commr Peshawar Division; 1964–71 Chairman Dacca Improvement Trust; 1971 Chairman East Pakistan, Water and Power Development Authority. 1971 elected Independent Member, Sind Provincial Assembly.
43. I. A. Khan, ICS (1915–2001); second of the three sons of Nawab Ismail Khanj q.v.; educated Aligarh Muslim University and

During the second half of 1953, entries in Jamal Mian's diary slackened off. But things livened up in early 1954. In February, he was enjoying the company of his old friend, the Raja of Mahmudabad, who was showing a group of Iraqi officials around Calcutta and Dacca.[44] In late February and early March, he often found himself in the company of Miss Jinnah who had come to bolster the Muslim League campaign in the first East Pakistan elections since Independence on 10 March. He dined in her company at least four times.[45] His friends, Khaliquzzaman, Muhammad Azfar, Ghufran Faruqi,[46] and Mirza Ahmed were all involved in entertaining

---

Cambridge; entered ICS in 1940; Iftikhar Ahmad Khan began his service in East Bengal and at Partition was the District Magistrate of Murshidabad; subsequently he was District Magistrate of the East Pakistan districts of Faridpur and Comilla; 1956–61, Chief Controller of Imports and Exports, Karachi; 1961 Chairman of the Jute Board, East Pakistan; 1966–69 Secy Economic Affairs Division, President's Secretariat, Rawalpindi/Islamabad; 1969–73 Chairman of the Water and Power Development Authority (Lahore); a keen sportsman from 1969–72 he was President of the Board of Control of Cricket in Pakistan. In retirement he was executive director of several companies and elected chairman of the Meerut Cooperative Housing Society in memory of his father.

44. Jamal Mian Diary, 22 February, 1 March 1954, JMP.
45. Ibid. 23 February, 7, 8, 10 March 1954.
46. Ghufran Ahmad Faruqi, ICS (1909–1985). From a landed family of Sandila (Sitapur) UP, he was educated at Jubilee College, Lucknow, Allahabad University, and King's College, Cambridge. Entered the ICS in 1933, serving in Ajmer, Allahabad and Lucknow, amongst other places. Opting for Pakistan in 1947 he served as Commissioner in the Rajshahi and Dacca divisions of East Pakistan, rising to become Chief Secretary. In the mid-1950s he was transferred to the central government, representing Pakistan in a range of international bodies. From 1960 to 1972 he worked for the UN in Sierra Leone, Yemen, and Lebanon. On retirement he settled in England.

her. Miss Jinnah's presence, however, seems to have made little difference to the outcome of the elections. After winning Bengal in a landslide victory in the 1945/46 elections, on this occasion, the Muslim League was crushed, winning only ten out of 309 assembly seats. The atmosphere, moreover, had turned hostile towards non-Bengalis, who were being killed.

We need to reflect on what Jamal Mian was doing as he mixed with the leadership of two states which were hostile to each other, indeed, had been briefly at war with each other. He was certainly seeing old friends and acquaintances from his political activist days before Independence. This was as much the case for his old Congress opponents in India such as Rafi Ahmed, Nehru, Azad, and Mahmud as it was for Khwaja Nazimuddin, Iskander Mirza, Khaliquzzaman, Chundrigar, and Miss Jinnah in Pakistan. At times, we know that his engagements were more than merely social. Certainly, Rafi Ahmed was a good friend and a relative but Jamal Mian was also seeing him at the behest of Mirza Ahmed to help resolve tax issues and other matters. Equally, his engagement with politicians and bureaucrats in Pakistan also served to advance the interests of the Ispahanis and, by the same token, himself. When in January 1953 he went with Hassan Ispahani to see Ghulam Mohamed, he was meeting the man who was probably the most powerful person in Pakistan at the time. Certainly, the civil servants such as Muhammad Azfar, Ghulam Faruque G. A. Madani, and I. A. Khan, who formed part of his circle in Dhaka, shared with him a common *sharif* Urdu culture, but they were also people whom it was crucial to keep onside if Ispahani enterprises were to flourish. Understandably, Jamal Mian was agitated when in 1955 a dispute broke out between Mirza Ahmed and Ghulam Faruque.[47]

---

47. Jamal Mian Diary, 4 February, JMP.

This said, Jamal Mian's engagements with the political elites
of India and Pakistan were rather more than was required by
Ispahani interest. They reflected his pleasure in the company
of his old political friends as well as his continuing fascination
with politics, even though he had foresworn active engagement
in them. They also reflected the value these elites, in particular
the Muslim elites, found in having Jamal Mian as part of their
circle. He brought the authority of Farangi Mahall to their
world, alongside his spiritual presence, his worldly wisdom, his
reputation as a former member of the Muslim League High
Command, and his accomplishments as a product of Lucknow
high culture. All treated him with respect; for instance, his
patron and senior in age, Mirza Ahmed Ispahani, always
addressed him with the respectful *aap* rather than *tum*. He,
himself, used entertainment to strengthen old relationships
as with, for instance, his party for Rafi Ahmed in Farangi
Mahall and his party for Khaliquzzaman on his arrival in
Dacca. Equally, he entertained to strengthen new relationships,
as with his party in Lucknow for the Delhi-based civil servant,
Ahmed Mohyuddin. In entertaining thus, however, we should
note that Jamal Mian was doing little more than following the
traditions of his ancestors who were famed for entertaining
visitors to Lucknow. Beyond Jamal Mian's personal concerns,
his movements and connections show how unreal, for people
of his class, the borders between India and Pakistan still
seemed to be. It was perfectly alright for members of the old
sharif elite to travel across them, to have frequent access to
the leadership of either side, and to discuss high politics as
though Partition had never happened.

The betwixt and between existence which Jamal Mian lived
was summed up in November 1952 when he, an Indian citizen,
felt able to give advice to the Pakistan Constituent Assembly.

This was the time when Maulana Maududi and his ulama allies, including Jamal Mian's fellow Lucknavi, Sulaiman Nadvi, were putting pressure on the constitution-making process to take it in an Islamic direction. His unsolicited advice was that the Constitution should be formed on the basis of the final agreement between Britain, the Congress, and the Muslim League of 3 June 1947, and the joint statement issued by the leaders of the respective parties on the eve of Partition, and such statement[s] issued by the leaders [as] were instrumental in giving shape to the final agreement ...' He was worried by the demand for an Islamic state; 'this cry of Nizam-e-Islam meaning a constitution based on books of Fiqa [sic] and a religious state has brought certain misgivings to my mind.' It meant going back on an agreement 'Movaheda' which was un-Islamic. 'In the case of Pakistan we achieved the State by agreement, and the leaders of the Muslim League before and after Partition declared that Pakistan would be a democratic state giving equal rights to all citizens. Now we cannot set aside this basic principle and it will be un-Islamic on our part [to do so].' A note in Urdu at the foot of the statement declared: 'I personally handed this to Tamizuddin Khan [President of the Constituent Assembly]. Also mentioned this to Shaheed [Suhrawardy]. Also informed Ghulam Mohamed and Nazimuddin on this matter. But no one listened to me.'[48]

48. Typed memorandum in English, Dacca, 8 November 1952, JMP. In his submission, Jamal Mian also referred to Liaquat Ali Khan's Objectives Resolution [a typing error mean he just wrote 'Objective'] to which, as the rest of his submission would suggest, he was profoundly opposed. His joke about it was that the 'Qarardad-e Muqassid [Objectives Resolution] is the Qarardad-e Mufassid [Disorder Resolution]'. Family tradition reported by Bari Mian.

Anxieties and deepening roots in Dacca

At the beginning of 1952, the confidence with which Jamal
Mian had ended 1951 was quickly undermined. First, he
heard a rumour that Mirza Ahmed was resigning from all his
companies. This led him to reflect on how much his position
depended on the Ispahanis. 'If Mirza Ahmed's jute goes down,'
he noted in his diary, 'I will go down.'[49] Fortunately, the news
about Mirza Ahmed's intentions turned out to be false. But,
a few days later, while admitting that trading in jute had both
exposed his ignorance and his lack of negotiating skills, he
complained that Mirza Ahmed had 'forced' him to buy 2,000
jute bale futures thus exposing him financially should the price
not rise.[50] He lost money and clearly did not have the stomach
for what he termed 'gambling' in the jute market. Then he
was worried by the growing opposition to the imposition of
Urdu on East Pakistan as the national language, a move which
he thought was quite wrong, and led to bloody clashes with
the policy on Dacca University campus on 21 February.[51]
In addition to these elements of uncertainty, Jamal Mian
heard on 14 January that the Lucknow Custodian of Evacuee
Property was asking him to show cause why he should not
be declared an evacuee and his property in Farangi Mahall
declared evacuee property. The Custodian had been tipped
off by his old antagonist, Muhammad Kamil Bahr ul-Ulumi,
who had told the legal inspector that he knew all about Jamal
Mian's movements and would declare them if the authorities
had the *Hamdam* Electric Press removed.[52] Jamal Mian was

---

49. Jamal Mian Diary, 13 January 1952, JMP.
50. Ibid. 18, 19, 22 January.
51. Ibid. 24 January 1952.
52. Order in the Court of Sri A. P. Tripathi, Assistant Custodian (Judicial)

in danger of the state sequestering property which had been in his family for over 260 years. A few days later, whether in response to the Custodian's request or by coincidence, he went with Ghulam Faruque to view a plot of land he might buy in New Eskaton Road, Magh Bazaar, Dacca.[53] These uncertainties set him worrying about whether he should be in Lucknow or Dacca, and whether he should become a Pakistani citizen or not:

I am in great difficulty because I cannot stay in Lucknow because of the growing situation at home. Lucknow brings emotional and spiritual turmoil which I do not feel in Dacca. However, staying on as an Indian in Pakistan with all my Muslim League connections, and doing jute business makes me anxious. Here I worry about politics and jute; there I worry about my financial troubles. I wish I had the true faith and spiritual strength of my ancestors to sustain myself ... But as soon as I decide to go to Lucknow I see a whole heap of problems: the situation at home [he refers to the illness of the current sajjadanashin, his cousin, Qutb Mian]; the unwelcoming environment of the muhalla, the lack of friends and close ones; the intrigues of the antagonists, and on all sides demands for money. That is why I do not like going. But the problem is how long can I live in Pakistan being an Indian national? My wife and children are eager to go back to Lucknow and Rudauli. I am worried that I have not been able to make a decision on where to be. I have started down this road. Let us see what will happen in future.[54]

E. P. Lucknow Circle, Objection Case No. 51 of 54 of Distt. Lucknow, 18. 6. 1955, JMP.

53. Jamal Mian Diary, 16 January 1952 Ibid.
54. Ibid. 24 January 1952.

In 1953, it seemed as though Jamal Mian was resolving the
problem of where he should live in favour of Dacca. He had
hired an architect and on 8 January was able to show off the
rising building to Hassan Ispahani.[55] Soon, he saw the roof
being put in place and his children were clearly pleased by the
development.[56] The family developed a comfortable routine by
which Jamal Mian dropped off his children at Sadri Ispahani's
house every day, then the children of the two families would
be taken together to school. Jamal Mian's mother, Ammi Dadi,
although increasingly unwell, was still with the family and
so was his driver and old family retainer, Irtiza. The arrival
of Khaliquzzaman as Governor of East Pakistan brought
another reassuring sense of Lucknow to this Dacca world.
Jamal Mian took him a hookah as a welcoming present. He
neatly closed one of life's circles when the very first party he
held in his completed house, which somewhat hopefully he
named Darul Qiam, or Place of Stability, was in honour of his
former political boss.[57] Darul Qiam was a tribute to his father,
Qiyamuddin Muhammad Abdul Bari, from whom so much
of his good fortune in life was derived.

Family life was developing too. By this time Jamal Mian had
five children—Farida, Bari Mian, Mahmood, Alauddin and
Amina; there was just Moin and Humaira to come. In spite of
his evident keenness to travel Jamal Mian missed his family. On
one occasion he admitted to 'feeling an emptiness because my
family is not with me'.[58] On another he declared: 'Now I realise
that not having one's family with one, not having resource, not
having health is a great loss for us.' Then he went on to reflect:

---

55. Ibid. 8, 9 January 1953.
56. Ibid. 14 January 1953.
57. Ibid. 6 April, 12 June 1953.
58. Ibid. 13 January 1955.

'Just like hunger for food, there is another hunger—the sexual one. Sexual desire increases with separation. One must have discipline not to give way. I now realise that being busy saves us from a lot of sin.'[59] But his family also missed him. In his 'personal file' where Jamal Mian kept correspondence that meant a lot to him, there is a collection of postcards from Asar. These are all undated but appear to be, for the most part, from the 1950s. They are typical of what a wife might write to a husband who is away and give us an insight into the relationship between the two. There are postcards in which Asar describes events on the home front:

We are all fine. I am very happy the children are fine [she refers to Bari and Farida who are travelling with their father] and hopefully they will arrive safely. Ali Husain did not come today. [She refers to his business manager who kept an eye on things when Jamal Mian was away]. The inauguration of the godown took place today. Some purchases were made but I do not know the detail. Mirza Ahmed will come at the end of the month from Calcutta. I have asked Sadri Sahib for his measurements for the kurta. Sadri phoned yesterday and said you were planning to go to Surat. Bari will miss a lot [of school] but Farida should be OK. You should return as quickly as possible.[60]

There are postcards in which Asar said how much she missed her husband:

Bring kurtas for all the children. Hope you have arrived in Lucknow safely. Bari Mian's school has opened and he goes

59. Ibid. 20 January 1955.
60. Asar to Jamal Mian, n.d. but from Darul Qiam. Personal File, JMP.

tomorrow. Now I feel your absence much more. Please write
and tell me when you are coming back.[61]

There are postcards saying why don't you reply:

I have written several letters to you at the Lucknow address;
you must have got them. But I have not had any letter from
you for four days. Juni [Sadri's sister] is getting married on 20
December. Faruque Sahib is leaving East Pakistan …. I don't
know when you are going to return. How *long* are you going to
be away? The children need two woollen trousers each. They
are missing you daily. Yours, Asar.[62]

There are postcards listing children's wants:

I was relieved to hear your voice on the phone. I have written
two letters to Bombay. I am very happy that you have shown
yourself to doctors there. Seen the doctor myself. I hope you
will finish your work in Lucknow and be here. The children
are very happy with the watches. They are also asking for kites
and kite-string. Alauddin is asking for a pigeon. Moddu [Moin]
wants almonds and raisins and a toy plane and a bus. Minoo
[Amina] wants a toy refrigerator. Farida wants a subscription
to a magazine called *Kalyan* from Lucknow.[63]

During the 1950s and 1960s, Jamal Mian tried to give his
children the essentials of the upbringing they might have had
in Farangi Mahall as far as possible. Although the children

61. Asar to Jamal Mian, n.d., Personal File, Ibid.
62. Asar to Jamal Mian, n.d., Personal File, Ibid.
63. Asar to Jamal Mian, n.d., Personal File, Ibid.

were sent to Western schools, they were taught Arabic, Persian, and the Quran at home. Among their teachers were: Jamal Mian himself, Maulana Mirajuddin, a former student of Farangi Mahall, and Maulana Abdul Rahman Kashgari who had been connected to Farangi Mahall. School commitments permitting, the children were expected to be home for prayers five times a day so that the family could pray in *jama`t*, that is together. Mahmood remembers that theirs was a much stricter household than those of their school friends. Of course the rituals of the Farangi Mahall devotional year were, as far as possible, replicated, that is *giyarhvin, milad, `urs, fateha, roza* in Ramadan, and *qawwali.*[64]

Return to Lucknow; the Evacuee Property Case

By early 1954, Jamal Mian seemed to be settling into a life based on Dacca. At the end of April, Jamal Mian was in Calcutta hoping to find Rafi Ahmed and had been to see the film based on Anthony Hope's novel *The Prisoner of Zenda*. He could not sleep. At 1 p.m. he was woken by a phone call from Lucknow telling him that Qutb Mian had died and asking him to come to the funeral. After taking the advice of Sadri, he decided not to go; possibly Sadri feared the impact of such an occasion on Jamal Mian's stability.[65] Nevertheless, Jamal Mian travelled to Lucknow as soon as he could. He was needed to oversee the succession to Qutb Mian and to assist in the affairs of the madrasah which was, as ever, short of funds. He

64. Note by Mahmood Jamal, 3 October 2016, Ibid.
65. Note by Jamal Mian, 30 April 1954, Personal File, Ibid.

moved his whole family back to Lucknow. His older children
were sent to Lucknow schools. Farida remembers a fun-filled
period. There were lots of ladies in the house and guests from
Rudauli and Baragaon kept coming.[66]

One of the first things Jamal Mian had to do was to settle
the succession to Qutb Mian as *sajjadanashin*. This is a role
he could well have filled himself, were he minded to stay in
Lucknow. But he placed his weight behind Qutb Mian's son,
Muhammad Mian. This led to strong criticism from Sadri for
prejudicing Bari Mian's future as a Farangi Mahalli leader.
'Leave Bari Mian in Lucknow in a good English school and
also to follow the teaching of your family. You have no right
to hand over what has been built by your forefathers—to the
winds. Do not take the responsibility to put an end [to] what
generations have built … Allah guide you in your hour of
need.'[67] On this matter, Jamal Mian was much better equipped
to judge than Sadri (Illustration 21). There was no world in
which he could be both *Sajjadanashin* and provide for his
family as a businessman in Dacca.

In May and June 1954, Jamal Mian seems to have sent
conflicting signals to Sadri about when he was going to
return to Dacca. On the one hand he seemed to be burning
some of his boats in Dacca, asking Sadri to sell his car and
his refrigerator. Within three weeks of Jamal Mian's arrival in
Lucknow, Sadri was accusing him of writing 'in such a manner
that one would think you had no intention of returning from
India!'[68] It seems that Jamal Mian replied encouragingly about
his return. On 31 May, Sadri wrote that he had spent a long

---

66. Farida Jamal, 'Recollections of Ammi Dadi' Ibid.
67. Sadri Ispahani to Jamal Mian 18 May 1954, 2nd letter 18 May 1954,
     Ispahani Correspondence, Ibid.
68. Sadri Ispahani to Jamal Mian, 20 May 1954, Ibid.

time with Iskander Mirza who 'was pleased to know that you might return shortly.'[69] But Jamal Mian did not. As the months went by, Sadri continued, at decreasing intervals, to press Jamal Mian. 'The longer you will be away', he joked on 14 June, 'the longer it will take to appoint you Sheikh ul-Islam.— The post will not be filled until you return.'[70] 'Do come', he wrote on 8 November, 'you must lead a Milad in Dacca. We will miss the Qawwali this year.' He then listed their mutual friends. 'What fun is there in Qawwali without all of you.'[71] By February 1955, he was going back to his youthful tactic of emotional blackmail. 'I want you to know that on my return yesterday from Calcutta I missed you in Dacca. The same was this morning at breakfast.'[72]

In spite of Jamal Mian's prolonged absence, his business in Dacca flourished. 'Ali Husain is looking well after the business', Sadri reported in November 1954. 'I think Habib [Mian Ansari] is still living of [sic] bluff as usual (Allah may forgive me if I have misjudged).'[73] By July 1955, matters seemed quite rosy. 'In the jute section of your organization', Sadri wrote, 'they are purchasing 300–400 maunds daily. Tea sales are continuing very satisfactory with about 2000lbs a month. Matches sale is the only item which remains unsatisfactory.'[74] In September, Jamal Mian noted that he was doing well in business: 'No new income, but much more from old sources. Why should we worry?'[75]

69. Sadri Ispahani to Jamal Mian, 31 May 1954, Ibid.
70. Sadri Ispahani to Jamal Mian, 14 June 1954, Ibid.
71. Sadri Ispahani to Jamal Mian, 8 November 1954, Ibid.
72. Sadri Ispahani to Jamal Mian, 15 February 1955, Ibid.
73. Sadri Ispahani to Jamal Mian, 19 November 1954, Ibid.
74. Sadri Ispahani to Jamal Mian, 18 July 1955, Ibid.
75. Jamal Mian Diary, 14 September 1955, JMP.

It was Jamal Mian's good fortune that the death of Qutb Mian brought him back to Lucknow at a moment when he really needed to be there. In 1952, he and Qutb Mian had filed objections to the show cause notice in the Evacuee Property case on the grounds (1) that Jamal Mian had not migrated to Pakistan, and (2) that five out of six of the properties mentioned in the show-cause notice belonged to Qutb Mian. On 10 December 1953, their objections had been dismissed. They had appealed and their appeal was upheld on 1 June 1954 and a fresh hearing ordered. Jamal Mian's closeness to the Indian political establishment was widely advertised when he led the prayers at the funeral of Rafi Ahmed Kidwai after his death on 24 October 1954. Nevertheless, he still worried about the outcome of the hearing, although this worry was slightly alleviated when on 2 February 1955 he had a dream in which he saw a bearded Jawaharlal Nehru coming to Farangi Mahall and lavishing on him great love and affection.[76] On 22 February, Jamal Mian gave evidence in his case at Kanpur. On the 18 June, Assistant Custodian A. P. Tripathi decided that Jamal Mian had not migrated to Pakistan with a view to settling there, indeed, his visit (only one was mentioned) was temporary and in connection with his profession as a commission agent. His property (Tripathi did not go into whose property it was) could not be declared evacuee property. On 7 July, Jamal Mian was informed of the favourable outcome.[77]

A rough estimate from Jamal Mian's diary suggests that in 1951 he spent thirteen weeks in India; in 1952, seventeen weeks; and in 1953, just four. On this basis, he was most

---

76. Ibid. 2 February 1955.
77. Order in the Court of Sri A. P. Tripathi, JMP.

fortunate that the Custodian's judgement was in his favour. Nevertheless, now that the judgement was made and the family property in Lucknow was still in family hands, he could return to Dacca, please Sadri and his other Dacca friends, and engage more fully in its social and political life. A further incentive was that the disturbances with their anti-*muhajir* tone, which had engulfed East Pakistan in 1954, notably the riots at the Adamjee Jute Mill and the Ispahani-owned Karnaphulli Paper Mill, had subsided.[78] In December 1955, the whole family with the exception of Ammi Dadi, who was now seriously ill, returned to their house in New Eskaton Road, Magh Bazaar.

As soon as Jamal Mian had given evidence to the Custodian's hearing on 5 March 1955, he seems to have felt free to travel widely. His first move was to join Mirza Ahmed and Ghulam Faruque on a trip to Baghdad where they were met by the Raja Mahmudabad (Illustration 18). Doubtless, this was a return of the visit paid by Iraqi officials in 1954. There appears to have been no business reason why Jamal Mian should have been part of the delegation although Faruque and Mirza Ahmed may well have valued his Arabic and his connections in the Sunni world of Iraq. Nevertheless, from his point of view there was the pleasure of travelling with friends and the opportunity to pay his respects at the shrine of Abdul Qadir Gilani once more. On his return in April, Jamal Mian spent four months in constant travel through the major cities of India and Pakistan. For the most part, the purpose

---

78. For a thorough analysis of the anti-*muhajir* nature of these riots see, Layli Uddin 'In the Land of Eternal Eid: Maulana Bhashani and the Political Mobilisation of Peasants and Lower-Class Urban Workers in East Pakistan, c. 1930s–1971', (PhD Dissertation, Royal Holloway, University of London, 2015).

of his travel is not obvious, although he would certainly have been trying to raise money to support the Farangi Mahall madrasah. At the beginning of August, he discovered that Ghulam Mohamed was to be replaced as Governor-General by his friend, Iskander Mirza. Within six weeks, Jamal Mian was in Karachi taking breakfast with the new Governor General (he called Government House the 'Coffee Shop') every day and introducing his friends, Muhammad Azfar; I. A. Khan; Ebrahim Zainal, the Bombay businessman who had been with him on the Middle East Delegation in 1947; and Yusuf Najmuddin of the Bombay Bohra community who was in Karachi on business.[79] While engaged thus, he heard that his supporter of many years, Saidur Rahman Qidwai, had died. He went from Karachi to Lucknow as quickly as he could. Saidur Rahman was buried in the family Bagh.[80]

We are not able to track Jamal Mian's movements in the first half of 1956; there is no diary. July found him in Dacca meeting I. I. Chundrigar several times.[81] In August, he noted that a new Chief Secretary to the East Pakistan Government had been appointed, one Hamid Ali Khan, to replace his friend Muhammad Azfar. Jamal Mian moved quickly to draw him into his circle, inviting him to dinner.[82] A few days later, Chundrigar was again in Dacca and Jamal Mian was taking him round. Chundrigar expressed his unhappiness at Prime Minister Chaudhuri Muhammad Ali's behaviour. But more pertinently, he wanted to meet Maulana Bhashani, the peasant and workers' leader. Jamal Mian was dead against this;

---

79. Jamal Mian Diary., 23, 24, 28, 30 September, 1 October, 1955, JMP.
80. Ibid. 1, 3 October, 1955.
81. Ibid. 10, 11 July 1956.
82. Ibid. 2 August, 1956.

he felt Bhashani to be most unreliable.[83] Two months later, he was deeply upset, indeed losing sleep, because Bhashani had launched a direct attack on Ispahani operations.[84] In the middle of October, he was mixing with the Pakistani leadership, all of whom were in Dacca.[85]

Relations with the Dawoodi Bohras

Since the death of Qutb Mian, Jamal Mian had been cultivating the Dawoodi Bohras of Bombay, whose relationship with Farangi Mahall went back to the time of his father. Soon after Qutb Mian died, he went to visit them to see if they would help fund the Farangi Mahall madrasah.[86] One reason why he might have had hope of success was that in 1953, Syedna Taher Saifuddin (Illustration 24), the Bohra Leader, had made major donations to Aligarh Muslim University in exchange for being appointed honorary Chancellor.[87] Jamal Mian was unsuccessful on this occasion. But this visit does seem to mark the beginning of a relationship with the Bohras which would last for the rest of his life. He probably saw the Bohras again when he visited Bombay for a fortnight in May and June 1955. Then in November, while tied up in business in Dacca, he heard that Syedna Taher Saifuddin was going to visit Farangi Mahall.[88] He was desperate to be in Farangi

83. Ibid. 7 August, 1956.
84. Ibid. 6 October 1956.
85. Ibid. 14 October 1956.
86. Ibid. 10 December 1954.
87. Asghar Ali engineer, *The Bohras* (Ghaziabad UP: Vikas Publishing House Pvt Ltd, 1980), 210.
88. Jamal Mian Diary, 11 November 1955, JMP.

Mahall to greet the Syedna, but the young Bari Mian was
there to present some Lucknow quilts his father had had made,
and his mother reported that the visit went very well.[89] We do
not know if Farangi Mahall actually received any support as a
result of this visit but the Bohras clearly felt able to ask Jamal
Mian for favours. In July 1956, Tyabji, the representative of the
Bohras in West Pakistan, asked him to open doors for them.[90]
In November 1956, when Jamal Mian went to Bombay there
was a reception committee of Bohras, led by Yusuf Najmuddin
(Illustration 25) and Tyabji, to greet him and to carry him to
Badri Mahal, the Dawoodi Bohra centre in the city.[91] In later
life, the Bohras were to provide important financial support
for Jamal Mian.

Jamal Mian's Indian international passport impounded

Jamal Mian next visited India in March 1957 when, with
Dr Faridi, he attended the `Urs at Ajmer. He then moved
to Karachi, via Bombay, where he spent April, May, and
June staying with the Raja of Mahmudabad in 2 Framroze
Road. On 13 May, he was present at the first 'Hasrat Day'
celebrating his friend Hasrat Mohani. In July, he returned to
Dacca and on the 19th, submitted his passport to the Indian
High Commission so that it could be renewed. On 25 July, the
Visa officer at the High Commission telephoned to say that
his passport had been impounded.[92]

---

89. Ibid. 18 November 1955.
90. Ibid. 14 July 1956.
91. Ibid. 30 November 1956.
92. Ibid. 19, 21, 25 July 1957.

From the moment Jamal Mian had begun to work in Dacca he had been worried about his passport. It would appear that initially he travelled on his old passport from the time of the Raj. Acquiring an Indian International passport would have been a clear statement of his Indianness. So, when in 1952 they became available, he applied for one. On 15 May, he was interviewed in Farangi Mahall by Inspector Babu Lal of the CID, who he later discovered had written a hostile report saying he was a Pakistani spy.[93] At the same time, he had applied for a No Objection Certificate which would enable him to return to India. This was in the gift of the District Magistrate and he received it on 5 June.[94] In his diary, he does not actually mention receiving an Indian passport, despite his anxiety about it. But, he clearly did receive one for five years as it was part of the evidence he gave before the hearing of the Custodian of Evacuee Property.[95] This may have been just an India-Pakistan passport.[96] This would explain why he applied for, and received, an Indian International passport at the Indian Embassy in Baghdad on 20 March 1955. It was valid only to 15 August 1957 which suggests that his Indo-Pakistan passport was replaced by the International passport but valid just for the same period.[97]

When the High Commission impounded Jamal Mian's

93. Ibid. 16, 27 May 1952.
94. Ibid. 5 June 1952.
95. Jamal Mian was granted in 1952 passport No A350493. Order in the Court of Sri A. P. Tripathi, JMP.
96. For the passport regime at this time see: Vazir Fazila-Yacoobali Zamindar, *The Long Partition and the Making of Modern South Asia: Refugees, Boundaries, Histories* (New Delhi: Penguin Books India Pvt. Ltd, 2007), 161–89.
97. Note by J. N. Mathur, Office of the Deputy High Commission for India (Dacca), 30 July 1957. Passport File, JMP.

passport, it was in effect confiscating what had become the new badge of citizenship in the post-Partition world. In its place, he was given an Emergency Travel Certificate and required to go to India by 31 August 1957 and prove his nationality. He was only permitted to enter India by land and via the Banpur crossing. On arrival, he was to report any change of address to the local Magistrate. The certificate was for one one-way journey. Even though Jamal Mian realized that he had been running risks in living between India and Pakistan, the response of the Indian state was unexpected and humiliating.

The immediate reason for the High Commission's action was a letter from the External Affairs Ministry of 17 May 1957. Indian diplomats had noted that Jamal Mian had been staying with the Raja of Mahmudabad in Karachi for nearly three months and, apparently, he had been overheard making disparaging remarks about India.[98]

Jamal Mian used his connections to try to get the decision revoked. He contacted Ahmed Mohyuddin, the civil servant in the central government whom he had befriended in Rafi Ahmed's company. 'I got your postcard', Mohyuddin replied. 'Very worried. Go as soon as possible to the High Commission and get permission to come to Delhi. Maulana Sahib is very worried. Ajmal [Ajmal Khan, Azad's private secretary] is saying please contact him quickly. If you come over Maulana Sahib will talk to Panditji.'[99] 'I am certain that you should now come to Delhi and meet Panditji and Maulana Azad', Mohyuddin declared in a handwritten note a few days later,

---

98. Jamal Mian to Chief Visa Officer, Indian High Commission, Dacca, 15 August 1957, Passport File, Ibid.

99. Ahmed Mohyuddin to Jamal Mian, 15 September 1957, Passport File, Ibid

'I have not been able to discover where this report has come from and where it is. ... [this matter] can only be resolved if you come over.'[100] Jamal Mian's response to Ajmal Khan's request that he come to Delhi to 'clarify his position' was to send the following couplet, asking him to present it to Azad:

Each speck of dust on your street is asking for my neck.
Even if I wanted to, how many could I clarify myself to?[101]

But Jamal Mian was not prepared to take the risk that Panditji and the Maulana would be able to resolve his situation. His mother lay dying in Lucknow and he needed to go there as quickly as he could, but he also needed to be sure that he could return to Dacca, his business, and his family. Therefore, he immediately got a Pakistani passport, effectively making him a Pakistani citizen. He then flew to Karachi to get an Indian visa. He preferred to trust C. C. Desai, the Indian High Commissioner there, whom he knew, rather than take a risk with his opposite number in Dacca. Such was his hurry that he woke the Indian High Commissioner at the dead of night to get his visa, and then flew to Delhi.[102] When the Government of India refused to extend his visa so that he could be with his mother for as long as possible, Jawaharlal Nehru arranged for it to be done.[103]

Thus, Jamal Mian became a Pakistani. His wife did not immediately follow suit. In applying to the Indian High Commission to renew her passport in February 1958, she explained that she wanted to maintain her Indian nationality

100. Ahmed Mohyuddin to Jamal Mian, 20 September 1957, Ibid.
101. Jamal Mian, Note on Hasan's *Legacy*, Ibid.
102. Ibid.
103. Jamal Mian, Note on Jawaharlal Nehru, 1964, Ibid.

and to keep her children with her. She did not become a
Pakistani until 1963.[104]

                    ★ ★ ★

Jamal Mian's life in the decade from Partition to 1957 reveals
that he did not, as Mushirul Hasan suggested, leave Farangi
Mahall 'overnight' and bereft of his crucial support. Although
occasionally he thought about taking Pakistani citizenship,
he firmly maintained his Indian citizenship, taking out what
appears to have been one of the new Indo-Pakistan passports
in 1952, and turning it into an Indian International passport
at the Baghdad embassy in 1955. Indeed, he maintained
his citizenship until he was forced into a corner by the
Government of India in 1957. This said, in the six years
and more that he lived between India and Pakistan, he did
slowly slide in a Pakistani direction, pushed by the hostility
he received in Lucknow and pulled by the relative ease and
pleasure of life in Dacca and Karachi.

Amongst the pleasures of these cities was being surrounded
by many old friends from his Muslim League past, who
were running the country, but also by cultivated senior
administrators. In Karachi, there was Iskander Mirza, Khwaja
Nazimuddin, Chundrigar, and Khaliquzzaman all holding
the highest political positions. In Dacca, there were many top
administrators from outside the region: Ghulam Faruque,
Ghufran Faruqi, Muhammad Azfar, and the two sons of
Nawab Ismail Khan, G. A. Madani and I. A. Khan. In both

---

104. Mrs Kaniz Fatima Asar to Mr Mahomed Rafique, Chief Visa Officer,
     Indian High Commission, Dacca, 15 February 1958, Passport File,
     JMP.

cities there would always be the Ispahanis, and sometimes
the Raja of Mahmudabad, and for a moment Khaliquzzaman.
Jamal Mian's standing amongst this elite was such that he
could get an immediate response when he sought it. On one
occasion, the two Alsatian dogs of his next door neighbour,
Jehangir Khan, the Ispahani general manager, savaged the
local milkman. Jamal Mian was furious and immediately
telephoned G. A. Madani, then Commissioner of Dacca, to
have Jehangir Khan punished. Within hours, Jehangir Khan
was imprisoned. After cooling down, Jamal Mian asked that
the man be released.[105] Jamal Mian's circle of businessmen,
administrators, and politicians in East Pakistan, in which only
Fazlul Huq makes a brief appearance, underlines the *muhajir/*
West Pakistani takeover of the Bengali world to which Bengalis
objected so strongly. This said, Jamal Mian, as Chapter Twelve
reveals, was probably rather less detached from the Bengali
world than his elite colleagues.

Through Jamal Mian's experience, we can sense the
stresses borne by Indian Muslims, particularly if they had
been League activists, as they tried to make their way in
independent India. They were 'fair game' for those who had
backed the nationalists; they also became fair game for rivals
in their locality. We have noted how his rivals harassed him
through the Evacuee Property Act and equally how Inspector
Babu Lal would appear to have prevented him from getting
an Indian International Passport, and how a report by
diplomats in Karachi led to the impounding of the Indian
International passport that he did get. But, on the other hand,
the Evacuee Property judgement was in his favour, which was
most fortunate, and he did seem to receive the No Objection

105. Jamal Mian Diary, 2 August 1956, Ibid.

Certificates he needed to travel between India and Pakistan
without too much bother. Jamal Mian was able to use his elite
connections in India to further the interests of the Ispahanis,
to ease the business of being in Delhi, to smooth the process
of Hajj, and to have his visa extended. However, when it came
to the central boon of Indian citizenship, this was either a
favour he did not feel Nehru was able to grant, or a favour
for which he did not wish to beg. When he saw Nehru after
he had become a Pakistani citizen, the Prime Minister asked:
'Why did you not come to me?' Jamal Mian gave no answer
and 'Nehru hung his head'.[106]

In Jamal Mian's life over the ten years between Partition
and the impounding of his passport, we see the machinery
of modern statehood—permits, no objection certificates,
passports, visas—steadily being imposed to create two
separate bodies of citizens where once there had been one.
Also, through his eyes, we witness the fashioning of different,
if only slightly different ways of being in real life, from the
differing values of the rupee in India and Pakistan through
to the differing roads in life on which the Muslims of the
two countries were now travelling. Eventually, it became
too difficult for Jamal Mian to be domiciled in India and to
work in Pakistan. Jamal Mian's 'long partition' in terms of
citizenship took a whole ten years. But, in fact, the process of
partition in terms of access to the places which gave meaning
to his life was to continue until he died.

---

106. Jamal Mian, Note on Hasan's *Legacy*, Ibid. Jamal Mian's note also
     states that Ishaat Habibullah told him that Sir Maharaj Singh's son,
     who worked in the Prime Minister's office, had reported that Nehru
     had written on top of Jamal Mian's file: 'the manner in which we have
     dealt with Jamal Mian shows what is wrong with us.'

18. The Raja of Mahmudabad, Ghulam Faruque, member of an Iraqi trade delegation, Mirza Ahmed Ispahani and Jamal Mian, Dacca 1954

12

Politics, business, international engagements, and the break-up of Pakistan, 1958–1971

FROM 1958 TO 1971 JAMAL MIAN WAS FIRMLY BASED IN DACCA. In the early years, his ties to India began to drop away although those that remained, in particular the spiritual ones, continued to be strong. Nevertheless, Jamal Mian increasingly came to focus on Pakistani and international matters. One theme was his growing engagement with Pakistani politics, at the heart of which was his relationship with the President Ayub Khan. A second theme was the growing international dimension to his existence, which was reflected in his membership of the Motamar al-Alam al-Islami (World Muslim Congress) of the Palestinian leader, Mufti Amin al-Husseini (Illustration 19) and the Rabitat al-Alam al-Islami (World Muslim League) of the Saudi government. The third theme was the development of his business career which both benefited and suffered from his engagement in politics. The high point of this was the bringing to fruition of his Shakarganj Sugar Mill project. All of these things took place against a backdrop of growing opposition to West Pakistani dominance in East Pakistan, and specifically to the *muhajir* presence in the region.

Finding his way in Pakistan

As soon as he gained Pakistani citizenship, Jamal Mian became
more involved in Pakistan's politics. In January 1958, the
National Assembly, founded under the Pakistan Constitution
of 1956, was meeting in Dacca. As a spectator, he attended
the debates every day and entertained leading figures at Darul
Qiam.[1] When on 10 January the action moved to Karachi, he
followed it. He met Iskander Mirza in the President's House
almost every day and, amongst other things, counselling him
not to declare martial law, which suggests that the President
had this in mind well before he took action.[2] At the same time,
Jamal Mian was meeting all of his old friends: Mahmudabad,
Ghulam Faruque, Madani, Ebrahim Zainal, Khaliquzzaman,
and Tyabji Al-Kayum. He went on with Ebrahim and Tyabji to
Bombay where on 30 January, Dr Faridi telephoned to say that
his mother had died. 'Before I knew my mother had died', he
told his diary, 'I saw her in a dream. She kissed my forehead.
She showed me her leg and said: "look it has all gone". At that
point I knew she had died.'[3] This brought an end to one of his
most important ties to Lucknow.

At the end of May 1958, Jamal Mian set out on his third
Hajj. He succeeded in annoying the Pakistan Hajj officer by
making contact with Prince Faisal, then heir to the Saudi
throne. 'The Pakistani Diplomatic Mission here', he noted,
'does not like any Pakistani to meet the king.'[4] He enjoyed the
irony that, when he was last on Hajj in 1950, he as an Indian
citizen had stayed with the Pakistani ambassador, but that

---

1. Jamal Mian Diary, 4, 5, 6, 7 January 1958, JMP.
2. Ibid. 1, 13, 14, 15, 16, 17, 18, 20 January, 1958.
3. Ibid. 30 January 1958.
4. Ibid. 7 June 1958.

now he was a Pakistani citizen, he was staying with the Indian ambassador.[5] In what was often his way, almost on a whim, Jamal Mian decided to go on to Cairo after Hajj. There, he was met with great affection by Mufti Amin al-Husseini, whom he had last seen in 1947.[6] Further evidence of his friendship with the current Pakistani President was an invitation he received while staying at the Cairo Embassy asking him to join Iskander Mirza in Tehran on 19 July. But Jamal Mian was not prepared to hang around in Cairo to make this date. He returned directly to Dacca via Karachi.[7]

Jamal Mian spent most of September 1958 in India. The morning of 7 October found him in Karachi with Iskander Mirza. In the afternoon, he was with him again, along with the Raja of Mahmudabad. On this occasion, the President made it clear that he wanted full control of the government in his hands. Hence, it should have come as no surprise to Jamal Mian when, the following day, he learned that the President had abrogated the constitution and declared Martial Law. General Ayub Khan was appointed Supreme Commander of the Armed Forces and Chief Martial Law Administrator.[8] Within three weeks, Ayub Khan had used his military muscle to overthrow Iskander Mirza, to pack him off in exile to London, and to replace him as President. Jamal Mian makes no comment on this coup, but, given his earlier counselling of Iskander Mirza against Martial Law, and his friendship with him, he was probably not happy.

Jamal Mian spent 1959 and 1960 travelling through India and Pakistan, meeting his friends, and following his

---

5. Ibid.
6. Ibid. 7 July 1958.
7. Ibid. 13, 14, 19 July 1958.
8. Ibid. 7, 8 October 1958.

devotional round, as he had done for much of the 1950s. There was one event on 1 March 1959 at Farangi Mahall for which he really wanted to be present. This was the opening of the Abdul Bari Academy which was to publish and market the works of his father. Jawaharlal Nehru was doing his family the great honour of inaugurating the Academy. It must have hurt Jamal Mian greatly not to be present, but he decided, probably because he was now a Pakistani citizen, that 'it would not be appropriate'.[9] He was very grateful to Nehru for his speech on the occasion and made sure that Rajeshwar Dayal, the Indian diplomat who was serving in Dacca at the time, carried his thanks to Nehru along with his signature gift of a hookah.[10] Feeling it unwise to attend this event would have brought home to Jamal Mian how he was becoming detached from his heritage, as would the death of Irtiza, his father's driver and his driver, who had cared for him in his early years. He was, however, able to do something positive about the past by preparing the first collected edition of Hasrat Mohani's poetry, his *Kulliyat-i Hasrat*. But the turmoil in his heart was expressed in these lines of Ghalib that he recited with some force to a startled Bari Mian as at this time they flew over Lucknow on a flight from Calcutta to Delhi:

Relinquishing the temple of my pride and ego
I once again circumambulate* the streets of infamy!
Once again, I assemble the broken pieces of my heart
It's been a long time since it was pierced by the beloved's lashes!

---

9. Ibid. 1 March 1959.
10. Ibid. 5, 7 March 1959.

*Ghalib uses the term 'tawaf' that is the term used for going
around the Kaaba.

In 1960, Jamal Mian went to London for the first time. His
diary for this period is thin but even then it is surprising that
no mention was made of his visit. It is very likely that he spent
time, as he did on other visits, with his friend Iskander Mirza,
who was condemned to a penurious exile.

In 1960, an event of no small interest was the evidence
Jamal Mian gave before the Constitution Commission,
which Ayub Khan had appointed to examine the reasons
for 'the failure of the parliamentary system in Pakistan'.
Notes in his papers indicate that Jamal Mian gave serious
thought to the process. On 21 July, he gave his evidence in
Dacca orally. He acknowledged, as everyone did at the time,
that the country faced major problems: 'In this abnormal
situation,' he declared, 'where the urgent need is for the
rapid development of the country and also for the solution
of other problems, which if not attended to in time and
satisfactorily, will endanger the safety of the country, it
appears to me unwise to think of any democratic form of
constitution. As a matter of fact', he continued reflecting
the Cold War concerns of the time, 'from Indonesia up to
Sudan democracy has been in difficulties in combatting the
influence of communism.'[11] He recommended that for 'a
temporary period, say five or ten years [his notes suggest
twenty years] as the Commission may consider it fit to
fix during which the economic uplift of the country can
be attended to, the present regime with some necessary

---

11. Copy of statement given by Jamal Mian, businessman, Dacca, Witness
    116, to the Constitution Commission, Dacca, 21 July 1960. Ibid.

modification should continue.'[12] These modifications were
that Fundamental Rights, which Ayub Khan in abrogating
the 1956 Constitution had abolished, should be recognized,
and that the Supreme Court should be given jurisdiction
over the complaints of the aggrieved. If the Commission
felt that the Supreme Court should not be drawn into this
matter, then it should devise some other means of restraint
on the President during the emergency period.

With regard to the issue of an Islamic state, Jamal Mian
said:

> Although on independence day Quaid-i-Azam made a speech
> which clearly indicated that he wanted a democratic state yet
> the events which took place subsequent to that date, i.e. the
> killing that went on and the questions which arose which were
> mainly based on communal difference, inclined him to the
> view that it was necessary that an objective should be a Muslim
> state. But no definite shape, [sic] was given to this and then
> unfortunately he fell ill and died. But I took the stand in the
> circles in which the question was debated that it would not
> be in accordance with the principles of Islam to make this
> [country] a Muslim state, after having achieved it on the basis,
> more or less, of a contract the laws of which do not justify our
> making it into a Muslim state. The idea was that we should
> treat Muslims and non-Muslims equally so that it may have a
> corresponding effect in India.[13]

Then Jamal Mian repeated the point he had made to the
Constitution Commission in 1952. With regard to people acting

---

12. Ibid.
13. Ibid.

in accordance with the Quran and Sunna, this should depend
on the example of those in the public eye, the implication being
that it should not depend on the machinery of the state.[14]

Jamal Mian and Ayub Khan

In retirement, Jamal Mian listed the friends he had made
throughout his life. One of them was Ayub Khan.[15] The
relationship can be traced only through Jamal Mian's papers;
no mention of it is made in any of Ayub Khan's published
writings. It seems that the Raja of Mahmudabad may have
been instrumental in their meeting. When Jamal Mian was
doubtful about attending the meeting, it was the Raja who
persuaded him to go and accompany him to Rawalpindi
from Dacca, via Lahore, on 7 October 1961. The meeting
went well. Ayub Khan approved of Jamal Mian's statement
that 'in Pindi there are no Pakistanis. Each active politician is
either a Punjabi, Baluchi, Pathan or Sindhi. The government
is nothing but an assembly of tribal leaders each trying to
propagate the interests of his "tribe".' Moreover, he remained
'warm and friendly' in spite of Jamal Mian's statement that
Ayub's government 'had not done much better than Iskander
Mirza's'. Ayub Khan then said that it would be good if people
like Jamal Mian were in Parliament. Jamal Mian replied that
'Maybe fifteen years ago he would have taken up the option but
that now he was too concerned about looking after his family
to take up such responsibilities ... the desire for sacrifice and
duty to country had been exhausted in him.' Ayub Khan

---

14. Ibid.
15. Biographical note, 1, 11, 1975, Ibid.

closed the meeting by asking Jamal Mian to go with him to
Dacca by plane. For a man who was fascinated by politics,
but had foresworn involvement, this was a sore temptation.
As he was wont to do on such occasions, he turned to Hafiz
for guidance. The Diwan fell open at the following couplet:

A Saqi whose mouth is sweet and a singer whose verses are
beautiful
A companion who is of good character and a friend who has
a good name.

Jamal Mian interpreted this as giving him the go-ahead to
join Ayub.[16]

On the plane, Jamal Mian spoke to Ayub Khan freely. He
said that 'this country was neither made by history or by
geography, nor indeed was it made by religion BUT BY A
POLITICAL MOVEMENT.' For this reason there was no
point in trying to copy Ataturk's example in Turkey or that
of the Shah in Iran. 'I also expressed my opinion freely,' he
noted, 'on the Ulama.' He did not say what his views were,
but they were unlikely to be favourable. He told Ayub 'if you
prefer I can keep my mouth shut for the next five years.' The
President said: 'You have been quiet long enough.'[17] This was
a clear invitation to Jamal Mian to lend his voice to supporting
the President's initiatives. When they were in Dacca, Jamal
Mian met Ayub Khan again, at the Governor's House, where
their conversation covered many topics. 'I then said to him',
Jamal Mian noted, 'I have talked a lot and often openly, if at

---

16. Note dated October 1961 in a notebook supplementing his 1961 Diary,
    Ibid.
17. Ibid.

any time I appear disrespectful, please forgive me.' At this, the President hugged him.[18]

Jamal Mian's diaries for 1962 and 1963 do not exist. Family tradition, however, maintains that he was very much part of Ayub Khan's entourage. He found new friends there. One was Amir Muhammad Khan, the Nawab of Kalabagh (1910–67), hereditary chief of the Awans of Mianwali district. He was chair of the Pakistan Industrial Development Corporation and Governor of West Pakistan (1960–66). He has been described as a 'perfect instrument for Ayub's authoritarian rule. A ruthless administrator and a wily political manipulator, the thick-moustached Kalabagh kept firm control over the press and used the police to silence his opponents. Stories of his tyrannical methods have passed into Pakistani folklore.'[19] With this reputation it may not be surprising that he was killed by one of his sons in a quarrel over the maintenance of his estate. Nevertheless, he was an important patron of Jamal Mian, making possible the Shakarganj Sugar Mill project which was to help make him comfortable in later life.

The second new friend was Mohamed Shoaib (1906–74), Ayub's Finance Minister from 1961–67. Shoaib hailed from Azamgarh in the UP and had been plucked out of the World Bank, where he was an Executive Director, to serve Ayub. Pakistan's economy did particularly well under his guidance. He was helpful to Jamal Mian in various ways. Jamal Mian represented the Darul Musannifin Shibli Academy of Azamgarh in Pakistan. The National Bank of Pakistan had

---

18. Ibid.
19. Ayesha Jalal, *The Struggle for Pakistan: A Muslim Homeland and Global Politics* (Cambridge Mass: Belknapp Press, 2014), 107.

donated Rs 25,000 to the Academy in recognition of its service to the literature of Islam, but there was difficulty in transferring the money. Shoaib made it happen.[20] Then, he was also helpful in larger ways, doing what he could to promote Jamal Mian's business career. Jamal Mian's diaries frequently mention Shoaib indicating the strength of their relationship, which was continued after Shoaib returned to the World Bank in 1967, in a vigorous correspondence. Shoaib's son married Jamal Mian's daughter, Amina.

In 1964, the relationship between Jamal Mian and Ayub Khan was illustrated in Ayub's campaign to be re-elected President. The constituency for the election were the basic democrats whom Ayub Khan, believing that Pakistan was not ready for direct democracy, had fashioned in 1959. Under the 1962 Constitution, the directly elected members of the Union Councils, which formed the lowest tier of Ayub's 'Basic Democracy', formed a constituency of 80,000 which would elect the President. In the election, the Convention Muslim League supported Ayub Khan while the Combined Opposition Parties—whose programme included the restoration of direct elections, adult franchise, and the democratization of the 1962 Constitution—supported Fatimah Jinnah, who hitherto had had little to do with politics. Jamal Mian remembered opening Ayub's campaign. In his speech, he quoted the following couplet in criticism of Miss Jinnah:

Anyone who crosses boundaries is bound to be destroyed
They wallow in the dust like the tresses of the beloved.[21]

---

20. Jamal Mian Diary, 10 January 1965, JMP.
21. Jamal Mian, undated note in 1964–65 notebook, Ibid.

December 1964 saw him speaking all over Pakistan. When in Karachi, he would, as usual, have breakfast with the Raja of Mahmudabad in 2 Framroze Road. Then, the Raja would go off and campaign for Miss Jinnah while he did so for Ayub. He was often employed as a speaker to warm up the crowd before Ayub spoke (Illustration 20). Not all his rhetoric was sophisticated. 'It was after a long time', he told an audience of Basic Democrats, 'that the Muslim world had produced a person who was a thinker and a soldier at the same time; as such President Ayub Khan deserves all the support of the people.'[22] One afternoon, the President sent him a message that he should go with him to Karachi. The following day, he had breakfast with the President. He reported their conversation:

I said to the President Sahib that whether it was a law case, a war or an election, a wise person, despite being 100% confident of victory, should think of what he would do in the event of defeat. The President's answer really impressed me. He said that he wanted to retire at some point, but considering the situation in the country he is loathe to hand over power into the hands of Miss Jinnah. That is why he is fighting the election. I then told him that if he is defeated, he should consult the army first, as it was as a representative of the army that he had declared Martial Law when he took power. [Jamal Mian had clearly forgotten that it was his friend Iskander Mirza who had declared Martial Law] I also said that the citizens of Karachi were antagonistic after the capital was moved away from there, and it will be difficult to get their support, but I will try.[23]

---

22. Clipping from the *Morning News*, 9 December 1964, Ibid. In the last week of the campaign he was often in the President's company.
23. Jamal Mian note dated 28 December 1964 covering recent events. Notebook 1964–65, Ibid.

The next day, after attending an event at the President's House, Jamal Mian flew to Karachi. In a short space of time he made numerous speeches. He spent much of election day, 2 January 1965, at Mohamed Shoaib's house, worried at first that Ayub might be losing, and then learned around 7 p.m. that Ayub was the clear victor.[24] In fact, there was no need for him to have worried. 'The entire administration was mobilized in Ayub's favour', Jalal tells us, 'What followed was a thoroughly rigged electoral process.'[25]

Looking back at the campaign, there was one particular incident which stuck in Jamal Mian's mind. 'While speaking in Multan I suddenly had this nursery rhyme in my head re. Khwaja Nazimuddin:

Humpty Dumpty sat on a wall
Humpty Dumpty had a great fall.

I was going to say it in my speech but thought it was a bit unbefitting so I resisted the temptation.'[26] After coming back from the meeting, he learned that Khwaja Nazimuddin had died. The following day at breakfast, with the President, people talked about the Khwaja. 'I said that anyone who utters La Ilaha Illalah is destined for heaven in my belief. Bhutto intervened and said something negative about him. I silenced him with one couplet:

Do not criticise someone else for what they are.
Look at the state of your hem and your buttons are undone.[27]

---

24. Jamal Mian Diary, 2 January 1965, Ibid.
25. Jalal, *Struggle*, 115.
26. Jamal Mian, entry for 5 January 1965, Notebook 1964–65, JMP.
27. Ibid.

Reflecting on his relations with Ayub Khan in 1969, Jamal Mian felt that immediately after the 1965 Presidential election, Ayub Khan began to distance himself from him. Indeed, after this, he met the President little. This was the time when the President was acting on the advice of Altaf Gauhar (1923–2000), the powerful information minister under Ayub Khan and de facto number two) and Zulfiqar Ali Bhutto (1929–1979, foreign minister 1962–67, President 1971–77) with regard to Kashmir and visiting China and Russia.[28] Jamal Mian does not mention the impact of the Indo-Pakistan war of 1965, but it was surely the reason why 'his behaviour towards me was careful as I was a Hindustani'.[29] 'For the past three years', he noted, the President, 'has been caught between two Gauhars.' By this he meant Altaf Gauhar 'his political guru' and Gohar Ayub, his son who wielded great influence in the administration.[30] Jamal Mian continued, stating that over the past few months when he had met the President at the airport, he had been 'aloof and distant'.[31] The most recent occasion had been just a week earlier when he had seen Ayub Khan off at Dacca after the Pakistan Muslim League meeting, which was the last time the two met.[32] He wondered if the latest frostiness stemmed from an incident, in Karachi on 28 August 1968, at the wedding of Sarvat Ikramullah to Prince Hasan of Jordan. Jamal Mian had read the *nikah*. He feared that his refusal to translate the *Khutba* which he had given, or more likely his criticism of the constitutional reforms while getting

---

28. Jamal Mian Diary, 17 February 1969, Diary 1968–69, Ibid.
29. Ibid.
30. Ibid.
31. Ibid.
32. Jamal Mian Diary, entries covering –13 February 1969, Ibid.

Ayub's signature for the *nikah,* had given offence.[33] Jamal Mian
may not have realized how sensitive the pressures of rule since
1965 had made an already thin-skinned man. Ayub Khan was
no longer able to cope with the straight taking which had been
a feature of their early relationship. Muhammad Shoaib urged
Jamal Mian to go and see the President in person and repair
the relationship. But Jamal Mian decided, according to Hafiz:

> The right thing to do at this time is
> To pack up and find a tavern and sit there quietly.[34]

Growing engagement with the wider Islamic world

While Jamal Mian was becoming involved in the high politics
of Pakistan, he was also travelling to the Middle East and to
Britain more frequently. He was beginning a pattern of life
that he would continue almost to his death. In 1965, the
government made him Pakistan's representative at a conference
of the Motamar al-Alam al-Islami (The World Muslim League)
in Cairo. The Motamar had been founded at a conference
hosted by Abdul Aziz ibn Saud at Mecca in 1926, to consider
ways of promoting the solidarity of Islam after the abolition of
the Turkish Caliphate. After its second meeting in Jerusalem
in 1931, the Motamar achieved organizational form. Mufti
Amin Al-Husseini, then Grand Mufti of Jerusalem, was elected
President. The birth of Pakistan revitalized the Motamar.
Congresses were held in Karachi in 1949 and 1951 and its

33. Jamal Mian Diary, 17 February 1969, Ibid.
34. Ibid.

headquarters were established there. We have already noted that Mufti Amin visited Farangi Mahall in the 1930s and Jamal Mian met him in Cairo in 1947 and 1958. From now on, their relationship was to deepen. Like Jamal Mian, Mufti Amin had good relations with the Dawoodi Bohra leader, Mulla Saifuddin, and his two sons. Moreover, it was through Jamal Mian that he came to meet Ayub Khan and Muhammad Shoaib.[35]

Not much of note actually happened at the Motamar meeting. Jamal Mian was met in Cairo by Abul Fazl of the Embassy, who happened to be Mustafa Qidwai's son. His co-representatives from Pakistan were Mufti Mahmud and Maulana Ghulam Ghaus, who both made speeches, and so somewhat uncharacteristically, he did not do so. Jamal Mian did, however, propose a motion in support of those suffering from a cyclone in East Pakistan. Towards the end of the meeting he spoke in Arabic on the Palestine issue.[36] After this, he moved on to Medina and then to Jeddah where he met the Indian Ambassador, yet another Qidwai, in this case Midhat Kamil, who insisted that he stay with him. After spending some days in Jeddah, he had hoped to meet Hafiz Wahba (1889–1969), who had visited Farangi Mahall before World War One and subsequently had a distinguished career including posts as Governor of Mecca and Ambassador to London. But the two failed to meet on this occasion. Jamal Mian went on to Beirut, via Jerusalem, where he made a point of praying for Maulana Mohamed Ali who was buried in the compound of the Dome of the Rock. From Beirut, Jamal Mian travelled into the mountains of Shtara where he met Mufti Amin. He noted that the Mufti was a very strong

35. Ibid. 5 July 1974.
36. Ibid.13, 17, 18 May, 1965.

supporter of Pakistan and wanted the Motamar to have much
closer ties.[37] He then returned to Karachi, via Tehran, where
he spent several days with the Raja of Mahmudabad.

Jamal Mian's next visit to the Middle East, of which we
have a record, took place in the shadow of the Arab defeat in
the war with Israel in June 1967. In September, he met Mufti
Amin and it was decided that a Motamar delegation should go
to King Faisal under the leadership of Dr Nasir, an Indonesian
scholar, to put a resolution on Palestine before him. From
Jamal Mian's record of the occasion it seems that little was
achieved. King Faisal opened the occasion by suggesting that
the reason the Jews ('Yahudis' was the term he used) had won
was because we were not good enough Muslims and the Arabs
were the very worst in this respect. Jamal Mian took up the
theme saying God acts in his own way; 'when the Arabs lost
Jerusalem a Kurd, Salahuddin Ayyubi, got it back for them'.
Then Jamal Mian said that his President had great respect
and regard for His Highness; the King reciprocated. By this
time, because Jamal Mian and others had not given Dr Nasir
the opportunity to speak as leader of the delegation he was
clearly very upset. After this exchange, the audience came to
an end. After reporting events to Mufti Amin in Beirut, Jamal
Mian returned to Dacca.[38]

Jamal Mian and the Shakarganj Sugar Mill Project

In the midst of his engagement in politics and his travels to the

---

37. Ibid. 25 May 1965.
38. Ibid. 23, 24, 30 September and 2 October 1967.

Middle East and London, Jamal Mian was also trying to run the business which supported him and his family. Jamal Mian saw a direct conflict between business and politics. When, for instance, in 1961 Ayub Khan asked him about his business, he replied that he would have to abandon his business because he could not pay enough attention to it.[39] Nevertheless, given the nature of the Pakistani system, there were some advantages to political involvement, as his fortunes bear out.

In the early 1960s, there was a hiccup in Jamal Mian's business. His relative, Habib Mian, who had become quite wealthy, declared that as Ansari Ltd. had been registered in his name, he would be the controlling influence and set about easing Jamal Mian out. The stress brought on by this treachery sparked a bi-polar incident in Jamal Mian, similar to that he experienced in 1949, for which Asar did not forgive Habib Mian. For his part, Jamal Mian refused to have anything further to do with his relative. As a result, he set up a separate business which, as he was now a Pakistani citizen, he could register in his own name. It was 'M. Jamaluddin Abdul Wahab (Jamal Mian), Merchant and Commission Agent'.

In the 1960s, this business built on what had been established with the help of the Ispahanis in the 1950s. So his core business was jute, gunny bags, and tea, to which in the 1960s he added fertiliser.[40] He also had a series of agencies, courtesy of Tyabji Abdul Kayum, his Dawoodi Bohra friend, who was Director of the Saifee Development Corporation. Jamal Mian received 5 per cent of the net profit made by Saifee on orders for metallic links received from the Director

39. Note, 1 October 1961, Jamal Mian Notebook, 1961, JMP.
40. Jamal Mian to H. Cooper, International Credit Information Bureau, 4 May 1967, Muhammad Shoaib Correspondence, Ibid.

General Defence Procurement. He was also an agent for the sale of Saifee gas cookers.[41] As we have already noted, Jamal Mian was the Pakistan agent for the Darul Musannifin Shibli Academy, Azamgarh. Moreover, in May 1966, Greaves Cotton & Co (Pakistan) offered him ½ per cent on the F.O.B. value of the order for assisting N.V. Energy Division, Almeto, Holland to obtain a power station contract at Habibganj, Sylhet.[42] In 1962, Jamal Mian was discussing with Hassan Ispahani the prospect of buying Russian tractors; Hassan insisted that he keep in touch with Qadri, the Chairman of the Agricultural Development Corporation.[43] Thereafter, in 1966, he seems to have created the Standard Shipping Company which applied to Pakistan's Industrial Development Bank, without success, for financial assistance in buying a vessel.[44]

We do not know how well Jamal Mian's business went but we do know that his personal financial position steadily deteriorated in the second half of the 1960s. In May 1967, he received a stern letter from the Manager of the Standard Bank in Dacca. He referred to Jamal Mian's overdraft of Rs 1,12,631, which had been outstanding since 1964. He noted that, despite many written reminders and personal contacts, Jamal Mian had done nothing about it. He went on to mention that the State Bank of Pakistan, in its recent audit, had taken strong objection to his long-standing liabilities; he

41. Tyabji Abdul Kayum to Maulana Jamal Mian, 22 January 1958 and 7 August 1963, Shakarganj Mill File, Ibid.
42. Greaves Cotton & Co (Pakistan) Ltd to Jamal Mian 16 May 1966, Ibid.
43. Hassan Ispahani to Jamal Mian, 14 March, 22 March 1962, Ispahani Correspondence, Ibid.
44. Chief Manager, Industrial Development Bank of Pakistan, to M/S Standard Shipping Co., PO Box No 230, Darul Qiam, New Eskaton Road, Dacca, 10 January 1966, Shakarganj Mill File, Ibid.

requested that they were liquidated within the next fortnight.[45] No evidence exists as to whether Jamal Mian was able to satisfy his bank manager or not. Nevertheless, we do know that, as the protest movement against Ayub Khan grew in the autumn of 1968, Jamal Mian was heading towards a serious financial crisis. On 20 November, he was worried about increased expenses.[46] Two days later, he could not 'figure out a solution to the financial problem. It is essential to lower expenses and increase income somehow. I have managed to survive for a few years in this way, now I feel I have to do something.'[47] On 17 December, Sadri gave Bari Mian Rs 4,000. 'The truth is', Jamal Mian told his diary, 'for the last two years this kind of help has been very handy in meeting the expenses of the household.'[48] The following day he was still worrying.[49] By the 26th, he was beginning to chastise himself and make small adjustments to his lifestyle.

Today I had this feeling that because of my own laziness and inability in business, I am not able to make any headway in arranging the means of survival. The coming few months are very delicate. I must be very careful about meddling in politics and focus seriously on my personal [financial] matters. In this light I have decided to postpone my trip to Karachi.[50]

Jamal Mian's diary contains graphic descriptions of the break down of order in Dacca in early 1969. On 21 January,

45. Lutfur Rahman Sarkar to Jamal Mian, 30 May 1967, Ibid.
46. Jamal Mian Diary, 22 November 1968, Ibid.
47. Ibid. 24 November 1968.
48. Ibid. 17 December 1968.
49. Ibid. 18 December 1968.
50. Ibid. 26 December 1968.

people were being asked to walk barefoot in the streets in sympathy with the strikers. On the night of the 23rd, there was a massive demonstration led by students and on the 24th, there was a general strike and an outbreak of fighting between Bengalis and non-Bengalis. On the 29th, he saw the 'horrid sight' of the burnt out *Morning News* building. By this time, he was very anxious and worried as to the outcome of the situation. On 16 February, there was smoke rising from the city in all directions; on the 21st, his next-door neighbour said he was moving to a safer location; on the 22nd, all of the windows in the Ispahani offices were broken.[51]

These developments, combined with Jamal Mian's financial worries led to a further bi-polar attack similar to those he had experienced in 1949 and the early 1960s. The illness hit him in Karachi where he spent a few days in hospital. Hassan Ispahani seems to have played a role in looking after him. He wrote the following aide-memoire for Jamal Mian on 14 May 1969:

1. Complete rest. Read and sleep—meet people and talk the minimum quantum.
2. Have one 2mg Valium after breakfast.
3. Have one 2mg Valium after lunch.
4. Have one 2mg Valium after dinner. After 2 or 3 days reduce the dosage to one tablet after dinner.
5. Keep off controversial talks—politics and business.
6. Read in your spare hours either the holy book or light literature.
7. Do not waste energy by talking unnecessarily.
8. Take half an hour's walk after breakfast—or sunrise and

---

51. Ibid. 21, 23, 24, 29 January, 16, 21, 22 February 1969.

sunset. Walk in a park with greenery—not on a traffic loaded road.

9. If you do not sleep well, I shall arrange [to] change your evening dose from Valium to some other effective and harmless drug.

10. You must have a full eight hours <u>undisturbed</u> sleep every night. Anything less is not enough.

11. Finally there is nothing basically wrong with you. Your condition has been brought about solely through worry, stress and strain. If you follow my advice above you will be as right as rain in ten short days. Hassan.[52]

Sensible measures were taken to bring Jamal Mian's finances under control. A mortgage was taken out in his wife's name and secured against the value of Darul Qiam, which was her property; the value was Rs 2,26,250. From this, Jamal Mian was to liquidate his existing liabilities which amounted to Rs 1,80,000. He was permitted to rent out his godown at Rs 13,000pm which was set against the expenses of the bank with the remainder being credited to his wife's account.[53]

With his health restored and his finances in better shape, Jamal Mian left for London where he spent June, July, and August passing time with his close friends, Mirza Ahmed Ispahani and Iskandar Mirza (Illustration 27). He tried to look after the latter 'as much as I could'. In September, he returned to Dacca. Reflecting on his illness in Karachi, he lamented that it was the cause of much disrepute for him and

---

52. Note by Hassan Ispahani, 14 May 1969, Ispahani Correspondence, JMP.

53. Typed note, signed by Jamal Mian, 8 June 1969, Shakarganj Mill File, Ibid.

he found out who his real friends were, namely Mirza Ahmed Ispahani, Hassan Ispahani, and Muhammad Shoaib.[54]

The Shakarganj Sugar Mill Project

Throughout the period of financial worry there had been one ray of hope. It was that his Shakarganj Sugar Mill Project would bring him a significant return. The project was the point at which Jamal Mian was unwittingly drawn into what Markus Daechsel has termed 'the dream of "development"—that great venture of transformation that gripped the world in the second half of the twentieth century' of which Ayub Khan's Pakistan was a model.[55]

Some time before July 1963, the Nawab of Kalabagh gave Jamal Mian a licence to develop a sugar mill and the Raja of Mahmudabad a licence to develop a cotton mill. Doubtless, this was a shrewd act of patronage designed to tie these two key *muhajir* figures to the regime. Jamal Mian was in very good company. The others who were given, or promised, licences for sugar mills at this time were: Mr Bhutto in Sind near Larkana; Pir Pagaro in Sind; Hasan Mahmud at Bahawalpur, Feroz Khan Noon at Bhyawal, Sargodha; and Shah Nawaz at Pasraur, Sialkot.[56] Jamal Mian set up a trust to act as the legal framework within which the development took place. Typically, he named it the Shakarganj Sugar Mill Trust in honour of Baba Farid of Pak Pattan and decreed that sugar

---

54. Jamal Mian Notebook 1969 entitled 'Story of illness and travels before the formation of Bangladesh' JMP, Ibid.

55. Markus Daechsel, *Islamabad and the Politics of International Development in Pakistan* (Cambridge: Cambridge University Press, 2015), 1.

56. S. M. Ahmed to Jamal Mian, 8 August 1965, Shakarganj Mill File, JMP.

from the mill should be presented to the *sajjadanashin* of the shrine every year.

Of course, Jamal Mian did not have the first idea of how to manage a project of this kind. First he brought in a disciple, Ataur Rahman Alvi of the Standard Bank to manage the project. He had already given him a power of attorney to develop some land for him. But one consultant was central to carrying the project forward. This was S. M. Ahmed, a US-trained MBA, whom the family nicknamed 'American Ahmed'. He did much of the legwork in getting the project moving. In all probability, he drafted the following letter which Jamal Mian sent to the Nawab of Kalabagh in July 1965:

My dear Nawab Sahib,

With reference to my recent interview with you at Lahore during which I outlined to my desire of setting up an industrial project in West Pakistan. I have considered the proposition in consultation with my adviser and have concluded that a sugar mill containing crushing and refining sections with ancillary plant to utilise molasses and bagasse of about 200 tons capacity to be located in the vicinity of Jhang Sadar would be a feasible proposition. Already some preliminary work has been done on the project and I feel that I will be able to finalise the details for the formal application for obtaining finance and foreign exchange in a short time. Therefore I would be most grateful if you would kindly consider my [*sic*] this proposal favourably and accord the necessary sanction for me to progress the project. I hope to submit the formal application within a few days.[57]

---

57. Maulana Jamal Mian Darul Qiam (Camp Karachi) 11 July 1965 to Malik Aamir Mohamed Khan, Nawab of Kalabagh, Governor of West Pakistan, Lahore, Shakarganj Mill File, Ibid.

300   JAMAL MIAN

In August 1965, Ahmed was particularly busy on Jamal
Mian's behalf. He had written an initial report on the
project.[58] In a revised version, he took into account what
he had learned from officials. The Punjab was preferable to
Sind for a new mill because Sind had enough capacity while
business interests in Chiniot and Lyallpur were pressing
for more in the Punjab. It was crucial that he got the mill
sanctioned for Jhang, thus, neutralizing the business interests
which favoured Toba Tek Singh.[59] By the middle of August,
he had sent three copies of the application and project report
to Jamal Mian.[60] He had checked on the status of Jamal
Mian's project. The Governor (Kalabagh) was the key figure
in the process. He had sanctioned the project in principle
and the Provincial Permission Committee would process the
formal application. He advised that some foreign capital or
involvement would be essential for the project to go forward.
As at the moment Jamal Mian had made no provision for
this, he should go to the Industrial Development Bank of
Pakistan (IDBP) for the foreign exchange element. The
next step would be to form a Private Limited Company
which ultimately would become a Public Limited Company.
Furthermore, the relationship of the Trust that Jamal Mian
had set up to the Company should be one of holding a block
of shares. Jamal Mian should move quickly to buy land in
Jhang with a tubewell unit, and it would be sensible to ask
the Governor to let the District Commissioner know and
ask him to help. He then reinforced the point that Jamal
Mian really needed to move quickly to ensure that a rival

58. S. M. Ahmed to Jamal Mian 8 August 1965, Ibid.
59. Ibid.
60. S. M. Ahmed to Jamal Mian, 17 August 1965, Ibid.

mill was not established nearby and that he should keep the provincial administration informed at all times.[61] By November 1965, S. M. Ahmed had visited Jhang. The local people were keen on the project and had promised to invest. The District Commissioner was also keen. The Governor was proposing to visit Jhang on 24 November and there were to be representations regarding industrial projects in the district. It was crucial that Jamal Mian clarified the location of his project before the Governor visited.[62]

In the summer of 1966, Jamal Mian was organizing the financing of the project. In April, he had been asked to make a formal application to the Pakistan Industrial Credit and Investment Corporation (PICIC).[63] At the same time, he also approached the IDBP for a foreign exchange loan of Rs 1,40,00,000 and a rupee loan of 15,00,000.[64] In July, things seemed to be progressing well. He wrote to his friend, Mohamed Shoaib, the Finance Minister, to thank him for making it possible for him to take a loan.[65] In August, he was told that the terms he had asked for were acceptable to the Ministry of Finance.[66] Then, two things happened which brought the project to a halt. The Nawab of Kalabagh was dismissed as Governor of West Pakistan. Soon after, Jamal Mian's licence for the sugar mill was withdrawn. He was furious and flew straight from Dacca

---

61. Ibid.
62. S. M. Ahmed to Jamal Mian, Camp Jhang, 14 November 1965, Ibid.
63. R. Gallyot to Jamal Mian, 7 April 1966, Ibid.
64. Jamal Mian to Managing Director, Industrial Development Bank of Pakistan, 26 April, 1966, Ibid.
65. Jamal Mian to Mohamed Shoaib, Finance Minister, Qasr-e-Naz, Club Road, Karachi, 15 July 1966, Ibid.
66. M. A. Siddiqi, Government of Pakistan, Ministry of Finance, to Jamal Mian, 1 August 1966, Ibid.

to Islamabad and, according to family tradition, PIA bag
in hand, he marched into the President's House and said
to Ayub: 'If this is the way you are going to insult me, why
did you give me the licence in the first place?'[67] Ayub Khan
ordered that the licence be restored immediately. But the
licence was not immediately restored. As late as May 1968,
he was complaining to Shoaib that nothing had happened.[68]
But a few days later, he had good news about the licence
from the Military Secretary to the President[69] and this was
followed by a letter from the provincial government saying
that 'on reconsidering the matter' it had now asked the
PICIC to finance his project.[70] The second development
was the outcome of a feasibility report on the capital
structure of the Shakarganj Sugar Mill by Associated
Consulting Engineers, one of whom was Muhammad
Razzaq, a disciple of Jamal Mian's from Hyderabad, which
indicated that if the PICIC provided the foreign exchange
for the purchase of machinery Jamal Mian would have to
raise Rs 20,00,000 of which 12,00,000 would need to be
in shares raised from the public and 8,00,000 would need
to be supplied by him.[71] In April and May, as Jamal Mian's
correspondence with Mohamed Shoaib and his business
acquaintances reveals, Jamal Mian desperately sought the

---

67. Family tradition according to Mahmood Jamal.
68. Mohamed Shoaib to Jamal Mian, 3 May 1968, Shakarganj Mill File,
    JMP.
69. Md Rafi Khan (Major-General) Military Secretary to the President to
    Jamal Mian, 12 May 1968, Ibid.
70. Government of West Pakistan, Industries, Commerce and Mineral
    Resources Department to Jamal Mian, 11 June 1968, Ibid.
71. ACE—Associated Consulting Engineers Ltd., Note on Capital
    Structure of the Shakarganj Sugar Mill, Feasibility Report, Ibid.

finance he needed to enable his project to run. But no one was willing to support him.[72]

Then Mian Bashir, of the powerful Mohd. Amir Mohd. Bashir Chiniot Shaikh trading and industrial family, who ran Crescent Mills, got into touch with Jamal Mian and asked for the Memorandum and Articles of Association of Shakarganj Mill Ltd.[73] We do not know how this happened but it is not improbable that the news got around that Jamal Mian was having difficulty in raising the finance for his mill. Even though the licence for the mill had not actually been returned, and had only been promised by Ayub Khan, he was able to make a deal with Mian Bashir. 'I met Mian Bashir', he noted in his diary, 'and it was agreed I hand over everything to them [ie the firm of Mohd. Amir Mohd. Bashir] in exchange for 12 lakhs of rupees which were deposited with Alvi' of the Standard Bank who acted for him.[74] Three weeks later, Jamal Mian cancelled the agreement with Ataur Rahman Alvi by which he acted for him in sugar mill matters.[75] Mian Bashir was now, in principle, in the driving seat as far as the sugar mill was

72. See the following correspondence: Mahomed Shoaib to Jamal Mian, 11 and 17 April 1967; George Naylor (International Development Consultant) to Jamal Mian 22 April 1967; W. E. Knox to Jamal Mian, 27 April 1967; Francois Corpet of Pierrefitte to Jamal Mian, 9 May 1967; Mahomed Shoaib Correspondence, JMP.
73. Zeeba Zafar Mahmood, *The Shaping of Karachi's Big Entrepreneurs (1947–98): A socio-political study* (Karachi: City Press, 2003), 71; and Mohd Amir Mohd Bashir Ltd, Karachi to Jamal Mian, 19 August 1967, Shakarganj Mill File Ibid.
74. Jamal Mian Diary, 19 August 1967, Ibid.
75. Countersigned agreement cancelled 12 September 1967, Shakarganj Mill File, Ibid.

concerned. Nothing could happen until the licence was
formally returned in the following year.

Once the licence was returned, Jamal Mian was on
tenterhooks as to when Mian Bashir would deliver, a feeling
driven, of course, by the dire state of his personal finances.
In December and January, acquaintances who knew Mian
Bashir assured him that he was reliable.[76] When no news had
come by early March, he told his diary: 'I want to forget about
the whole business, but keep thinking about it.'[77] But then a
week later, key papers, probably those formally transferring
ownership to Mian Bashir, had been signed and returned.[78]

In January 1970, Mian Bashir was as good as his word.
He deposited Rs 12,00,000 in Jamal Mian's account against
which Jamal Mian pledged to Mian Bashir 1,20,00,000 shares
in Shakarganj Mill Ltd. For some reason, Jamal Mian wanted
to hold on to his shares for a year; the shares were to be
purchased at Rs 20.50 per share on or after 20 January 1971.
On 22 January 1971, Jamal Mian completed the deal with
Mian Bashir. Jamal Mian received Rs 24,00,000 for his shares.
Half the sum paid off Mian Bashir's original deposit. The
other half went to Jamal Mian. On 21 February, he was invited
to the first board meeting of what was now Shakarganj Mills
Ltd at the Company's office in Karachi. Its main business was
to approve a prospectus to be issued to the public inviting
a subscription of Rs 100,00,000.[79] What had been largely a
paper exercise for many years was now moving towards reality.
Jamal Mian had turned his licence into real money. Mian
Bashir was now in the business of building a real sugar mill.

---

76. Jamal Mian Diary, 5 December 1968 and 6 January 1969, Ibid.
77. Ibid. 10 March 1969.
78. Ibid. 15, 17 March 1969.
79. Invitation dated 22 February 1971, Shakarganj Mill File, Ibid.

The mill exists to this day and, as Jamal Mian intended, sends sugar to Baba Farid's shrine every year.

Jamal Mian was immensely fortunate to have twelve lakhs of rupees at his disposal at this juncture. He was about to experience the greatest upheaval in his life since the move to Dacca. This was of course South Asia's second great partition of the twentieth century (ignoring the partition of Bengal right at the beginning), which derived from the emergence of Bangladesh in East Pakistan and the consequent partition of Pakistan. When Jamal Mian completed his deal with Mian Bashir he was actually in hospital in Karachi. He returned to Dacca in February to face a massive civil disobedience movement demanding independence for East Pakistan after Yahya Khan's regime refused to allow Sheikh Mujibur Rahman's victory in the all-Pakistan elections of 1971 to stand. It was a situation which was increasingly hostile to non-Bengalis.

Jamal Mian was deeply saddened by the emergence of the Bengali independence movement and the harshness of the Pakistani response. He had always made a point of being close to the Bengalis, and certainly much closer than most of his *muhajir* contemporaries. He mixed regularly with Bengali Sufis and had his own Bengali disciples; regular meetings with Dr Ibrahim, a specialist in diabetic medicine particularly between 1967 and 1971 kept him up-to-speed, in a personal way, with Bengali aspirations; he employed the Eskaton Imam to teach him Bengali with the aim of giving speeches in the language; and he encouraged his children to sing the Bengali *na`t*s they learned at school. But he clearly did not feel that his goodwill to Bengalis and their aspirations would protect him and his family if order broke down. For their safety, he sent his daughters with his wife's brother's family to Karachi.

He was deeply critical of the army action against the Bengali independence movement which began on 25 March, making his views clear to his children.[80] He himself was very unwilling to leave Dacca. But eventually, he yielded to pressure from Mirza Ahmed Ispahani and left for Karachi on 14 April with his wife and Bari Mian. The strain and his great sadness at the turn of events brought about a recurrence of his bi-polar illness which forced him to stay in Karachi until September.

Even before the Pakistani army surrendered in December 1971, it must have been clear to Jamal Mian that he would not be able to return to Dacca. He had lost his business, his house, and the world that he had created for himself and his family in Dacca. There was the deeper blow that much of the effort and sacrifice of his life had been brought to nought; the Pakistan which he had spent many of the best years of his life trying to create had been destroyed. It is significant that he refers to none of the remarkable events of 1971 in his diary. Nor are there any of the reflective overviews of events which appear in earlier diaries. We must assume that he was just too depressed to write. There were just two bright points to lighten the gloom. First, he did succeed in rescuing his books and family papers which meant much to him. With Mirza Ahmed Ispahani's help, he was able to hide his books and family papers in a Shia imambara. Later, with the help of his daughter's (Farida) uncle-in-law, who was the Malaysian High Commissioner to Dacca, they were transferred to Kuala Lumpur. Only the bound files of *Hamdam*, his newspaper, were lost. Second, he did have Rs 12,00,000, less the mortgage on Darul Qiam which, to his friends' amazement, he insisted on paying off, to help him and his family start again.

---

80. Communication from Farida Jamal, 2 October 2016, Ibid.

19. Jamal Mian with Mufti Amin al-Husseini of Jerusalem in the 1960s.

20. Jamal Mian electioneering with Ayub Khan in 1965.

21. Sadri Ispahani with his son, Sajid,
in Dacca.

22. Jamal Mian in Morocco where he received the Kifalatul Fikriya
in 1968 from King Hassan.

23. Jamal Mian on a Rabita mission to East Asia.

24. Important supporters: Jamal Mian with Syedna Taher
Saifuddin of the Dawoodi Bohras.

25. Important supporters: Jamal Mian with Dr Yusuf Najmuddin of the Dawoodi Bohras.

26. Important supporters: Jamal Mian speaking at a function hosted by Hakim Said.

27. Jamal Mian with former president Iskander Mirza in London.

درگاه شریف اجمیر   اعجاز بی   جمال   باری میاں   انیس میاں

28. Jamal Mian at Ajmer with Bari Mian and Ejaz and Anis Ajmeri attending the `Urs.

29. Jamal Mian in Tokyo with Inamullah Khan, when the Motamar
received the Niwana Peace Prize.

30. Jamal Mian and Asar in retirement in Karachi.

31. Jamal Mian's funeral, Clifton, Karachi, 2012.

13

Life in Karachi, 1971–2012

THE MOVE TO KARACHI IN 1971 MARKED THE END OF JAMAL
Mian's business and political involvement. In Karachi, he set
about building a new home for himself and recreating his
social and cultural life. His public life was now mainly bound
up with his work for the Motamar and the Rabita for both
of which he travelled widely. He also travelled to London
almost every year. Until 1982, the old holy places in India
maintained their powerful attraction for him. However, after
his last climactic bi-polar incident in Lucknow, he swore never
to go to India again. From now on, he continued the pattern
of life he had developed since 1971, but found spiritual
sustenance in part in Pakistan but primarily at Medina to
which he travelled as often as he could.

Settling into Karachi

After returning from London, via Jeddah, in November 1971,
Jamal Mian began to establish his life in Karachi. He and his
family stayed with his old friend from Dacca, Muhammad
Azfar. This distinguished civil servant, who in the mid-1960s
had been Establishment Secretary of the Government of
Pakistan and Secretary to the National Assembly, had been
forced into retirement by Ayub Khan, who objected to his

307

views on the impact of the transfer of the capital from Karachi to Islamabad. Now he chaired the Urdu Dictionary Board.

In February 1972, in spite of the large sum that had come to him, Jamal Mian was still worrying about spending too much. 'The car mirror broke', he noted in his diary, 'had to spend five hundred rupees. I am spending inordinate amounts. God help!'[1] After paying off debts from the Rs 12,60,000 he received for his Shakarganj Mill shares, he had Rs 10,00,000 left which probably wisely he had deposited in different places. He had made what he termed a fixed deposit investment through his bank of Rs 3,50,000, he had a further fixed deposit investment of Rs 3,50,000 in his and Asar's name, then Rs 1,00,000 in the bank in his name, and Rs 50,000 in Bari Mian's name. In addition, he had lent Bari Mian Rs 16,000 for business purposes, and had made loans to the son of a friend of Rs. 25,000 and to Manzur, his father's disciple of the General Boot House, Rs 20,000. Beyond this, he had spent Rs 20,000 buying a car. After this mention of money worries disappears from his diary, doubtless reflecting, in part, the increasing responsibility that Bari Mian was taking in his area. He just mentions donations he receives from well-wishers, for instance, Mufti Amin al-Husseini or Dr Burhanuddin, the Bohra leader.[2]

Jamal Mian then set out to find somewhere to live. He looked at properties in amongst other places: Defence, Mahomed Ali Society, and Sir Syed Road.[3] On 29 June, he moved into a rented property on Kashmir Road and changed his plan; he would no longer buy a house but would build one.

---

1. Jamal Mian Diary, 14 February 1972, JMP.
2. Ibid. 5 July 1974, 29 July 1981.
3. Ibid. 10, 18 March, 9, 10 June 1972.

By March 1973, Bari Mian had identified a plot of land next to Kamal Azfar's[4] house in Clifton, which he bought in his mother's name.[5] The gifted young architect, Arif Hasan[6] was engaged to design the house; he found Jamal Mian a somewhat fussy client. By June 1975, the new house was finished. This meant that Jamal Mian could do something of enormous importance from his point of view. His books, but more important his family papers, which had been sent to Farida in Kuala Lumpur for safekeeping, could now be reunited with him. Among these papers were not just his own papers but those of his father, of some of his ancestors, including early farmans relating to Farangi Mahall. Surrounded by the family archive, and his library, Jamal Mian felt re-attached to his past; their presence meant a great deal to him.

It was serendipitous that, at the time that Jamal Mian had fully re-established his personal world in Karachi, we should have met. He was in London for May, June, and July 1976,

---

4. Kamal Azfar (1940–) Born Chandauli, UP, the son of Muhammad Azfar (see p. ? fn ?) Educated, Government College, Lahore, and Balliol College, Oxford. Called to the Bar in 1963. 1961–63, research assistant to Gunnar Myrdal; joined the Pakistan Peoples Party in 1970; Minister for Finance, Planning and Development, Sind; Federal Minister for Local Government and Rural Development; Chairman of the Prime Minister's Task Force on the Social Contract under Prime Minister Benazir Bhutto; Governor of Sindh 1995–97. He married Naheed, the daughter of the distinguished civil servant, S. S. Jafri.

5. Ibid. 11 March 1973.

6. Arif Hasan (1943–). Hasan migrated with his parents to Karachi in 1947. Studied architecture at Oxford Polytechnic 1961–65, and worked in architectural practices in the UK, France, and Spain for three years before starting his own practice in Karachi. The practice gained a national and international reputation for dealing with urban planning and development issues.

and on 18 May he asked me to come and see him in Farida's
rented flat close to Regent's Park.[7]

Jamal Mian wanted to meet the author of *Separatism Among
Indian Muslims: The Politics of the United Provinces' Muslims,
1860–1923* (Cambridge: Cambridge University Press, 1974).
He was particularly keen to do so because the book was the
first to set out the major role played by his father in the politics
of the period 1912–26. This said, there were one or two points
of fact which he wished corrected. Once these issues were
settled, we got on well and talked for hours. As we parted,
Jamal Mian told me that he had family papers in Karachi and
I was welcome to come and see them whenever I wanted. As
Jamal Mian's diary attests, I worked on them, microfilming
large quantities in January 1977 and 1978.[8] This generous
act, for Jamal Mian devoted his time to me when I was in
Karachi, both enabled me to write *The `Ulama of Farangi
Mahall and Islamic Culture in South Asia* (Delhi: Permanent
Black, 2001) and also influenced everything else I have written
on the Islamic world. It helped to shape a worldview as well
as an approach to writing Islamic history.

While Jamal Mian was becoming physically and perhaps
psychologically established in Karachi, a circle was also
forming around this very sociable man. There was an intimate
group of people he met regularly, the connections being both
long-term friendship and religious. There was Muhammad
Azfar and his family, whom he had known well in Dacca and
who was his host at the beginning of his Karachi life. Azfar's
son, Kamal, was a rising lawyer and politician. There was also

---

7. Jamal Mian Diary, 18 May 1976, JMP.
8. Ibid. 1–12 January 1977, 17 August 1977. There is no diary for early
   1978.

Ebrahim Zainal, from the eminent Ali Reza business family
of Jeddah who had accompanied him on the delegation to
the Middle East in 1947, and whose uncle, Muhammad,
had been so distressed in 1950 when he thought that Jamal
Mian was having to work in a jute mill to survive.[9] There
were two descendants of the founder of the Qadiriyya Sufi
order, Abdul Qadir Gilani of Baghdad: Pir Abdul Qadir
Gilani, former Iraqi ambassador to Pakistan, who settled in
Karachi, and Pir Najmuddin Gilani, the son of Pir Ibrahim of
Bombay, who had been very close to Maulana Abdul Bari. So,
too, was the father of Ataur Rahman of the Standard Bank,
and Mr Manzur of the General Boot House. Then there were
two devotees of Jamal Mian himself, Niazi Sahib and Ahmad
Mian Ansari, a descendant of Mulla Haider (see Chapter
2 p. 17). Jamal Mian also went frequently to see Hakim
Nasiruddin, the owner of the Nizami Dawakhana, a Unani
Tibb Pharmacy. Finally, there were two further notable civil
servants. First, there was S. S. Jafri, who Jamal Mian met
as the returning officer for the Bara Banki constituency in
the 1946 elections. He had had a distinguished career in
Pakistan, becoming Federal Secretary under Ayub Khan.
He was also Kamal Azfar's father-in-law. Second, there was
Ghulam Faruque, who Jamal Mian had known as Chairman
of the Jute Board in Dacca. Something of a mentor to Jamal
Mian, he was in the process of carving out a major political
and business career in West Pakistan (see Chapter 11 note 2).

Beyond this intimate circle, there were others who Jamal
Mian saw less frequently, or so his diary would suggest. Those
mentioned are only those whose names appear in his diary;
there is no doubt that his acquaintance ranged much more

9. See Chapter 10, 13.

widely. One group in this category was formed by relations and friends he had known for many years. There was Habib Mian Ansari, Maulana Sibghatullah's son, who had cheated him out of his business in Dacca.[10] In Karachi, he was in desperate straits and begged Jamal Mian for a loan of Rs 20,000; Jamal Mian showed forgiveness and accommodated him.[11] There was Usman Mian, his wife's brother, who had escorted his daughters to Karachi in 1971.[12] Hassan Ispahani was now based in Karachi, although Jamal Mian's relationship with him seems to have been less intimate that it had been in Calcutta and Dacca in the 1940s and 1950s.[13] This said, he extended his Ispahani acquaintance to Hassan's son, Zia, who was to become a distinguished Pakistani diplomat. There was also his former political boss, Choudhry Khaliquzzaman, on whom he took pity in his last illness,[14] and another Lucknavi, Shaddan Faridi, the brother of his great friend, Dr Faridi. Then, there was Nawab Ismail Khan's eldest son, G. A. Madani, whom he had known in Dacca (see Chapter 11 n. 43). In 1971, he retired from the civil service and was elected as independent member of the Sind Provincial Assembly.[15]

The second element of this less intimate circle of acquaintances consisted of the great and the good of Karachi, whom he had come to know as he settled there. K. M. Bashir of Hysons often invited Jamal Mian to preside

10. Jamal Mian Diary, 5 February 1972, 28 June 1977, 21 July 1977.
11. Ibid. 28 January 1977.
12. Ibid. 20 January 1972, 23 March 1977; Communication from Mahmood Jamal 28 August 2016.
13. Jamal Mian Diary, 5 January, 5 February, 25 February, 18 May 1972, 21 April 1973, 17 February 1977.
14. Ibid. 1, 24, 29 April 18 May 1973.
15. Ibid. 11 October, 1973.

over *qawwali* at his house.[16] There were notable academics: I. H.Qureshi (1903–81) the historian whose writing on Muslim South Asia amounted to propaganda, talking of a separate Muslim and Hindu communities and suggesting the inevitability of the emergence of Pakistan;[17] the political scientist A. B. A. Haleem (1897–1975) who was the first Vice-Chancellor of Karachi University;[18] and Akhtar Hameed Khan (1914–99), who, after resigning from the ICS in disgust at the Bengal famine of 1943, developed a second career as a social scientist and development practitioner, amongst other things developing his Comilla model of development in East Pakistan and designing the famous Orangi Town in north Karachi.[19] Another ICS man was Syed Hashim Raza (1910–2003), who had been the administrator of Karachi from 1948 to 1951 and had played a leading role in the construction of Jinnah's Mazar.[20] He told me that he had injected the idea of the Moroccan arch into the design. Another figure was Mr Justice Qadiruddin (1908–95), Chief Justice of both the Sind High Court and the West Pakistan High Court, whom Jamal Mian had met on his exploration of Pakistan in 1950.[21] There were also Shaikh Abdul Majid Sindhi (1889–1978), a convert to Islam who had figured in the Silk Letters Conspiracy in World War One and who had fought in the 1930s for the separation of Sind from the Bombay Presidency[22] and Inamullah Khan (1912–97), the

---

16. Ibid. 15 January, 5 February 1972, 6 July 1977.
17. Ibid. 20 January 1972.
18. Ibid. 23 April 1973.
19. Ibid. 25 February 1972.
20. Ibid. 23 March, 11 October 1973.
21. Ibid. 11 April 1973.
22. Ibid. 13 May 1972.

founder of the Motumar al-Alam al-Islami in Karachi, with
which Jamal Mian was much involved into the 1990s.[23] There
were in addition notable cultural entrepreneurs in this group.
One was Hameed Haroon (1952–), the grandson of Abdullah
Haroon, with whom Jamal Mian had stayed when he and the
Raja of Mahmudabad attended the Sind Provincial Muslim
League Conference in October 1938. Hameed was on his
way to becoming the CEO of Pakistan Herald Publications
which publishes the daily newspaper, *Dawn*. In his address
at the condolence ceremony after Jamal Mian's death, he
recalled how, after he had injured his spine and been confined
to bed, Jamal Mian would come and visit him every day.[24]
The second was Hakim Said (1920–88), an Unani Tibb
physician from Delhi, who had established the Hamdard
Foundation on his arrival in 1948, where he pursued research
into herbal medicine. This grew into his Medinat al-Hikmah
Centre for education, science, and culture, and Hamdard
University. Hakim Said had broad cultural interests and Jamal
Mian was to speak on several occasions under his auspices
(Illustration 29).[25]

There were also distinguished women who were part of his
world, Lady Ross Masood[26] and Begum Ikramullah, (1915–

23. Ibid. 23, 30 April 1973, 30 April 1977.
24. Address by Hameed Haroon, Conference of Condolence for Jamal
    Mian Firangi Mahali, Arts Council of Pakistan, 14 November 2013,
    JMP.
25. Jamal Mian Diary, 7 March 1977, 14 July 1978, Ibid.
26. Lady Ross Masood, was the wife of Syed Ross Masood (1889–1937),
    Vice-Chancellor of Aligarh Muslim University from 1929. Second, she
    married Rahat Said Chhatari, son of Nawab Ahmed Said Chhatari
    (1888–1981), a major landlord in Bulandshahr, UP. Rahat was Pakistan
    ambassador to Jordan and Chief of Protocal in the Foreign Ministry.

2000).[27] Jamal Mian took me to tea with them in January 1978
and I was able to see the lively, indeed spirited, relationship
the three had. Except for K. M. Bashir, Abdul Majid Sindhi,
and Hameed Haroon, all of this elite group were *muhajir*s.
Many of them would have come together on 13 May each
year to celebrate Hasrat Mohani Day.

Jamal Mian's society was not restricted to Pakistan. As
the years went by, there were increasing visits from friends
outside Pakistan. A notable early visitor was Mufti Amin al-
Husseini who came twice in the early 1970s. On the first
occasion, he stayed for nearly three weeks and Jamal Mian
was with him every day.[28] In early 1974, Sulaiman, the son
of his great friend, the Raja of Mahmudabad, who had died
in the previous year, was in Karachi. Amongst other things,
he was in town to attend a memorial service for his father.[29]
The occasion would have been one of no small significance
for the *muhajir* community. Then there were visits from his
relatives and the wider connections of Farangi Mahall in India.
Mufti Raza Ansari, the scholar and family historian, who was
a lecturer in the Department of Theology, Aligarh Muslim
University, stayed for at least three months.[30] Matin Mian,
his nephew, came as well as his close friend from madrasah

27. Begum Ikramullah was the daughter of Dr Hassan Suhrawardy, and the
    first Muslim woman to receive a PhD from the University of London.
    One of the two women who sat in Pakistan's Constituent Assembly, she
    was also Pakistan's Ambassador to Morocco 1964–67 and a delegate
    to the United Nations on several occasions. She was also an author an
    essayist. Jamal Mian presided over the *nikah* of her daughter to Prince
    Hasan of Jordan.
28. Jamal Mian Diary, 30 April to 18 May 1973, JMP.
29. Ibid. 6 January 1974.
30. Ibid. 8 October, 12 December 1977.

days and business partner in Dacca, Ali Husain Mohani.[31]
Then there was Mushir Mian Razzaqi from the holy family
of Shah Abdul Razzaq of Bansa, who was currently living
in Farangi Mahall[32] and Muhammad Mian Allahabadi from
the family of Muhibullah Allahabadi, long associated with
Farangi Mahall. Towards the end of the 1970s, there were
visits from Haider Husseini, the son of the late Mufti Amin,
and Dr Dwalibi who were arranging on behalf of the Motamar
an Asian Muslim Conference in Karachi.[33] Two further
visitors of great importance were Mulla Burhanuddin, who
had succeeded his father, Syedna Tahir Saifuddin, as leader
of the Indian Dawoodi Bohra community and his brother,
Dr Yusuf Najmuddin. Jamal Mian made a point of celebrating
Mulla Burhanuddin's presence in Karachi.[34] Again, he showed
great respect for the Mulla and his brother when he visited
Karachi in 1981.[35]

Jamal Mian was able to maintain his wider South Asian
connections, to some degree at least, by travelling to India and
Bangladesh. In 1975, he travelled to Bombay and Lucknow.
In Bombay, his prime concern was to pay his respects to
his Dawoodi Bohra friends; he made a special visit to the
tomb of Mulla Tahir Saifuddin, who had shown goodwill to
Farangi Mahall in the 1950s.[36] While in Bombay, he went into
a reverie about his many previous visits to the city, sparked
perhaps by the fact that the city was so much less accessible
to him now. 'When I got up this morning memories of earlier

31. Ibid. 18 March 1981, 28 April 1978.
32. Ibid. 25 February 1982.
33. Ibid. March (no precise date), 7 July 1978.
34. Ibid. 26 March, 12 May 1978.
35. Ibid. 27, 28, 29 1981.
36. Ibid. 5 August 1975.

visits to Bombay came flooding back. In 1938 the friendship
of Maulana Shaukat Ali and Raja Sahib Mahmudabad, Pir
Ibrahim, Jinnah Sahib and after that till Partition—the various
journeys I made to Bombay, staying at Ispahani's flat, Mohd
Ali Manyar, and the stay at Khilafat House.'[37] He left Bombay
for Lucknow where, as his father would have done, he went
straight to Bagh Maulana Anwar to pray in the company of
his ancestors. He saw Sulaiman Mahmudabad and his uncle,
Nabbu Mian, paid his respects to the Faridi household,
and saw his nephews Matin Mian and Muhammad Mian
in Farangi Mahall. At the cost of Rs 5,000, he recovered
family books which the latter had sold to a collector.[38] On 7
April 1980, Jamal Mian dreamed that he was in India 'and
everybody is very happy to see me'. The following day, he
was delighted to learn that the Rabita had selected him to
tour India as a member of its Mosques Committee. He saw
this as an interpretation of his dream and was pleased by the
thought that 'I will be able to pay my respects at Ajmer `Urs
… This is something I have been deprived of for some time.'[39]

A few months earlier, there was an example of how
subcontinental elites might still help each other across national
boundaries as they had done in the 1950s and 1960s. Jamal
Mian had been given a visa to enter and leave India through
Delhi, but he was not sure whether he might enter India
from Malaysia through Bombay. Mani Shankar Aiyar, the
Consul-General in Karachi who was later to become a leading
Congress politician, wrote to the Indian High Commissioner
in Malaysia, introducing him to 'M. M.Jamaluddin Abdul

37. Ibid.
38. Ibid. 8, 9 August 1975.
39. Ibid. 18 April 1980.

Wahhab, a close friend of Ambassador Bajpai, and a leading
figure in the Pakistan Movement'. He had given him a visa
for Delhi but 'I would be grateful, if he is to visit Bombay, if
you will instruct your consular secretary to amend the visa.'
The civility behind this letter is telling, given the often fraught
relations between India and Pakistan, but perhaps more telling
was the fact that Aiyar thought Jamal Mian's role as a leader
in the Pakistan movement a suitable calling card.[40]

In 1975, there was an extraordinary moment in which
Jamal Mian became the unofficial envoy of the Bangladeshi
government. After Sheikh Mujib was assassinated, Sadri
Ispahani asked Jamal Mian to come to Bangladesh to meet
the new President, Khondkar Mushtaq, and then to try to
persuade the Saudis to recognize Bangladesh at the Rabita. In
September, Jamal Mian went to Dacca, being admitted even
though he had been refused a visa.[41] 'The Dacca journey', he
told his diary, 'was beneficial and pleasant in every way ....
Everyone met me with affection, love and regard.[42] He picked
up the message from President Mushtaq and it seems that his
welcome may have healed some of the wounds of his losses
in 1971. A couple of weeks later, he travelled to the Hejaz
and delivered the President's message in an open session of
the Motamar along with an invitation to Shaikh Saleh, the
Secretary-General of the Rabita, to visit Bangladesh. Some
objected strongly that Jamal Mian should be representing
Bangladesh in this way. Jamal Mian proposed that Ali Ashraf
should be nominated to represent Bangladesh, a proposal

---

40. Mani Shankar Aiyar (Govt. of India) to Shri S. S. Chatwal, High
    Commissioner of India in Malaysia, 13 August 1979, Misc. File 1980–
    81, JMP.
41. Jamal Mian Diary, 31 August 1975, Ibid.
42. Ibid. 17 September 1975.

which was accepted even though Saudi Arabia was yet to recognize the new country.[43]

Spiritual Life in Karachi

Settling into Karachi did not mean simply establishing and sustaining networks of friends, it also meant fashioning a world of religious engagement and spiritual practice which was now largely lost to Jamal Mian in India and Bangladesh.

In Karachi, there were two new focuses for Jamal Mian's spiritual devotion: the two descendants of Abdul Qadir Gilani, *Ghaus-e A`zam,* Pir Najmuddin, and more important from Jamal Mian's point of view, Najmuddin's cousin, Pir Abdul Qadir Gilani. Until Pir Gilani's death in March 1976, whenever Jamal Mian was in Karachi, he would pay his respects at least once a week.[44] Then, the Farangi Mahall custom of saying *fateha* on *Giyarhwin,* the 11th of each month, for *Ghaus-e A`zam* was continued while, of course, his `Urs on 11 Rabius Sani was celebrated. Such was the respect that Pir Gilani's family had for Jamal Mian that it was he who recited the prayers at the Pir's funeral in March 1976.[45] The Pir's tomb in Karachi became a spiritual focus for Jamal Mian, who celebrated his `Urs in subsequent years. In his early years, in Karachi, Jamal Mian was supported in his devotion by another Qadri *pir,* and friend of many years, Pir Mohiuddin of Golra.[46]

---

43. Ibid. 24 September 1975.
44. For instance, in May and June 1972, according to his diary, Jamal Mian saw the Pir eight times. 5, 24, 25, 27 May, 8, 9, 10, 13 June 1972, Ibid.
45. Ibid. 27 March 1976.
46. Ibid. 22, 23 April 1972, 30 June 1974.

Jamal Mian also recreated important aspects of the
Farangi Mahal devotional year. The main Farangi Mahall
saints' 'Urs were remembered on 25, 26, 27 Safar, as they
would have been in Lucknow. In 1973, for instance, two
devotees of Farangi Mahall, Yusuf and Idris Khan, arranged
a major celebration on 25 Safar at his house on Kashmir
Road. More than fifty people attended, including Pir Abdul
Qadir Gilani, Pir Najmuddin, Muhammad Azfar, Kamal
Azfar, Shahab Azfar, Rashid Mian from the family of Shah
Abdul Razzaq of Bansa, and several Hyderabadi followers
of Farangi Mahall.[47] The highlight of this devotional year
was, as in Farangi Mahall, the remembrance of the Prophet
on the first twelve days of Rabiul Awwal, culminating in a
performance of *Milad* on the 12th. This was organized by his
wife, Asar, who had a great tent erected in the garden of his
Clifton house, and many came from Karachi to participate.
Increasingly, however, Jamal Mian's attention turned towards
Medina which he visited in most years. In 1978, for instance,
he could see no reason to attend the Rabita Conference that
October but 'for me a chance to visit Mecca and Medina is
something I cannot miss.'[48]

Travels Abroad

What enabled Jamal Mian to go to the Hejaz so often was his
involvement with the Rabita which held an annual conference
there. This was just part of an increasing programme of
international travel involving delegations on behalf of the

---

47. Ibid. 31 March 1973.
48. Ibid. 11 October 1978.

Motamar as well as the Rabita, journeys to see his eldest daughter in Kuala Lumpur, and journeys to London to see his other children and friends.

From 23 May to 15 July 1973, Jamal Mian was a member of a Rabita delegation which visited Malaysia, the Philippines, Japan, Australia, and Sri Lanka (Illustration 23). The Rabita chief, Ibrahim Saqqaf, supported by Ibrahim Qahtani, was the leader of the delegation. They met government officials at all of the countries visited and occasionally met a head of state such as President Marcos in the Philippines. It appears that the prime purpose of the delegation was to inspect Islamic practice and, following one of the main objectives of the Rabita, to call on individuals, communities, and states to abide by the *shari`a*. Jamal Mian was asked to translate the speeches of the Arabs into English. He felt uneasy doing so when the two leaders of the delegation were taking a strict Wahhabi line and failing to respect the Sufi understandings of local people. Indeed, he threatened to leave the delegation. Before returning to Karachi, the delegation also visited Myanmar where Jamal Mian saw how drab things looked and how depressed the people were. 'If socialism and military dictatorship lead to this kind of condition', he told his diary, 'may God protect people from these things.'[49]

In June and July 1974, Jamal Mian went on a visit, funded by the Motamar, to Malaysia. His diary does not tell us the purpose of the visit but it was memorable from his point of view as this was the time when he heard of the deaths of two of his greatest supporters, Pir Ghulam Mohiuddin of Golra and Mufti Amin al-Husseini.[50] While he was in Kuala Lumpur,

49. Ibid. entries covering the period 18 May to 15 July 1973.
50. Ibid. 30 June, 5 July 1974.

his daughter, Farida, gave him a diary. In the front of it he noted with the wisdom of experience: 'Writing a diary is no easy matter', and followed this with a statement with which his biographer could only agree 'in fact a diary can only give brief impressions and hints.'[51]

In August 1975, Jamal Mian went to Australia again, on the invitation of Sadiq Baksh, an Australian businessman from Pakistan, whom he had met on his previous visit. Sadiq Baksh had a *halal* meat business and was probably, through Jamal Mian, seeking a Rabita stamp of approval, which would enable him to export his meat to Saudi Arabia and other Muslim countries. Jamal Mian found himself in the position of having to defend Sadiq Baksh against his business opponents, which endeared him to the Baksh family. On the same visit, he was delighted to meet Mukarram Jah, the grandson of the last Nizam of Hyderabad, in part because his grandfather had been a great patron of the Farangi Mahall family, and in part because his maternal grandfather had been Sultan Abdul Majid of Turkey, the Caliph.[52]

At least once a year, Jamal Mian would go to the Hejaz for the annual Rabita meeting. Obligations to the Motamar might also take him there. In September 1975, he supported a resolution at a Motamar meeting that the Turkish government should turn the Aya Sofia into a mosque but opposed another part of the same resolution which objected to the creation of a Christian centre in the Aya Sofia complex.[53] In 1977, he travelled on behalf of the Rabita to Kuala Lumpur and Sri Lanka.[54] In 1980, he accompanied the Bohra leader,

---

51. Ibid. 29 September 1974.
52. Ibid. 31 August 1975.
53. Ibid. 24 September 1973.
54. Ibid. overview of the year, 1977.

Dr Najmuddin, to Cairo to attend the inauguration of a Bohra centre there.[55] In spring 1981, he attended a Motamar meeting in Sri Lanka devoted to Muslim-Christian relations.[56] Then, in June of that year, he was part of a joint Rabita/Motamar delegation to Tokyo.[57]

Every year, Jamal Mian went to London in the summer months, following the pattern of 'transhumance' common amongst the Karachi elite. Often he stayed with his second son, Mahmood, who had settled there. His third son, Alauddin, also settled there, as did his youngest daughter, Humaira. His youngest son, Moin, also lived there for a time in the 1970s. A notebook for 1972 gives details of how he spent his time. He visited the India Office Library frequently, and also the School of Oriental and African Studies. On 4 September, he recorded an interview on Jinnah with Athar Ali, head of the BBC Urdu Service. He also gave speeches in various gatherings. He clearly enjoyed travelling by bus and by the underground. But most important, in addition to seeing his children in London, he was also able to see some of his closest friends. For instance, he saw the Raja of Mahmudabad, now the Director of the Islamic Centre in Regent's Park, almost every day.[58] Later in life, he recalled a particular exchange he had with the Raja. This was the only time the Raja gave him cash and he could not refuse. 'Unusually he himself was in financial worries as he had had to send money to Lucknow,' he recalled. 'In any case I went to see him in Regent Lodge where he used to stay. After lunch he said "Mian I am going to do something and you must accept". Saying this he took out

55. Ibid. 2–8 September 1980.
56. Ibid. 23 March–1 April 1981.
57. Ibid. 19–21 June 1981.
58. Jamal Mian Notebook, 1972, JMP.

150 or 250 pounds and handed them to me. I knew he was financially worried so I took out my wallet and showed him my travellers' cheques and said: "I have enough on me and do not have any difficulty. Please don't do it." He started crying and said: "I fear you are refusing because you consider me a faqir." I was so moved I took the money. ... What a man!"[59] He also saw Mirza Ahmed Ispahani on this visit, and in all probability, Sadri.[60] Correspondence of a few years later reveals that Sadri was keeping an eye on Jamal Mian's children in London.[61] It also reveals that Sadri had suffered some kind of mental breakdown as a result of the turmoil in Bangladesh. 'All his troubles are due to his nerves', Mirza Ahmed wrote to Jamal Mian. 'They have been shuttered [sic]. He could not take the loss which the upheaval brought in Bangladesh and in a [sic] organization of which he was the Chairman.'[62] After his brutal and somewhat conceited fashion, Mirza Ahmed continued: 'To me it has no effect. My trust in God is so complete that nothing worries me.'[63] Correspondence from Sadri later in the year shows him trying to gather strength and will to return to Bangladesh.[64] He was not to know that under his leadership down to his death in 2004, M. M. Ispahani was to play a major role in the industrialisation of Bangladesh and to become one of the largest and most respected businesses in the country with a strong record of social responsibility. Mirza Ahmed, on

---

59. Jamal Mian Tape 5B, Ibid.
60. Jamal Mian Notebook, 1972, Ibid.
61. Sadri, Kew, to Jamal Mian, Karachi, 24, 25 February, 26 March 1975, Ispahani Correspondence, Ibid.
62. Mirza Ahmed Ispahani, Dacca, to Jamal Mian, Karachi, 10 March 1975, Ispahani Correspondence, Ibid.
63. Ibid.
64. Sadri, Kew, to Jamal Mian, Karachi, 14, 23 April, 12, 22 May 1975, Ispahani Correspondence, Ibid.

the other hand, remained his Olympian self, full of confidence
in his capacities aged seventy-seven[65] and contemptuous of
the future of Britain. 'Unfortunately your son [Mahmood]
and my grandson [Sajid] are most foolish in settling down in
England which is already a third-grade European country—a
welfare state.'[66]

Comments on Pakistan's Politics

From time to time, in the 1970s, Jamal Mian commented
on Pakistan's politics in his diary. As far as we know, what
was written in private was not made public. One theme was
his continuing disapproval of the way in which the current
political leadership was deserting the principles of those who
founded the state. In 1974, the Majlis-e-Ahrar and the Jamaat-
e-Islami launched a violent campaign against the Ahmadiyya.
This led to constitutional changes promoted by Prime
Minister Bhutto which criminalized the religious practices of
the Ahmadis, preventing them from claiming that they were
Muslims, or behaving as such. 'Personally', Jamal Mian wrote,
'I did not subscribe to this campaign because it threatens
Pakistani unity as a nation.'[67] After General Zia ul-Haq seized
power, Jamal Mian became increasingly concerned about the
way that religion was being used for political purposes. 'I am
unhappy with the government and Pakistani politicians', he
told his diary, 'because being unaware of the journey that

65. Mirza Ahmed Ispahani, Dacca, to Jamal Mian, Karachi, 14 March 1975,
    Ispahani Correspondence, Ibid.
66. Mirza Ahmed Ispahani, Dacca, to Jamal Mian, Karachi, 13 February
    1975, Ispahani Correspondence, Ibid.
67. Jamal Mian Diary, 7 September 1974, Ibid.

the Muslims of the subcontinent began, they are relying heavily on religious sloganizing instead of moving the people towards modern knowledge.'[68] When Zia ul-Haq introduced the Hudood Ordinance as part of his Islamic window-dressing Jamal Mian was adamant in opposition:

> Pakistan Hudood Ordinance and desire to adhere to Shari`a is one thing and the thoughts of those who campaigned for the Muslim League and the thoughts of their leaders is another matter. Unfortunately it is no longer possible to relate candidly the truth about the Muslim League campaign. Nor is there any point to it. But I have no doubt that those who were founding fathers of Pakistan would never have accepted such a law in this country as it will divide the Muslims and cause friction among the different sects.[69]

A second theme was Jamal Mian's reflections on Bhutto, which went alongside a certain fascination with the man. His diary traces the final tragedy of Bhutto's life from his calling of a general election for 7 March 1977 to his hanging in April 1979. On election day, he noted that 'there was trouble and violence in places so no one went to vote. I consider this form of voting (with intimidation etc...) wrong so I had already decided that I would not go out to vote.'[70] By morning, he had discovered from the television that the Peoples Party had won in Karachi and all the people he knew, meaning Kamal Azfar, Hakim Said, and Akbar Liaqat Ali Khan, had lost.[71] In spite of the fact that the Pakistan National Alliance

68. Ibid. 5 January 1978.
69. Ibid. 14 March 1979.
70. Ibid. 7 March 1977.
71. Ibid.

(PNA), the opposition party, had been able to demonstrate strong support before the election, it was trounced at the polls. There had clearly been considerable vote-rigging. The PNA responded by launching a national strike on 11 March and a continuing campaign of resistance to Bhutto and the election result. This ended with the declaration of Martial Law on 5 July 1977.[72] Jamal Mian followed Bhutto's various expedients to preserve his position and noted the similarity between this situation and the last days of Ayub Khan, when Bhutto had been leading the opposition.[73] In September, he noted that Bhutto had been arrested and charged with murder.[74] In January of the following year, he thought that the army must be careful in how it deals with Bhutto. On 30 March 1979, he declared: 'These days the whole country is caught up in Bhutto's trial. Everyone I meet seems concerned about the impact of the outcome. On 5 April he noted: 'Yesterday Bhutto Saheb was hanged.'[75]

Despite his political differences with Bhutto, Jamal Mian was visibly shocked by Bhutto's hanging and found it upsetting that a civilian prime minister had been hanged.[76] This led to the following reflection:

I had first heard his name from General Iskander Mirza. During Ayub's rule I had numerous arguments with him. I don't know why but from the start I was not keen on his attitude. And I used to criticise him often. One time Ayub Khan even complained to

72. Ian Talbot, *Pakistan: A Modern History* (London: Hurst & Co., 1998), 239–44.
73. Jamal Mian Diary 13, 14, 15 April, 14 May, 1 June 1977, JMP.
74. Ibid. 3 September 1977.
75. Ibid. 5 April 1979.
76. Recollection of Mahmud Jamal, 23 January 2017.

me that I had no appreciation of Bhutto's services to Pakistan
and had a wrong opinion of him. But, when Bhutto started
opposing him after Tashkent, he too complained about him and
turned against him. After Bhutto came to power, I made every
effort to avoid meeting him because I knew that he was quite
harsh in settling old scores. However, when I went to meet
him because of Begum Khaliquzzaman's insistence regarding a
Sirat conference, he was very warm and gracious and respectful
towards me. I feel sad that after he came to power he made
such mistakes that the army ... ended up removing him. ...
There is no doubt that he was a man of unique qualities and
his end was astonishing and shocking.[77]

A third dimension to Jamal Mian's attitude to politics from
the post-Ayub period onwards was that, while he enjoyed
the recognition of the powerful, he really did not wish to be
involved in the workings of power. This was brought to a head
in June 1977 when Maulana Kausar Niazi invited him to join
the Islamic Ideology Council, which reviewed legislation in
the light of its adherence to Islamic principles.[78] His wife, Asar,
was very much against his joining it; doubtless she knew the
worries it would bring to the household. Jamal Mian excused
himself on health grounds. Kausar Niazi, however, insisted.
But when, in spite of Niazi's insistence, nothing further
happened, Jamal Mian expressed his ambivalence about the
whole thing: 'If now my name is there, I feel very anxious and
uncertain, and if it is not included, I feel they did not consider
me important enough to be a member.'[79] Jamal Mian's desire

---

77. Ibid. 5 April 1979.
78. Ibid. 23 June 1977.
79. Ibid. 2 September 1977.

not to be forgotten, even though he was no longer a front line
player in Pakistan's politics, was reflected in his response to his
first meeting with President Zia ul-Haq, which took place in
the context of the Asian Muslim conference, organized jointly
in 1978 by the Motumar and the Government of Pakistan. He
was standing with Haider Husseini and a Mujtahid, and when
Zia passed he said in Persian 'We too await to catch your eye'.
Zia turned, he noted in his diary, 'and very warmly shook my
hand and when I praised his speech he was very happy and
at dinner he greeted me with great warmth and affection. ...
Thank God most of the people who are now in power are
familiar with me from Ayub and Iskander days.'[80]

The Crisis 1982

1982 saw the major crisis of Jamal Mian's later life. At the heart
of it was one of the worst bi-polar incidents he experienced.
The following year he described the onset of the illness thus:

> ... disturbed sleep, forgetting the *rakat*s of *namaz*, eating too
> much, smoking hookah more than usual, or drinking more
> tea than I usually do. Talking incessantly and so on. The most
> critical sign is over-listening to *qawwali*. When I start listening
> to too much *qawwali* that is the sure sign that I am reaching
> the danger point.[81]

In April 1982 Jamal Mian set out to visit the places in India
of great spiritual importance to him—Ajmer, Lucknow and

---

80. Ibid. 7 July 1978.
81. Jamal Mian 'Reflections', Karachi 25 May 1983, JMP.

to a lesser extent Rudauli. The symptoms of his illness, at this stage inability to sleep, began to affect him during the `Urs at Ajmer and became pronounced when he reached Lucknow on 4 May. Soon, he reached a manic phase, displaying superhuman energy in arranging the family books and papers which remained in Farangi Mahall, behaving badly towards his relations, and refusing to leave India even though his visa was running out. Those around him realized that he was seriously ill. Bari Mian was summoned to Lucknow to take charge of matters. After he arrived on 18 June, doctors were consulted, treatment was prescribed, and on 26 June he accompanied his father to Farida's house in Kuala Lumpur, via Delhi and Bangkok. Bari Mian then returned to Lucknow to mend fences with his relations.

Once in Kuala Lumpur, Jamal Mian began to reflect on what had taken place in Lucknow and the damage it had done to his reputation. He had no doubt that 'it was because of Bari Mian my life was saved and I managed to come home from Lucknow. Slowly I am beginning to become aware of the extent of my mad act. Now I am thinking that I must take any step to avoid putting myself in that kind of situation.'[82]

One reason for the mistakes of Lucknow 'which began with my suppliant journey to Ajmer' was, Jamal Mian concluded, his spiritual arrogance. 'Why should such a journey with its elevated spiritual purpose end in such a disaster? I think this was the punishment of my pride which made me feel that I was the *murshid-e tariqat* and the Khalifa of Pir Ibrahim and my father. That arrogance made me err.'[83]

---

82. Entry entitled 'The journey to Lucknow, the mistakes that were made there, and the result of them. Jamal Mian Notebook 1982B, Ibid.
83. Ibid.

Jamal Mian returned to Karachi on 22 July. He soon came under pressure from Inamullah Khan of the Motamar to attend the upcoming meeting of the Rabita.[84] After coming under heavy pressure from Bari Mian he decided not to go.[85] A few days later, he came to a sensible decision. Realizing that travelling alone left him particularly exposed should his illness return, he decided that 'from now on I shall travel with my wife.'[86] Moreover, Jamal Mian knew he had not completely recovered. 'I am in a strange situation', he confided to his notebook. 'In the morning I do not wish to travel, but in the afternoon I do. This shows that I have not completely recovered.'[87] But it was not long before he completely recovered.

At no point in his reflections on what had happened did Jamal Mian explicitly say that it was the psychological pressure of returning to Farangi Mahall that triggered his bi-polar illness. He did not admit to feeling, as probably the most gifted man in his Farangi Mahalli generation, some sense of responsibility, however unfair that might have been, for the decline in the family fortunes—for the decline in their traditions of scholarly and spiritual leadership.

Nevertheless, his actions while in Lucknow, for instance, his manic gathering together of family papers and books, and his subsequent decision never to return to Lucknow for fear of the inconvenience to others of another bi-polar incident, suggests that he knew that he would find it difficult to endure the psychological burden of returning to the place where his family had flourished for three hundred years. Three years

---

84. Ibid. 26, 27 July 1982.
85. Ibid. 27 July 1982.
86. Ibid. 3 August 1982.
87. Ibid. 10 September 1982.

earlier, he had made a note in his diary which suggests that
he was reconciled to the end of Farangi Mahall. 'The Farangi
Mahall issue is very complex', he noted in April 1979. 'May
God give a long life to Matin. I do not know what will happen
to our house after him. To make Farangi Mahall an institution
of religious scholarship now is very difficult. If it remains as
a token of our past, it will be enough.'[88] What took place in
Lucknow in 1982 suggests that, although rationally he knew
the days of Farangi Mahall were over, he still had to come to
terms with the fact emotionally and psychologically.

Jamal Mian Moves Further into Retirement 1982–2012

The year 1982 was the last major turning point in Jamal
Mian's life. From now on he seems to have put his concerns
over Farangi Mahall behind him. He may have yearned for
the family's holy places in India, but he was not going to visit
them. In the same way, stuck in Karachi's vast conurbation,
he may have yearned for the villages and qasbahs in the
countryside outside Lucknow, but they were no longer to
be visited. He now lived a life based in Karachi, but with
regular visits to the Hejaz and London. In Karachi, he
continued to move in the social circles he had established in
the 1970s. There was a regular round of `Urs celebrations, of
Milad recitations, of presiding over nikah ceremonies, and the
funerals of friends. Three organizations absorbed at least some
of his energies: Hakim Said's Hamdard Foundation, with its
Hamdard evenings; the Hasrat Mohani Memorial Society with

88. Entry, 20 April 1979, Jamal Mian Notebook 1978–79, JMP.

its annual gatherings in May; and the Motamar. Jamal Mian was one of the founding members of the Motamar Foundation established in Karachi in 1982 and engaged in its activities such as its conference on drugs in Karachi in 1986. When the Motamar al-Alam al-Islami was awarded the Niwana Peace Prize, Jamal Mian went with Inamullah Khan to Tokyo to receive the award (Illustration 29). As always, his visits to the Rabita conference were an opportunity to pay his respects to the Prophet at Medina. Now that he no longer visited India, this became an even more important spiritual exercise. He continued to go to London every year where he would see his children, Mahmood, Alauddin, and Humaira. On occasion, he would also see Farida whose daughter, now married to a man of Norwegian origin, was established in London as a General Practitioner.

In his address to the Condolence Meeting for Jamal Mian at the Karachi Arts Council in 2013, Hameed Haroon described Jamal Mian as an enigma. His reason was that this last surviving member of the All-India Muslim League High Command, known for his powerful public speaking, had remained silent for decades.[89] We cannot speak for Jamal Mian but can reckon that he thought that he had already contributed much and sacrificed much to the cause of Pakistan, He probably felt, too, that interventions by him in contemporary politics were unlikely to be well-received, and that it would be best, from all points of view, if he maintained his silence and kept to his family, his friends, and his spiritual devotions.

Jamal Mian was not entirely forgotten. In 1999, he was awarded the *Nishan-e-Imtiaz*—the highest honour in the gift

---

89. Address by Hameed Haroon, op. cit.

of the Government of Pakistan—for his contributions to the
Freedom Movement. This award went alongside his award of
the *Kifalatul Fikriya* in 1968 by King Hasan of Morocco for
his contributions to scholarship. In keeping with his decision
to stay out of the public eye, Jamal Mian asked Bari Mian to
collect the *Nishan-e-Imtiaz* on his behalf.

On 31 December 2009, Jamal Mian's wife, Asar, who had
done so much for over sixty years to hold the family together
and to support her husband, died. She was buried in the
Defence Gizri Cemetry in Karachi. By this time, Jamal Mian
himself was already ill. Unable to read because of failing sight,
he spent his last months listening to tapes of *qawwali*. He died
on 14 November 2012. It might be thought that tradition
required that he be buried alongside his ancestors in Bagh
Maulana Anwar in Lucknow. But in his will of 1992, he left
instructions that no attempt should be made to bury him in
any particular place; his body was dispensable but his soul
would remain. This was in keeping with his Sufi beliefs. So he
was buried beside his wife. In this decision, which represented
both a continuation of the family Sufi tradition and a break
with Farangi Mahall practice, the last stage in Jamal Mian's
experience of the 'Long Partition' was reached.

14

The nature of the man and the meaning of his life

JAMAL MIAN WAS BROUGHT UP IN ONE OF THE BEST KNOWN *sharif* families of northern India, which traced its ancestry back through Abdullah Ansari of Herat to Ayub Ansari, the host of the Prophet at Medina. The family had established itself in India under the Delhi Sultanate; family members were amongst those who, like the descendants of the Normans who settled in Britain after 1066, had 'come over with the Conqueror'. This said, because their tradition was one of scholarship and spiritual leadership rather than warfare and rule, their wealth lay in cultural capital as opposed to material means. Against this background, Jamal Mian was brought up as an `alim and a Sufi in a Farangi Mahall tradition that was largely untouched by Islamic reform. He entered politics as a teenager, working for the All-India Muslim League, and at the age of twenty-three became an official member of the League's High Command. He went through the highs of the League's campaign for Pakistan and the lows of its aftermath in India. Feeling compelled to go to East Pakistan to earn money to sustain his family, as an Indian citizen, he travelled frequently between the two countries. until the Government of India placed him in a situation in which the only way in which he could continue to do so was by becoming a Pakistani citizen. Through the 1950s and 1960s, he conducted business

335

in Pakistan, by his own account not very efficiently, while mixing with the *muhajir* and West Pakistani political elite. The emergence of Bangladesh brought this phase of his life to an end. He spent his last forty years in Karachi, which was a base for his engagement with international Islamic organizations and his annual visits to London. In assessing his life we shall, first, explore more closely the nature of the man and, second, see what meaning we may attach to the passage of his life.

The nature of the man

To engage with the man, we will examine the following aspects of his life: his personal library, his reading habits, and his annotation of books; his approach to family life, the upbringing of his children, and the freedoms they were permitted; the close friendships he cultivated throughout his life, and the pleasure which friends found in his company and in helping him; the centrality of his spiritual life, which was fashioned from a young age and which was informed by his association with holy men and holy places to the end of his life; and finally the basic principles which underlay his approach to the demand for Pakistan and measures relating to Muslims, and indeed people in general, in India and Pakistan.

The man and his Library

Jamal Mian left a personal library of just over 2,000 volumes, which has recently been catalogued. Roughly 55 per cent of the titles were in Urdu, 30 per cent in Arabic, 10 per cent in English, and 5 per cent in Persian. If the library had been put together in the nineteenth century, a much larger proportion of the books would have been in Persian; Urdu, Arabic, and most certainly English books would have figured less prominently. So, the makeup of the library reflects the decline of Persian as an influence over Indian Muslim civilization that came with the decline of the Mughal Empire. But, before we make too much of this, we should also note that: first, up to 1982, Jamal Mian still had access to the Persian books and manuscripts in the Farangi Mahall library, and second, while over the past one hundred years Urdu had taken the place of Persian, it still remained a channel of Persianate influences. Of course, the large number of Arabic and English titles reflected, in part at least, Jamal Mian's frequent travels both to the Hejaz and West Asia, and more generally to London.

Jamal Mian's library came together, as most libraries do, in various ways. There were gifts from friends. For instance, there was *The Standard English-Urdu Dictionary*, which the Raja of Mahmudabad had given to him when they both attended the Sindh Provincial Muslim League Conference in Karachi in October 1938. It was inscribed 'Braber bejane Jamal Mian (May God keep him safe) Mohammed Amir Ahmed 26 Shaban 59 hijri 22 October 1938 AD'.[1] There was also Ibn Rushd's commentary *Bidyat al-Mujtahid* which the ruler of Qatar had given him in Mecca in 1954 and which he found to be a very useful work on *fiqh*.[2] Then there were publications which came from his relations, for instance, Maulana Inayatullah's collective biography of the Farangi Mahall family

---

1. Catalogue of the books in Jamal Mian's personal library at the time of his death, held with his private papers, henceforth JM Catalogue, and in this case number 1758, JMP.
2. Ibid. 0002; annotation Mecca 19.12.54.

or Mufti Raza Ansari's biography of Mulla Nizamuddin.[3] Of
course, publications for which Jamal Mian himself had been
responsible figure among the volumes such as his collection of
Hasrat Mohani's poetry; his publication of his sister, Sughra's,
poetry; and stray volumes of the newspaper, *Hamdam*, from
his father's time.[4] Another category of books is those left in
Jamal Mian's house and subsequently incorporated into his
library, for instance, school maths and economics textbooks[5],
or *Notes on George Eliot's Mill on the Floss*, left by Mahmood,
and *The Encyclopedia of Golf Technique* left by Bari Mian.[6]
This said, the vast majority of titles were bought by Jamal
Mian and reflect his interests and tastes. In his annotations
to books Jamal Mian from time to time tells us about how he
came to buy them. In his copy of Burhanuddin Marghinani's
Hidaya he tells us that he bought it on the 18 December
1963 from the Imdadia Library, Dacca, for 90 Rupees.[7] In
his copy of *Amalnama*, the autobiography of The UP politician
Sir Syed Raza Ali (1882–1949) he tells us that he had been
looking for this book for a long time, that he and the Raja of
Mahmudabad used to stay with Raza Ali in Moradabad when
on League business, and that Raza Ali had a rich African wife

3. This was Mawlana Mawlawi Muhammad `Inayat Allah, *Tadhira-yi
   `Ulama-i Farangi mahall* first published Lucknow, 1348/1929–30 which
   Jamal Mian had republished in Karachi, no date. Jamal Mian Catalogue
   no. 1305 and Mufti Rada Ansari, *Bani-yi Dars-i Nizami* (Lucknow,
   1973), Jamal Mian Catalogue no. 0074.
4. *Kulliyat-i Hasrat Mohani* Jamal Mian Catalogue no. 0581; Fatima
   Sughra, *Nawa-yi Agahi* (Lucknow: Muhammad Jam, 1948) Jamal
   Mian Catalogue no. 1223; Sayyid Jalib Dihlawi, Ruznama-i Hamdam
   Lakhnaw. 2 volumes from 1919, Jamal Mian Catalogue nos. 625, 626.
5. Jamal Mian Catalogue nos. 1334, 1246.
6. Ibid. 1267, 0760.
7. Ibid. 0473, 0474.

who was twice his size. He bought the book probably on 22 January 1997 for 500 Rupees in Ferozesons.[8] Jamal Mian reveals his booklover's instincts in his response in October 1959 to the arrival in Dacca of Amir Khusrau's *Mathnawi-yi Hasht Bihisht* which had been published in Aligarh in 1918. The Vice-Chancellor of Aligarh had located a copy for him and left it with his ICS friend, Ahmed Mohyuddin. 'My dear brother ... Muhammad Azfar ... went to New Delhi to attend a conference', he noted, 'and brought back with him this rare treasure. May God Bless him.'[9] Jamal Mian was a determined builder of his library.

Let us consider the Urdu materials in the Library. It emerges straightaway that Jamal Mian had a huge interest in poetry. Among those Urdu poets who appear in his library, either in single volumes or collected editions, are: Ghalib, Zauq, Momin, Hali, Shibli, Iqbal, Jigar Moradabadi, Josh Malihabadi, Rais Amrohavi, Zafar Ali Khan, Aziz Lucknavi, Dagh Dihlavi, Akbar Ilahabadi, Hasrat Mohani, and Raja Kishen Pershad Shad. Bulleh Shah and Waris Shah also appear but in Punjabi/Siraiki editions. He also subscribed to literary magazines such as *Nuqqush* of Lahore which produced numbers focussing on particular poets. Letters form another interest which might be religious as much as literary or political. Amongst these collections he had those of: Rashid Ahmed Gangohi, Sir Saiyid Ahmad Khan, his friend Amir the Raja of Mahmudabad, Abul Kalam Azad, Begum Hasrat Mohani, Sulaiman Nadvi, Pir Mehr Ali Shah of Golra Sharif, and Shah Sulaiman of Phulwari Sharif.

Of course there are works of religious scholarship in Urdu,

8. Ibid. 920, Jamal Mian annotation Karachi 22.1.97.
9. Ibid. 1448, Jamal Mian annotation, 19.10.59.

for instance, the following classical work on jurisprudence which figured in the *Dars-i Nizami*, Shahr-i Wiqaya, which was Ubaidullah ibn Masud's (d. 1346–47) commentary on Wiqaya by his father Tajul Sharia Mahmud.[10] But what are more notable are works written by scholars outside the Farangi Mahall tradition. The great eighteenth-century reformer Shah Waliullah's masterwork, *Al-Hujjat Allah al-Balighah* in Urdu translation; the *Ahl-i Hadith* scholar, Nawab Siddiq Hasan Khan's *Sham-i Anjuman*; Rahmatullah Khairanavi's *Izhar al-Haqq;* the Deobandi, Ashraf Ali Thanvi's *Bihishti Zewar* and his commentary on Rumi's *Mathnawi* in ten volumes; and Abul Kalam Azad's *Tarjuman al-Quran*.[11] For Azad's *Tarjuman,* Jamal Mian had the highest regard and urged me to read it. Alongside the works of the ulama, there are Sufi materials which reflect Jamal Mian's attachments. Hence, there are works on the traditions of Ajmer; on those of Abdul Qadir Gilani; plus the *malfuzat* of Pir Mehr Ali Shah of Golra; that of Nizamuddin Aulia, *Fawaid al-Fawad,* which he would quote frequently; and published collections of *Na`ts*.[12]

Works of history figure, not least the works of family history mentioned above. But there is also a good number of volumes on Islamic history published in the 1950s by the Maarif press of the Darul Musannifin of Azamgarh. Jamal Mian represented this press in Pakistan and it is not clear the extent to which these works represented a genuine interest, which is not at all unlikely, or were the remnants of the books he was promoting. Bound files of newspapers are also present. Notable are volumes of Hasrat Mohani's *Urdu-e Mualla,* both

---

10. Ibid. 472
11. Ibid. in order of mention, 1536, 563, 702, 1197, 194–203, 325–6.
12. Ibid. Ajmer 980–87, Gilani 739, Golra 349, *Na`ts* 1339, 1580, 1368–9.

early numbers published from Aligarh between 1909 and 1913 and later ones published from Cawnpore between 1927 and 1932.[13] We do not know for certain but it seems likely that Jamal Mian inherited these files, some of which may be unique, from Hasrat. Then there are 153 volumes of *Haftawar-i Sidiq Lakhnaw*, edited by Abdul Majid Daryabadi.[14]

Biographies of various kinds are present in the Library. As might be expected, there are biographies of the Prophet. There are also biographies of Sufis from Abdul Qadir Gilani to Pir Mehr Ali Shah of Golra. There are the lives of major figures in the Aligarh movement such as Saiyid Ahmad Khan and Mohsinul Mulk. There are the lives of leading twentieth century figures such as the educationist, Akhtar Husain Raipuri, and the Deoband leader Husain Ahmad Madani. And finally, there are the lives of friends: Ishtiaq Asghar's life of Hasrat Mohani, an Urdu translation of Khaliquzzaman's *Pathway to Pakistan*, and a life of his friend and patron in Karachi, Hakim Said.[15]

There are relatively few Urdu novels but Jamal Mian did possess classics. There was Munshi Saiyid Muhammad Husain Jah's version of the *Dastan-i Amir Hamza* in seven volumes; Ratan Nath Sarshar's *Fasana-yi Azad*; the didactic novels of Nazir Ahmad; the historical romances of Abdul Halim Sharar, who was educated at Farangi Mahall; a novel by Ismat Chughtai; and Mirza Hadi Rusva's *Umrao Jan Ada*. Jamal Mian thought highly of this love story. At his last meeting with Abul Kalam Azad, he asked him if he felt there was any truth behind the story. Azad was doubtful. It is a testament to

---

13. Ibid. Aligarh1395, 1397, 1401; Kanpur 1388–92, 1396.
14. Ibid. 1037–1190.
15. Ibid. 163, 1821,47.

the range of interests of both these men that they should have discussed such a matter.[16]

Jamal Mian's Arabic books covered a narrower range of subjects; not surprisingly there was little on Sufism. The books divided into three categories: religion, literature, and general interest. As far as religion was concerned, his holdings were straightforward. In *Hadith* he had two of the great collections, the *Sahih* Muslim in seven volumes and the *Sahih* Bukhari in four volumes.[17] As we might expect, there are several biographies of the Prophet. In Quran commentary, there was Muhammad bin al-Tabari's *tafsir* in ten volumes alongside the *Jalalayn* of the two Jalals.[18] Nevertheless, Jamal Mian did not restrict himself to these classical works; he also had a copy of the Egyptian Islamist, Saiyid Qutb's, Quran commentary. In *fiqh*, he possessed Imam Alauddin's seven volume work on Hanafi *fiqh* and Abdul Rahman al-Jaziri's four-volume work on contemporary points of comparative *fiqh*.[19] Classic works in the Awadhi tradition are also there, for instance, Abdul Hai Farangi Mahalli's Shahr-i Wiqaya and Muhibbullah Bihari's *Musallam ath Thubut*, and a commentary on Bihari by an Egyptian.[20] There were, of course, collections of *fatawa*. Most striking among these were the *fatawa* of Abdul Aziz Bin Baz (1913–99), the Salafi Grand Mufti of Saudi Arabia (1993–99) renowned for his support for the Muslim resistance to the Soviet invasion of Afghanistan. Given Bin Baz's conservative jurisprudential record, it is hard to see Jamal Mian being

---

16. Jamal Mian annotations, dated 7.7.82 and 3.1.92 in Mirza Hadi Rusva, *Umrao Jan Ada*, Ibid. 1751.
17. Ibid. 27–33, 355–8.
18. Ibid. 1027, 1028; 443–54; 483.
19. Ibid. 1364; 320–7; 369–72.
20. Ibid. 348, 192, 1547.

drawn to him, so one must assume that he may have been given Bin Baz's *fatawa* when he attended the Rabita and kept them out of interest.[21]

In Arabic literature, as we might expect, Jamal Mian had the works of the classical poets al-Mutannabi and Abu Niwas. It is no surprise either to find the works of the Abbasid man of letters, al-Jahiz and the Mamluk scholar, Imam al-Busiri's *Qasida al-Burda*, his great poem in praise of the Prophet. Ibn Battuta's *Rihla* is also there.[22] But surprisingly, in view of his father's high regard for it and its strong presence in the Farangi Mahall world, there is no copy of Ibn Khaldun's *Muqaddima*. A notable presence, however, are works by Butrus Bustani (1819–93), the Maronite Christian whose research on Arabic literature helped to lay the foundations of Arab nationalism.[23] Alongside these classics there were works of contemporary Arabic literature and literary criticism.

Finally, there are books which would have caught Jamal Mian's interest from time to time. For instance, there was the thirteenth-century Arab scholar, Al-Zarnuji's, work on learning and the pupil-teacher relationship: *Ta`lim al-Muta`allim Tariq al-Ta`allum*; Jamal Mian's father's advice some 800 years later, as we have noticed, was very similar.[24] There was Al-Zamakshari's advice on how to give a good sermon, which would have been of no small interest to a man who prided himself on his public speaking skills.[25] Then there were those items which Jamal Mian would have picked up on

21. Ibid. 13, 237, 381.
22. Ibid. 109–13, 1217, 78–80, 970, 128.
23. Ibid. 554, 558 568.
24. Ibid. 159, and see Chapter 4, pp.00.
25. Al-Zamakshari, *Atwaq al-Dhahab fi al-Mawa`iz al-Khutab* (Egypt, n.d.), Jamal Mian Catalogue 1521.

his regular journeys to the Hejaz and West Asia: a history of Mecca; a guide to Mecca; a collection of lectures given at the Rabita; Muhammad Abduh on Islam in Egypt; a history of al-Azhar; the collected works of Baba Khanov, Chief Mufti of the Soviet Union; and interestingly a biography of Ataturk.[26]

As far as his books in Persian go, Jamal Mian had the great classics one might expect. We have already noted Amir Khusrau's *Mathnawi-yi Hasht Bihisht* and the trouble he went to acquire it. Alongside this there was the *Diwan* of Najmuddin Hasan Sanjari (known as Sizji) of Delhi, whom Khusrau referred to as 'teacher'. Rumi's *Mathnawi* was, of course, there, as was his *Diwan* in the name of his inspiration, *Shams-i Tabrizi*. Then there was the work of the great eighteenth-century poet, Bedil, who epitomized the Sabki Hindi style, a *Diwan* of Ghalib which embraced Persian poetry, and the Persian poetry of Iqbal.[27] Hafiz does not appear in the catalogue although we know that his *Diwan* never left Jamal Mian's side, and he was particularly pleased when in May 1973 Mufti Amin al-Husseini gave him a copy from his personal library.[28] But there is Saadi's *Bustan*, his verse work in *mathnawi* style which, along with the *Gulistan*, his mother loved to quote. In an annotation, he recalled that Maulana Ruhullah had read some chapters with him in his madrasah days, but reading it again he was bowled over:

Saadi is unique and is for all times. A garden of eternal spring this masterpiece of Persian poetry has been an authentic tutor of Islamic civilisation for centuries. Those who study *Gulistan*

26. Ibid. 138, 317, 541, 516, 66, 1548, 460.
27. Ibid. 59, 702, 90, 312, 316. NB re. 59 the catalogue suggests it is Hasan Sanjari, but it is probably Sizji.
28. Jamal Mian Diary, 2 May 1973.

and *Bustan* acquire special views and values. For high level education in good conduct and spirituality and training of the mind and heart these two books are matchless.[29]

Beyond this, there were a few prose works worthy of note. Saadi's *Gulistan*, of course, which is a mixture of prose and poetry. Tajuddin ibn Shihab Yazdi's *Jami` Tawarikh-i Hasani*, which suggests an unsuspected interest in Timurid history, and two copies of the letters of Aurangzeb, which leave a favourable impression of the controversial Mughal ruler's concern for good government. But then, again, like Yazdi's work they are an odd presence in the library.[30]

Jamal Mian's English collection contains much literature and history but also reaches through biography and religion to matters of general interest. In literature, as we might expect from his tastes in the Islamic languages, there was a good quantity of verse: Tennyson; Wordsworth; Hardy; Frost; various anthologies; the poems of the Palestinian, Mahmood Darwish; Arberry's *Modern Arabic Poetry*; and a collection of Azarbaijani poems. His interest in the theatre is demonstrated by Vyvyan Holland's complete edition of his father, Oscar Wilde's works and J. M. Synge's *Playboy of the Western World*. There are no Bernard Shaw plays although we know that he was very keen on them; whenever he was in London he would try to see one. In prose there were the novels of Dickens, a great favourite, all of whose works, according to Mahmood Jamal, he read. In addition there were novels by Jules Verne, Alexander Dumas, James Joyce, Leo Tolstoy, Jane

29. Sa`adi's *Bustan*, Jamal Mian Catalogue no. 604; Jamal Mian annotation 11.1.66 Dacca.
30. Ibid. 1185, 172, 933.

Austen, R. L. Stevenson, Alberto Moravia, George Orwell, and
Mikhail Sholokov. There were also works by James Boswell,
Mark Twain, and Samuel Pepys. Arguably he had many of
the works in his library that a native Englishman of his time
might have had, notable omissions being perhaps, Shakespeare,
Wodehouse, Agatha Christie, and Dorothy Sayers. But, he did
have two copies of the *Complete Sherlock Holmes.*

As both Jamal Mian and his father had been much involved
in the politics of Muslim India, it is not surprising that the
historiography of the Pakistan movement was another major
interest. He possessed many of the numerous books published
on Jinnah in English. He also had a considerable interest in
the Khilafat Movement in general and Maulana Mahomed
Ali in particular. After reading Afzal Iqbal's *Life and Times of
Mohamed Ali* he commented that 'it was painful to read the part
about the publicized disagreement and its spiced up reporting
between my father, Maulana Abdul Bari and Mohamed Ali.
In this matter Abdul Majid Daryabadi demonstrated the
ugly side of his writing skills and personality.'[31] Jamal Mian
had the works of key players at the time: Viceroy Wavell's
Diary, Choudhry Khaliquzzaman's *Pathway to Pakistan*, and
Chaudhuri Mahomed Ali's *Emergence of Pakistan* plus works by
Jawaharlal Nehru such as *A Bunch of Old Letters* and his *Letters
from a Father to his Daughter.*[32] He also kept up with Western
scholarship in the field. Hence, he had on his shelves: Francis
Robinson's *Separatism Among Indian Muslims*, Judith Brown's
Gandhi's Rise to Power, David Page's *Prelude to Partition*, and
Stanley Wolpert's *Nehru* and *Jinnah of Pakistan*. After reading

31. Afzal Iqbal, *The Life and Times of Maulana Mohamed Ali* (Lahore:
    Institute of Islamic Culture, 1974), Jamal Mian Catalogue no 1001;
    annotation 22.10.77. For this incident, see Chapter 3 pp 00.
32. Jamal Mian Catalogue nos. 1794, 1801, 1793, 1630, 853.

the American scholar Gail Minault's *The Khilafat Movement* he lamented 'the best and most authentic writings are by the English and the foreigners'.[33]

Amongst biographies there are some improbable companions on Jamal Mian's shelves. This said, biographies of Abdullah Haroon and the Raja of Mahmudabad are good company. Gandhi's autobiography and that of Bertrand Russell might seem odder companions, although they both showed an unusual frankness for their time: Gandhi admitting to guilt at making love to his wife while his father was dying and Russell being unusually candid about his sexual relationships. On the other hand, the lives of Hasrat Mohani and Muhammad Shah Pahlavi of Iran had absolutely nothing in common, as the biographies by K. H. Qadri and Kapuscinski reveal. The same could be said for Maxim Gorky's life as revealed in *My Universities*. The Duchess of Windsor's *The Heart has its Reasons* is a most odd presence in this company, demonstrating perhaps the widespread appeal of royal scandals.[34]

In religious matters in English, Jamal Mian had several works on and by Abdul Qadir Gilani, emphasising yet again the importance of this saint to his spiritual existence. There are works by Western scholars, Bruce Lawrence and Annemarie Schimmel on Sufism, and various works on the Quran and the Prophet by Muslims. He also possessed *Islam and Idealism* by Muhammad Qutb, the brother of Saiyid Qutb, who is said to have had a considerable influence over Usama Bin Laden whom he taught in Riyadh. Most striking, however, is the

33. Ibid. 1633, 1808, 1009, 1003, 1805; Gail Minault, *The Khilafat Movement: Religious Symbolism and Political Mobilization in India* (New York: Columbia, 1982) Jamal Mian Catalogue no. 1811; Jamal Mian Diary 11 August 1983.
34. Jamal Mian Catalogue nos. 605, 217, 1802, 1253, 1810, 1998, 1284.

evidence of his interest in Christianity and the relationship between Islam and Christianity. His Bible was the *New Oxford Annotated Bible*.[35] Moreover, he had the classic Bible commentary, Peake's.[36] He possessed the *Gospel of Barnabas*, the controversial manuscript which emerged in early-modern Europe and offers an Islamic interpretation of the origin of Christianity and contradicts its teachings. More significantly, perhaps, he possessed Geoffrey Parrinder's highly-regarded comparison of Islam and Christianity, *Jesus in the Quran*.[37]

The remainder of Jamal Mian's English books offer an eclectic mix. They range from his friend, Hassan Ispahani's, *Twenty-Seven Days in China* through to the management of Pakistan's frontier tribes as demonstrated in *Resistance and Control in Pakistan* by the anthropologist-cum-administrator, Akbar Ahmad. Further titles which reflect Jamal Mian's interests are: Misbah ul-Islam Faruqi's *The Jewish Conspiracy and the Muslim World* and M. Adams and Christopher Mayhew, *Publish it Not: the Middle East Cover Up*. Both speak to his concerns, widely shared amongst Muslims, that the Muslim world had not received even-handed treatment at the hands of the West. The first book identified a Jewish conspiracy in the management of world affairs, a view which unfortunately retains considerable credence in Pakistan. The second was a famous indictment of Western press coverage of the Israel-Palestine issue.[38] Kapuscinski's *The Emperor* covers the life of Hailie Selassie of Ethiopia who was a hero to many of Jamal Mian's time for his resistance to Italian imperialism and his

35. Ibid. 620, 1634, 1308, 1192.
36. M. Black and H. H. Rowley eds., *Peake's Commentary on the Bible*, 8th ed. (London: Nelson, 1977). Jamal Mian Catalogue no. 1783.
37. Ibid. 1338, 1827.
38. Ibid. 1826, 1833, 1311, 1247.

leadership in Pan-African affairs until he was brought down in 1974. Thesiger's *Arabian Sands* is said by some to be the finest book about the Arabs. It was natural reading for a man thoughtful about two of the greatest achievements of the Arab peoples: Islam and the Arabic language. Finally, there were two further books by Bertrand Russell. First, his *Outlines of Philosophy* with its claim of the role of humanity in discovering the universal world would have been of interest to anyone well-educated in the Farangi Mahall tradition. Second, there was his *In Praise of Idleness*, a collection of essays. Two themes run through them which would have been attractive to Jamal Mian: the idea that the value of knowledge lies not just in its utility but in its capacity to foster a contemplative mind; and Russell's belief that the world was suffering from intolerance and bigotry and the way to confront them was to question dogma and do justice to difference points of view.[39]

The man, some reading habits, and annotations

It is possible from Jamal Mian's diary, and other evidence, to get an idea of what he read, when, and sometimes why. In the 1940s, when occasionally he worked as a translator of Jinnah's speeches, Jamal Mian seems to have been working his way through Gibbon's *Decline and Fall of the Roman Empire*, borrowing volumes, one by one, from the Ispahanis.[40]

Fortunately, the great historian's orotund style seems to have left no mark on Jamal Mian. After this we hear little of what

39. Ibid. 850, 1283, 1259, 302.
40. Sadri to Jamal Mian, 3 November 1944, Ispahani Correspondence, JMP.

he is reading until he is in Karachi in the 1970s, has virtually retired, and regular visits to the British Council Library have become part of his routine. So in June 1973, he was reading Felix Greene's *The Wall has Two Sides* about China.[41] It seems that Jamal Mian would escape into books when he was disturbed by events in the wider world. In March 1977, for instance, during Bhutto's election campaign, and the outrage that followed the rigged polls, he was reading Badauni's history of the first century of Mughal rule and following that with all the plays of Oscar Wilde.[42] In 1978, when Bhutto's trial and appeal were actually taking place, he was having a great Dickens phase which was leavened by reading *The Thousand and One Nights* in Arabic.[43] In 1982, when he could not sleep on account of the Israeli bombardment of Beirut, he was reading Sherlock Holmes.[44] In 1987, for much of October, he was reading Viceroy Linlithgow's *Memoirs*.[45] In general, Jamal Mian only noted the English titles he was reading, but there is no doubt that he was reading in all languages. 'At this moment', he told his diary in August 1979, 'I am reading stuff in four languages.'[46]

There is information, as we have noted in this chapter and earlier in the work to be gleaned from Jamal Mian's annotations. Two books in his library were especially heavily annotated: Khaliquzzaman's *Shahrah-i Pakistan*, the Urdu translation of his *Pathway to Pakistan*, and Wolpert's *Jinnah of Pakistan*. In both cases, the annotations fill the front matter

---

41. Jamal Mian Diary, 7, 8, June 1973, Ibid.
42. Ibid. 7, 11, 14 March 1977.
43. Ibid. 5 April, 27 May, 19 August 1978.
44. Ibid. 16 August 1982.
45. Ibid. 5–28 October 1987.
46. Ibid. 19 August 1979.

with extra pages added. In the case of the former, most of the matter was repeated in the tapes which Jamal Mian left with his papers, and we have made good use of these. In the case of the latter, Jamal Mian, while making clear his great admiration for Jinnah, made three criticisms of his former leader, two of which betray the disappointment of a Muslim who stayed in India. They may be summarised thus:

1. He thought Jinnah could be cold and harsh at times, a fact he used to discuss with the Raja of Mahmudabad;
2. He thought it unfortunate that Jinnah had sold No 10 Aurangzeb Road to Dalmia who turned it into a Cow-Protection Centre.
3. He felt that, after Partition, Jinnah did not care enough about the fate of the Indian Muslims.[47]

The man and his children

Jamal Mian's relationship with his seven children—Farida (b. 1944), Bari Mian (b. 1945), Mahmood (b. 1947), Alauddin (b. 1950), Amina (b. 1953), Moin (b. 1956) and Humaira (b. 1957) reveals his attitude to family life and his liberal views. When away from his family, he would tell his diary how much he missed them.[48] While away, he would correspond with Asar about what presents he should bring them.[49] They remembered him

---

47. Annotations by Jamal Mian 12.10.84 to Stanley Wolpert, *Jinnah of Pakistan* (New York: Oxford University Press, 1984), Jamal Mian Catalogue no. 1805.
48. Jamal Mian Diary, 8 November 1951, 11 November 1953.
49. Series of undated postcards from Asar to Jamal Mian, Personal File, JMP.

equally. On 5 December 1968 (his birthday by the Gregorian calendar), the children organized a celebration for which Farida knitted him a sweater and Humaira made him a cake.[50]

In Dacca, the boys were sent to St Joseph's, a Roman Catholic school run by the American Brothers of the Holy Cross and the girls were sent to Viqarunnisa Noon School. Later, Farida went to Holy Cross College. This was a clear indication that Jamal Mian wanted his children to have a Western education and that he had no worries about that education being within a Christian framework. The boys and girls, as we have noted, were taught the Quran, Arabic, and Persian out of school. School programmes permitting, as we have also noted, all children were expected to be at home for family prayers five times a day. Purdah was also observed, much to Farida's distress when she had to wear a burqa to school. There was also a separate ladies entrance to the house. In Karachi, however, Amina successfully resisted Jamal Mian's 'weak attempts' to impose the burqa. By the time it became Humaira's turn, the tradition had been dropped. Even Asar had given it up in favour of a shawl.[51]

Jamal Mian's liberal approach extended to the choices his children made in their lives. Bari Mian became a businessman. Arguably, he had excellent training through his association with the Ispahani family who literally breathed business. Ultimately, he became a leading figure in Karachi society, becoming his father's representative and that of Farangi Mahall in Pakistan. He officiates at religious ceremonies—*milad*s, weddings, and funerals, and is known to be a lover of Urdu and Persian poetry. Mahmood went to England in

50. Jamal Mian Diary 5 December 1968, Ibid.
51. Farida Jamal, Note on Asar, 30 November 2016, Ibid.

1967, to train as an accountant, but while there succeeded in developing a career as a man of letters and of film. He is a poet with six published collections of his work and three anthologies—the Penguin *Modern Urdu Poetry* (1986), the Penguin *Islamic Mystical Poetry* (2009), and *Faiz: 50 Poems* (2013). He is also a script writer and film producer with much work for the BBC and Channel 4. Alauddin, after doing an MA in English at Karachi University, started a career in advertising and then went to the London Film School in the UK. When he graduated, he and Mahmood joined together in film work before founding separate companies. Two of Jamal Mian's daughters became leading consultant physicians. Farida, after studying at Dacca Medical College and the London School of Hygiene and Tropical Medicine became a member of the Royal College of Pathologists and has retired as a Professor of Microbiology in the National University of Malaysia in Kuala Lumpur. Humaira, after studying at the Dow Medical College in Karachi, also moved to London where she gained a doctorate it endocrinology and became a member of the Royal College of Physicians. She is now a consultant in Palliative Medicine. Amina, who won the President's gold medal for being the best child writer in Pakistan in 1964, began her working career as a journalist. Later, after she moved to North America, she studied sociology at the University of Toronto. She currently holds a post in the Department of Sociology at Ryersons University and has one major book to her name on Jamaati Islami women in Pakistan, *The Vanguard of the New Modernity* (Syracuse NY: Syracuse University Press, 2013).

It is when we come to his daughter's marriage choices that Jamal Mian's liberalism is fully revealed. In one of his reflective moments, when kept awake at night, worrying about his children's marriages and the future of Farangi Mahall, he declared: 'I was hoping that my children would marry among my relatives ... [but this is] only possible if children agree to that.'[52] When a proposal came in January 1968 for Farida's hand, Jamal Mian was not surprised that she turned it down. But, more significantly, he flatly refused, despite considerable pressure, to try to persuade her to change her mind.[53] He was initially shocked when Farida admitted to wanting to marry a fellow student at the Dacca Medical College, Syed Mohamed Noori bin Syed Hussain Jamalulail from Kuala Lumpur. However, after going to see Noori's parents in Malaysia, Jamal Mian set aside his reservations and Farida was married in 1970.[54] In April 1979, Jamal Mian turned down requests from within his family for Amina's hand, in all probability following Amina's wishes.[55] Twenty months later, she was married to Ahmed Khan, the son of his old friend Muhammad Shoaib.[56] Humaira married Rohinton Jamshed Mulla, from a Parsi background, whom she met at the Dow Medical College and with whom she had continued to study in London at the Hammersmith Hospital. Jamal Mian's one condition was that Rohinton should convert to Islam. They married in London.

Amina was the only one of Jamal Mian's children who, to her mother's pleasure, had a traditional and partially arranged marriage. His sons all made their own arrangements: Bari Mian was briefly married to Sherry Rahman, the Pakistani politician; Alauddin married a Hindu, Veena Obhrai; Moin married Samina Ata; and Mahmood has still to marry.

There was just one point where Jamal Mian's liberal

---

52. Jamal Mian Diary, 20 April 1979, Ibid.
53. Ibid. 1, 3, 4, 5 January 1968.
54. Farida Jamal, Note on Asar, Ibid.
55. Jamal Mian Diary, 20 April 1979, Ibid.
56. Ibid. 9 January 1981.

approach to his children's choices found its limit, if only in his discourses with himself. This was when Moin became a singer, appearing with his guitar on television. This made Jamal Mian very upset. 'I am being punished that my son is a common singer', he told his diary, revealing his pride in his breeding and his background. But then he chastised himself for his snobbery. 'It is my selfishness and egocentricity that I would think it beneath me that my son would be a singer. If there were *shari`a* reasons it would be alright. But I object because I believe it to be beneath my status. I pray to God to forgive me for this.'[57] Here we see Jamal Mian trying to come to terms with Moin's decision psychologically. Eventually, Moin made a career for himself in the media in Toronto, Canada.

The man, his friends, and patrons

As we have noted, Jamal Mian had the gift of friendship. For much of his life, he had the emotional, and sometimes the material, support of close friends. It was his misfortune that he should outlive them all. There was the Raja of Mahmudabad, whom he came to know as he helped to organize the All-India Muslim League meeting in Lucknow in October 1937, and with whom he worked together closely in League campaigns down to 1947. Theirs was a relationship built on a shared sense of humour and a shared love of Urdu and Persian verse, which they sustained in Lucknow, Dacca, Karachi, and London until the Raja died in 1973.

There was Dr Faridi, who was as committed to defending the interests of Muslims as Jamal Mian was. He travelled

---

57. Ibid. 14 March 1991.

with Jamal Mian to witness the inauguration of Pakistan in
Karachi in 1947 and emerged as a Muslim leader in the UP
in the 1960s. He shared Jamal Mian's devotion to the saint of
Ajmer and would aim to meet him at the `Urs each year. This
friendship is continued through the descendants.

Of course, there was Hasrat Mohani, a family devotee and
Jamal Mian's companion on several pilgrimages. Together
they campaigned for the Muslim League and sat in the UP
Legislative Assembly. Jamal Mian was at his bedside when he
died in Farangi Mahall in 1951. In later life, Jamal Mian was
persistent in keeping the flame of Hasrat's memory alive by
publishing his *Diwan*, by supporting the construction of a hall
and library, in Karachi, in his honour, and by celebrating his
life every year on 13 May.

Another good friend was Iskander Mirza to whom Jamal
Mian became close when he was President of Pakistan. He
saw him every year while he was exiled in London. A further
cementing of the relationship was derived from the fact that
Iskander Mirza enjoyed entertaining him in restaurants
called Knights in Knightsbridge (there were four of them),
which were run by Hadi, who was married to Mirza Ahmed
Ispahani's daughter, Juni.

A mentor who became a close friend was Mufti Amin al-
Husseini of Jerusalem. We have noted that Jamal Mian first
met him when he came to Farangi Mahall in the 1930s, and
subsequently in Cairo in 1947 and 1958.[58] They came to meet
more frequently after that. 'During Ayub's time my friendship
with Mufti Sahib became very close.'[59] It was the Mufti who
put Jamal Mian forward to be a member of the Rabita and

---

58. Ibid. 5 July 1974.
59. Ibid.

it was Jamal Mian who arranged for the Mufti to meet Ayub Khan. 'He was the equal of Mohamed Ali and Iqbal and the great men of the Islamic world,' he told his diary on hearing of the Mufti's death, 'and he shared the qualities of greatness with such men.'[60]

Arguably, the man who was Jamal Mian's closest friend was Sadri Ispahani. We have noted the youthful ardour of Sadri's letters to Jamal Mian as their relationship developed in the early 1940s and their change of style as Sadri became involved in the affairs of M. M. Ispahani from the mid-1940s onwards. There is no doubt that Sadri was a great support to Jamal Mian and his family as he set up his home and business from the 1950s. Sadri kept a watching brief over Jamal Mian's health, being concerned to avoid situations which might spark a bi-polar attack, and also kept an eye on his children when he was in London in the 1970s. 'Among my benefactors', Jamal Mian wrote in a biographical note, 'top of the list is Sadri Ispahani who year in and year out helped me in every way and manner. My children's education, my living in Dacca, and every comfort was because of him.'[61]

There were less close friends and patrons who played an important part in Jamal Mian's life. By adding these to those above, I mention a good number of those who appear in an exhaustive list drawn up by Jamal Mian in his biographical note.[62] First, there were the associates of the Farangi Mahall family as a family of ulama long present in Lucknow and Bara Banki: Altafur Rahman Qidwai, who was his father's secretary and virtually a foster father after Abdul Bari's death, and

---

60. Ibid.
61. Jamal Mian, Biographical Note, 1 November 1975, JMP.
62. Ibid.

notably indulgent to Jamal Mian's children; Saidur Rahman
Qidwai, who made a monthly donation to Jamal Mian from
his salary and for whom Jamal Mian wrote his travelogue
of Pakistan in 1950; the Raja of Jahangirabad, who helped
him financially and of whose estate he became a trustee; and
Rafi Ahmad Kidwai, opponent for all his political life but a
generous host to Jamal Mian when he stayed in Delhi after
Partition and whose funeral prayers Jamal Mian led. Then,
there were political associates largely inherited from his father:
Shaukat Ali, who whisked the young Jamal Mian off to the
Palestine Conference in Calcutta in 1936; Nawab Ismail
Khan, leader of the UP Muslim League, who, as Chancellor
of Aligarh Muslim University after independence, was to make
Jamal Mian a member of its Court; Khaliquzzaman, who was
at the heart of Lucknow's politics from the second decade of
the twentieth century and was a major figure in Jamal Mian's
political firmament until his death in 1973; Jinnah, who gave
Jamal Mian good advice as he entered politics in the 1930s,
worked behind the scenes to get him a source of income,
refused to accept his resignation from the honorary assistant
secretaryship of the League in 1943, and tolerated his speaking
up for his beliefs at League meetings. No less important were
the brothers Mirza Ahmed and Hassan Ispahani who were
friends and supporters from the early 1940s to their deaths in
the 1980s. Mirza Ahmed had a stern but ultimately benevolent
oversight of Jamal Mian's attempts to sell tea. Hassan offered
more emotional support and stepped in to help when Jamal
Mian was ill. Although these brothers were Jamal Mian's
patrons, as well as his seniors, he did have the personal
authority, when differences between them threatened to
destroy their business, to step in and facilitate a reconciliation.
A further group was represented by people from the Bombay

world: the distinguished businessman Ebrahim Yusuf Zainal, who travelled with him on the Middle East Delegation; and Mulla Tahir Saifuddin and his sons, Mulla Burhanuddin and Dr Najmuddin of the Dawoodi Bohra community, who helped Jamal Mian financially. Pir Mohiuddin of Golra should also be added to this list. The son of a close associate of Abdul Bari, Pir Mehr Ali Shah, he was always looking for ways to help Jamal Mian. Later on, in Pakistan, Ghulam Faruque and Muhammad Azfar were amongst those formerly of the ICS who helped Jamal Mian. And finally, there was Ayub Khan, with whom Jamal Mian had an increasingly edgy relationship. Without Ayub's intervention in the Shakarganj Mill issue, it is unlikely that Jamal Mian would have been able to make up for his losses after the Bangladesh disaster and live in a financially secure retirement.

All these men were Muslims, but there was also a Hindu who took a fatherly interest in Jamal Mian throughout his life—Jawaharlal Nehru. It was Nehru who took the adolescent Jamal Mian with him to the platform of the Congress in 1936; it was Nehru who overlooked ten years of political attacks from Jamal Mian to take him in his personal plane from Lucknow to Delhi in September 1947 so that he could see the communal situation for himself; it was Nehru who gave instructions to Pant in 1949 that Jamal Mian's resignation from the UP Assembly should be refused; it was Nehru who instructed the Indian consulate in Jeddah to assist him while on Hajj in 1950; it was Nehru who had Jamal Mian's visa extended in 1957 when he visited India to see his mother; and it was Nehru who would have done much more than this if Jamal Mian had let him.[63] Through much of his life,

63. Jamal Mian, 'Note on Jawaharlal Nehru's Death', JMP.

Jamal Mian was the beneficiary of unusual levels of personal, financial, and political support.

The man, his faith

There can be no consideration of Jamal Mian the man without addressing his faith. According to Mahmood Jamal, the family household was dominated by the shadow of Abdul Bari, which perhaps is a way of saying that in life in general, and certainly in religious matters, the family was well aware of the continuing impact of Abdul Bari on Jamal Mian. We should remind ourselves of the first two sentences of Abdul Bari's will:

> All relatives and friends should fear God, obey and love the Prophet, his associates and seek their blessing and consider this the part of their worship. They should never avoid congregational prayer, should never compromise with their conscience, they should seek forgiveness of their sins, and remember death and the Day of Judgement.[64]

This was precisely the code by which Jamal Mian strove to live.

As we have noted, the whole Farangi Mahalli devotional year, as far as possible, was translated to Dacca and to Karachi. Love of the Prophet was always a central focus with its celebrations of *milad* in particular in the first twelve days of Rabiulawwal. The celebrations of Abdul Qadir Gilani, *Ghaus-i A'zam,* remained immensely important for him. It was a mercy that in mid-life he was able to come to close to the Qadri Pir Mohiuddin of Golra and that in Karachi he

---

64. `Abd al-Bari's will, 29 Ramadan 1341 (1923), ABP.

should be able to become a disciple of Pir Abdul Qadir Gilani. Equally celebrating the `Urs of Moinuddin Chishti at Ajmer was a central part of his annual calendar. The family saints, moreover, in Bagh Maulana Anwar and Rudauli Sharif were not forgotten, while particular attention was paid to Shah Abdul Razzaq of Bansha.

Jamal Mian's decision, in 1982, never to return to India meant that he lost contact with all of his traditional sources of spiritual comfort there. The impact would have been exacerbated by the fact that his Karachi pir, Abdul Qadir Gilani, had already died. As we know, he compensated for his by focussing much more intently on the Prophet's shrine in Medina. His love of Sufi poetry, however, remained as strong as ever. As we have noted, in his last days, he had tapes of *qawwali* playing continuously. One he listened to repeatedly was a manqabat to Shah Abdul Razzaq of Bansa, the family saint. Jamal Mian feared God, living as he did according to the *shari`a*. But his faith was also instinct with the humanity, and dare one say the balance, which he derived from his spiritual development.

The man, his political views

Jamal Mian's beliefs were expressed in his political views. Arguably, the essential humanity which was derived from his Sufi understandings was expressed in positions which supported humanity—which supported the 'common good'. Implicitly, although not explicitly, he was following the classic jurisprudential concept of *maslaha*. As always, the common good was defined in different ways in different contexts.

So, from 1937 to 1947, Jamal Mian worked for the

All-India Muslim League. He saw this, as did many, though not all of his friends and relations, as the best way of protecting the interests of Indian Muslims as British India moved towards independence. For this reason, he supported the League's demand for Pakistan, although he admitted that forming a Pakistan out of India's Muslim majority provinces would leave Muslims in the minority provinces exposed. He used the 'hostage' argument, as he did in his 1945–46 election campaign, to explain how the danger would be nullified. In 1946, in the UP Legislative Assembly, his principle of the common good acquired a new expression when he attacked the Congress ministers for putting forward a bill to increase their salaries while the common people, Muslim and Hindu, were suffering from want. In a similar vein, at the last meeting of the Muslim League Council in Karachi in December 1947, he opposed a resolution referring to Pakistan as a 'Muslim state' because its new government ministers were living well amidst the poverty and squalor of hundreds and thousands of refugees, which was not how the leaders of Muslim states in the past behaved.

The idea of the 'common good' also lay behind Jamal Mian's approach to Islam and the Pakistani constitution. It was for this reason that he opposed Liaquat Ali Khan's 'Objectives Resolution' which opened the door to an Islamic state, declaring that it would be the source of chaos. So in his evidence to the first Constituent Assembly, he opposed the idea that Pakistan should become an Islamic state because both before and after Partition the League had declared that Pakistan was to be a democratic state, giving equal rights to all citizens whatever their religious beliefs, which an Islamic state would not. He made the same point to Ayub Khan's

Constitution Commission in 1960. The same principle, moreover, underlay his objections to Bhutto's amendments to the Constitution in 1973, which made Ahmadis non-Muslims. He said it would be divisive. Time proved him right.

★ ★ ★

Jamal Mian was a bright flower of Islamic culture in its North Indian manifestation. His library reveals the depth and breadth of his Islamic culture in its religious and literary forms. It also reveals, in its holdings in English, how he followed the basic Islamic principle of pursuing knowledge wherever it might be found. Indeed, he went beyond English literature to English humour, or better put, an English sense of humanity as expressed in the British media; a much-loved entertainment in later life was box sets of the BBC sitcom about the Home Guard in the Second World War—'Dad's Army'.

Jamal Mian was respected as the leading representative of the Farangi Mahall tradition in his day, which he upheld in his family life and in his spiritual life. Later on, he had added respect as a member of the Muslim League High Command which achieved Pakistan. Through much of his life, because of his cultivation, because of his personal qualities, and because of what he represented, many people were drawn to him and so were powerful patrons. As Muhammad Ali Zainal declared in 1949: 'Jamal Mian is the kind of person who only appears rarely'.[65]

---

65. Statement repeated in a letter from Saidur Rahman Qidwai to Jamal Mian, Bombay, 2 January 1950, JMP.

The meaning of Jamal Mian's life

Jamal Mian's life embraces the dying embers of the old Mughal dispensation and the triumph of new forces in Indian society—Islamic reform, a Western elite culture within the framework of British rule, and Indian nationalism which sheltered within it Hindu revivalism. Jamal Mian's struggle to maintain the Farangi Mahall madrasah, the Congress attack on Urdu in the UP after 1947, the removal of the Persian verses decorating the UP Legislative Council chamber, and the takeover of the great Muslim Princely State of Hyderabad were all manifestations of this, great and small.

In microcosm, Jamal Mian's life offers the twentieth-century story of the Mughal service class which, over previous centuries, had been formed for the most part by migrants into India from Arabia, Iran, Central Asia, and Afghanistan. Like many, but not all members of this class, he supported the Muslim League and its demand for Pakistan. Many members of this class opted for Pakistan, becoming citizens. Jamal Mian, on the other hand, went to Pakistan to earn a living, but never intended to become a Pakistani citizen until he was practically forced to do so by the Government of India. In Jamal Mian's circle in Dacca, in the 1950s and 1960s, and in Karachi from the 1970s onwards, we can see the descendants of the old Mughal service class reshaping themselves as an elite in the new state. Furthermore, with the rapid development of air travel from the late 1950s we also see them developing their pattern of international travel, involving regular visits to Europe and, in Jamal Mian's case, to the Hejaz as well. At the same time, they came to acquire positions in international organizations—the UN, the World Bank, and international businesses. The spread of Jamal Mian's children through

Toronto, London, Karachi, and Kuala Lumpur is symptomatic
of this.

Jamal Mian's life also reveals the complex and nuanced
nature of the Partition process. For some it was a brief and
extremely traumatic event. For others, amongst them Jamal
Mian, it was a slow tearing apart of the fabric of a whole way of
life and spiritual being. We have noted how in the 1950s, Jamal
Mian and members of his class felt they could travel between
India and Pakistan easily as though the new boundaries did
not exist. We have noted, too, the extraordinary access he
had to the leaders of the new states. So, as an Indian citizen,
he could have close relations with presidents Nazimuddin
and Iskander Mirza of Pakistan, and then, as a Pakistani
citizen, have privileged access to the Indian Prime Minister,
Nehru. Less striking, but another dimension of this freedom
of movement, was the way in which he was able, while based
in Dacca and Karachi, to continue much of the Indian part
of his devotional routine.

Alongside the mindset which floated above the emerging
nation-state system, there was an increasing awareness
of different systems and growing barriers. There is his
awareness in 1950 that the rupee had a different value in
India and Pakistan, and, as the 1950s progress, there is
his growing entanglement in the new instruments of state
control—passports, no objection certificates, and visas.
While the new states were refining their administrative
barriers, much as he loved to visit India, Jamal Mian found
an emotional barrier rising within him over visiting Lucknow.
In 1982, this made him so ill that he decided never to visit
India again, thus, finally ripping apart the fabric of his
spiritual life. Against this, the undoubted trauma of the
second Partition and emergence of Bangladesh was a lesser

affair. For the last thirty years of his life, cut-off from his
holy places in India, he found spiritual sustenance in the
Hejaz. This tearing apart was completed by his decision,
following his Sufi beliefs, to break with the Farangi Mahall
tradition and be buried in Karachi and not in the family
Bagh in Lucknow.

For those who despair of madrasah education, Jamal
Mian's life demonstrates that such education, at its best,
could produce a man of great cultural breadth who was
open to new possibilities and who believed implicitly that
the purpose of religion was to serve the welfare of humanity.
Serving humanity also meant respecting the individual. Thus,
and it was not always easy, he respected the decisions that
his children made about their marriages and their lives. But,
before we surrender to this picture of the 'modern' liberal
`alim`, we should also note that, as is often the case in the
so-called modern personality, there was at least one element
of superstition, his practice of *fal*, of seeking guidance from
the verse that first appeared to him as the *Diwan-i Hafiz*
fell open.

Jamal Mian was sustained through his life by the
extraordinary cultural capital he gained from his Lucknow
upbringing. His education in Farangi Mahall at one of the
highest points of its existence, his guidance at the hands of
many able relatives and friends, his command of Islamic
culture in both its religious and literary forms, and his
unpretentious spiritual authority earned him respect from
those amongst whom he moved in his long journey through
life, while giving him both signposts and pleasure along
the way.

Appendix 1

Milad written by Maulana Ruhullah for Jamal Mian

Translated by Mahmood Jamal

Bismillah Al Rahman Al Rahim

Hamidan Wa Musalyan Wa Musalyman

Laqad ja'akum Rasulun min anfusykum azizun aliyhey ma anittum harisun alaikum bil momineena' rauufur rahim

(Surely, there has come to you a Messenger, from amongst you, hard on whom is your suffering, for the good of you he craves and for the believers he is kind and merciful (128))

All praise and deserving of all reverence is Allah who has bestowed innumerable blessings and favours upon us. He indeed is deserving of worship and prayer who has created the universe and adorned it with His will. He indeed is the Creator of the worlds.

Love and affection are His adornment who is eternal and who is never dependent or contingent. It is his wrath and anger that we must fear for he is powerful and fearless and is never weak or subservient to any.

Durud and *Salaams*, and bouquets of devotion are for *Rahmatul lil alameen* who for all humans and for the elevation of *Deen* and *Dunya* showed us a simple and straight way, Islam; and whose character and actions and whose goodness and beauty, and His manners and ways, still create light and tranquility in our hearts, still light up and make fragrant the Universe. Allahumma Salley! Salaams be upon Him!

Nearly fourteen centuries have gone by when Arabia had two tribes, the Qahtani (who were inhabitants of Yemen and who were later forefathers to the Ansars of Medina) and Adnani (who were inhabitants of Hijaz) who like the rest of the world, were spending their lives in sin, and were busy spending their days in ignorance and sinful deeds. The land was barren; water was scarce; civilization and culture were hardly evident, they spent their lives like nomads and savages. Undoubtedly, they had certain qualities exhibited in those who had not been touched by civilization. They were brave; they were decent; they protected their neighbours; they were courageous and brave, true and loyal, and men of their word. But with this, their sins exceeded their virtues by far.

They were idol worshippers; they worshipped wine and song. They worshipped rank and tribe, in other words they worshipped all sinful things and were shameless and crude in their ways. It was part of their character to bury young girls alive, kill infants for fear of hunger, to fight and feud over small things.

But from this very dark pit of evil and sin a stream of goodness and virtue was to spring forth.

The tribe of Adnanis which was also known as Quraish who dwelt in God's first house in the city of Mecca, was hiding in its embrace that sun whose light would shine out of Arabia and envelop the world.

The dawning of this sun was to be the household of Abdul Muttalib, and the sky of this moon was to be Bibi Amina's home.

Just as Abdullah, Abdul Mutallib's son and Abdul Mutallib, Hashim's son, were related to Hazrat Ibrahim and Ismail, so in the same way Abdullah's wife, the venerable Amina daughter of Wahb, was also a rosebud of the garden of Ibrahim.

In 571 AD, in Abdullah's household, came that respected orphan through whom the universe would be released from a greater orphanhood.

His respected age was only six when he suffered the loss of his mother. When he was only eight, Abdul Mutallib took him under his wing and after that Abu Talib's poverty turned to wealth through this wealth of joy. The day Abu Talib took this venerable child into his home, from that day God increased his fortunes.

In youth he spent time shepherding the flock then he started trading and became so well known for his honesty that at the age of twenty-five, he became a representative of a rich business woman, Bibi Khadija who sent him to Syria as her manager. In this journey her profits doubled. After his return from the journey, this rich lady became his loyal wife.

When all those stages of life which an ordinary human passes (and which he had been sent to teach men) had been traversed, and his respected age was forty years, then Hazrat Jibril, the angel sent by God, delivered God's first message to him on Monday, 27th of Ramzan in the cave of Hira:

Iqra Bisme Rabbikal lazi khalaq
Khalaqal insaana min alaq
Iqra wa rabbuka alakramul lazi
Allama bil qalam-e
Allamal insaano maalam yalam.

(Recite in the name of your Lord Who created
He made man from a clot of blood
Recite for your Lord is the Most Generous
Who taught writing by the pen
Taught man what he knew not.)

After being endowed with Prophethood and Risalat, he first started privately to call people to worship God and abandon the idols.

Among the first to embrace the faith were Hazrat Bibi Khadija, close friend Hazrat Abu Bakr Siddique and cousin, Hazrat Ali ibn Abi Talib and Zaid bin Harisa.

After 4 years of Prophethood, he was ordered to make a public call.

He climbed mount Safa and called on the Quraish to hear him and said:

'I am the Messenger of Allah for you and for all mankind. Fear the Day of Judgement and mend your ways'

This timely and apt admonition and proclamation, offended the other mushrikeen including Abu Lahab who exceeded all in his enmity and opposition.

When Abu Talib saw this increasing hostility, he asked his nephew (Muhammad SAW) to desist; he replied that if the moon were placed in his one hand and the sun in the other, even then he could not be stopped from his work. *Alla huma Salle ala Muhammad wa ala ale Muhammad.'*

In those early days, the Prophet and his companions were subjected to innumerable hardships. They had stones and garbage thrown at them.

He and his companions showed the same restraint and forbearance that they showed when hunger or thirst had struck them.

In the seventh year after Prophethood, *Rasulallah sallahe alaihe wasallam* and, for their closeness to him, his relatives of Banu Hashim, were made prisoners in a valley of Mecca.

They were excluded from all commerce and exchange, virtually ex-communicated.

There were hangings on the walls of the Kaaba and they said that unless Bani Hashim declare a truce and hand over Muhammad [PBUH] for execution, they shall remain banished. After three years the Tyrants relented and these restrictions were removed.

In the Hajj season a few people came from Medina who having seen the honest ways, accepted the truth and had embraced Islam. On one occasion, a few people just accepted to do good deeds and returned. And then one group promised to practice righteous acts and fight for them and went back to Medina.

During this period, another proof of Prophethood was delivered that God, as He had done with other Prophets, blessed Muhammad SAW with his presence; and through his special Angel Gabriel, mounted him on Buraq, via Palestine, and journeyed him to the heavens, where he met other Prophets and led the Namaz(prayers). This great height was called Miraj.

This gift from Allah further aggravated and inflamed the enemies and in the storm of their denial, they showered untold hardships on the Prophet.

He also went to Taif. There too, like the *mushrikeen* of Mecca, the cruel enemies of truth, insulted and opposed him, the children stoned him, the adults taunted him. And without taking benefits of God's blessings, they turned him away.

When the trouble and pain reached its limit, the Prophet asked his followers to migrate to Medina. When all had left, and the Quraish had plotted to finally kill him, and surrounded his residence, he left Hazrat Ali in his place and took Abu Bakr as his companion and left for Medina.

After thirteen years in Mecca and preaching Islam lovingly and peacefully, the time had come that he go to Medina and raise the banner of truth and start a Jihad in the way of Allah.

The Meccan enemies could not tolerate him living peacefully in Medina and preaching Islam.

Led by Abu Sufyan, the battles of Badr and Uhud were imposed and fought near Medina, but finally, God helped his messenger and he became victorious over the Quraish and Arabia; and in the sixth year of Hijrat, at Hudabia, the famous peace accord was signed, which on the surface seemed like a defeat, but in fact proved to be a great victory for Islam. *Alla huma Salle ala Muhammad wa ala ale Muhammad.*

In the eighth year of Hijra, the Quraish broke the agreement, and *Rasullah sallah wali wassalam* entered Mecca with ten thousand courageous followers, in total victory.

Those who had been cruel to him were shown mercy, those who had been harsh were treated with kindness. Those who had denied him shelter, their homes were declared as sanctuaries of peace.

Those who had refused to give him the keys of the Kaaba for a moment's worship were bestowed the honour of being keepers of the keys till judgement day. In other words, he forgave all his enemies.

To the extent that even those eleven men and seven women who had been declared to be put to death by any mean, were spared under the blessing of *Rahmatul lil alameen.*

Alla humma salle ala Muhammad wa ala aley Muhammad

Then the prophet went to Medina and in the tenth year of Hijra, performed his last Hajj. There were approximately 90,000 devotees assembled around him when he rose up in Arafat to deliver his address.

He said:

Ya ayyuhan nasa innau qauli fa inni la adhri le alli la alqaaukum bada aamin haza behazal muqafi abadan...
Listen to me o people, for I do not know if I shall be ever again here after this year.

That is why it is called Hajjat ul Wida

In this speech he said:

Inna dimaukum wa amwalakum haramun alikum ila un tallaqu rabbukum

(Verily, your blood and possessions of fellow beings are forbidden to you till you meet your Creator)

And also said *Innamal mominuna ikhwatun.*

(All Momins are brothers) ... and in this it was also stated,

La uhillo le imraa mala akhihey illa un tayyaba nafsan

(Your brother's property is forbidden to you except that which he gave to you himself)

As soon as he completed Hajj he returned to Medina and after Muharram and Safar, the call came for a return to God.

In the veil of a fever, at the age of sixty-three of which fifty-three were spent in Mecca and ten in Medina.

After a revolution in Arabia and after giving a complete way of life to the world, the beloved of Allah, veiled himself from this world.

Alla humma salle ala Muhammad wa ala aley Muhammad

The venerable Prophet was the bravest of the brave; when the most courageous and strong ran away, he stood firm in Battle.

He was generous in a way that he would never fear lack of wealth. He was calm. When a *mushrik* (Da'saur) raised his sword and asked, 'Who is going to save you from me now!?'

The Prophet answered 'Allah'

The sword shook in his hands and fell.

Then the Holy Messenger (SAW) picked up the sword and asked the unbeliever

'Now who is going to save you now?'

He answered 'No One'.

The Prophet forgave him as he had done to all Quraish after the conquest of Mecca by uttering

'*Izhabu fa antum tulaqa*'
(Go you are Free)
and freed them all.

He was patient and kind, so much so that when the people of Quraish used to cause him pain, even then he would say
'*Alla humma ahdi qaumi fa innahum la yalamun*'
(Oh Allah guide my people because they are ignorant)
Alla humma salle ala Muhammad wala aley Muhammad

In short, Allah had bestowed upon him the highest state of creation. He had adorned him with the highest qualities and attributes of humanity. '*Innaka la ala khulqin azeem* bears witness to that.

In looks, he was the most beautiful, in height he was not too tall or too short. In intelligence he was foremost of all.

His visage was such that no eye could rest on it fearful of its august beauty. His tongue (language) was so perfect that despite being an illiterate, a miracle such as the Quran emerged from it.

Hazrat Ali described his total appearance and concluded thus:

Lam ara mithlahoo qablahoo wa la baadahoo salla allah alihay wassallam.
(I have not seen the like of Him either before or after Him SAW).

The most fearful of God; fighting only for God, and merciful to his creation like God Himself would be merciful.

From his glowing body would emerge such fragrance that for devotees like Anas, even amber and musk would seem bland in front of it.

His tawwakal (contentment) and steadfastness was such that Bibi Aisha states that he often went hungry, and for months the fire was not lit (for cooking) in his home.

He would not talk unnecessarily. Whatever he uttered was brief and full of meaning.

True belief and its conditions were expressed in one sentence:

'*Qul amanto billahe summas taqim*'
(Say you believe in God and be steadfast thereafter)
In one sentence good and bad actions were recognized:
'*Innamal aamalo bin niati*
(Actions depend on your intentions)
One of the essentials of belief was revealed thus:
'*Al hayyao minal iman*'
(Modesty is the essence of belief)
The sign of the obedient and dutiful is:
'*Assaido mun Wo izzo be ghairi hi*'
(Happy is he who respects the advice of others)
For his devotees he pointed out the way of salvation with:
'*Al marro maya mun ahabbo*'
(An individual will accompany in the hereafter those whom he loves)
He taught us to recognize strength thus:
'*Laisa shadeed bil sarriati innama al lazi yamlik naafsahu indil ghazabh*'
(He is not strong in character who conquers others, but he who controls himself (his *nafs*) when he is angry)
In beautiful brevity, he defined a *munafiq* (hypocrite) thus:
'*Iza hadasa kaziba wa iza wada khalafa wa iza aatumina khana?*'
(When he speaks he lies; he breaks his promise and is untrustworthy)
With one sentence,
Almuslimu mun salimul muslamoon min lisaanihi wa yadehi
(A Muslim is he from whom other Muslims are safe: from his tongue (speech) and hands (actions))

He fortified Islamic unity and organization for our guidance.

The whole essence of mercy and kindness was explained in a simple sentence:

Sil man qata'kaWa affo amman zalamak wa ahsin ila mun assa al alyka

(Establish your relationship with he who breaks from you and forgive him who is unjust to you. And be good to one who is unkind to you.)

With '*Hasib qabla an tuhasib*' (Be accountable before you are held accountable)the essence of civility and goodness, with '*Khairakum khairikum le ahlakum*' showed us the strategy for reaching our goal.

And with, '*Afzalul ashghalay khidmatul naas*'
(The best occupation is the service of humanity)
and
Kullukum rayin wa kullukum mas'oolun an rayiatihi
(All for one and one for all)
Explained to us the entire subject of culture of politics.

It is these priceless sayings and extraordinary civility and treatment of others and unequalled qualities and habits which converted the idol worshipping Arabs into accepting his God as their God and his faith as their faith and made each utterance of his their lifeblood and their soul. (*Hirze jaan aur vird-e zaban*)

Wine drinking was deeply embedded in their nature, but those drunk on their beloved's love, were willing to shatter the vats of wine at one word from the Prophet.

Those inhabitants who would refuse to bow even before God, started to bow their heads before the slaves of Muhammad ur Rasoolallah (SAW)

Not just the Arabs, many powerful and proud bow their heads when they hear his name even today!

The mansion of love, unlike buildings of stone and brick, does not grow derelict and old with the vicissitudes of time. In fact, the more time passes, the stronger and more sturdy become its foundations. The evergreen garden of the memory of the beloved is impervious to autumn and spring. This flower never wilts; the more time passes it becomes even more fresh and alluring and tender (*shagufta*).

Love and memory (of the Beloved) are things that day by day grow stronger and deep.

Even in this day and age, those who have only a tiny ember of belief hidden under the ashes of their hearts become restless and intoxicated upon hearing:

Marhaba Syyed Makki Madani ul Arabi
Dil o jann baad fidayat cheh ajab khush laqabi!

And the light of knowledge shines in their desolate eyes:

Qad-e raana ki ada jama-e zeba ki phaban
Surmagi aankh ghazab naz bhari woh chitwan
Woh aamamy ki sajawat woh jabeen-e raushan
Aur mukhray ki tajalli woh bayaz-e gardan
Woh aba-e arabi aur woh neecha daman
*Dilrubayana woh raftar, voh besakhta pan***

(The stature of beauty the robes of adornment
The dark surma eyes and the alluring gaze
That style of your turban and the glowing forehead

---

*   Quotation from Jan Muhammad Qudsi, poet of Shah Jahan's court.
**   Tentatively attributed to Shaheed Lucknavi (fl. twentieth century).

The brightness of your face and the graceful neck
That Arab abaya and that flowing hem
That alluring gait, that open friendly manner ...)

And before their eyes that sun becomes alight on which when
seeing a red blanket, according to Ibn Aaazib, the light of the moon
seemed to be eclipsed.

Allah o Akbar!
Fourteen centuries have passed! what is the allure that makes an
itinerant wanderer of the streets proclaim:

Meray maula bulalo Madinay mere!
(My Lord! Call me to Medina!)

The sign of faith and the name of Islam now resides in this
passionate devotion and this slavery (to the Prophet). That is why
it is essential for every believer (Muslim) to keep the Messenger of
God closer to him than his life, his property, his relations, his nation
and everything else.

When we consider Allah's other prophets we ascribe qualities to
them: some we praise for their power, some for their beauty and
attraction, some for their courage and some for the quality of their
mercy and kindness but when we look at our Lord (Muhammad
SAW) we find him replete and complete with all qualities and a
perfect human being.

It is true indeed:

Husn-e Yusuf Dam-e Isa Yad-e bayza dari
*Anche khuban hama darand tu tanha dari**

---

*   Quotation from Saadi Shirazi (d. 1291).

(The beauty of Yusuf, the spirit of Isa, the bright hand of Moses
All those attributes they had we find in your person)

And this too is a miracle of his perfection, that the Puritan
rubbing his forehead in the dusty floor of his mosque, when he
rises and utters '*Assalam o aliaka ya ayyuhan nabi wa rahmatullah
wa barkathu*'.

Then even a poor stone grinder or a humble worker can imagine
that his Lord and Master had also ground stones and lifted weights
for others with His holy hands.

And on the field of battle, a mujahid performing his ablutions
with blood and offering the namaz of love, can see Muhammad ur
Rasool Allah (SAW) with his powerful visage (*Paikar-e Jalal*) in the
battle of Hunain, defeating his enemies with a few pebbles.

So can one who loves children imagine that the Holy Prophet
always put his hand of loving protection on children, especially
orphans.

In short, at home, in the mosque, in the bazaar, in the field of
battle, in the madrasah, in the religious gathering, in the company
of friends, in the graveyard, where ever you care to imagine and see
with discerning eyes, the light that emerged from Mecca and found
rest in Medina will be a lamp of guidance for you.

Alla humma salle ala Muhammad wa la aley Muhammad

Thanks be to Allah, that we are the lucky people of this Ummah.

This is the blessing and tufail (largesse) of this enslavement that
today when many great empires of the world are crumbling and
civilized and cultured nations are being annihilated, and those more
deserving than us are being destroyed, at this time we who are the
devotees of *Rahmatul lil alimeen* (Prophet) are dwelling in peace
and tranquility and dignity. Everywhere new life is emerging and
awakening and progress is being manifested, we stand proudly and
say loudly:

Ta daagh-e gulami tu dareem
*Har ja ke rawem badshaheem**
(Since I received the stamp of your slavery
I am a king wherever I may go!)

The holy month of Rabiul Awwal is spent in celebration of (the Prophet's birthday)

The desolate settlements of the heart become green with the arrival of this guest and our dark gatherings are lit up by this lamp of guidance and light.

This birth which at one time was a moment of joy only for Abdul Muttalib and his household, is today a moment of joy and celebration for 75 crores (750 million) devotees. And is indeed without doubt a blessing for the whole world.

Alla humma salle ala Muhammad wa la aley Muhammad

In Abdullah's house, from the womb of Bibi Amna it happened thus that on the 12th of (Rabiul Awwal), on Monday in the early morning when thousands of innocent orphans with faces uplifted waited patiently for the blessing of God, widows were lamenting their loss, looked to the heavens, and the subject and slaves were raising their lament, when the lamps of goodness and civility had been extinguished, when the abodes of mercy and loyalty were in desolation, the furrows of humanity and decency had dried up.

Everything under the heavens was thirsting and waiting for the rain of God's blessing:

Yakayak hui ghairat-e-haq ko harkat
Barha janib-e Bu Qubais Abr-e-rahmat

---

* Quotation from Abdur Rahman Jami (d.1492).

Hui pahloo-e-aamna say huvaida
*Dua-khalil aur naved-e-masiha**

(Suddenly was moved the hand of Truth
And towards Bu Qubais moved the cloud of Mercy
And from Amna's womb emerged
The prayer of Abraham, the good tidings of Jesus!)

Fourteen hundred and ten years ago from today the Leader of
the World, the Pride of Humanity, the Emperor of Prophets and
Messengers, the Curer of Ills, the Blessings of the Worlds, Lord
Mohammad Mustafa Ahmad Mujtaba Sallalaho Alihey Wassalam
with his happy presence and advent made this world proud and joyful.

---

* Quotation from the *Musaddas Madd-o Jazr-e Islam* (Musaddas on the Flow and
Ebb of Islam of Altaf Husain Hali, d. 1914).

Appendix 2

Khutba Part 1 delivered at Calcutta Maidan by Maulana Jamal Mian who led the Eid ul Fitr prayers there on 2 October 1943

Translated from Urdu by Mahmood Jamal

بسم الله الرحمن الرحيم

الله اكبر الله اكبر لا اله الا الله والله اكبر الله
اكبر ولله الحمد في كل أوان   الحمد لله الذي هدانا
لهذا وما كنا لنهتدي لولا ان هدانا الله نا ما لنا
الله اكبر الله اكبر لا اله الا الله والله اكبر الله اكبر
ولله الحمد في كل زمان ومكان   والصلوة والسلام
على جميع الانبياء والمرسلين سيما على سيدنا
والاخرين رحمة للعالمين محمد المصطفى احمد المجتبى
وعلى آله واصحابه اجمعين •

All praise is Yours and doings Yours! It is You who has created everything with Your power and all qualities O Merciful Creator are Yours. It is You who has adorned everything and blessed them with Your favour. O Merciful and Beneficient, we thank You and are

383

indebted to You for making us Muslims and showing us the sacred month of Ramadan and giving us joy in the happiness of Eid ul Fitr.

We send our *Salaams* and *Salawat* to all Your prophets and messengers who showed us the way to please You and delivered to us Your commands.

In particular, Hazrat Muhammad Mustafa and his heirs and companions on whom O Lord bestow Your blessings for it is they who delivered Your last and most complete message and Your favoured religion, Islam, to us so we can have success in this world and happiness in the next.

Friends! Eid Mubarak to all of you! This joy and happiness, and the celebrations fixed by God and the happiness celebrated by the Prophet, all joy Mubarak to you.

Your satisfaction and joy tells us that despite the sufferings and troubles you understand the importance of fasting and the greatness of Eid.

But the true celebrators of this joy are not those who wear attractive clothes or have smiles on their faces and are expressing happiness by rituals.

The true celebrators of Eid are those whose hearts and souls have been cleansed by the *barkat* of Ramzan, whose foreheads have been brightened with the mark of repentance, whose tears of repentance have given rise to the sun of salvation. Those who say *'Man saam Ramadan imanan wa ihtisaban ghafralah ma taqqadam min zambin'* have repented.

Today, the real congratulations are deserved by they who know and accept God, and recognize and love God's beloved Messenger, Muhammad Ibn Abdullah, performed their prayers, enjoyed the trials of fasting; and if they were wealthy, they earned the treasures of belief and the wealth of blessings in exchange for giving charity and zakat.

Friends! The real Eid is for those soldiers of God whose days of instructions came to an end with the month of fasting yesterday;

and with the coming of a new year, they started their *Jihad-e-Akbar* on a new front against their *Nafs Ammara*.

It is for those who defeated the lure of wealth and worldly pleasure, and whose absorption in God was a sword which gave them victory over hearts.

It is through the blessings of these deserving ones that we too can celebrate Eid and we are hopeful that our Eid also becomes a true Eid and delivers us from the troubles of this life and saves us from the deprivations of the next.

(O You who are believers. Let not your wealth or offspring make you forgetful of Allah. Whosoever does this, will be the loser. And spend from what Allah has given you and before you face death and say O my Creator why did You not give me time to do it. So I could give charity and become amongst Your good slaves. Allah will not give more time than what is allotted. And Allah is mindful of what you do.)*

In the Eid khutba it is essential to mention the rituals and manners of celebrating Eid. Hence I would like to mention some important aspects in keeping with the Sunnat.

---

* *Surah Al-Munafiqun* (the Hypocrites) Quran, 63; 9–11).

Today, bathing, brushing your teeth, wearing your best clothes, using pleasant fragrances, going to the Eid Gah by one route and returning by another, and before leaving your house, eating a few dates or any other sweet is desirable.

The purpose of all this is that today Muslims must celebrate; and express their joy and happiness through their dress and actions. But to be profligate or wasteful or to take loans to make fancy clothes etc is definitely not appropriate.

In fact doing this is against the greatness of Eid and is contrary to the teachings of Islam.

In Eid prayers, like *Juma*, two *rakats* in *jamaat* is obligatory.

In the *namaz* of Eid, there are three *Takbirs* in the first *rakat* after *Sana* and in the second *rakat*, three before *Ruku*.

The time of Eid prayers is from the rising of the sun to its decline. To listen to the Khutba after Eid is a sunnat.

Like the *namaz*, it is also obligatory to give fixed *fitra* and alms. The measure of this alm is one seer two chatanks of wheat or 2.25 ser of jao just to be sure you should give 1.75 ser wheat or 3.5 ser of jao.

It can also be done with other cereals and should be similar in amount.

Today in Bengal it is rice instead of wheat so the measure of *fitra* here would be 1.75 seers of rice.

Fitra can also be paid in monetary value instead of cereal.

So in today's terms 1.75 seer rice will equal 12 annas. In ordinary times, giving it in the form of money, but considering today's conditions, it would be better that whoever can, should give it in form of cereal.

Fitra should be given before prayers but is acceptable after it too.

Eid *fitra* is only obligatory on those who are able, or on behalf of their non-adult or insane children and are owners of wealth of more than 39 rupees. And it should be given to those whom such *fitra* is due.

According to the *Hanafi maslak, fitra* can also be given to needy non-Muslims but to give it to needy Muslims or poor relatives is considered better.

Namaz is the prayer of the body and spirit, *fitra* is a way of prayer for wealth and well-being. It is in this way that the month of fasting's charity is activated and purity completed.

The reason why this tax has also been imposed particularly on Eid day is that no Muslim should remain deprived of the celebration and happiness of Eid. And so our needy brothers can also participate in the joy.

Like Eid and *Fitr* all Islamic duties increase the unity and brotherhood organization and togetherness of the Muslims.

In the book of education for Muslims each page emphasizes the unity and organization of Muslims.

Other religions of the world emphasize worship in solitude but in Islam the nearest route to reaching God is through gathering together and closeness to others.

Namaz is a pillar of Islam. It is the zenith of the believer, and it is the conversation of the slave with his Lord.

Yet even that, God prefers us to perform shoulder to shoulder with each other.

The reason why thirty days of fasting in one specific month are made obligatory is so that all Muslims according to God's command struggle together against their baser urges.

The house of God (Kaaba) is there. We can worship there throughout the year, but the day for Hajj was fixed on one particular day so that all the lucky Muslims of the world can gather there in one dress and circumambulate the house together.

Zakat is certainly for the unity and collective relief of Muslims.

To the extent that even after death, the togetherness of Muslims has been emphasized by the burial party standing side by side and praying for the departed, together.

Today's great and wonderful gathering is an awesome expression of the unity and brotherhood of Muslims. In this vast Maidan, we the rich and the poor, the great and the small are calling God with one heart and one voice.

All our worldly differences and our ranks are hidden away. This lesson of unity and organization is not just for Eid grounds and mosques, but is a lesson for homes, bazaars, and societies.

The Quran states unambiguously that all Muslims are brothers and asks us to make peace and unity among them. And the Prophet has said that creating friendship and peace among Muslims is a greater form of worship than *namaz*, *roza*, or giving of alms. The truth is that all the ills and decline of our Ummah is because we have forgotten this lesson.

Muslims progressed and prospered while they remained united. But once they divided into sects, classes, occupations, and ethnicities, they were dishonoured, dispersed, and they declined.

It does not become a *momin* to be proud of the fact that he is an Indian, a Hijazi, or Irani, or a Turk. For us our pride is our religion.

What is the secret of the devastation of Islamic countries? Why are they helpless and friendless? It is because they have become unattached and indifferent to each other.

Nations who are Godless are getting together in new associations based on economic interests and common enmities, the unity of some nations is being strengthened. And many Muslim individuals are seeing the false nationhood of the Western countries as a way of salvation. In India the untouchables who had been excluded for 5,000 years are being united with higher castes.

But among Muslims there are even today, those who spout slogans of Bengali and non-Bengali!

'Look in the mosque the broken prayer beads of the sheikh
In the temple see the strength of the string of the Brahman
Look at the caravans and their speed of travel
And also see this weary traveller's disillusion with his
destination!'*

But thank God, the Islamic countries are also awakening to the
desire for unity.

A few days ago the agreement of Saadabad took place and though
it did not produce desired outcomes, it made these countries realize
their helplessness and peripheral status. Nowadays the campaign
for Arab Federation is gaining momentum. We hope that these new
efforts will not just end with centralization of governments and
countries but will free Muslims from the curse of nationalism and
sectarianism. Because, unless the desire of Muslim brotherhood
does not take birth in our hearts, the unity will be illusory and
short lived.

Most encouraging is the truth that today, Indian Muslims have
made great gains in political unity and organization. They have a
strong party and a separate identity.

And thank God that the Muslims have freed themselves from the
greatest political folly of power sharing etc. Now they are neither
interested in forming a partnership government with non-Muslims
nor are they willing or desirous to accept the guarantees of foreign
powers protecting their rights and interests.

Their hearts are alive with the desire to be the vice regents of
God on earth and a free independent Muslim nation has become
their central objective.

---

*   Quotation from the poem *Hilal-e Eid* (The New Moon of Eid) of Muhammad
    Iqbal (d. 1938)

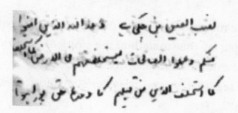

Everywhere the Muslims are awakening and their weakened body is coming alive with a new spirit. In commerce and politics, and in worldly knowledge they are progressing rapidly. The leaves of autumn are beginning to turn green.

Kitab-e millat e beza ki phir shiraza bandi hai
Yeh shakha Hashmi karney to hai phir barg or bar paida!
(The book of the nation of light is once again being revived
This Hashmi branch is about to flower again)*

If with this worldly progress, we also progress in spiritual and moral terms then the prophecy will be seen to be fulfilled.

Today, many laws and systems are clashing. Empires and nations are hell bent on establishing their power and are using every means and every form of knowledge to achieve this. But their achievements are devoid of spirituality.

Their new-fangled charters and international agreements cannot produce true equality and inclusivity.

If there is any hope out of the present destruction and darkness, it is the feint star of the caravan of the Islamic Ummah.

Today it is far from its destination, powerless and needy but we must never despair of God's blessing and bounty. Who knows after the end of all these wars the banner of victory and leadership might be in the Ummah's hand!

---

*   Quotation from Tulu-e Islam (The Dawn of Islam) of Muhammad Iqbal (d. 1938).

'It is not impossible that this sunken vessel rise again and sail.
For we have also seen such revolutions under the skies.'

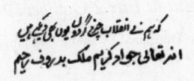

Indeed Allah is Most beneficent and Most Merciful

End of Part 1 of Khutba.

APPENDIX 2

Khutba Part 2 delivered at Calcutta Maidan by Maulana Jamal Mian on Eid ul Fitr 2 October 1943

Translated by Mahmood Jamal

خطبة ثانية

الحمد لله نحمده ونستعينه ونستغفره ونؤمن به

ونتوكل عليه ونعوذ بالله من شرور أنفسنا ومن

سيئات أعمالنا من يهده الله فلا مضل له ومن

يضلل فلا هادي له ونشهد أن لا إله إلا الله وحده

لا شريك له ونشهد أن سيدنا محمداً عبده ورسوله

أرسله بالحق بشيراً ونذيراً بين يدي الساعة من

يطع الله ورسوله فقد رشد ومن يعصهما فلا

يضر ولا يضروا الله شيئاً إن الله وملائكته

يصلون على النبي يا أيها الذين آمنوا صلوا عليه

وسلموا تسليماً اللهم صل على سيدنا محمد صاحب

أبي بكر وعمر وعلى آل بها اللهم صل على سيدنا

محمد صاحب عثمان وحيدر وعلى آل محمد وصل

كذلك على جميع الانبياء والرسلين وعلى ملائكتك
المقربين وعلى سائر الصحة من الانصار والصابين
وعلى اهل طاعتك اجمعين الى يوم الدين يا ايها
الناس اتقوا ربكم واخشوا اليوم لا يجزى والد
من ولده ولا مولود هو جاز عن والده شيئا ان وعد
الله حق فلا تغرنكم الحيوة الدنيا ولا يغرنكم بالله
الغرور

In these verses, we are enjoined to abstain from sinful activity and are told to fear that day when the father will not be the son's and the son will not be the father's. All worldly relations will be useless and the only thing that will matter are our good deeds. Those who have made worldly pleasures and acquisitions the object of their lives are admonished not to forget that promise by God, and not to indulge in worldly pleasures.

We can see everywhere the temporariness of this world and the inherent poverty of worldly wealth!

These huge sky scrapers, these broad avenues, the varied inventions of man's industry, these places of comfort and pleasure, have we not seen them turned to painful and ineffective wilderness by a few attacks by evil men? And even today the darkness of fear and uncertainty envelops us and the glimmering lights of metropolis are dim.

How ironic that we still do not learn from this and wake up.

We hide our lights from these enemies in the skies (bomber planes) but are not willing to extinguish the raging fire of our sins!

O you who fear the bombs, learn to fear the fire of hell where there are no shelters, no escape routes, no defending armies. Look, the signs of God's wrath are before you! The quicksand of disease and the clouds of troubles are overhead.

If there is anything that can thwart these clouds and eradicate this growing darkness, it is the light of God's mercy and the glow of God's forgiveness.

And to please God, the best route is to make honest repentance for your sins and to give alms.

Come let us with a true heart ask for God's forgiveness:

O Creator of Ours we have sinned against ourselves. And if You do not forgive us and bless us not, we will surely be destroyed. Oh Allah guide us to success in religion. And forgive our sins for we are not ones who can bear the loss.

Oh God, make us true Muslims. [So]We live for you, and die in your way, and rise under the banner of your Prophet on judgment day.

Mushkilen ummat e marhum ki asan karde
Mur-e-bemaya ko hmadosh e sulaiman karde
Jins-e-nayab muhabbt ko phir arzan karde
*Yani hum dair nashinon ko musalman karde**

(O lord make the difficulties of the Ummah easy
Make the humble ant equal to Sulaiman
Make the rare commodity, love, abundant
In short, make us temple dwellers, Muslims again!)

O Allah! Protect us from the calamities and troubles of this world. O Lord of the Universe, provide us with a way of earning

---

* Quotation from the *Shikwa* (Complaint) of Muhammad Iqbal (d. 1938).

our livelihood so our Eid becomes a true Eid. And this celebration
(of yours) becomes a harbinger of happiness and joy for us.

اسن بنائے   اللهم انزل علينا مائدة من السماء تكون
نا عيدا لاو لنا واخنا واية منك وارقنا وانت خير
الرازقين

*Alla humma anzal alyna Maidata Min us sama'a takunu lana eida
la walna wa akhazna wa aita minka wa razzaqna wa anta khair ur
Raziqeen.*

(O Allah, our Lord, send down to us from heaven the table spread
(with bounty) so that (the day of its descent) becomes (Eid) a festival
day for us., and for our predecessors (as well as) successors, and that
(the spread table) comes as a sign from You, and provides us with
sustenance, and You are the Best Sustainer.)*

Before I end this khutba, please listen to this story of an Eid in
Medina.

It is stated by Ibn Abbas according to Muslim and Bukhari that
on Eid Day the Holy Prophet (PBUH), came to the Eid ground and
after the Eid prayers and khutba he addressed the women and
admonished them and reiterated to them the essentials of religion,
sadqa, fitr, zakat and charity etc. he ordered them.

When the women heard these words of the Prophet they removed
their jewelry and handed it over to Bilal.

---

* *Surah Al-Ma'idah* (The Food), Quran, 5:114).

From this incident we conclude that today the dearest act is the act of charity and the greatest sunnah is to alleviate the needs of humanity.

Come fellow Muslims! Let us celebrate this Eid as that Eid in Medina and despite our strained circumstances, give a part of our wealth to our poorer brothers so that we can be called true slaves and servants of the Prophet. The Prophet has said they are incomplete in their religion who have filled their stomachs and spent their lives in comfort while their brothers lie starving and the Prophet has given the good news that he who dresses a poor person will remain in Allah's protection until the garment is not in shreds.

It is in reliable Hadith that once a tribe came, half naked and starving; Came to the Prophet and he was so disturbed at their sight that he became restless and his face changed and became yellow with grief.

He ordered people to be assembled and when Bilal had assembled a number of people, the Prophet led the prayers made a speech and enjoined abstinence and chastity and emphasized the equality of all human beings and ordered that some provisions be made for these people.

When they heard the Prophet's speech, some people gave dirhams and gold coins, some gave wheat, others dates or other eatables. The great and the small, all gave according to their capacity to the point that one person who had nothing came with one date! On both sides of the Prophet the gifts of food and money were stacked up and he became so pleased with the generosity and dutifulness of his followers that his face lit up with joy.

Is there anyone in this city who can donate to the poor and afflicted here as by doing so they earn the *ziarat* of the Prophet's shining face in the hereafter.

There is a hadith that '*Al Khalq o Ayyal lillah*' meaning his slaves are Allah's family.

Today in your city and province how many are there that are homeless and destitute, how many young are exhausted with starvation, how many mothers and widows are driven with hunger, and how many innocent infants are an unbearable weight of suffering and pain for the parents to bear?

On the streets and alleys of Calcutta, in Bengal and other cities and villages the calamity stricken family of God lies helpless.

Is there anyone amongst you who will go forward and look after them?

ان الله یامرکم بالعدل والاحسان و ایتاء ذی القربی و ینهی من الفحشاء والمنکر والبغی یعظکم لعلکم تذکرون ولذکر الله تعالی اکبر واولی وارفع واکبر الله اکبر الله اکبر لا اله الا الله والله اکبر الله اکبر ولله الحمد

(Indeed Allah commands us to be just and good and to give to our relatives and forbids us to avoid the bad and unjust deeds. He guides you to understand.* God is most high and most elevated and great. Allah is Great. Allah is Great. There is no god but Allah and is deserving of all praise.)

---

* *Surah al Nahl* (The Bee), Quran, 16:90.

Glossary

adab	etiquette, good or appropriate manners.
adhan	the call to prayer
ajnabiyya	outsider, or foreigner; one outside the *baradari,* the patrilineal group within which within which marriage is preferred.
`alim	(pl. *`ulama*), a learned man, typically a man learned in Islamic legal and religious studies.
asr	afternoon (prayer)
bai`at	oath of allegiance to a *pir* as his disciple.
bida`	innovation in religion, heresy.
chauk	a market place or cross roads in a town or city.
chobdar	a beadle
dars	a course or curriculum
dars-i nizami	the course established by Mulla Nizamuddin of Farangi Mahall.
diwan	a collection of poetry, usually of a single poet.
Eid	religious festival; there are two: Eid al-Adha in the pilgrimage month and Eid al-Fitr at end of Ramadan.
fateha	the opening chapter of Quran, often recited at the tombs of Sufi saints or on other customary occasions.
fal	an omen, in Jamal Mian's case using the *Diwan-i Hafiz,* to gain guidance.

fiqh	jurisprudence, the discipline of drawing guidance from the Quran and *Hadith*.
ghilaf	covering, hence *ghilaf-e-Kaaba* for the embroidered cloth covering of the Kaaba.
ghusul	washing, the washing of a saint's tomb during the `Urs.
giyarhvin	literally 'eleventh', the celebration of the death of Abdul Qadir Gilani.
Hadith	tradition. The sayings and doings of the Prophet Muhammad [PBUH] based on the authority of a chain of transmitters. *Ahl-i Hadith*, the people of tradition.
hafiz	one who has memorized the Quran.
halal	lit. permissible, for instance meat from animals slaughtered according to the *shari`a*.
hijra	withdrawal, the emigration of the Prophet from Mecca to Medina in 622, which marks the beginning of the Islamic era.
hikmat	wisdom, particularly in Sufi circles.
`*ijaza*	a licence or permission to teach, classically granted to a student after completing a book in the *dars* but also used to described the permission given by a *pir* to a *murid* to take on *murid*s in his own right.
ijma	consensus, classically of ulama on a point of law.
iman	faith
`*Isha*`	night (prayer)
i`tikaf	retreating from the world in the last ten days of Ramadan to focus on reciting the Quran and the names of God.
kalam	theology
kalima	the creed, or confession of faith.

khalifa	the successor of the Prophet as the leader of the Muslim community, or alternatively the successor of a Sufi *pir*.
khilafat	the successorship to the Prophet, or to a Sufi *pir*.
khirqa	the cloak or robe worn by a Sufi *pir*.
khutba	the sermon given at zohar prayer on Fridays and at the two Eids.
kiswah	the embroidered covering of the Kaaba.
kufr	disbelief/profanity, the practice of non-Muslims.
madad-i ma`ash	a revenue-free grant.
maghreb	sunset/evening (prayer)
mahfil	a gathering for the purpose of enjoying poetry or music.
mahzarnama	a witness statement.
majlis	lit. a place of sitting, a council, an assembly, a Parliament.
manqabat	a poem in praise of the Prophet's companions or saints.
mansab	a rank in the Mughal imperial system.
mantiq	logic
maqbara	monument raised above a grave.
ma`qulat	the 'rational sciences' in classical Islamic knowledge.
maslaha	public interest or the common good.
milad	lectures in praise of the Prophet, typically on the first twelve days of Rabiulawwal, but also on other auspicious occasions.
millat	religious community. In some circumstances in modern times it is has come to convey idea of 'nation'.
mufti	an `alim qualified to give a fatwa, or legal opinion.

muhajir	a refugee; in the context of South Asia someone from India who settled in Pakistan.
muhalla	quarter of a town or city
murid	a disciple of a Sufi *pir*.
murshid-e tariqat	the master, or rightful guide, of a particular Sufi path.
namaz	prayer
na`t	poem in praise of the Prophet.
nazr	a gift of respect to a religious or political figure.
nahw	grammar
nikah	literally 'conjunction' but in Islamic law it means marriage contract.
pandal	a large fabricated structure, usually temporary, to house political religious or social events.
parwana	an order, often renewing a grant of revenue.
pir	a Sufi master who leads disciples along his Sufi path.
pugri	turban
purdah	the custom of veiling and seclusion of women
qaumi adat	national custom
qaumi ruh	national spirit
qawwal	a singer of *qawwali*s, devotional songs
qawwali	the singing of devotional songs, often inducing ecstasy amongst listeners.
qiyas	in legal terms, arguing by analogy.
qul	the four Quranic verses beginning with Qaf.
rang	the performance in *qawwali* which records the passing down of mystical knowledge from Abdul Qadir Gilani to the saint who is being remembered. It was first written by Amir Khusrau for Nizamuddin Auliya.
rakat	prostration, a cycle of daily prayer.

roza	fasting during Ramadan.
sahur	the meal taken before dawn during Ramadan.
sajjadanashin	literally 'the sitter on the carpet', the current master of a particular local Sufi tradition.
sama` khana	auditorium, place for listening to *qawwali*.
sanad	certificate.
shagird	pupil, often of a poet.
shamiana	a tent or awning used for marriages or feasts.
Shams ul-`Ulama	lit. 'Sun of the learned men', a medal given to ulama by the British in India.
shari`a	the body of rules derived from the Quran and *Hadith* governing the behaviour of Muslims. Ulama, using *fiqh*, interpret these rules in specific situations.
sharif	noble, pl. *ashraf* meaning nobility, in India, mainly but not entirely those descended from those who came from outside the subcontinent.
shirk	worshipping another besides God.
shirmal	a saffron-flavoured flatbread for which Lucknow, and also Hyderabad, was famous.
silsila	lit. chain, for Sufis the chain of succession down which spiritual knowledge travels.
sirat	biography of the Prophet.
tafsir	commentary on the Quran.
takhullus	pen name, usually of a poet.
tarawih	extra prayers performed at night during Ramadan.
tasawwuf	'to become a Sufi', Sufism.
tawaf	the ceremony of circumambulating the Kaaba.
`urs	'wedding', the celebration of the death of a saint, the point when he became joined to God.
usul-i fiqh	the principles of jurisprudence.

wahdat ul-shuhud	the oneness of witness
wahdat ul-wujud	the oneness of being.
waqf	religious endowment.
ziarat	a form of pilgrimage.
zuha	midday (prayer).

Note on Sources

Jamal Mian Papers, Karachi (JMP)
The main sources for this book are the papers of Maulana Jamal Mian which currently lie with his family in Karachi and London. These contain:

- Diaries and notebooks from c. 1939 to the 1990s
- Correspondence with particular friends:
  The Raja of Mahmudabad
  Mirza Ismail Ispahani
  M. A. H. Ispahani
  Sadri Ispahani
  Muhammad Shoaib
  NB. Most of the time Jamal Mian did not keep copies of letters he sent, so the correspondence is almost entirely of letters received.
- Files relating to particular issues e.g.
  Passport
  Personal matters
  The Middle East Delegation
  Evacuee Property Case
  Shakarganj Sugar Mill
  His own life
  Speeches and Radio presentations

- Notes on particular individuals on their death:
  Dr Faridi
  Jawaharlal Nehru
  Pir Mohiuddin of Golra
  Mufti Amin al-Husseini
- A number of tapes on which he recorded his recollections, largely of political events.
- An excellent album of photographs of leading figures and events in his life.
- The Diaries of Hasrat Mohani which bring great depth to the years 1947–50.
- These materials are supported by Jamal Mian's personal library, in particular annotations to some of his books. The library catalogue, (Jamal Mian Catalogue) forms a part of the papers.
- These materials are also supported by the following unpublished mss. in Urdu and English:
  Farida Jamal, 'Recollections of Ammi Dadi' n.d. but given to the author in 2014. (English)
  Farida Jamal, 'Communication' 2 October 2016. (English)
  Farida Jamal, 'Note on Asar', 30 November 2016. (English)
  Jalal al-Din `Abd al-Matin (Matin Mian), 'The Farangi Mahall Year'. (Urdu CD)
  Jamal al-Din `Abd al-Wahhab, 'Awraq-i Parashan', August 1950. (Urdu)
  Mahmood Jamal 'Note', 3 October 2016. (English)
  Muhammad Shafi Hajjat Allah Ansari, 'Memoir', 15 August 1977. (Urdu)
  Nafiseh Ispahani, 'Edited Memoirs of Mirza Ahmed Ispahani: 5.8.1898–12.3.1986'. (English)

A second source is the Abdul Bari Papers, which also lie with his family in Karachi and London (ABP)

These papers contain elements of the early history of the family going back to Akbar's first known farman of 1559. But the prime element lying behind this book is Abdul Bari's correspondence from the beginning of World War One to his death in 1926.

Farangi Mahall, Lucknow.

The following mss. lie in the hands of Maulana Jalaluddin Abdul Matin:

ʿAbd al-Bari, 'Nisab Taʿlim Nizami' dated 1328/1910, no pagination. (Urdu).

ʿAbd al-Bari, '12th Report of Madrasah-yi Aliya Nizamiyya Farangi Mahall, no pagination. (Urdu).

Qutb al-Din ʿAbd al-Wali, 'Nisab Nizami' 1946, no pagination. (Urdu).

Nadwat ul-Ulama, Lucknow.

Wali Allah Farangi Mahalli, al-Aghsan al-Arbaʿa, nd. Ms.

Bodleian Library, Oxford.

Newspaper:

Dawn

British Library, London

Newspapers:

Pioneer

Statesman

Sind Archives Karachi

Shamsul Hasan Papers

Dissertations:

Moin Nizami, 'Reform and Renewal in South Asian Islam: the Chishti-Sabiris in 18th and 19th c. North India' (Cambridge, PhD Dissertation, 1910).

Layli Uddin, In the Land of Eternal Eid: Maulana Bhashani and the Political Mobilisation of Peasants and Lower-Class Urban Workers in East Pakistan c. 1930s–1971' (Royal Holloway, University of London, PhD Dissertation, 2015).

Bibliography

Works in Urdu

`Abd al-Bari, Muhammad Qiyam al-Din, *Malfuzi-i Razzaqi* (Cawnpur: Ahmad Press, 1926).

`Abd al-Bari, *`Urs-i Hadrat-i Bansa* (Lucknow: n.d).

Ajmiri, Nur al-Hassan, *Khadimana Guzarish* (Lucknow, 1923).

Farangi Mahalli, Muhammad Jamal al-Din `Abd al-Wahab ed., *Qulliyat-i Hasrat* (Karachi: Mass Printers, Nazimabad, 1976).

Farangi Mahalli, Muhammad Jamal al-Din `Abd al-Wahab ed., *Nawa-yi Agahi Kalam-i Sughra* 2nd ed. (Karachi: Maktaba Khatoon-i Pakistan, 1967).

Muhammad Askari, *Maan Kestum?* (Lucknow: Uttar Pradesh Urdu Academy, 1985).

Muhammad `Inayat Allah, *Risala-yi Hadrat al-Afaq ba Wafat Majmu`at al-Akhlaq* (Lucknow, 1929)

Muhammad `Inayat Allah, *Tadhkirah-yi `Ulama-i Farangi* Mahal (Lucknow: Ishat ul-Ulum, 1928).

Nadwi, S. A. H., *Hindustan ki Qadim Islami Darsgahain* (Azamgarh: Ma`arif, 1971).

Nizam al-Din, Mulla, *Manaqib-i Razzaqiyya,* Urdu trans. Sibghat Allah Shahid Farangi Mahalli, (Lucknow: n.d.).

Qidwai, Altaf al-Rahman, *Anwar-i Razzaqiyya,* (Lucknow: n.d.).

Qidwai, Altaf al-Rahman, *Qiyam-i Nizam-i Ta`lim* (Lucknow: Nami Press, 1924).

Rada Ansari, Mufti, *Bani-yi Dars-i Nizami* (Lucknow: Nami Press, 1973).

Rada Ansari, Mufti Muhammad, 'Mawlana Muhammad `Ali aur Mawlana Farangi Mahall' in *Jami`a Mawlana Muhammad `Ali Numbar,* Vol II, 77, February 1980.

Salamat Allah, Maulana, *Islah-yi Tariq-yi Mawlud Sharif* (Lucknow: Mujtaba`i Press, n.d.).

Shah Muhammad Husayn, *Bil Tanzim-i Nizam al-Ta`llum wal Ta`lim* (Allahabad: n.d.)

Sibghat Allah Shahid Ansari, *Sadr al-Mudarrisin* (Lucknow, 1941).

Works in English

Afzal, M. Rafique, *A History of the All-India Muslim League 1906–1947* (Karachi: Oxford University Press, 2013).

Alam, Muzaffar. *The Crisis of Empire in Mughal North India: Awadh and the Punjab 1707–1748* (Delhi: Oxford University Press, 1986).

Ali, Khalid, *Ali Brothers: The Life and Times of Maulana Mohamed Ali and Shaukat Ali* (Karachi: Royal Book Company, 2012).

Ansari, Mufti Raza, 'A Very Early Farman of Akbar', cyclostyled paper, Centre of Advanced Study, Aligarh Muslim University.

Austin, Granville, *The Indian Constitution: Cornerstone of a Nation* (London: Oxford University Press, 1966).

Bearman, P., *et al.,The Encyclopaedia of Islam,* 2nd ed. (Leiden: Brill, 1954–2004)

Burhan al-Din Zarnuji, *Ta`lim al-muta`allim-tariq at-ta`allum, Instruction of the student: the method of learning,* trans. G. E. Von-Grunebaum and Theodora M. Abel, (New York, 1947).

Cole, J. R. I., *Roots of North Indian Shi`ism in Iran and Iraq: Religion and State in Awadh, 1722–1859* (Berkeley & Los Angeles: University of California Press, 1988).

Currie, P. M., *The Shrine and Cult of Mu`in al-din Chishti of Ajmer* (Delhi: Oxford University Press, 1989).

Datta, V. N. and Cleghorn H., eds., *A Nationalist Muslim and Indian Politics* (Delhi: The Macmillan Company of India Ltd., 1974).

Daechsel, Markus, *Islamabad and the Politics of International Development in Pakistan* (Cambridge: Cambridge University Press, 2015).

Dhulipala, Venkat, *Creating a New Medina: State Power, Islam, and the Quest for Pakistan in Late Colonial North India* (New Delhi: Cambridge University Press, 2015).

Douglas, Ian Henderson, Gail Minault, and Christian W. Troll eds., *Abul Kalam Azad: An Intellectual and Religious Biography* (Delhi: Oxford University Press, 1988).

Edib, Halide, Mushirul Hasan ed., and introd., *Inside India* (Delhi: Oxford University Press, 2002).

Engineer, Asghar Ali, *The Bohras* (Ghaziabad UP: Vikas Publishing House Pvt Ltd., 1980).

Gandhi, M. K., *The Collected Works of Mahatma Gandhi*, Vol. XXIV, (Ahmedabad: Director of the Publications Division, Government of Indias, 1967).

Gould, William, *Hindu Nationalism: The Congress in North India* (Cambridge: Cambridge University Press, 2004).

Habib, Irfan, *An Atlas of the Mughal Empire* (Delhi: Oxford University Press, 1982).

Hasan, Mushirul, *Legacy of a Divided Nation: India's Muslims since Independence* (Delhi: Oxford University Press, 1997).

Iqbal, Afzal, *The Life and Times of Maulana Mohamed Ali* (Lahore: Institute of Islamic Culture, 1974).

Ispahani, M. A. H., *Quaid-e-Azam Jinnah As I Knew Him*, 2nd ed. (Karachi: Forward Publications Trust, 1966)

Jalal, Ayesha, *The Sole Spokesman: Jinnah, the Muslim League and the*

Demand for Pakistan (Cambridge: Cambridge University Press, 1985).

Jalal, Ayesha, *The Struggle for Pakistan: A Muslim Homeland and Global Politics* (Cambridge Mass: Belknapp Press, 2014).

Jones, Justin, *Shi`a Islam in Colonial India: Religion, Community and Sectarianism, 1722–1859* (Cambridge: Cambridge University Press, 2012).

Karim, Al-Hajj Maulana Fazlul, *Al-Hadis: An English Translation and Commentary of Mishkat-ul-Masabih* (Lahore: The Book House, n.d.).

Khaliquzzaman, Choudhry, *Pathway to Pakistan* (Karachi: Longman's Pakistan Branch, 1961).

Khan, Amir Ahmad, 'Local Nodes of a Transnational Network: a case study of a Shi`i family in Awadh 1900–1950', in Justin Jones and Ali Usman Qasmi eds., *The Shi`a in Modern South Asia: Religious History and Politics* (Delhi: Cambridge University Press, 2015), 57–79.

Khan, Yasmin, *The Great Partition: The Making of India and Pakistan* (New Haven and London: Yale University Press, 2007).

Lakhnavi, Ghalib and Abdullah Bilgrami, *The Adventures of Amir Hamza,* introd. Hamid Dabashi (New York: Random House, 2007).

Lutfullah, *Autobiography of Lutfullah, a Mohamedan Gentleman and his Transactions with his Fellow Creatures,* Edward B. Eastwick ed. (London: Smith, Elder and Co., 1858).

Mahmood, Zeeba Zafar, *The Shaping of Karachi's Big entrepreneurs (1947–98): A socio-political study* (Karachi: City Press, 2003).

Mahmudabad, Raja of , 'Some Memories' in Philips, C.H. and Wainwright M. eds, *The Partition of India: Politics and Perspectives 1935-1947* (London; Geo. Allen & Unwin, 1970).

Mann, E. S., *Boundaries and Identities: Muslims, Work and Status in Aligarh* (Delhi: Sage, 1992).

Metcalf, Barbara, 'The Madrasah at Deoband: A Model for Religious Education in India', *Modern Asian Studies*, Vol. 12, Part 1, February 1978, 111–34.

Minault, Gail, *The Khilafat Movement: Religious Symbolism and Political Mobilization in India* (New York: Columbia, 1982.

Moosa, Ebrahim, *What is a Madrasah?* (Edinburgh: Edinburgh University Press, 2015).

Naim, C. M. *The Muslim League in Bara Banki: A Suite of Five Sentimental Scenes* (Shimla: Indian Institute of Advanced Study, 2010).

Noorani, A. G. *The Destruction of Hyderabad* (New Delhi: Tulika Books, 2013).

Pirzada, Syed Sharifuddin, *Foundations of Pakistan: All-India Muslim League Documents: 1906–1947*, 2 Vols. (Karachi: National Publishing House Ltd., 1970).

Qadiri, K. H., *Hasrat Mohani* (Delhi: Idarah-i Adabiyat-i Delli, 1985).

Robinson, Francis, 'Education' in Robert Irwin ed., *New Cambridge History of Islam, Volume 4, Islamic Cultures and Societies to the End of the Eighteenth Century* (Cambridge: Cambridge University Press, 2010), 497–531.

Robinson, Francis, 'Living Together Separately: The Ulama of Farangi Mahall c. 1700–1950' in Mushirul Hasan and Asim Roy eds., *Living Together Separately: Cultural India in History and Politics* (New Delhi: Oxford University Press, 2005), 354–65.

Robinson, Francis, *Separatism Among Indian Muslims: The Politics of the United Provinces' Muslims 1860–1923*, (Cambridge: Cambridge University Press, 1974).

Robinson, Francis, *The `Ulama of Farangi Mahall and Islamic Culture in South Asia* (Delhi: Permanent Black, 2001).

Schimmel, Annemarie, *Mystical Dimensions of Islam* (Chapel Hill: University of North Carolina Press, 1975).

Sharar, Abdul Halim, *Lucknow: The Last Phase of an Oriental Culture* trans. and ed., by E. S. Harcourt and Fakhir Hussain (London: Paul Elek, 1975).

Sherman, Taylor C., *Muslim Belonging in Secular India: Negotiating Citizenship in Post- Colonial Hyderabad* (Cambridge: Cambridge University Press, 2015).

Siddiqui, *Landlords of Agra & Avadh* (Lucknow: Pioneer Press, 1950).

Sumner-Boyd, Hilary and John Freely, *Strolling Through Istanbul* (Istanbul: Redhouse Press, 1972).

Talbot, Ian, *Pakistan: A Modern History* (London: Hurst & Co., 1998).

Wolpert Stanley, *Jinnah of Pakistan* (New York: Oxford University Press, 1984).

Zaidi, Z. H. ed., *M. A. Jinnah-Ispahani Correspondence 1936–1948* (Karachi: Forward Publications Trust, 1976).

Zamindar, Vazir Fazila-Yacoobali, *The Long Partition and the Making of Modern South Asia: Refugees, Boundaries, Histories* (New Delhi: Penguin Books India Pvt. Ltd., 2007).

Index

Persian Literature at Lucknow University 71; learns English 71–2; scholarship recognized by King Hassan II of Morocco 73; his library 336–9, 341, 344–5; Urdu works 336–7, 339–40, 350, 352; Arabic works 336–7, 342–3, 345; Persian works 336–7, 344, 352; English works 336–7, 344–8, 350; annotations in books 336, 338, 344, 349–50; and Hassan Ispahani 3, 113, 125, 145, 156, 188–9, 195, 231, 252, 255, 260, 294, 296, 298, 312, 348, 358; and Mirza Ahmed Ispahani 82, 125, 167, 225–6, 231–2, 234, 243, 256, 297–8, 306, 324; and Sadri Ispahani 114–6, 128, 132, 137–8, 144, 146–52, 167, 230, 253, 260–5, 267, 295, 318, 324, 357; Ispahanis and the Bengal Famine 313, delivers the Eid sermon on the Calcutta Maidan (1943) 123; relations with Raja Amir Ahmed Khan of Mahmudabad 104, 135, 137–8, 140, 142, 161, 234, 241, 254, 270, 272, 275, 278–9, 287, 292, 315, 317, 323, 337, 339, 351, 355; relations with Dr Faridi 138–40, 147, 197–9, 230, 245, 249, 253, 270, 278, 312, 355; relations with Hasrat Mohani 18, 48, 82, 90–100, 103, 107, 109–11, 167–8, 178, 187, 198, 201, 206–7, 211, 215, 217–9, 222, 224–5, 229, 241, 245, 249, 270, 280, 315, 332, 338–9, 340–1, 347, 356; relations with Iskander Mirza 252–3, 255, 265,

268, 274, 278–9, 281, 283, 287, 327, 329, 356, 365; relations with Mufti Amin al-Husseini, Mufti of Jerusalem 195, 277, 279, 290–2, 308, 315–6, 321, 344, 356; interprets the Lahore resolution 159–0, 163–4; opposed to Pakistan as an Islamic state 155, 161–2, 237, 257, 282, 362; quarrels with Hasrat Mohani over Begum Habibullah's nomination 168, 276; and Bara Banki election of (1946) 172; and Middle East Delegation 187–8, 268, 359; visits Eyup on the Golden Horn (Istanbul) 9, 194; meets Hasan al-Banna 195; attends inauguration of Pakistan in Karachi (14 August 1947) 140, 188, 197–8, 356; attends All-India Muslim League Council, December 1947, Karachi 188, 207, 214; attacks the use of the term 'Muslim State' 208, 362; asked by Khaliquzzaman to join Peace mission to Karachi 205; and death of Gandhi 152, 187–8, 210–5, 347; verse opposing the imposition of Hindi 218, 344; elegy on the dire straits of Lucknow 225; publishes his sister, Sughra's, poems 338; and Jawaharlal Nehru 101–2, 105, 156, 166, 203, 224, 230, 241, 251–2, 266, 273, 280, 346, 359; and Jinnah 2–5, 72, 99, 103–6, 108, 111, 112, 114–5, 117, 123, 126, 134, 155–62, 176, 190, 195, 197, 202, 204, 207–10, 214, 235,

Muhammad Husain Jah, Munshi Saiyid 341

Muhammad Husain of Allahabad, Shah 54

Muhammad Husain of Phulwari Sharif, Shah 250

Muhammad Shafi, Maulana (Farangi Mahalli) 34, 40, 43, 93–4, 171

Muhammad Yusuf, Mufti (Farangi Mahalli) 21

Muhammad Yusuf, Nawab Sir 167

Muhajir 238–9, 275, 277, 298, 305, 315, 336

Muhibullah, Shah of Allahabad 15–6, 316

Mukerjee, Shyamprasad 117

Mujibur Rahman, Sheikh 305

Mulk, Mohsinul 341

Mumtaz Ahmad Razzaqi, Shah of Bansa 17, 48–9, 82, 89

Muqaddimah of Ibn Khaldun 57, 343

Muslim League Council 3, 188, 206–7, 214, 362

Muslim Students Federation 171–2

Mysore 151

N

Nadvat ul-Ulama 54, 161

Najmuddin, Dr Yusuf 268, 270, 316, 323, 359

Naqvi, Ali Naqi (Shia Mujtahid) 71

Nasir Yar Jung 236

Nasir, Dr of Indonesia 292

Nasiruddin, Hakim 311

Nasiruddin, Nawab 58

National Herald (Newspaper) 204

Naushad Ali Khan, Raja 173

Nazimuddin, Khwaja 118, 234, 250, 253, 255, 257, 274, 288

Nehru, Jawaharlal 101, 105, 156, 166, 203, 224, 230, 241, 251, 266, 273, 280, 346, 359

Nehru, Motilal 44

Nishtar, Abdur Rab 208

Niwas, Abu (poet) 343

Nizami (Poet) 90

Nizamuddin, Makhdum (Ansari) 11

Nizamuddin, Mulla (Farangi Mahalli) 14, 17, 29–30, 58, 338

Nuqqush 339

O

Obhrai, Veena 354

Orient Airways 134, 233, 236, 245

Orwell, George 346

P

Page, David 346

Pahlavi, Muhammad Shah of Iran 347

Pakistan 26, 82, 111, 134, 140, 144–6, 155, 157–64, 166, 172, 183, 188, 195, 197–8, 200, 202–4, 209–10, 212, 215–16, 220, 222, 226, 231–3, 235, 237–41, 244, 246–7, 249–50, 252–60, 262, 266–8, 270, 272, 274–9, 281, 285–7, 289, 290–2, 294, 298–301, 305–7, 311, 313–15, 318, 322, 326, 328–9, 333–6, 340–1, 346, 348, 350, 352–3, 356, 358–9, 362–5; as an Islamic state 155,